Domesticating the Dharma

Domesticating the Dharma

BUDDHIST CULTS AND THE HWAŎM SYNTHESIS IN SILLA KOREA

Richard D. McBride, II

 University of Hawai'i Press
Honolulu

© 2008 University of Hawai'i Press
All rights reserved
Printed in the United States of America
13 12 11 10 09 08   6 5 4 3 2 1

LIBRARY OF CONGRESS CATALOGING-IN-PUBLICATION DATA
McBride, Richard D.
Domesticating the Dharma : Buddhist cults and the Hwaŏm synthesis in Silla Korea / Richard D. McBride, II.
p. cm.
Includes bibliographical references and index.
ISBN 978-0-8248-3087-8 (hardcover : alk. paper)
1. Buddhism—Korea—History—To 935. 2. Hua yan Buddhism—Korea—History. 3. Buddhist cults—Korea—History. I. Title.
BQ661.M33 2008
294.3'920951909021—dc22
                                                                2007031669

University of Hawai'i Press books are printed on acid-free paper and meet the guidelines for permanence and durability of the Council on Library Resources.

Designed by Paul Herr
Composition by Tseng Information Systems, Inc.
Printed by The Maple-Vail Book Manufacturing Group

Contents

Preface vii
Abbreviations and Conventions xi

Introduction 1

CHAPTER ONE: Buddhism and the State in Silla 13

CHAPTER TWO: The Cult of Maitreya 33

CHAPTER THREE: The Cult of Avalokiteśvara 62

CHAPTER FOUR: The Rise of Hwaŏm Buddhism in Silla 86

CHAPTER FIVE: The Hwaŏm Synthesis of Buddhist Cults 109

Concluding Reflections 139

    Appendix 1: The Divine Assembly from the *Avataṃsaka Sūtra* in Sixty Rolls / 147
    Appendix 2: The Divine Assembly from the *Avataṃsaka Sūtra* in Eighty Rolls / 149

Notes 151
Glossary of Sinitic Logographs 179
Selected Bibliography 193
Index 217

Preface

This book began as a study of mainstream Mahāyāna Buddhism as it was practiced on the ground in Silla Korea. In pursuing this course of research I originally intended it as a counterbalance to the detailed descriptions of scholastic Buddhism available on Silla Korea because I had long been fascinated by the anecdotes and narratives about the devotional practices performed by both eminent Buddhist monks and lay Buddhists in Korea during the Three Kingdoms and Unified Silla periods (traditional dates, 57 B.C.E.–935 C.E.). Because of the scarcity of early Korean primary sources, I sought to combine work in areas of Buddhist studies that particularly interested me: Sinitic Buddhist hagiography and Korean Buddhist thought, especially exegeses associated to the Maitreya and Amitābha cults that are traditionally labeled Pure Land Buddhism. In seeking to understand the East Asian historical context of the origins of Buddhist institutions and mainstream practices in Silla, I became convinced that Silla Buddhism preserved and further developed many attributes of Buddhism under the Chinese Northern dynasties (ca. 317–589), despite the protestations of certain literary sources that their legitimacy derived from the Southern dynasties. Furthermore, my participation on the translation team associated with the forthcoming *Collected Works of Wŏnhyo* Project for nearly all of the past decade caused me to question the utility of the academic discourse on "schools" as a useful methodology in explaining the nature of medieval Sinitic (that is, Chinese and Korean) Buddhism. The Silla monk Wŏnhyo (617–686), for instance, wrote essays crossing the full gamut of Buddhist sūtra literature and participated in a shared Sinitic discourse on intellectual Buddhism with Chinese colleagues. I became increasingly convinced that he belonged to no school in particular and that it would do harm to the evidence to suggest that he was the founder of his own school of Buddhist thought. Buddhist scholar-monks, whom I prefer to describe as exegetes, assuredly existed in Silla, as they did in medieval China, but they were not strictly affiliated with particular schools—a fact becoming progressively more evident in studies on medieval China as well. Also, it became increasingly clear that many exegetes were enamored by the conceptions of reality and practice on the bodhisattva path promoted by the *Avataṃsaka Sūtra* or *Flower Garland Sūtra:* Hwaŏm Buddhism.

If the sectarian-oriented schools approach was not fruitful, what bound Sinitic Buddhism together? The answer was found in the anecdotes preserved in Buddhist hagiography and in epigraphy: the cults of buddhas and bodhisattvas. Originally my research also included treatments of Buddhist spells (dhāraṇī) and thaumaturgy and the cult of Amitābha. To do justice to these topics, however, I will have to set them aside for another occasion. Although coverage has been curtailed in this respect, it has been expanded on the other hand to encompass the entirety of Buddhism in the Silla period, roughly the fifth through the tenth centuries C.E. It had previously concluded at the end of the eighth century, when Silla's hereditary aristocracy wrested the kingship of Silla from Kim Ch'unch'u's line in 780.

I would like to take this opportunity to thank all of my academic advisers at the University of California, Los Angeles, for their guidance, support, and fellowship during the course of my graduate studies there. I am particularly grateful to Robert E. Buswell, Jr., John B. Duncan, William M. Bodiford, and Richard von Glahn, the four readers on the dissertation to which this book owes its origins. I will be satisfied if my work even partially emulates the superb model of scholarship each of them has provided. I would also like to recognize the influence of Gregory Schopen, who arrived at UCLA while I was in the process of writing my dissertation. His emphasis on sources for the study of Buddhism on the ground, as well as appropriate models of scholarship on topics of religion in the West, has been an enduring benefit to my research and methodology. I would also like to thank Kim Sang-hyun of Dongguk University for offering valuable comments and for alerting me to certain key studies that have had important bearing on my research. His examinations of Silla's Buddhist culture and the Hwaŏm tradition have been the most influential in the formation of my views, although I do not always agree with his interpretations. Several individuals have also read portions of the manuscript and offered valuable comments and suggestions, especially my colleagues from graduate school George Keyworth and James Benn. I would also like to thank the two anonymous readers for the press. Their comments helped me improve the book and to make its insights clearer and more accessible. Finally, I would like to thank my colleagues at Washington University in St. Louis, in particular Robert E. Hegel, for mentoring me through the publishing process. I, of course, take full responsibility for any errors of fact or interpretation that may remain.

Research on this book was sponsored by a postdoctoral fellowship from the Visiting East Asian Professionals Program at Washington University in St. Louis. Also, much of the research upon which this book is based could not have been performed without the generous support of the Korean Cultural Center, Los Angeles, where I worked during my tenure as a graduate student at UCLA.

Finally, I would like to thank my wife, Younghee, who has been supportive through the entire process. The impending birth of our son David provided the impetus to complete my revision of the manuscript, and since his birth she has sacrificed frequently to allow me time and opportunity to bring this project to completion. The dedication of this book to her is but a small token of my debt of gratitude for her patience, love, and support.

Abbreviations and Conventions

Ch.   Chinese
HPC   *Han'guk Pulgyo chŏnsŏ*
IBK   *Indogaku Bukkyōgaku kenkyū*
Jpn. Japanese
Kor. Korean
K   *Koryŏ taejanggyŏng*
Skt. Sanskrit
SYKY *Samguk yusa kyogam yŏn'gu*
T   *Taishō shinshū dai zōkyō*
X   *Xuzangjing*

Citations from the *Taishō shinshū dai zōkyō* (Taishō edition of the Buddhist canon) are listed in the following manner: title (with Sanskrit title, if relevant, in parentheses) and roll number; Taishō serial number; Taishō volume number; page number, register (a, b, or c), and if applicable, line number(s)—e.g., *Da Tang xiyu ji* 9, T 2087, 51.946c4–5.

Citations from the *Han'guk Pulgyo chŏnsŏ* (Complete works of Korean Buddhism), *Koryŏ taejanggyŏng* (Korean Buddhist canon), and *Xuzangjing* (Hong Kong reprint of *The Kyoto Supplement to the Canon*) are listed as follows: title and roll number, volume number; page number, register (a, b, c, or d), and if applicable, line number(s)—e.g., *Tae hwaŏm sujwa wŏnt'ong yangjung taesa Kyunyŏ chŏn pyŏngsŏ* 1, K 47.259c4–5.

Citations from traditional East Asian historical or literary works are listed in the following manner: title of the work and roll or chapter number: page, and if applicable, register (a or b), and/or line number(s)—e.g., *Wei shu* 60:1421.

Citations to the *Samguk yusa* (Memorabilia of the Three Kingdoms) will be executed in the following manner. Since this is a primary source with several standard editions, I will cite the *Taishō* edition and the new critical edition by Ha Chŏngnyong and Yi Kŭnjik—e.g., *Samguk yusa* 5, T 2039, 49.1010c–1011a; SYKY 5:380–384.

Transliterations of Asian languages follow the romanization systems commonly used in the scholarly community: Pinyin for Chinese, revised Hepburn for Japanese, and McCune-Reischauer for Korean. All Buddhist terminology that appears in Webster's Third New International Dictionary I regard as English and leave unitalicized. This includes such technical terms as dhāraṇī, stūpa, and tathāgatagarbha. For a convenient listing of a hundred such words, see Roger Jackson, "Terms of Sanskrit and Pali Origin Acceptable as English Words." In rendering Buddhist technical terms, where the Chinese is a translation I translate; where it is a transcription, I transcribe. East Asian personal names appear with family names first. Characters are not given in the text; please consult the glossary or bibliography. Titles of books originally composed in East Asian languages or Buddhist books referred to in Chinese translation will be discussed in running text using standard English translations (e.g., *Lotus Sūtra*), English translations of my own making, or the accepted Sanskrit titles (e.g., *Avataṃsaka Sūtra*). Reconstructed Sanskrit names and titles will be placed in parentheses and indicated by an asterisk before the title (e.g., Skt. *Raśmivimalaviśuddhaprabhā Dhāraṇī*). A transliteration of the title's characters will be given the first time the title appears. For the English translations of official titles I have followed those given in Charles O. Hucker's *Dictionary of Official Titles in Imperial China* for the Northern dynasties, Sui, Tang, and Silla. For Silla titles not found in Hucker I have developed my own translations based on his model. Following the advice of Robert Buswell, I have generated some of my own English translations of official Buddhist titles for the Northern Chinese dynasties and Silla (e.g., Buddhist Overseer [Ch. *datong* or *tong*, Kor. *sŭngt'ong* or *kukt'ong*]). Aristocratic rank titles found in ancient Korean and Japanese society have usually been transliterated only because of the difficulty in assigning concise English meanings to these terms.

English translations of historical and hagiographical narratives, Buddhist exegeses, and epigraphy, which are presented in the body of the book or in the appendices, are all my own and have been translated from the original literary Chinese and literary Sino-Korean (Ch. *hanwen*, Kor. *hanmun*), unless stated otherwise in an accompanying footnote. For the sake of convenience, the Sinitic logographs comprising Korean and Japanese proper nouns that appear in traditional Chinese sources and Chinese proper nouns that appear in traditional Korean and Japanese sources will be transliterated according to the pronunciation of the individual or institution's original ethnic origin. Other words, compounds, phrases, or sentences singled out for discussion or for comparative purposes will be transliterated according to the original language of the source text. Hence, when discussing the biography of an ethnic Korean monk that is contained in the *Further Lives of Eminent Monks (Xu gaoseng zhuan)*, although his name will be transliterated according to its Korean pronunciation, his religious activities will be discussed using the Chinese pronunciation of the Sinitic logographs. Sexagesimal cycle dates are treated in the following manner: if the source text is Chinese, I transliterate the sexagesimal year using Chinese pronunciation (e.g., *jiazi*); but if the source is Korean, I transliterate it using Korean pronunciation (e.g., *kapcha*). In both cases the transliteration will be followed by an approximation to Western calendrical dates in parentheses following Xue Zhongsan's *Liangqiannian Zhong-Xi li duizhao biao* (A Sino-Western calendar for two thousand years).

Introduction

Chajang lamented that he had been born in a borderland. He longed to go to the West [to China, to participate in] the Great Transformation. In the third year of the Inp'yŏng reign period, the *pyŏngsin*-year [636], he received royal permission and, together with his disciple Sil and more than ten junior colleagues, went West, entering Tang, and visited Mount Qingliang [Mount Wutai].

On the mountain there was a clay form [statue] of the Great Saint Mañjuśrī. The traditions of that country say that the Lord Śakra, king of the gods, had artisans come fashion it. Chajang supplicated before that image for resonance from the unseen world. In his dream-state, the image rubbed his forehead and conferred on him a Sanskrit gāthā [verse]. When he awoke, he did not yet understand [what the verse meant]. When morning came, a strange monk came and explained it. Furthermore, [the monk] said, "Even though you study myriads of teachings, nothing will ever exceed this [gāthā]." Moreover, entrusting him with a *kaṣāya* [monk's robe] and *śarīra* [relics], he vanished.[1]

This anecdote about the aristocratic Silla monk Chajang's worship of and spiritual encounter with Mañjuśrī, a bodhisattva important to the Hwaŏm tradition, illustrates several of the themes with which this book is concerned: the adoption and adaptation of religious practices by elites and the role, in this process, of imported deities and systems of understanding the cosmos. This book deals with the origins, composition, and function of Buddhist cults in the early medieval Korean state of Silla (ca. 300–935).[2] In this connection it touches on a few themes and topics that inhabit the overlapping boundaries between several fields in the study of history and religion: questions of class and cultural context, the role of literature, and ritual studies. Fundamentally, it calls into question a scholarly assumption that the nameless masses are responsible for the dissemination of "popular" religious practices and that those practices are a static heritage of man's primordial polytheism.[3] More precisely, it challenges the two-tiered model of religion that divides the concept into two distinct groups based upon imagined perceptions of religious practitioners: elite versus folk religion, intellectual versus popular religion, philosophy versus vulgar practices, and other such designations deployed usually as heuristic devices.

Although the limitations and inefficacy of the two-tiered model have been shown repeatedly by scholars in recent years—most notably in Peter Brown's study of the cult of saints in Latin Christianity; Gregory Schopen's work on the cults of the book, relics, and images in medieval Indian Buddhism; and Michel Strickmann's research on the interconnections between Buddhist and Daoist rituals and medical practices in medieval China[4]—this model has been and is still pervasive among students of the history of religion.

The conventional wisdom offered by the two-tiered model is wrong. Neither material nor literary evidence supports its conclusions. In this book I demonstrate the role that religious and social elites played in the domestication of the religion. I also consider the place of objects, images and icons, dreams, spells, repentance rituals, and devotional practices associated with buddhas, bodhisattvas, and other sundry deities in the religious life and organizations of lay and monastic Buddhists in Silla Korea between the sixth and tenth centuries C.E. The thesis of this work is that the popularity of Buddhist cults among Silla's social and religious elites was the primary cause behind the successful domestication of Buddhism and that this form of the religion achieved its ultimate phase when codified with the observances of Silla's Hwaŏm tradition, which provided a compelling vision of the relationship between ritual and reality by incorporating key cultic practices. The attractive potency and legitimating power of Buddhist symbols motivated the social and religious elites of Silla to rename the country's famous sites in Buddhist fashion, re-inscribing the local geography as a past Buddha-land. In time this gave way to a Hwaŏm-inspired vision of Silla topography that imbued the country with a deeper religious significance that has remained to this day. The power and potency of these sites was made accessible to the people of Silla through cultic practices.

The practices of Buddhist cults became so ubiquitous in the traditions of East Asian Buddhism in succeeding times that we tend to take their presence for granted. Although the origins of some of these Buddhist cults in China and their importation and development into Japan have received a certain amount of scholarly attention, the Buddhist history and heritage of Korea have often been overlooked. This study seeks to recognize the contributions of Silla Buddhists to the shared East Asian

Buddhist heritage and to emphasize the vital role that cults and Hwaŏm symbolism played in Korean Buddhism.

Buddhism as Cultic Practices and Rituals

The Buddhism that entered the Korean peninsula was a cosmopolitan religion that linked the Indian cultural sphere with the Sinitic cultural sphere through Central Asia. Mahāyāna Buddhism practiced in China was not a simple, coherent belief system but a vast assemblage of practices.[5] A richer picture of medieval Chinese Buddhism is now emerging in which cult and ritual play a central role in the dissemination of the religion. Although he is addressing Chinese perceptions of India, Michel Strickmann encapsulates a seminal aspect of the way that Buddhism transformed the religious practices of the Silla people:

> The therapeutic aspect of Buddhism, in the medical as well as the spiritual sense of the word, lent powerful support to capital formation in promoting the religion's eastwards diffusion. But for the special circumstances attendant upon the end of Buddhism, which was also to be the end of the world, material means alone of dealing with disease were not adequate. It was necessary to channel the full resources of the spirit-realm against the demonic menace, and this could best be done through ritual. Indian scriptures offered potent *mantras* towards this end, each to be recited under the proper ritual conditions, and each embodying the concentrated force of a particular Buddha, Bodhisattva, or a benevolent guardian deity.[6]

Buddhism provided the people of Silla, particularly social and religious elites, with a cosmopolitan weltanschauung that enabled them to assimilate Indian and Chinese culture and technology, both material and spiritual, and yet preserve many of their indigenous aristocratic traditions in a new Buddhist form. The ritual aspects of Buddhist culture that were indigenized by the people of Silla included new ways to generate blessings and benefits, quell demons and ghosts, deal with illness and death, and protect family interests. Catherine Bell's theoretical work on ritual suggests that Silla society would have been profoundly changed in the process of acculturating new ritual practices: "Ritual can be a strategic way to 'traditionalize,' that is, to construct a type of tradition, but in doing so it can also challenge and renegotiate the very basis of tradition to the point of upending much of what had been seen as fixed previously or by other groups."[7]

The missionary monks who went from China and India to the ancient and early medieval Korean kingdoms of Koguryŏ (traditional dates,

37 B.C.E.–668 C.E.), Paekche (traditional dates, 18 B.C.E.–660 C.E.), and Silla not only brought the widely varying religious teachings attributed to the historical Buddha, Śākyamuni, and his followers, but also technology, skills, rituals, and religious practices from throughout China and the Indian subcontinent. These skills, including the use of literary Chinese, had trickled into the peninsula in the sporadic waves of immigration from the Chinese cultural sphere over preceding centuries. It was, in fact, the transmission of Buddhism by royally or imperially sanctioned monks to the courts of the Korean kingdoms that truly began the process of normalizing relations between the Chinese dynasties and peninsular kingdoms during China's period of disunion (ca. 220–589).

The Chinese monk Shundao (Kor. Sundo) introduced Buddhism to the Koguryŏ court, having been sent by the Former Qin emperor Fu Jian (r. 357–384), and, notwithstanding the fact that Chinese monks had been corresponding with Koguryŏ monks since the early fourth century, the religion was received "officially" by the king and made a state religion in 372.[8] In 384 the Serindian monk Maranat'a (Skt. *Mālānanda), an emissary of the Jin dynasty, introduced Buddhism to the court of Paekche, where it was also made a state religion.[9] Monks of various ethnic origins then traveled from Koguryŏ to bring Buddhism to the kingdom of Silla during the fifth century, but it was not officially accepted until about 535. For several hundred years, monks from the Korean kingdoms traveled to China and India in search of the Buddhist teaching and brought back Chinese and Indian culture and technology as well. This process was more or less concluded during China's greatest cosmopolitan age of the Tang (618–907). Thus, Buddhist monks were the purveyors of Chinese culture—from architecture, calendrics, literature, and clothing to statecraft and government institutions—and Koreans, in turn, transmitted their knowledge and understanding of "Buddhism," which included their mastery of Sinitic culture, to the Japanese islands. Monks sent under the direction of the Paekche king officially introduced Buddhism to the Japanese ruler in the mid-sixth century (552 or 538). Unofficial correspondence between monks on the continent and the peninsula and official diplomatic relations between the Korean kingdoms and Chinese states brought a flood of Chinese books and manuals other than Buddhist scriptures and commentaries, such as the Confucian classics and works on statecraft, which inspired the aristocratic rulers of the early Korean kingdoms to attempt to form centralized, authoritarian polities based on textual Chinese models.

The promotion of Buddhism by royalty and aristocracy in many Asian countries created a cosmopolitan culture linking India, Central Asia, and East Asia in much the same way that Christianity unified and defined the culture of medieval Europe. The kingdom of Silla was profoundly influenced by the diverse Buddhist culture of the continental kingdoms, and the cults of many buddhas and bodhisattvas began to develop during the sixth and seventh centuries. Like the Chinese and the Japanese, the Koreans of the Silla kingdom built massive monasteries in their capital to house large images of these deities, and carvings of buddhas and bodhisattvas in stone multiplied on rocky hills and mountains around the country. The cults of Maitreya, the future Buddha and lord of Tuṣita Heaven; Amitābha, the Buddha of the Western Paradise Sukhāvatī; and Avalokiteśvara, the bodhisattva of compassion, in Silla, which shared similar practices, were the most diffused of the cults of buddhas and bodhisattvas during the Silla period. All of the cults included meditative and visualization exercises, devotional practices, such as making offerings and chanting the names of buddhas and bodhisattvas, and the recitation of dhāraṇīs or Buddhist spells. When Hwaŏm Buddhism was established in Silla at the end of the seventh and early eighth centuries, it quickly became the most powerful and influential approach to Buddhist practice on the peninsula because of royal and aristocratic patronage. The purveyors of Hwaŏm Buddhism in Silla assimilated the practices and rituals of the preexisting cults of buddhas and bodhisattvas, thereby enabling Hwaŏm to develop into the most influential tradition in Korean Buddhism during the first half of the eighth century.

Exegetical Literature and Cultic Practices

Making merit and the efficacy of Buddhist practices appear to have been just as important to monastic Buddhist intellectuals as to lay Buddhists. For instance, in his *Commentary on the Three Maitreya Sūtras (Sam Mirŭk kyŏng)*, the monk-scholar Kyŏnghŭng, who served as Silla's supreme Buddhist overseer (*kungno,* "state elder") in the late seventh century, provides a list of practices believed to cause rebirth in Tuṣita Heaven in the presence of the future Buddha Maitreya:

> (1) The practice of discussing the precepts *(tam'gye)*, which means acting in dignified manner without fail; (2) the practice of worshipping stūpas *(kyŏngt'ap)*, which means sweeping stūpas and painting the precincts; (3) the practice of making offerings *(kongyang)*, which refers to precious incense and wondrous flowers; (4) the practice of absorption *(tŭngji)*, which means all samādhis enter the correct feelings *(chŏngsu);* (5) the practice of sūtra-chanting *(songgyŏng);* and (6) the practice of sūtra-recitation *(tokkyŏng).*[10]

It is clear that Kyŏnghŭng conceived of Maitreya worship as encompassing all facets of Buddhist worship. In a long passage explaining these six practices in greater detail he describes how the cult of Maitreya and the desire for rebirth in Tuṣita are conducive to the three essential goals of classical Buddhist practice, the three teachings—morality, meditation, and wisdom—and that all merit-making practices from the maintenance of stūpas to sūtra recitation can also be marshaled under its head. The first three practices are associated with the precepts or morality, the third with meditation, and the final two with the development of wisdom. He says that if you cultivate six or five practices you will be reborn in the highest grade of the highest class in Tuṣita Heaven, if you cultivate three or four practices you will be reborn in the middle grade of the highest class, and if you cultivate one or two practices you will be reborn in the lowest grade of the highest class.[11]

Scholarship on Buddhism has typically subordinated descriptions of monastic exegetes' interest in cultic practices to their doctrinal views and philosophical speculations. It is somewhat similar to the case of classicists' discomfort with and disbelief of Augustine's description of the efficacy of the cult of Saint Martin of Tours at the end of his philosophical masterpiece *The City of God*. This is the legacy of what Gregory Schopen calls "Protestant presuppositions" in Western scholarship that privileged idealized, canonical descriptions of what a monk is and does. Renewed interest in archeology, material culture, and the ritual dimension of religion are causing scholars such as Schopen to rethink the image of the medieval Buddhist monk:

> A picture of the actual Indian Buddhist monk and nun is gradually emerging; he and she differ markedly from the ideal monk and nun who have been presented on the basis of textual material alone. The actual monk, for example, unlike the textual monk, appears to have been deeply involved in religious giving and cult practice of every kind from the very beginning. He is preoccupied not with *Nirvāṇa*, but, above all else, with what appears to have been a strongly felt obligation to his parents, whether living or dead. He appears, in short, as very human and very vulnerable.[12]

Eminent monks and exegetes in East Asia were much like their Indian brethren described above. They were first and foremost practitioners who hoped to gain spiritual and thaumaturgic power from their cultic activities. Although these practices are usually labeled "popular Buddhism," this designation is ultimately unsatisfactory and creates more problems than it resolves because it presumes that religious elites perform different Buddhist practices. The terms "popular" and "folk" give the impression that these practices were marginal or subaltern with respect to the "great tradition of elite Buddhist scholars," who purportedly indulged solely in philosophical musings on spiritual liberation and their concomitant ascetic and meditation practices. A review of the hagiography on the major figures in East Asian Buddhist history shows that this was far from the actual situation. The Chinese pilgrim, translator, and Yogācāra exegete par excellence Xuanzang (ca. 602–664), for instance, venerated Maitreya and worshipped Avalokiteśvara in a variety of practices, including spells and ritual procedures, throughout his life.[13] Another monk, Daoshi (ca. 596–683) devoted an entire encyclopedia to canonical descriptions and stories devoted to all aspects of Buddhist practice and belief, *A Grove of Pearls in the Garden of the Dharma (Fayuan zhulin)*.[14] The aristocratic and intellectual monks of Silla, such as Chajang (d. between 650–655), Wŏnhyo (617–686), and Ŭisang (625–702), whose rituals and performances are described in the chapters that follow, were no different. Even the most renowned intellectual monks were intimately associated with various culturally informed, "popular" Buddhist practices. Thus, "popular Buddhism" is really mainstream Mahāyāna Buddhism, and the cultic practices that comprise it were promoted and patronized by eminent Buddhist exegetes and religious elites, aristocrats, and royalty.

In this book, literary materials are the primary sources used to construct episodic histories of the cults of Maitreya, Avalokiteśvara, and Hwaŏm Buddhism in Silla. As in the case of other studies of topics in Sinitic Buddhism, scholarly exegesis, hagiography, epigraphy, and the writings of literati are the most common sources.[15] Although a complete picture of what Gregory Schopen calls "Buddhism on the ground" would also include a detailed discussion of art historical materials dating from the Three Kingdoms (traditional dates, 57 B.C.E.–668 C.E.) and Unified Silla (668–935) periods, some architectural and art historical material will be used to describe the way that Hwaŏm symbolism was assimilated to Silla's topography.

The two main literary sources for the study of ancient Korea are the *History of the Three Kingdoms (Samguk sagi)* and *Memorabilia of the Three Kingdoms (Samguk yusa)*. The former was compiled by Kim Pusik (1075–1151) during the years 1136 to 1145 and follows the pattern set by Sima Tan (ca. 180–110 B.C.E.) and Sima Qian's (146–86 B.C.E.) *Historical Records (Shiji)*. As in the other Chinese dynastic histories in this genre, Buddhist themes are not treated in great detail and are ignored in many respects. Nevertheless, the *History* preserves important facts regarding the Silla royalty's deployment of Buddhist symbolism in order to provide legitimacy vis-à-vis the powerful hereditary aristocracy.

Although late in comparison to such works as Daoxuan's (596–667) *Further Lives of Eminent Monks (Xu gaoseng zhuan)*, which was completed in 649 and further revised afterward, and Kyōkai's *Miraculous Stories of Japan (Nihon ryōiki)*, which was first compiled in 787, *Memorabilia of the Three Kingdoms* is the major source of the hagiographical anecdotes that provide much of the detail in this book. It was compiled initially by the Buddhist monk Iryŏn (1206–1289), most likely in his final years after the devastating Mongolian invasion and subjugation of Korea in the mid-thirteenth century. The collection was further amended by his disciple Mugŭk (Hon'gu, 1250–1322) and also later by other unknown hands. The work of is a hodgepodge of legends of historical people, places, and events, short stories, local narratives, poetry, songs, and so forth, similar to some Chinese works of the *yishi* genre.[16] Though most scholars trained in Korea do not question its validity, Western scholars are typically skeptical of the value of *Memorabilia of the Three Kingdoms* not only because of its late date, but also because of its fanciful subject material and anachronisms.[17] *Memorabilia of the Three Kingdoms* was compiled originally during the mid-Koryŏ period (918–1392), but many of the narratives it includes are derived from accounts contained in earlier historical documents, biographies, stele inscriptions, gazetteers, and collections of wonder tales emphasizing the traditions and local discourse of the ancient Silla domain. Although the hand of Iryŏn and other later editors is obviously evident, *Memorabilia of the Three Kingdoms* preserves much of the original language of its sources as far as such sources can be checked.[18] Despite its shortcomings, and the inescapable fact that what was selected for inclusion in the text must have been influenced somewhat by concerns and interests dating to the Koryŏ period, I believe that it preserves much useful information on Buddhist cults in the Silla epoch when used carefully and judiciously.

Epigraphy from the Silla period, composed by both Buddhists and non-Buddhists, has been preserved in various sources, such as monastic records *(saji)*, and is compiled in a number of modern collections. Such literature provides much germane detail regarding religious communities and practices at particular religious sites. The shortcomings of *Memorabilia of the Three Kingdoms* are remedied, in part, through this useful material. The collected writings of the Silla literatus Ch'oe Ch'iwŏn (857– d. after 908) are also particularly useful in fleshing out the nature of the Hwaŏm tradition in the late ninth and early tenth centuries. Many of Ch'oe's stele inscriptions and poems composed at Buddhist monasteries were preserved in several kinds of premodern sources, particularly those seeking to present noteworthy examples of literati writing. Ch'oe's writings provide important information on the relationship between local elites, Buddhist cultic practices, and the Hwaŏm tradition.

Buddhist sūtras and sections of exegetical materials composed by Silla and contemporary Tang Chinese monks that treat Buddhist practices associated with the worship of particular buddhas and bodhisattvas are also frequently consulted. Such literature not only fleshes out what contemporary Buddhist monks thought appropriate practices were and the significance of cultic observances but also serves a useful heuristic device giving insight into how Silla Buddhists understood and applied Buddhist beliefs their own way.

Buddhist Cults and the Hwaŏm Synthesis in Silla Korea

It is commonly accepted that the actual establishment of Buddhism in Korea began in the sixth and seventh centuries when the doctrinal schools of Sino-Indian Buddhism were established in Koguryŏ, Paekche, and Silla. Silla's unification of the Three Kingdoms by conquest in the mid-seventh century and close relations with Tang China thereafter are the background to the importation of new practice-oriented schools in the seventh and eighth centuries. Emphasis on "schools" defines Korean Buddhism until Sŏn (Chan/Zen) became the dominant form of Buddhism at the end of the Unified Silla period. This model of early Korean Buddhism not only fails to do justice to what Buddhists were actually doing but also projects artificial boundaries that obscure the mutual interaction between many groups of Buddhists. It likewise neglects how the aristocrats and royalty deployed Buddhist rituals, practices, and symbolism to provide legitimacy. My principal objective here is to rectify this outdated model by emphasizing the role of cults in the domestication of Buddhism. I will show how Buddhist cults were deployed by social elites and religious leaders first before passing down to the common people. I will start with the deployment of Buddhist symbolism and ritual practices by Silla's royalty and then evaluate the cults of Maitreya and Avalokiteśvara as case studies. I will conclude by showing how the cosmology and widespread worship of buddhas, bodhisattvas, and deities associated with the Hwaŏm tradition provides the most compelling evidence of how Buddhism became completely entwined with Silla culture.

Chapter 1 reevaluates the introduction of Buddhism to the Korean peninsula and several ways in which the religion became inextricably tied to the Silla state. I identify various kinds of Buddhist symbolism and cultic practices that were deployed by the Silla royalty to legitimate the acquisition of power and by aristocrats to maintain their hereditary ascendancy and privileges. I emphasize interactions between the practices of native institutions and the nascent Buddhist church. I also address the role of native Buddhist propaganda suggesting how sites associated with pre-Buddhist religious practices were transformed and how Silla became portrayed as a land with an ancient Buddhist past, not as a barbarous country on the fringes of civilization. I likewise treat the position of rituals and monasteries associated with the protection of the state. A by-product of the topics covered in this chapter is clear evidence that the Buddhism adopted by the Silla state shares the same aristocratic characteristics as those observed in such early medieval Chinese states as the Northern Wei (386–534). Many Chinese Buddhist practices from the Northern dynasties probably entered Silla through the assistance of monks from the northern Korean state of Koguryŏ.

Chapter 2 examines the role of the cult of Maitreya in the domestication of Buddhism in Silla and describes how Maitreya worship, which was the dominant Buddhist cult among the Chinese Northern dynasties, encompassed several types of Buddhist practices. The early assimilation of the cult to the *hwarang* (flower boys) institution enabled Buddhist reinterpretations of native practices to permeate the sociocultural fabric of the Silla aristocracy and allowed Maitreya to become an important symbol of state protection during Silla's conquest of the other peninsular kingdoms. Funerary practices involving images of Maitreya and the use of Maitreya as an object of vision quests punctuate early aristocratic deployment of the cult in the sixth and seventh centuries. The appropriation of Maitreya by the elite of Silla was the main reason why no millenarian revolution in Silla drew upon this imagery until the early tenth century. Commoners of Silla would have seen images of Maitreya at Buddhist monasteries, but there are no narratives that suggest they participated in the cult until the eighth century. In this connection I introduce ties between the cults of Maitreya and Amitābha. After Buddhism became established in Silla, the popularity of the cult of Maitreya enabled it to become a vehicle through which fashionable Buddhist repentance rituals linked to imported Chinese divinatory observances were introduced to Silla. The veneration of Maitreya with offerings of tea and song suggests ways in which Silla Buddhists adapted Chinese developments to suit their needs.

Chapter 3 assesses the worship of Avalokiteśvara, which emerged as a cult easily accessible for people of all social strata in Silla during the seventh and eighth centuries. Available evidence demonstrates that supplication of this bodhisattva in Silla followed the recommendations for worship found in the chapter of the *Lotus Sūtra* that encourages people to invoke the bodhisattva's matchless power of compassion in a creative manner. In this chapter I develop the nature of the interrelationship between the cults of Avalokiteśvara, Amitābha, and Maitreya, which derives, in part, from the fact that the methods of worship of these three personages were roughly the same: verbal recitation of the bodhisattva's or buddha's name, visualization practices, the adoration of images, the commissioning of images, the chanting of spells (dhāraṇīs), and the making of offerings of songs. The hagiographical accounts suggest that a proliferation of images, both icons and paintings, of the various incarnations of the bodhisattva—such as the thousand-armed, thousand-eyed Avalokiteśvara or the eleven-headed Avalokiteśvara—existed in royal palaces and in monasteries on the peninsula just as they did in contemporary China and Japan. Aside from making offerings of all sorts, including tea and songs in one's native tongue, Silla Buddhists worshipped Avalokiteśvara through recitation of the Great Compassion Spell, a practice that has continued to the present. The promotion of the Avalokiteśvara cult by Silla monks steeped in the teachings of the *Avataṃsaka Sūtra* foreshadows the role that the Hwaŏm tradition will play in reconfiguring Silla's Buddhist landscape.

Chapter 4 examines the origins and development of Hwaŏm Buddhism in Silla. I describe the growing importance of the sūtra in medieval China and the role played by Silla monks in the rise of the tradition in both China and Japan from the standpoint of practice primarily and also intellectual developments. I argue against the position that the Silla royalty in the eighth century drew upon Hwaŏm symbolism to bolster the power of an autocratic ruler at the expense of the hereditary elites. I demonstrate instead how aristocrats and religious elites together gradually promoted the *Avataṃsaka Sūtra* as the most excellent explanation of the Buddhadharma and as a powerful talisman for the protection of the state by describing several projects of royal patronage directly associated with Hwaŏm themes. The evidence indicates that the promotion of Hwaŏm Buddhism increased after the royalty became dominated by a hereditary aristocracy. The importance of the disciples of Ŭisang, an early promoter of Hwaŏm Buddhism, is discussed, as is the role of Hwaŏm societies in the veneration of the founders of the Hwaŏm tradition in late Silla, especially in relation to the writings of the Silla scholar Ch'oe Ch'iwŏn. I conclude the chapter with a discussion of three inscriptions on the backs of images of Vairocana, the central Buddha of the *Avataṃsaka Sūtra,* in which the rhetoric on the decline of the Buddhist teaching and the cultic belief in the coming of Maitreya are combined using Hwaŏm imagery.

Chapter 5 provides several examples of how the Hwaŏm tradition was successful in organizing various Buddhist cultic practices within the conceptual framework of the *Avataṃsaka Sūtra*. When applied to topography, Hwaŏm cosmology further reinforced native propaganda that sought to transform Silla from a backward country on the fringes of civilization to the status of a Buddha-land on earth and demonstrated that it was a country with deep connections to the past, present, and future of Buddhism. The importance and pervasiveness of Hwaŏm views in Silla are made manifest in hagiographical, epigraphical, and architectural sources. To this end the chapter addresses the importation and appropriation of the cult of Mount Wutai (Odaesan) by royal monks of Silla and the establishment of royally sponsored rituals on the various peaks of the mountain range. The associated practices of erecting Hwaŏm monasteries on Silla's five sacred mountains and of locating mountains mentioned in the *Avataṃsaka Sūtra* in Silla are also examined. Hwaŏm and Pure Land symbolism became intertwined at monasteries founded by the royalty and elite and suggests ways in which cultic practices were combined under the umbrella of Hwaŏm cosmology. I conclude the chapter with a discussion of the role of the Hwaŏm cult of the Divine Assembly that flourished in late Silla times. Because the Hwaŏm tradition was successful in accommodating Sillan particularity into Buddhist universality and providing meaning for elite Buddhists on multiple levels, it became the most dominant and influential expression of Buddhism on the peninsula.

CHAPTER ONE
Buddhism and the State in Silla

In the early tenth century, a legend circulated on the Korean peninsula that the Silla king had three treasures *(sambo)*. These treasures—the sixteen-foot image of the Buddha *(changnyuk chonsang)* at Hwangnyong Monastery, the nine-story wooden pagoda *(kuch'ŭng mokt'ap)* erected at the same monastic complex, and the jade belt bestowed by heaven *(ch'ŏnsa oktae)* upon Silla king Chinp'yŏng in 579—not only putatively protected the state from invasion and destruction but conferred legitimacy upon the possessor. They functioned symbolically like and, perhaps, were figuratively modeled after the three treasures of the ancient Chinese Zhou dynasty (ca. 1045–256 B.C.E.): the Hall of Light (Mingtang), the imperial seal *(chuanguoxi)*, and the nine tripods *(jiuding)*.[1] In contrast to the Zhou objects, however, two of Silla's three treasures are items of Buddhist material culture; the selection of such objects emphasizes the importance of the religion in this early medieval Korean state. How did Buddhism come to enjoy such an exalted place in Silla and, more important, why did these objects of Buddhist worship come to represent the power and authority of the Silla state? What did Buddhism offer Silla kings that made it such an indispensable tool of governance?

The rise of Buddhism in Silla is linked to the social and political tensions surrounding the Silla royalty and aristocracy during the sixth century as well as to the royal use of cultic practices associated with cakravartin kings and the cult of Śākyamuni. Buddhism was adopted and deployed by Silla kings to enhance their power, prestige, and authority—their symbolic resources—that resulted from the thaumaturgic power associated with the religion. Silla kings were essentially primus inter pares, and their power was limited as a result of the tradition of assemblies of aristocratic governance known as *hwabaek*. Royal power was checked by the chief minister, the official representative and protector of aristocratic interests. Acts of Buddhist piety combined with military

13

success demonstrated that Silla kings followed the model of the Chinese Northern dynasties in yoking the respect of the Buddhist church to the authority of the state. The first Buddhist kings of Silla used the symbolism of the cakravartin king; but as the state cult began to flourish, they linked it to a special royal version of the cult of Śākyamuni to counterbalance the aristocracy's deployment of symbolism from the Maitreya cult in the native *hwarang* tradition. In this chapter, I will describe the rise of Buddhist cults in Silla by reviewing the introduction of Buddhism to Silla, the deployment of Buddhist symbolism by the Silla royalty and aristocracy, and the role of Buddhist propaganda and state-protection Buddhist rituals.

The Introduction of Buddhism to Silla

Traditional Buddhist narratives tell us that monks from Koguryŏ were the first to preach Buddhism in Silla. During the reign of King Nulchi (r. 417–457), the Koguryŏ monk Mukhoja (lit. "son of a dark barbarian"), who was probably a dark-skinned Central Asian, reportedly came to Silla and stayed in a village in the northern border areas, propagating Buddhism secretly. A later tradition says that an official envoy from the southern Chinese state of Liang (502–557) brought incense to Silla, but neither the king nor his ministers knew what it was or how to use it. They dispatched an emissary bearing the incense to find someone in the country who knew how to use it. Mukhoja instructed the emissary in its use, saying, "If you burn this when you make a vow there will certainly be a numinous response." At this time, the king's daughter had become seriously ill. The king summoned Mukhoja and had him burn incense and make an oath. When the king's daughter recovered, the king was overjoyed and rewarded him liberally with gifts. Suddenly, however, the monk vanished.[2] Although anachronism is a fundamental problem with the story—the Liang came to power almost fifty years after the death of King Nulchi—it is not far-fetched to accept the role that monks from Koguryŏ must have played in the early encounter of the Silla people with Buddhist beliefs and practices.

Another tradition reports that later, during the reign of King Soji (r. 479–500), another monk from Koguryŏ named Ado came and preached among the people, making a few converts before he passed away. After his death, his disciples continued the work, making converts from time to time.[3] A number of monks named Ado were known to Iryŏn, who, in his *Memorabilia of the Three Kingdoms,* attempts to sort out the confusing narratives associated with this figure. Particularly problematic to Iryŏn is that another monk named Ado is said to have first preached in Silla in 263, established the sites of seven monasteries, performed miracles, and prophesied that Buddhism would fail in Silla until the reign of a king who was a Buddhist sage.⁴ Modern scholars have suggested that the name Ado may really be a title referring to a tonsured monk, since at least three monks named Ado—the one who served in Koguryŏ and two who served in Silla—are mentioned in Korean sources.⁵

The Korean sources are silent with regard to the progress of the religion among the general population of Silla. By the time of Silla king Pŏphŭng (r. 514–540), however, the royal family wanted to adopt Buddhism as a state cult, despite the opposition of the conservative aristocrats who sought to maintain the ancient tribal system and indigenous beliefs.⁶ Perhaps they recognized that if King Pŏphŭng used Buddhism to enhance his symbolic resources, linking the king with spiritual entities supposedly stronger than the native gods and spirits, their political prerogatives and hereditary rights would be diminished in the process. Buddhism was ultimately made a state religion about 535, after the miraculous martyrdom of Pak Yŏmch'ok in 527. Better known as Ich'adon, Pak was a devoutly Buddhist aristocrat, official, and confidant of King Pŏphŭng.⁷

According to conventional scholarly wisdom, Buddhism was introduced to Koguryŏ and Paekche from the nobility down to the populace; in Silla, the direction was reversed. Conventional scholarly wisdom takes its position because the *History of the Three Kingdoms, Lives of Eminent Korean Monks,* and *Memorabilia of the Three Kingdoms* all state that Buddhism was introduced to the Koguryŏ court in 372 by Shundao and to the Paekche court in 384 by Maranant'a. On the other hand, hagiographic sources state that monks such as Ado and Mukhoja came to Silla and enjoyed some success because of their thaumaturgic healing powers among the people in remote areas outside the capital region of present-day Kyŏngju but that the ruling elites rejected Buddhism. It took a miracle performed by an aristocrat to cause the Silla elite to relent and accept Buddhism as a state religion.

I would argue that this sort of analysis is too simplistic and is based on the deployment of a handful of questionable narratives as historical facts. Evidence from Chinese sources suggests that Buddhist monks who had contacts in north China were active in Koguryŏ roughly fifty years prior to the time that Buddhism was made a state religion. Furthermore, various sea routes connecting southern Chinese states and Paekche were open during this period. Thus, Paekche's contacts with China through trade and tribute missions also suggest that Buddhist monks arrived in Paekche before 384.⁸

In fact, the traditional accounts of the acceptance of Buddhism by the three Korean kingdoms are not useful for deciding exactly when Buddhism was transmitted to the peninsula or the social status of the first converts. They are valuable, however, for suggesting a rough time period when the kingdoms on the peninsula began to imbibe Chinese culture at a more rigorous pace and saw the benefits of participating in cosmopolitan social, political, and religious practices.

Koguryŏ and Paekche had regular relations with the various states in northern and southern China. Koguryŏ maintained relationships with several kingdoms in north China to maintain a balance of power in their interstate relations. The Koguryŏ king may have accepted Buddhism from Fu Jian of the Former Qin (351–394) also because of the symbolic benefits Buddhism can lend to a hegemon seeking to establish authoritarian rule. Paekche's importation of Buddhism from the Jin (317–420) demonstrates its relations with the Chinese Southern dynasties, a connection that is reflected in the extant art; however, artistic influences are also evident from the northern Turko-Mongol dynasties. The fact that Silla did not officially recognize Buddhism until about 535 suggests that Silla did not have normal contact with Chinese kingdoms and was culturally backward. If Silla did send diplomats to China, they usually tagged along with the envoys from Paekche or Koguryŏ. The Silla state, however, was moving into a period of great expansion, lasting from about 514 through 780, which coincides with the early period of the domestication of Buddhism. This important transitional period of Silla history also included the amassing of territory, the forging of political and cultural links with China, the rise of authoritarian rule by Silla kings, the assimilation of the confederated Kaya states (532–562), and the conquest of Paekche (660) and Koguryŏ (668) with the aid of Tang China.

Buddhism and the Royalty of Silla

When King Pŏphŭng ascended the throne in 514, his attempt to fashion royal support for Buddhism can be seen as one of several actions directed at developing his symbolic resources to enhance royal prestige at the expense of the aristocrats. He established a military bureau in 517, promulgated a legal code in 520, and sent envoys to Liang in 521.[9] According to tradition, he wanted to construct a Buddhist monastery as well, and he clandestinely planned with the Buddhist Pak Yŏmch'ok (Ich'adon), a young, low-ranking official, to construct such a structure. They both knew that the aristocrats would strongly oppose construction of the monastery, but Pak, as the earliest version of the story goes, persuaded the king that he would be able to perform a miracle that would ultimately remove all opposition. According to their plans, Pak would secretly begin work on a monastery. When discovered, the king would deny complicity and move to execute Pak. Under these circumstances, Pak would testify about the power of Buddhism and perform a miracle that would convert the aristocratic officials. Pak was executed by beheading. As the story goes, when this was done his blood gushed forth milky white, and in a more mature version of the narrative, his head flew away north to the sacred Mount Kŭmgang, which was just north of the Kyŏngju plain in Yŏngch'ŏn.[10] The Buddhist tale says that all the conservative officials were impressed and awed by the power of the Buddhist faith and surrendered their opposition to Buddhism.[11]

Although the miraculous martyrdom of Pak Yŏmch'ok occurred in 527, Silla's official acceptance of Buddhism probably did not begin until nearly eight years later, with the establishment of Silla's first Buddhist structure, Hŭngnyun Monastery, in 535.[12] Instead, an aristocrat named Ch'ŏlbu was named chief minister (sangdaedŭng) in 531 and was entrusted with the affairs of state. No biography of Ch'ŏlbu has been passed down, so we cannot know of his attitude toward Buddhism. Some Buddhist ideas were apparently incorporated into the ruling apparatus, because the king was able to prohibit wanton killing in 528.[13] Nevertheless, it is apparent that construction of Hŭngnyun Monastery did not recommence until after Ch'ŏlbu's passing in 534.[14] What is significant is that the post of chief minister was created by King Pŏphŭng in 531. Perhaps this position was established to deal with the mounting conflicts arising between the aristocrats and the king. Since the king was insecure at this moment, as evidenced by the execution of Pak Yŏmch'ok, this post may have been created as an institutional compromise between the king and the hereditary aristocracy. In reality it consisted of the king's turning over powers and responsibilities previously entrusted to him to an aristocratic representative. Thus, the aristocracy was willing to allow Buddhism to be an official religion only if there was to be an exchange of actual power.[15]

Although King Pŏphŭng may appear to have lost power by creating the office of chief minister, in the long run royal authority was greatly enhanced by the royal family's patronage of Buddhism. No immediate successor to Ch'ŏlbu is listed in the historical documents, and in 536, Silla announced its first independent reign name Kŏnwŏn, "Establishing Prime," an auspicious title suggesting great power for the king.[16] This, however, was not to be a final victory of the royalty over the aristocracy. King Chinji (r. 576–579), for instance, was dethroned by the aristocracy putatively for licentious behavior. Buddhism could not have received official recognition in Silla by means of royal support alone. There must have been some compromise between the two competing groups.[17]

King Pŏphŭng's successors King Chinhŭng (r. 540–576) and King Chinp'yŏng (r. 579–631) enhanced their prestige and authority by drawing upon Buddhist imagery and symbolism and the cults of Śākyamuni and the cakravartin king. Veneration of the Buddha Śākyamuni, the historical Buddha Siddhārtha Gautama, is an ancient and enduring practice of Buddhism. Śākyamuni often represented all of the buddhas and in this guise was symbolically linked to royalty. The symbolic linkage of Śākyamuni to the royal family was first used by the Northern Wei, who featured images of the Buddha prominently in grottos constructed for its kings at Yungang and imagined their kings as living buddhas. The royal family of Silla, however, took their deployment of symbolism one step further by making connections to the Indian concept of the cakravartin king, an ideal Buddhist monarch. A ruler who deserved this epithet was one who ruled over the whole world (comprising the Four Continents). The Indian prototype is King Aśoka (r. 268–232 B.C.E.), and some scholars have accentuated the parallels between the two.[18] The term "cakravartin" means "wheel-turner" and suggests that the whole world submits to him because he turns "the wheel of the Dharma." Buddhist literature lists four wheels turned by such a king: golden *(jinlun)*, silver *(yinlun)*, copper *(tonglun)*, and iron *(tielun)*.[19] King Chinhŭng drew upon this imagery directly, giving two of his sons the names of Tongnyun (copper wheel) and Saryun (or Kŭmnyun, golden wheel).[20] Saryun later succeeded to the throne and reigned as Chinji before he was deposed by the aristocracy.

King Chinhŭng's military conquests and religious patronage more fully demonstrate his adherence to the model of the cakravartin king. Chinhŭng's military accomplishments include the extension of Silla's borders through the conquests of the Han River Basin in 551 and Tae Kaya in 562.[21] He is also credited with organizing the *hwarang* order.[22] His Buddhist patronage is also compelling. Hŭngnyun Monastery was completed in 544. In the spring of 549 the Chinese Liang court dispatched an emissary bearing a Buddhist relic. He was accompanied by the Silla monk Kaktŭk, who returned to his homeland after studying Buddhism in China. King Chinhŭng met them publicly in the presence of one hundred ministers on the road in front of Hŭngnyun Monastery.[23] Although Chinhŭng dispatched emissaries to the courts of the Liang and Chen (557–589) dynasties, from whence Silla reportedly acquired scores of Buddhist scriptures and treatises, he was invested as king of Silla by the Northern Qi (550–577).[24] Although these reports emphasize contact with the Chinese Southern dynasties, influences from the Northern dynasties were greater.

Lavish patronage of the Buddhist church was also a key component of Chinhŭng's rule. After sighting a yellow dragon on an auspicious site where he had planned to build a palace, he set aside the land and established Hwangnyong Monastery in 553. This monastery was partially completed in 566, when two more monasteries were announced.[25] The first Assembly of the Eight Prohibitions *(p'algwanhoe)* was held in Silla in 572.[26] This dharma assembly was held under the direction of the monk Hyeryang, who had emigrated from Koguryŏ in 551 when Silla conquered the Han River Basin. The last years of his reign include the casting and enshrining of a large sixteen-foot Buddhist image in the Golden Hall of Hwangnyong Monastery.[27] Thus, his lavish patronage of Buddhism and his military conquests made him a prototypical cakravartin king in the eyes of his subjects.[28]

The Northern Wei emperor was regarded by the Buddhist church as a living buddha, thus engendering a close relationship between the church and the state.[29] Silla rulers took the symbolism of this sort of relationship between the church and the royal family one step further: the royal family of Silla became the literal embodiment of the family of the Buddha Śākyamuni by taking upon themselves the names of the Buddha's family members. King Chinp'yŏng was the son of crown prince Tongnyun (d. 572) and had the same given name as the father of Śākyamuni, Śuddhodhana (Kor. Paekchŏng); his queen was given the same name as the Buddha's mother, the Lady Māyā (Kor. Maya puin); and even the names of Chinp'yŏng's brothers Śuklodana (Pāli Sukkodana, Kor. Paekpan) and Drotodana (Pāli Dhotodana, Kor. Kukpan) corresponded to those of Śākyamuni's uncles.[30] Following this method of symbolic reasoning, a son born to King Chinp'yŏng and Queen Maya would correspond to Śākyamuni. Ironically, they had only daughters. Nevertheless, this relationship between the family of the Buddha and the royal Kim family of Silla must have had some effect on the circumstances surrounding the ascension of Queen Sŏndŏk (r. 632–647; given name Tŏngman, Skt. *Guṇamālādevī?) to the throne.[31] Queen Sŏndŏk was succeeded by her cousin Queen Chindŏk (r. 647–654), who had a Buddhist given name, Śrīmālā (Kor. Sŭngman), the same as that of a famous female ruler appearing in Mahāyāna Buddhist literature. The concept of royalty prevalent in the Northern dynasties, where the king is a buddha, influenced Silla royalty. The rulers of Silla probably received this conception of royalty through the influence of Koguryŏ.[32]

The Silla holy-bone royal family also identified themselves as being of the Indian *kṣatriya* (warrior) caste *(ch'alli chong)*, even though no son was born to King Chinp'yŏng. According to a later Buddhist tradition, when the aristocratic monk Chajang visited Mount Wutai in China and encountered Mañjuśrī there, the bodhisattva of wisdom said, "The queen of your country (Sŏndŏk) belongs to the *kṣatriya* caste and has already received a prophecy of her future buddhahood. Because of this special destiny, his [Chinp'yŏng's] family is not like the rest of the Eastern Barbarians *(tongi).*"[33] Although these associations between the royal family and India's kingly and warrior caste and the Buddha's family accrued symbolic resources to the holy-bone elites, the power of the Silla aristocracy was not broken. Silla's true-bone aristocrats quickly realized the benefit that Buddhist doctrine and symbolism could provide in the maintenance of their hereditary privileges.

Buddhism, the *Hwarang,* and the Aristocracy of Silla

The royalty of Silla were able to increase their power and prestige by drawing upon the model of the cakravartin king and the cult of Śākyamuni. They were, however, not the only social group in Silla to enhance their symbolic resources by using Buddhist symbols. The aristocracy drew upon the unique relationship between the cakravartin king and Maitreya, the future Buddha, to counterbalance royal power. Studies on the Maitreya cult in Silla have shown that it was focused on the teaching of the *Sūtra on Maitreya's Rebirth Below (Mile xiasheng jing)* rather than on the *Sūtra on the Visualization of Maitreya's Rebirth Above in Tuṣita Heaven (Guan Mile shangsheng jing)* and that Maitreya was incarnate as a *hwarang* in Silla.[34]

Most scholars agree that Silla's bone-rank system—its rigid system of hereditary status and social stratification—did not become fixed until the sixth century and, more important, that the youth of Silla society learned the order of the bone-rank system *(kolp'umje)* through their participation in the *hwarang* institution.[35] The system consisted of two bone ranks and, in theory, six head ranks. The Silla royal family comprised those of holy-bone *(sŏnggol)* status, and the capital-based aristocracy held the true-bone *(chin'gol)* position. Local elites of the provinces comprised the head-rank six *(yuktup'um)* category, and local functionaries head ranks five and four. Head ranks three, two, and one, which seldom appear in the extant materials, are thought to have consisted of peasants and slaves. The *hwarang* are presumed to have developed out of local, village, or rural youth organizations of the Three Kingdoms era that were reformulated into the more centralized *hwarang* order to promote royal and aristocratic prerogatives.[36] The basic purpose and structure of the *hwarang* order may be outlined as follows:

> The *hwarang* were a means of cultivating and educating elite youths that might later become strong leaders.
> Each *hwarang* band was made up of a leader, known as a *hwarang,* who was of true-bone descent; a *sŭngnyŏ nangdo* (monk follower or attendant to the *hwarang*), who functioned as an adviser or spiritual mentor and teacher; and ranks of commoner *nangdo* (followers) underneath.[37]
> From the ages of fifteen to eighteen, *hwarang* received specialized training, which included music and wandering in the mountains. This training is called *p'ungnyu,* a polysemous term that is under-

stood best in the general sense of aristocratic "customs and traditions" of the *hwarang*.³⁸

Blood oaths were made between members of each *hwarang* band.

The *hwarang* were associated with the cult of Maitreya but not with Maitreya as a messianic figure.

The *hwarang* acted as a buffer for the changes taking place in Silla's status-oriented society.

The *hwarang* mediated between various competing traditions and sources of power in Silla: the royal family and the aristocracy, the regional and capital aristocracies, elites and commoners, the traditions and cultures of Silla and Kaya, and Buddhism and the indigenous religious practices of Silla and Kaya. After the peace inaugurated by Silla's "unification" and the development of the State Academy (Kukhak) in 682 for the instruction and cultivation of Silla's elite sons, the *hwarang*'s efforts and activities turned from "war" to "play." The *hwarang* became more intellectual, artistic, and effete, though they still officiated at official state rituals such as the Assembly of the Eight Prohibitions. They ultimately disappeared as a meaningful institution during the Koryŏ period (918–1392).³⁹

The relationship between Maitreya and the *hwarang* is manifest in the traditional narratives: that of the monk Chinja (fl. 576–579), who set out to find Maitreya incarnate as a *hwarang* and was directed to a mysterious youth named Misi (often read Miri = Mirŭk), who became the leader of Silla *hwarang*;⁴⁰ of Kim Yusin (595–673), who as a youth led a *hwarang* patrol known as the Dragon Flower Aspirants *(yonghwa hyangdo)*, referring to the *nāgapuṣpa* (Ch. *longhua*), the bodhi tree of Maitreya;⁴¹ and of the *hwarang* Chukchi (fl. 692–702), whose parents placed a stone image of Maitreya over the grave of a youth who they dreamed would be reborn as their son.⁴²

A key point that defines the special relationship between the king, the aristocracy, and the Maitreya cult in Silla derives from an early teaching found in the Buddhist scriptures that Maitreya will manifest himself in the world during the reign of a cakravartin king.⁴³ This relationship between the king and Maitreya showed that religion and politics could be complementary. The king of Silla functioned in the role of the cakravartin, and the *hwarang* were representative of Maitreya; however, because the *hwarang* were typically the sons of true-bone aristocrats and head-rank six elites, they were, in the words of Lee Ki-baik, "the flower of Silla's aristocracy and were symbolic of the power of this social class."⁴⁴ Thus, modeled on the relationship between Maitreya and the cakravartin king, both the royalty and the aristocracy of Silla were able to draw upon Buddhism to enhance their symbolic resources.

Silla's Buddha-Land Propaganda

The Silla royalty and aristocracy collaborated in creating and disseminating propaganda "verifying" that Silla had been the abode of buddhas in previous ages of the Dharma. Many places held sacred in the pre-Buddhist religion of the people of Silla, such as the three sacred mountains and sundry forests and valleys, were reconfigured as places where they had discovered traces of past buddhas.[45]

There were three sacred mountains around the Kyŏngju plain[46] and four hallowed spots in Silla where aristocratic ministers would gather to discuss important affairs of state. These four places were Mount Ch'ŏngsong in the east, Mount Oji in the south (on Kyŏngju's Namsan), P'ijŏn in the west, and Mount Kŭmgang in the north (modern Yŏngch'ŏn in North Kyŏngsang Province). Namsan, or South Mountain, and Mount Kŭmgang, in particular, which must already have been cultic sites of some importance, were then recast in a new role as Buddhist sites of a previous age in order to propagandize Silla as a Buddha-land with karmic connections to the Buddhist teaching stretching back many eons. The land northeast of South Mountain was the heartland of the Silla capital city. The Dragon Palace (Yonggung) was east of the royal palace, Moon City (Wŏlsŏng). To the south pious Buddhists discovered "the meditation stone" (*yŏnjwa-sŏk*) of Śākyamuni's forerunner, the Buddha Kāśyapa, who had become enlightened on that spot eons before. It was on this site that Hwangnyong Monastery, the Monastery of the August Dragon, was erected.[47] These claims to Silla's purported Buddhist past, along with the subsequent diffusion of Hwaŏm (Avataṃsaka) cosmology, served as the basis for Silla's Buddha-land propaganda.

Probably sometime during the late seventh or early eighth century, members of the royalty and aristocracy created and disseminated a tale about the Buddhist past of the land of Silla. This propaganda was codified in a stele inscription for the previously discussed monk Ado, who putatively brought Buddhism to Silla at great personal risk in the mid-third century. This inscription, which is preserved in *Memorabilia of the Three Kingdoms* with Iryŏn's editorial interpolations, records that Ado's mother prophetically informed him of seven locations in Silla where vestiges of past buddhas could be found and where he should found monasteries:

> His mother said, "This state [Koguryŏ], even up to this point, does not grasp the Buddhadharma, but after 3,000 moons a sage king will be born in Kyerim [Silla], who will greatly promote Buddhism. There will be seven vacant *saṃghārāma* [monastery] sites within his capital city. The first is Ch'ŏn'gyŏng [Heavenly Mirror] Forest east of Kŭm Bridge. ([Interlinear note by Iryŏn:] This is the present-day Hŭngnyun Monastery. Kŭm Bridge is called the West River Bridge. In the local dialect it is called Pine Bridge.)

The monasteries first founded by Ado were all abandoned. From the *chŏngmi* year of his reign [527] King Pŏphŭng first began [re]building it; its grand opening was in the *ŭlmyo* year [535] and King Chinhŭng eventually completed it.) The second is Samch'ŏn [Three Rivers] Fork. ([Interlinear note by Iryŏn:] This is the present-day Yŏnghŭng Monastery. It was opened at the same time as Hŭngnyun Monastery [535].) The third is south of Dragon Palace. ([Interlinear note by Iryŏn:] This is present-day Hwangnyong Monastery. King Chinhŭng first opened it in the *kyeyu* year [553] of his reign.) The fourth is north of Dragon Palace. ([Interlinear note by Iryŏn:] This is present-day Punhwang Monastery. [Queen] Sŏndŏk first opened it in the *kabu* year [634].) The fifth is Sach'ŏn [Sand River] Promontory. ([Interlinear note by Iryŏn:] This is present-day Yŏngmyo Monastery. Queen Sŏndŏk first opened it in the *ŭlmi* year [635].) The sixth is Sinyu [Spirit Wandering] Forest. ([Interlinear note by Iryŏn:] This is present-day [Sa]ch'ŏnwang Monastery. King Munmu opened it in the *kimyo* year [679]). The seventh is Sŏch'ŏng [Son-in-Law's Request] Patty. ([Interlinear note by Iryŏn:] This is present-day Tanŏm Monastery.) All of these were monastery sites in the previous Buddha's age."[48]

The important fact is not whether the prophecy of Buddhism's reflourishing in Silla "after 3,000 moons" (equals 250 years) is accurate, since there is at least a 265-year period between Ado's coming to Silla in 263 and King Pŏphŭng's bid to build a monastery in 527. This is most certainly an ex post facto concoction; we have already reviewed how work on Hŭngnyun Monastery did not actually begin until 535. The important issue at hand is that some influential people of Silla presented this as the truth during the seventh and eighth centuries. Faithful Buddhists developed these stories as a means of adding symbolic value to the monasteries they were constructing while Buddhist culture prospered in Silla. Furthermore, although the historical validity of the stories is disputable, they show how completely portions of the Silla aristocracy were converted to Buddhism.[49]

This inscription also provides evidence for the way in which cultic sites associated with Silla's indigenous gods and spirits may have been transformed into protectors of the Buddhadharma as Buddhism grew in power and prestige on the peninsula. Of these seven sites, the Dragon Palace where Hwangnyong Monastery (fig. 1) was eventually constructed was the most important locus of ritual and Buddhist learning. Iryŏn stresses the layered nature of this site in his narrative on the meditation stone of the former Buddha Kāśyapa, the mythical buddha of the remotely distant past under whose influence the future Śākyamuni vowed to become a buddha. This spot, which may have originally been the center of a royal dragon (or snake) cult for the propitiation of rain, acquired a Buddhist prehistory to enhance its prestige as a site worthy of a royally sponsored monastery. Iryŏn says,

> According to the *Jade Dragon Collection (Ongnyong chip)*, the *Biography of Chajang (Chajang chŏn)*, and various other sources, the meditation stone of the Buddha Kāśyapa was located south of the Dragon Palace, east of Moon City. It was a vestige of a monastery dating from the time of the past buddha. The present site of Hwangnyong Monastery is one of the seven *saṃghārāmas*.
>
> According to the [official] *State History (Kuksa)*, in the second month of the *kyeyu* year (1–29 March 553), the fourteenth year of King Chinhŭng's reign and the third since the foundation of the state, when the king wanted to construct a new palace east of Moon City an "august dragon" appeared there. The king reconsidered and converted the palace into August Dragon Monastery (Hwangnyongsa). The meditation stone was located near the rear of its Buddha Hall. From what I have seen, it [the

FIGURE 1. Model reconstruction of Hwangnyong Monastery, Kyŏngju National Museum.

stone] is about five to six palms high and only three cubits in circumference. It stands erect like a flagstaff and its top is flat. Having endured two fires since its construction by King Chinhŭng, the stone was cracked, and monks sealed it with iron in order to protect it.[50]

The traditional narrative regarding the image of the Buddha enshrined within Hwangnyong Monastery also stresses the dynamic nature of the legends developed by the royalty and aristocracy to highlight the karmic connection between Silla and the Buddhist homeland of India. This account is slightly different from the foregoing, because it records that in 553 the king planned to build a Purple Palace (Chagung) on the site of the Dragon Palace, but instead commissioned a Buddhist monastery, which he named Yellow Dragon Monastery (Hwangnyongsa). The monastery was finally completed in 569 and enclosed with a fence. Soon after the monastery's completion, a mysterious unmanned boat drifted into the port of Sap'o in Hagok district from the distant region of the "south seas" (Namhae). The boat was found to contain a sealed letter that said the Indian king Aśoka gathered 57,000 *kŭn* of yellow iron and 30,000 *pun* of gold and tried, without success, to cast an image of Śākyamuni. Believing that Buddhists elsewhere would fare better, he placed the materials in a boat and set it adrift, expressing the following wish: "May it reach some karmicly connected country *(yŏn kukt'o)* and that an image of the venerable [Śākyamuni measuring] sixteen feet will be made with it." Smaller images, one of the Buddha and two of bodhisattvas, were also placed on board to serve as models. When word reached the king, he dispatched commissioners to found a monastery on auspicious high ground; it was called Tongch'uk (East India) Monastery, and there the smaller images of the Buddha and bodhisattvas were enshrined. The metals were transported to the capital. The skilled artisans of Silla succeeded immediately in casting the Śākyamuni image in 574 (or 573 according to the monastery record). The main image contained 35,007 *kŭn* of iron and 10,198 *pun* of gold, while the bodhisattva images contained 12,000 *kŭn* of iron and 10,136 *pun* of gold. A year after these three images were enshrined at Hwangnyong Monastery, tears miraculously flowed from the eyes of the statue, running down to the heels of the image and moistening the ground at the base of the icon. These tears were taken to be a sign of mourning over the death of the "great king." Iryŏn then remarks that another source, which says that the images were cast during the reign of King Chinp'yŏng, is wrong. Iryŏn next relates another tale regarding King Aśoka's difficulty in casting an image of the Buddha and his subsequent setting adrift a boat filled with the materials from which to make the image. The boat floated to all the countries, large and small, of Jambudvīpa; however, in each and every place the casting was unsuccessful. At long last it reached Silla; the images were cast in Muning Forest under orders from King Chinhŭng and displayed all the special marks of a buddha.[51]

Later, when the aristocratic monk Chajang went to China in search of the Dharma during the years 636 through 643, he climbed Mount Wutai in hopes of encountering the bodhisattva Mañjuśrī and obtaining wisdom from him. He returned to Silla telling of an experience of his communing with Mañjuśrī in which the bodhisattva reminded him of the karmic connection between India and Korea:

> Hwangnyong Monastery in your country is the place where the Buddhas Śākyamuni and Kāśyapa preached. The "meditation stone" [of Kāśyapa] is still there. For this reason, King Aśoka of India, having amassed a great amount of yellow iron, sent it on a boat over the seas. After more than 1,300 years it reached Silla and [the images] were completed and enshrined in that monastery. This was brought to pass by an impressive chain of causality.[52]

The account continues, informing us that the three smaller statues, which had originally been placed in Tongch'uk Monastery, were moved to Hwangnyong Monastery. Iryŏn then refers to the monastery's records to inform us that the Golden Hall was erected in the sixth year of King Chinp'yŏng (584). The first abbot, or "monastery overseer" (saju), Master Hwanhŭi, was installed during the reign of Queen Sŏndŏk; the second was Buddhist Overseer (kukt'ong) Chajang. He was succeeded by Buddhist Overseer Hyehun and Vinaya Master Sang. Although most of these images were lost to wars and fires over the centuries, Iryŏn remarks that the small statue of Śākyamuni still remains.[53]

All of the foregoing accounts suggest that they were composed at a time when Buddhism was flourishing in Silla, yet lacked sufficient prestige to be accepted as a new religious movement. Silla Buddhists, like their Chinese brethren, were sensitive to the fact that they were removed from the Buddha temporally and spatially.[54] These stories demonstrate that Buddhists wanted to justify their conversion to the Buddhist faith by acknowledging a hitherto unknown prehistory that was revealed through the enlightened and inspired prophecy of the faithful and karmic linkage with India, the mainspring of Buddhism. This preliminary stage was aimed at confirming the people in their belief that Silla, far from being an isolated, backward country on the edge of the known world, was, actually, originally a Buddha-land.[55] The conceptualization of Silla as a Buddha-land became more sophisticated with the importation and assimilation of the Chinese cult of Mount Wutai and the application of Hwaŏm cosmology to the Silla landscape. More closely linked with Buddha-land propaganda, however, were rituals performed by elite monks to ensure the longevity and prosperity of the Silla state.

State-Protection Buddhism

There was a close relationship between the state and the Buddhist monastic establishment during the Chinese Northern dynasties period. The state supported official monks who benefited the state by performing rituals promising the longevity of the dynasty. The belief by politically minded monks that the Northern Wei emperors were living buddhas fostered a close relationship between the state and the monastic community. This deployment of Buddhism became a key component in the ideology of imperial legitimation under the Northern dynasties.[56] Despite periods of suppression, the Northern dynasties held special Buddhist assemblies for the protection of the state, a concept that has become known as state-protection Buddhism (Ch. *huguo fojiao*, Kor. *hoguk pulgyo*).[57] State protection was an important aspect of Silla Buddhism as well. Several aspects of this form of Buddhism in Silla are especially important: special dharma assemblies, monasteries, and the early government organs for controlling the Buddhist monastic community.

Two special dharma assemblies were held from time to time on behalf of the Silla court and kingdom: the Assembly of the Eight Prohibitions and the Convocation for the Recitation of the *Sūtra for Humane Kings* by One Hundred Eminent Monks *(paekkojwa kanghoe)*. They were introduced to Silla by the Koguryŏ monk Hyeryang, who emigrated to Silla after the conquest of the Han River Basin in 551. The first Assembly of the Eight Prohibitions was held in the tenth lunar month of 572 at an unnamed monastery *(oesa)* on behalf of deceased soldiers, and it lasted for seven days.[58] Āgama literature suggests that the eight prohibitions refer to a special dharma assembly for laymen, particularly kings, in which they empower themselves by fasting and following eight precepts that a monk would follow for a specified period of time. Full-fledged monks usually reviewed and rededicated (i.e., empowered) themselves to the monastic precepts (Skt. *vinaya, śīla*) twice a month on the seventh and fifteenth days in a special dharma assembly (Skt. *poṣadha*) in which the monastic code was recited. Although scholars are not sure what was contained in the Silla assembly, they suggest that the Assembly of the Eight Prohibitions in Silla was used to empower the Silla kings and prosper the country and that it included worship of the native gods and spirits of Silla. The assembly may have been held in conjunction with royal veneration of the future Buddha Maitreya because three principal Mahāyāna sūtras treating the past and future ministry of this popular bodhisattva encourage aspirants to hold "fasts of the eight precepts" *(bajiezhai)*, which is another name for the same type of assembly.⁵⁹ Emperor Wu (r. 502–549) of the Liang dynasty held similar assemblies *(baguanzhai hui)* to expiate the sins of his people and to ward off calamities.⁶⁰ Korean Buddhist literature suggests that the assembly was held only once more, at a ceremony celebrating the completion of the nine-story wooden pagoda at Hwangnyong Monastery, perhaps in 646. It later became a regular Buddhist ritual held by the Koryŏ court.⁶¹

The Convocation for the Recitation of the *Sūtra for Humane Kings* by One Hundred Eminent Monks has its basis in the "Protecting the State" chapter *(Huguo pin)* of the *Perfection of Wisdom Sūtra for Humane Kings (Renwang bore boluomi jing)*. This scripture stipulates that whenever a country is faced with difficult or threatening circumstances, the humane king should first prepare one hundred images and one hundred high seats. Eminent and worthy monks of equal number are then to be invited to recite and expound upon this sūtra.⁶² This convocation was held perhaps twice during the seventh century at Hwangnyong Monastery and purportedly featured the lectures of the eminent monk Wŏn'gwang (d. ca. 640) in 613 and 636.⁶³ King Sŏngdŏk (r. 702–737) founded Pongdŏk Monastery in order to perform rituals on behalf of his ancestor Kim Ch'unch'u (604–661), the posthumous King T'aejong Muyŏl (r. 654–661). At that monastery he erected the Humane Kings' Enlightenment Site (Inwang toryang)—a hall for the recitation of the *Sūtra for Humane Kings*—and as part of the festivities lasting seven days he granted amnesty to prisoners.⁶⁴ The recitation assembly was held again in 779 in response to an earthquake that killed a hundred people in the Silla capital and other inauspicious omens in the sky. The state-protection ritual was conducted more frequently at Hwangnyong Monastery in the final years of Silla in 876, 886, 887, and 924, where it was held in conjunction with general amnesties and vegetarian feasts of Buddhist monks.⁶⁵

Three monasteries were directly associated with state-protection Buddhism in Silla: Hwangnyong Monastery, Sach'ŏnwang (Four Heavenly Kings) Monastery, and Kamŭn (Responsive Grace) Monastery. Hwangnyong Monastery held a special place among all monasteries in Silla because it functioned as the state palladium. Hwangnyong Monastery was a massive structure; built south of the main palace of Silla, it took nearly ninety years of sporadic construction to bring to its final form, before being burned down by the Mongols in 1238 in an act of cultural terrorism. Construction on the monastery began in 553, and the nine-story pagoda was completed in 645.⁶⁶ It not only served as the location for the Assembly of the Eight Prohibitions and the Convocation for the Recitation of the *Sūtra for Humane Kings*, but was also the principal residence for the monastic leaders selected by the government and the location where Silla kings attended the Lantern Festival and other Buddhist gatherings. The monastery's most important asset, though, was the nine-story pagoda constructed at the behest of Chajang, a monk of the true-bone social strata linked to the Silla royal family.[67] Two narratives purport to provide the reasons for the construction of this wooden pagoda. The first and apparently older story was recorded in 872 on a reliquary container placed under a large stone marking the base of the central or main pillar *(simch'o)*. It says that when Chajang desired to return to Silla, he bowed as he took his leave from an otherwise unknown meditation master named Yuanxiang on Mount Zhongnan. In parting, Yuanxiang gave him the following instruction: "By observing your mind I have observed that of your country. Build a nine-story pagoda at Hwangnyong Monastery, and all the countries east of the [Yellow] sea (Haedong = Silla Korea) will surrender completely to your country." Chajang memorized his words and reported them to the Silla court when he returned.[68]

The second and more popular legend was recorded by Iryŏn. According to that legend, Chajang went to Tang China to study Buddhism during the years 636 to 643, during which time he had an encounter with the dharma-protecting dragon of Taihe Lake. When the dragon asked him why he had come, Chajang responded that he was in search of enlightenment. The guardian then asked him what difficulties his country faced. Chajang told the dragon that his country was surrounded by enemies on all sides and that incursions by foreigners were bringing hardships on the people, and he asked what he could do to benefit his country. The dragon informed him that the dharma-protecting dragon at Hwangnyong Monastery was his eldest son and instructed Chajang to build a nine-story pagoda at that monastery and, when the pagoda was complete, to perform an Assembly of the Eight Prohibitions. When all this was accomplished, the dragon promised, Silla would prevail over its neighboring states, and the expansionist designs of Silla would be secured. The nine stories of the pagoda were later said to represent the various states and tribal peoples with which Silla had dealings, such as Japan, China, Wuyue, the Malgal (Ch. Mohe), and the Yemaek.[69]

Silla's nine-story wooden stūpa, which was designed by a Paekche architect named Abiji, was probably modeled after another large nine-story pagoda built at Yongning Monastery in Luoyang, the capital of the Northern Wei dynasty, in 516.[70] The opulence of Hwangnyong Monastery probably inspired the Yamato court in Japan to compete with the holy-bone kings of neighboring Silla by building its own nine-story wooden pagoda on the site of the Kudara Ōdera (Great Paekche Monastery), also called Daikan Daiji, situated near Kibi Pond in the capital at Asuka in 639.[71] The building of this monastery and its large pagoda shows the wealth, opulence, and power of Silla and Queen Sŏndŏk's court and their promotion of Buddhism for the success of the Silla state.

Although later Korean legends attribute the "unification" of the three Korean kingdoms of Paekche, Koguryŏ, and Silla to the nine-story stūpa at Hwangnyong Monastery, the pagoda by itself was not able to protect the state from invading Tang Chinese armies. Silla was able to defeat its rivals, Paekche in 660 and Koguryŏ in 668, only with the intervention of Tang China; and the mighty Tang was able to bring Koguryŏ to submission only with the assistance of Silla. Once the allies had completed their conquest, however, Silla had designs to rule the peninsula itself, and Tang had plans to annex and administer all of the regions they conquered jointly. This difference led to war between the erstwhile allies in 671, and the Chinese dispatched a large invasion fleet across the Yellow Sea. Chajang's relative, the monk Myŏngnang (fl. 632–671), also of true-bone rank, who had apparently studied Buddhist rituals in China at the same time as Chajang, instructed King Munmu (r. 661–681) to construct a makeshift monastery dedicated to the four heavenly kings, the protectors of the Dharma in this world, south of Mount Nang in the sacred Sinyu Forest. It was initially made with colorful silks instead of wood and images of the spirits of the five directions *(obang sin)* out of grass. There, Myŏngnang conducted an esoteric ritual procedure *(munduru pimil chi pŏp)* with twelve other Yoga monks.[72] According to tradition, a violent storm wrecked the invasion fleet, causing the Chinese to make peace with Silla and recognize Silla's hegemony over the former Paekche lands and the southern portion of the former Koguryŏ domain. King Munmu later reconstructed the monastery and called it Sach'ŏnwang Monastery.[73]

King Munmu's obsession with the protection of his newly conquered territory continued to his death. According to legend, prior to his passing, he swore an oath that he would be reborn as a dragon protecting Silla's coast from invasion and piracy and commanded that he be cremated, according to Buddhist custom, and his ashes scattered in the East Sea (Sea of Japan). A turtle-shaped rock was placed in a rocky crag off the coast of the present-day small fishing village of Kamp'o to commemorate his vow. This is known as the Tomb-Rock of the Great King (Taewangam). His son, King Sinmun (r. 681–692), constructed Kamŭn Monastery less than a mile inland on a spot that is connected to the coast through an underground channel so that the dragon-spirit of his father could rest at the monastery. All that remains of this monastery are the twin stūpas constructed in front of the Golden Hall, which are the largest extant stone stūpas dating from the Unified Silla period. Because Kamŭn Monastery was specially administered by the state, scholars think that Buddhist rituals for the longevity of the royal family of Silla and the protection of the state were also regularly performed at this monastery.[74]

Throughout this section I have touched on the symbolic ties between the Buddhist monastic community, the royalty, and the aristocracy in Silla and concluded that it followed primarily Chinese Northern dynasties models. One final example of this trend is the establishment of the Silla government's organs for controlling the Buddhist community. State-protection Buddhism included not only the use of Buddhist rituals on behalf of the state, but also the state's safeguarding or official administration of the Buddhist monastic community. Studies have shown that the names selected by the rulers of Silla for ecclesiastical positions followed precedents set in the Northern Wei. For example, the positions of Saṃgha Overseer or Buddhist Overseer (*sŭngt'ong, kukt'ong*; glossed as *saju*, "overseer of monasteries"), Chief Buddhist Monk *(taedoyuna)*, Chief Buddhist Nun *(toyuna-nyang)*, and Chief Monastic Scribe *(taesŏsŏng)*, established during the reign of King Chinhŭng, correspond quite well to the Northern Wei and Northern Qi offices of Buddhist Overseer *(datong, tong)* and Chief Buddhist Monk *(duweina)*, but not to the Liu-Song (420–478) and Southern Qi (479–502) offices of Saṃgha Overseer *(sengzhu)*, Saṃgha Rectifier *(sengzheng)*, and Saṃgha Chief *(sengdu)*. Although the names of the titles of the Silla offices follow those of the Northern dynasties, scholars suggest that they functioned more as honorific titles than as actual administrative posts—but this may also have been the case in China.[75] They did not become actual positions of power until the time of Chajang, who, after his return from Tang China, was named Supreme Buddhist Overseer *(taegukt'ong)*, was empowered to establish a precepts platform *(kyedan)* at T'ongdo Monastery, and was authorized to inspect and rectify the Buddhist monastic establishment in Silla.

The reason these official positions in Silla's Buddhist church were probably honorific was most likely a result of the Silla government's waiting for a monk tied to the royal family, like Chajang, to acquire enough prestige in the Buddhist community to be respected by the aristocracy and the monastic community alike. Regardless, this approach was soon discarded. After Kim Ch'unch'u's true-bone line ascended the throne of Silla and initiated the peninsular wars of expansion, which pitted the Silla-Tang alliance against Paekche and Koguryŏ, Silla kings appear to have used the position of Buddhist Overseer, later called State Elder or State Preceptor *(kungno, kuksa)*, to create religious harmony in their expanded domain won by conquest. According to tradition, on his deathbed, King Munmu admonished his son King Sinmun to make the eminent scholar Kyŏnghŭng (fl. late seventh–early eighth centuries), a monk from the old Paekche capital region of Ungch'ŏn, the State Elder.[76] Perhaps Kyŏnghŭng was installed in this high position to assuage or compel the people and Buddhist community of the former Paekche kingdom to submit to Silla rule and religious administration. Apparently Kyŏnghŭng did not oppose collaborating with the Silla conquerors, and he seems to have adjusted well to his responsibilities in the Silla capital. Kyŏnghŭng was succeeded by Hyet'ong (fl. 692–702), who is remembered as a powerful Buddhist thaumaturge.[77] Because he was renowned throughout the country, his being named State Preceptor may have helped stabilize the Silla court as it attempted to control and perhaps assimilate disparate elements of society.

Silla history indicates that its society and culture were dominated by the prerogatives of the aristocratic elite. That the Silla royalty and aristocracy accepted Buddhism as a state religion much later than Koguryŏ and Paekche suggests Silla's tardiness in assimilating continental Chinese culture. Nevertheless, once a compromise was made and the elites decided to support their primus inter pares king and promote Buddhism, they competed in their absorption of mainland culture and in their domestication of Buddhist practices. Both groups deployed Buddhist symbolism to enhance their symbolic and political resources and charisma to perpetuate their positions of social ascendancy. The royal family of Silla presented itself symbolically as the family of the Buddha Śākyamuni, forging a link with the cult of Śākyamuni. Meanwhile, the aristocracy fostered connections with the cult of Maitreya, which flourished at this time in Northeast Asia, by means the royally instituted *hwarang* order. The aristocracy and elites also collaborated in spreading stories about Silla's prehistory as a bona fide Buddha-land, which removed Silla from its marginal position in Northeast Asia to a central and important role in propagating the Buddhadharma. Furthermore, as in China and Japan, Silla Korea constructed lavish monasteries and held special Buddhist assemblies and rituals for the protection of the state. In all these things, and even in their choice of terminology for official monastic positions, they followed the general patterns of elite Buddhist practice found in Buddhism under the Chinese Northern dynasties. When established in Silla, these patterns enabled the Korean state to participate in the cosmopolitan Sinitic world. The religion provided new and powerful forms of legitimacy and prestige for its royalty and elites and predisposed the people, both elites and nonelites, to a wealth of cultic practices associated with the images and icons enshrined with great pomp and circumstance in monasteries and shrines, such as those associated with the cults of Maitreya and Avalokiteśvara. I will now turn to the cult of Maitreya, whose practices are most representative of what it meant to be Buddhist in Silla Korea in the sixth, seventh, and eighth centuries.

CHAPTER TWO

The Cult of Maitreya

If there were just one cult that could be said to characterize Buddhist practice on the Korean peninsula during the beginnings of the religion, it would have to be that of Maitreya (Mirŭk, Chassi). The veneration of the Bodhisattva Maitreya, the future Buddha, is a practice common throughout the Buddhist world and is probably the first personality cult that emerged historically after that of Śākyamuni. The worship of Maitreya was also the first Buddhist cult in which Silla elites and aristocrats actively participated in the sixth century after its introduction from China, where it was in vogue during the Northern dynasties period. The cult entered Silla through the medium of its sister Korean states Koguryŏ and Paekche. All three states exercised influence on the contemporary Japanese Maitreya cult during the Asuka and Nara periods (552–794).[1] From the sixth through the eighth centuries, the Maitreya cult was inextricably linked to the task of projecting and legitimating royal and aristocratic power in Silla.[2] During the ninth and tenth centuries, however, the cult underwent a period of transformation, being assimilated gradually into the rising Hwaŏm tradition. When the declining Silla domain was divided with the rise of the Later Three Kingdoms, the political and millenarian aspects of the cult were redeployed by would-be kings seeking to reunify the peninsula.

The Veneration of Maitreya in Medieval Northeast Asia

The Origins of the Cult in China under the Northern Dynasties

The cult of Maitreya in medieval China was originally associated with the vows of monastic exegetes to be reborn in Tuṣita Heaven (Doushuaitian, Kor. Tosolch'ŏn). This heaven is connected to our realm of existence and is where Maitreya waits to be reborn into our world. Adherents also vowed to be reborn in Ketumati (Jitoumo, Kor. Kyeduma, or Chitoumo, Kor. Sidumal), the pure land created by Maitreya when he is born on earth in the distant future. In this case aspirants hoped to be among the three assemblies of beings that will attend Maitreya's future preaching of the Buddhadharma. The goal for both monastics and laypeople in either case was that they might hear the Buddhist teaching directly from the mouth of the future Buddha Maitreya and thus attain buddhahood. These elite monks, and the aristocrats and royalty who patronized them, commissioned images of Maitreya, both standing and seated in meditation, as objects of worship and as aids for visualization and contemplation. Standing images of Maitreya were indicative of his preaching in Ketumati; seated images, usually in the so-called half-seated pensive pose (Jpn. *hankashiyui-zō*), portrayed Maitreya's waiting in Tuṣita. Both styles of Maitreya are found closely connected in the art of the Northern dynasties and demonstrate that these two aspects of the cult of Maitreya were interrelated in early China.[3] Because many sūtras about Maitreya prophesy that he will descend from Tuṣita to inaugurate a peaceful Buddhist millennium after years of warfare and the decline of the Dharma (Ch. *mofa*, Kor. *malbŏp*), worship of Maitreya began to spread throughout Chinese society in the Northern dynasties because of the frequent warfare between the northern Chinese states that had been founded by the invasions of Turko-Mongol tribal peoples. The sūtras associated with the cult of Maitreya describe both devotional and meditative practices to be reborn in the presence of Maitreya. The sūtras encourage people to do one or more of the following: (1) visualize themselves in the presence of Maitreya in Tuṣita now, (2) make vows to be reborn in Tuṣita later (at their death), (3) make vows to be reborn on earth when Maitreya comes later, (4) perform devotional practices in order to see incarnations of Maitreya here on the earth.[4] All of these practices were popular among the elites during the Northern dynasties, and at the height of the cult in the sixth century, they were transmitted to Silla.

The cult of Maitreya in China emerged in connection with the practices promoted by Shi Daoan (312–385). Prophecies of Maitreya's presence in Tuṣita Heaven and of his future descent to the world had begun to emerge in the Buddhist literature of the period.[5] One aspect of the cult for Daoan was his desire to be reborn in Tuṣita Heaven in the presence of Maitreya so that his doubts concerning the Buddhist scriptures could be resolved. Daoan's faith in Maitreya was well known. Fu Jian, hegemon of the Former Qin dynasty, sent Daoan a portrait of Maitreya pieced together out of pearl as well as gilded icons and other gifts. Daoan and his disciples pronounced vows in front of images of Maitreya expressing their desire to be reborn in Tuṣita. Daoan's veneration of Maitreya by vowing to be reborn in Tuṣita, the veneration of images of Maitreya, and the deployment of visual aids in lecturing became some of the basic practices of the cult.[6]

The cult of Maitreya continued to flourish under the Northern dynasties. In the Buddhist grottos inaugurated under the Northern Wei—the Yungang (mid- to late fifth century) and Longmen caves (late fifth to the tenth centuries), where some of the oldest surviving examples of Chinese Buddhist art were found—images of Maitreya, along with images of Śākyamuni, were the most numerous.[7] The Longmen caves preserve some spectacular examples of art from the golden age of the Maitreya cult in northern China. Succession, the inheritance of social position, and dynastic authority are important themes in the worship of Maitreya, who is seen as the legitimate heir to the Buddha Śākyamuni. After the first half of the Northern Wei, the Śākyamuni cult, most graphically depicted at Yungang, gave way to the Maitreya cult, most prominent at Longmen; however, the Longmen caves also signal the beginning of the rise of the Amitābha cult that would surpass the Maitreya cult during the early Tang. Tsukamoto Zenryū thinks that Buddhists of this period conceived of heaven, particularly Tuṣita Heaven, as a "Daoistic Pure Land," a hybrid of Buddhist and Daoist ideals. This is not strange when one considers that Buddhist cosmology has always incorporated local belief systems.[8] The preeminence of the Maitreya cult in medieval China transformed as a result of the rise of and its interactions with the cult of Amitābha and his Pure Land Sukhāvatī. Lay Buddhists, and probably some monastics as well, saw both Sukhāvatī and Tuṣita as "Pure Lands" where Buddhist faithful were reborn. These two Buddha-lands or Buddha-fields (Skt. *buddhakṣetra*) were often confused with each other, a confusion that seems to be a striking characteristic of the representations of Buddhist paradise at Dunhuang. The Maitreya cult had been dominant since the Northern Wei, but the Amitābha cult became more widespread during the Northern Qi (550–577) and Sui dynasties (581–618). As doctrinal understanding of the differences between the two world systems developed, the stage was set for competition between the cults during the early Tang.[9]

While Daoan and his small circle of worshippers of Maitreya may have provided the original influence for the cult of Maitreya, it was affected more by the concurrent translations of scriptures dealing with the Pure Land of Amitābha and the rise of Amitābha's cult. Nevertheless, the original appeal of a cult of Buddhism focused on the belief that one could become a Buddhist sylph (like a Daoist *xian*) and dwell in the company of Maitreya just as a Daoist immortal might reside in the Daoist heavens. Thus, the cult seemed to appeal to many people during the Northern dynasties and played an important role in the initial conversion of the people to Buddhism.[10]

Maitreya Worship in Koguryŏ and Paekche

Although the evidence is slight, the Korean states of Koguryŏ and Paekche followed the model of the Northern dynasties in promoting the cult of Maitreya. A recent collection of Korean Buddhist images registers nineteen extant Koguryŏ Buddhist images, four of which have been identified as Maitreya. The sampling is too small to present conclusive evidence, but an extant inscription suggests a similar type of combination of the cults of Maitreya and Amitābha. The inscription is carved on the back of a gilt-bronze buddha triad, dated to 571, that was discovered in Koksan County, Hwanghae Province. It says that several monks commissioned an image of Amitāyus (Muryangsu), another name for Amitābha, but vowed to meet Maitreya and to be reborn in a place to see and hear the Buddhadharma.[11] Although some scholars hold that there was confusion in the understanding of the proper relationship between these two figures,[12] the cults of Maitreya and Amitābha were not necessarily mutually exclusive. As in medieval China, the characteristic of combining the worship and supplication of Maitreya and Amitābha later became an important characteristic of the Buddhist cults of Silla.

Like the inscription given above, an inscription on an image of Maitreya in Koguryŏ is similar to those found at Longmen and other Northern Wei–period images. The donors hoped that the deceased individuals for whose benefit these images were made would be reborn in the presence of Maitreya, that they would achieve enlightenment through hearing the Dharma preached in Maitreya's Tuṣita Heaven, and that all their sins would be destroyed by the wholesome karma generated by making and worshipping these images.[13] An image of Śākyamuni dated to either 594 or 654 also manifests these same characteristics and also shows how desire for rebirth in the Pure Land was a strand of belief found in the Śākyamuni cult as well.[14] A few gilt-bronze images of a meditating bodhisattva, in the "pensive pose," seated on a lotus throne with one foot touching the ground and the other crossed over his knee, have been found that date to the mid-sixth century in Koguryŏ.[15] Although this type of image was commonly used in depicting Prince Siddhārtha and Maitreya in China, in Korea it usually represented the Bodhisattva Maitreya only.

In Paekche, the worship of Maitreya was closely linked to the projection of royal power. The Paekche court introduced the cult of Maitreya to Japan, and Paekche kings venerated the bodhisattva in a majestic monastic complex. In 584, Japanese emissaries returned from Paekche with a stone statue of Maitreya and another image. Later, Soga no Umako (d. 626), a powerful aristocrat, chief minister, and promoter of Buddhism, acquired these two images, enshrined the image of Maitreya in a Buddha hall, and commanded nuns to make offerings to it.[16]

Paekche King Mu (r. 600–641), the subject of many popular tales pieced together by Iryŏn into a miracle-filled biography, is said to have erected a Mirŭk Monastery with the assistance of a monk-thaumaturge. This Mirŭk Monastery has been linked traditionally to a monastery site outside the present-day town of Iksan in North Chŏlla Province where a large stone stūpa dominates the site. Recent excavations show that Mirŭk Monastery was among the largest monastic complexes in East Asia during the middle of the seventh century.[17] Iryŏn, however, conflates the dates of construction for this Mirŭk Monastery with those of Wanghŭngsa, which was built in the Paekche capital and initiated by Mu's father King Pŏp (r. 599–600) in 600 and completed in 634. Iryŏn claims that the two monasteries are the same, though the claim contradicts strong traditional and architectural evidence.[18]

The account of the founding of Mirŭk Monastery found in *Memorabilia of the Three Kingdoms* shows how the cult of Maitreya provided the impetus for its construction. The anecdote says that Paekche King Mu and his queen, who was the third daughter of Silla king Chinp'yŏng, planned to visit a monastery on a certain Mount Yonghwa, an allusion to the bodhi tree of Maitreya. When they reached a pond at the foot of the mountain a Maitreya Buddha triad emerged from the pond. After halting their carriages and paying homage to Maitreya, the queen asked the king to build a monastery there. Three images of Maitreya were made for use in three different halls at the monastery. The queen's father, the king of Silla, was said to have dispatched a hundred craftsmen to assist in the construction and consecration of the monastery.[19]

Both textual evidence and extant sculptural evidence indicate that the cult of Maitreya—who was worshipped as the future Buddha and as a bodhisattva—was the dominant form of religious veneration during the Korean Three Kingdoms period (ca. 300–668). This is because the existing images identified as Maitreya constitute the largest single group of images depicting any particular buddha or bodhisattva. A recent catalogue of Korean Buddhist images contains fifteen sculptures dating to the Three Kingdoms period that are recognized as the Bodhisattva Maitreya, ten of which are of Silla manufacture. Only three images of the bodhisattva remain from the Unified Silla period, however, all of which can be dated to the first fifty years after Silla's conquest of Paekche and Koguryŏ. To some, this evidence suggests that the veneration of Maitreya may have declined following Silla's forced unification of the peninsula in the late seventh century, and some have advanced theories that the cult of Maitreya began to decline during the late seventh and early eighth centuries in China and later in the eighth and ninth centuries in Japan.[20] Active aristocratic worship of Maitreya in Silla continued well into the eighth century, but veneration of Amitābha and Avalokiteśvara also became more widespread. I assert that instead of declining, the context of belief in Maitreya was transformed as a result of its gradual assimilation by Hwaŏm Buddhist practices. Widespread evidence of the Maitreya cult endured during the Koryŏ and Chosŏn periods and thrives in contemporary Korea.[21]

Flower Boys, Vision Quests, and Images of Clay and Stone

The Hwarang *and the Maitreya Cult*

The earliest accounts of the worship of Maitreya in Silla are associated with the *hwarang*. As bands of aristocratic and elite youths of Silla, the *hwarang* performed religious and military functions—often connected with protecting Silla from encroachments from its enemies Paekche and Koguryŏ. These accounts of the cult of Maitreya in Silla demonstrate that the people of Silla associated *hwarang* with incarnations of Maitreya from the late sixth century to the mid-seventh century. Furthermore, aristocrats commissioned and buried images of Maitreya in hopes that sons would be born to them who would protect the kingdom. Even the name of one *hwarang* band implies a direct link with the cult of Maitreya.

Iryŏn reports that during the short reign of King Chinji (late sixth century), the monk Chinja of Hŭngnyun Monastery supplicated before the image of Maitreya, begging that Maitreya incarnate himself as a *hwarang* so that he might be near him and serve him. He continued to pray fervently day after day and was ultimately rewarded with a vision in which a monk told him to go to Suwŏn Monastery in Ungch'ŏn (now Kongju in North Ch'ungch'ŏng Province), which was then part of Paekche territory, where he would behold Maitreya. At the monastery gate Chinja met a handsome and friendly youth, who showed the monk to his quarters in the monastery. Chinja thought it was strange that he would be treated so nicely—not realizing that this was Maitreya. The youth explained his kindness by saying that he too was from the Silla capital.

Later, Chinja told the monks at the monastery about his dream and desire to see Maitreya. They encouraged him to go south to Mount Ch'ŏn, the traditional abode of the wise, to ask the mountain spirit *(sallyŏng)* for answers. When Chinja arrived, the mountain spirit, in the form of an old man, informed Chinja that he had already encountered Maitreya at the gate of the monastery. The monk hurried back, but it was too late—the young man had disappeared. Since the boy had said that he was from the Silla capital, Chinja thought that he might see him again there. The monk, aided by his attendants, searched for the youth in the villages surrounding the capital. They finally found him playing under a tree northeast of what would become Yŏngmyo Monastery. Chinja told him that he was Maitreya and then asked the boy about his family. The youth said that his name was Misi (also read Miri),[22] but that he did not know his surname because he had been orphaned as a child. Chinja took the boy to the royal palace in a palanquin; there he was honored by the Silla king. The king made him a *kuksŏn* (state sylph), a *hwarang* leader. The narrative ends by saying that Misi vanished after a brilliant career lasting seven years, during which time his teachings and personality were revered by the other youths.[23]

Although nearly nothing is known about the monk Chinja, we may conjecture from information provided in the hagiographical account. Some scholars have suggested that Chinja was a *hwarang*,[24] but I feel safer asserting that Chinja was probably of holy-bone or true-bone status, and even may have been a lesser member of the Silla royal family, because he had physical access to the image of Maitreya enshrined in Hŭngnyun Monastery, which had been built by King Pŏphŭng, and because he had the ability to appropriate royal palanquins for direct access to the Silla throne. The main image in the monastery was probably that of the Bodhisattva Maitreya. This anecdote links the Silla polity to the cult of Maitreya and defines the uniquely Korean relationship between mundane manifestations of Maitreya and the elite Silla youths that constituted the *hwarang* order.

The monk Chinja's worship of Maitreya is surprisingly international in its scope and brings together some aspects of traditional Korean religion that predate Buddhism. Although he worshipped the cult image of Maitreya at the Hŭngnyun Monastery, he was instructed by the monk-figure of his dream to travel to a monastery in Paekche territory to encounter Maitreya, who had been incarnated as a youth suitable to lead the Silla *hwarang*. Furthermore, when Chinja does not recognize Maitreya at first in the handsome youth, the Paekche monks direct him to pay a visit to the local mountain god for answers. Thus, traditional Korean gods and spirits of nature have become supporting actors to the Buddhist cult figures. While the account explicitly states that the youth Misi, like Chinja, was also of the Silla capital, it seems strange that an orphaned youth, apparently of noble parentage, would have wandered so far from his home by himself. Silla monks who worshipped Maitreya may have recognized the superiority or developed nature of the Maitreya cult in Paekche and wanted to bring it back to Silla. Nevertheless, Misi, the Maitreya youth, next appears in the vicinity of another monastery in the Silla capital, and his connection to Silla is assured.

With the association between Maitreya and handsome male youths of the *hwarang*, the cult of Maitreya was coupled with the perennial desire of military men for strong and able sons and with the protection of the state. Some nobles of Silla expressed their desires for sons by erecting images of Maitreya at the tombs of deceased youths of noble bearing in hopes of forming karmic connections with the deceased youths so that they might be reborn in their families as their sons. Thus, in effect, the son born through this karmic affinity is an incarnation of Maitreya. The following account of Lord Sulchong (active ca. 600) is emblematic of this trend, which must have developed during the late sixth and early seventh centuries.

Lord Sulchong was on his way to Sakchu (in present-day Kangwŏn Province) to assume the post of governor. He led a retinue of three thousand soldiers because there were armed rebels in the land. They stopped at Chukchi Pass because a young man, a Buddhist lay devotee, was repairing the road. Sulchong was impressed by the youth, and the boy took a liking to the aristocratic lord. They parted, having formed a karmic connection. A month after taking office, Sulchong and his wife both had the same dream, in which the youth he had met at Chukchi Pass entered their room. Perplexed by the dream, the lord sent a messenger to inquire after the youth and learned that he had died a few days before. The governor ascertained from the report that the day of the youth's death was the same as that of his dream. Thinking that the youth might be reborn as his son, Lord Sulchong sent soldiers to bury the youth on the northern crest of Chukchi Pass and had a stone image of Maitreya erected before the grave. The lord's wife, who had conceived on the day she had her dream, gave birth to a son whom they named Chukchi. Chukchi later became a *hwarang* and served his country honorably as a military commander and high government official.[25]

The wording of this story, nevertheless, is misleading. It says that Lord Sulchong was granted the "post" of "governor" of Sakchu and was given a large escort because of "armed rebels." At this time Sakchu included the northern border area recently conquered by Silla during the reign of King Chinhŭng that was probably contested by Koguryŏ. The armed rebels probably refer both to Koguryŏ military units and to Koguryŏ's allies, the Malgal (Ch. Mohe) tribesmen, and the three thousand troops attending Sulchong were probably a consignment of subordinate troops to keep the region pacified. Because Lord Sulchong was awarded the post of governor, we can assume that he was of true-bone status, but this was really more like the installation of an aristocratic war leader. Lord Sulchong's erecting a Maitreya image at Chukchi Pass, which was also apparently in the Sakchu territory, signifies the transmission of the cult of Maitreya to these hinterlands far north of the capital. The significance of this with the cult of Maitreya is that Maitreya-like youths may be conceived in all areas of the Silla domain to protect the heartland from hostile invasion. The imagery of the cult of Maitreya's descent into the mundane world is deployed by the Silla elites to serve their prerogatives.

The relationship between the *hwarang* and the cult of Maitreya centers on the idea that *hwarang* are incarnations of Maitreya. According to the Buddhist sūtras, the Buddha Maitreya will descend to earth from his abode in Tuṣita Heaven after the period of the decline of the Buddhadharma and inaugurate a long period of Buddhist peace and prosperity. The sūtras encourage people to perform devotional practices in order to see incarnations of Maitreya here on earth. In both China and Korea, this devotional aspect was deployed to support political agendas, but it was done in the opposite manner in Silla. In medieval China, rebels frequently claimed to be Maitreya as a means of garnering support from the common people to overthrow the government. In Silla, the aristocrats appropriated the Buddhist concept of an incarnation of Maitreya on earth to maintain their sociopolitical influence. In early Korea, Maitreya, as a *hwarang*, does not establish a new kingdom; he supports the Silla aristocrats in expanding Silla's boundaries and promoting peace and prosperity within its growing borders. In this sense, all *hwarang* represent Maitreya, although certain individuals, such as the previously discussed Misi, were believed to be direct incarnations of Maitreya.

Kim Yusin and the Maitreya Cult

Maitreya imagery is also prevalent in the *hwarang* band of Kim Yusin, an aristocrat of true-bone status and joint architect of the Silla-Tang conquest of Koguryŏ and Paekche with his brother-in-law Kim Ch'unch'u, whom he also engineered to ascend the throne as King Muyŏl (r. 654–661).[26] Kim Yusin became a *hwarang* when he was fifteen years old and had developed a great following. They were called the Dragon Flower Aspirants. The name of Kim's *hwarang* band shows a direct connection to the cult of Maitreya: "the Dragon Flower Aspirants" is an allusion to the bodhi tree of Maitreya and implies that he and the youths of his band aspired—perhaps vowed—to be present at the future threefold assembly where the future Buddha Maitreya would preach the restored Dharma and begin a millennial reign of Buddhist peace in this world system.[27] In 611, when Kim was seventeen years old, all the enemies of his country— Koguryŏ, Paekche, and the Malgal tribes—invaded Silla. He traveled alone to the rocky crags of Chung'ak (Central Peak), fasted for purification, and prayed for a divine response to his desire to protect his country. An old man named Nansŭng appeared to him, and Kim begged him to teach him some method or technique to protect and rectify his country. The old man eventually taught Kim a secret ritual procedure *(pibŏp)* and then disappeared in a flash of colorful brightness.[28]

The *hwarang* traveled to the famed mountain areas of Silla to develop the skills of quasi-religious resources of singing, dancing, physical health and beauty, and an appreciation of natural beauty. Central Peak was one of the five sacred mountains of Silla *(oak)* and is in the P'algong Mountains near present-day Taegu in North Kyŏngsang Province.²⁹ The old man, Nansŭng, who appeared to the young warrior may be seen as either Maitreya himself or as the mountain god of Central Peak. Although the appearance of Maitreya would be more dramatic, I think that the characteristics of the figure indicate that he was a mountain god appearing as an old monk or attendant bodhisattva, because Maitreya in Silla is more often presented as a youthful figure, as seen in the half-seated, pensive images of Maitreya remaining from the period and in the foregoing tale of Chinja. The old man's transmission of a secret formula is particularly intriguing and probably denotes a special dhāraṇī, or spell designed for the protection of the Silla state.

Images of Maitreya

Images of Maitreya also flourished in the vicinity of Kyŏngju's South Mountain, a site long regarded as a sacred mountain by the Silla people. They were commissioned by various groups of Silla's elite, both monks and laity. Like similar developments in Latin Christianity's cult of saints, the images of some monasteries developed or inherited mysterious genealogies that must have enhanced their appeal as cult sites associated with particular cultic figures. The following account suggests such a development in the cult of Maitreya spurred by a monk.

During the reign of Queen Sŏndŏk, the usual residence of monk Sŏk Saengŭi was Tojung Monastery. One night he dreamed that a certain monk dragged him up to the top of South Mountain and made him bind some grass together to mark the spot. When they came back down the mountain, the monk said that he was buried on the spot they marked and begged him to dig him up and place him on the top of the ridge. When Saengŭi awoke he dragged a companion up the mountain where they searched for the marker. When they found it, they dug up a stone image of Maitreya. Following the instructions given by the monk in the dream, they enshrined it on top of Samhwa Ridge. They later built a monastery named after Saengŭi nearby so that they might provide the proper ritual care of the image. During the eighth century the monastery on the ridge became a popular pilgrimage site where monks made offerings of tea.³⁰

Though Saengŭi or a fellow monk probably commissioned this image of Maitreya and buried it for the purpose of its later miraculous discovery as the result of a dream of Maitreya appearing as a monk, there is also the possibility that it was an image enshrined in a crude earthen chamber by a nobleman for the purpose of obtaining a son (such as performed by Lord Sulchong above) that was later appropriated by the monastic community to serve its own purposes. Regardless, South Mountain was specially associated with Maitreya; one of its vales was even named Maitreya Valley (Mirŭkkok). Samhwa Ridge is just northeast of this valley where still today is a Buddhist triad of images: a seated Maitreya, flanked by two unidentifiable bodhisattvas.³¹

A legend about Kim Yangdo emphasizes the continued relationship between Hŭngnyun Monastery, the first monastery built by the Silla royal family in the capital Kyŏngju, and the cult of Maitreya. Kim Yangdo was a true-bone elite related to the Silla royal family who served as an emissary to the Tang court in six diplomatic missions during the reign of King Munmu. Noted for his literary attainments, he had been raised to the rank of *p'ajinch'an* by 669 and may have held a high office during the reign of King Sinmun.³² When he was a young man, as the story goes, he was possessed by evil and afflicting spirits, which robbed him of the ability to speak. When exorcisms by male and female shamans proved ineffective, his parents sent for Milbon (fl. 632–647), a Buddhist thaumaturge noted for his ability to cure illness through sūtra chanting. Kim Yangdo was cured immediately through his ministrations and became a devout believer in the monastic community for the rest of his life. He reportedly commissioned a clay Buddhist triad (of Maitreya flanked by two bodhisattvas) and golden paintings for the main hall of Hŭngnyun Monastery.³³ This was the same monastery in which the monk Chinja previously petitioned Maitreya to incarnate himself as a *hwarang* so that the monk could serve him. Hŭngnyun Monastery, besides being the first monastery built by the Silla royalty of holy-bone status, was an important center of the Maitreya cult in Silla because it united royal power with Buddhist authority in its representation of Maitreya. Given that it was built in the mid-sixth century, when the worship of Maitreya was at its apex in Northeast Asia, this monastery probably also displayed artistic influences from the Korean kingdoms of Koguryŏ and Paekche, as well as from the Chinese Northern dynasties, centering on the cult of Maitreya.

By the mid-seventh century, although the Maitreya cult was an important religious force, trends in Buddhist worship on the Asian continent were shifting. The Chinese period of disunion ended with the Sui unification of China and, later, the Tang succession. The Silla court sought political and cultural connections and tributary relations with both of these powerful Chinese dynasties as a means of counterbalancing political and military pressures from its peninsular rivals Koguryŏ and Paekche. Buddhist monks such as Wŏn'gwang, Chajang, and Ŭisang, who went to China to study with Sinitic Buddhist masters, were instrumental in introducing Chinese Buddhist practices and securing Chinese goodwill for Silla. Koguryŏ and Paekche were ultimately defeated through Silla-Tang alliance. Monks, such as Ŭisang, who returned to Silla brought with them new Buddhist practices associated with the cults of Amitābha and Avalokiteśvara. Silla Buddhists did not discard their earlier practices but instead, in the case of the Maitreya cult, synthesized their worship of Maitreya with the veneration of Avalokiteśvara and Amitābha.

Devotion, Divination, and Offerings of Tea and Song

During the long reign of King Sŏngdŏk, the cult of Maitreya began a period of transformation. At this time recitation of the name of the Buddha Amitābha began to emerge as the dominant form of Buddhist practice in Sinitic Buddhism. Furthermore, the social composition of people worshipping Maitreya appears to have widened to include some commoners. The first account of the cult of Maitreya in the eighth century involves two men who became famous for their spiritual attainments but whose names indicate humble social origins. Nohil Puduk and Taltal Pakpak were both commoners; the names of their parents in the narrative have been altered to forge a link to the names given to the parents of Maitreya and Amitābha in Buddhist scriptures. Nohil Puduk's father's name was said to be Wŏlchang, his mother's name, Misŭng. Taltal Pakpak's father's name was given as Subŏm, his mother's name, Pŏmma. Scholars have indicated that the names of the men's parents may be compared to the names of Maitreya and Amitābha's parents as found in Buddhist literature. Maitreya's parents are Xiufanma (Kor. Subŏmma) and Fanmayue (Kor. Pŏmmawŏl); Amitābha's parents are Yueshang Zhuanlun Shengwang (Kor. Wŏlsang Chŏllyun Sŏngwang) and Shusheng Miaoyan (Kor. Sulsŭng Myoan). They did not, however, emphasize that the names of the parents of Puduk, who worships Maitreya, correspond to the names of Amitābha's parents, and that the names of the parents of Pakpak, who worships Amitābha, correspond to the names of Maitreya's parents.[34] Considering that the finale of the tale is that Puduk and Pakpak literally become Maitreya and Amitābha respectively "in their present bodies," it is a curious editorial mistake that Amitābha's parents should give birth to Maitreya and Maitreya's parents give birth to Amitābha. If we take a more positive view of the literary situation, on the other hand, it provides further evidence of the interrelationship and interchangeability between the cults of these two figures. More important, the narrative concerning Puduk and Pakpak's practice describes a close and friendly relationship among the practitioners of the cults of Maitreya, Amitābha, and Avalokiteśvara in Silla.

Although these two men were married and had families, they had made commitments to assist each other in acquiring their desired religious goals. They led simple lives as faithful householders for a time but eventually decided to reject the world of men for a reclusive life in a deep mountain valley. One night they both dreamed of a thin ray of white light that came from the west. A golden arm emerged from the light and touched both their foreheads. When they awoke and shared their dreams they were amazed. They then decided to leave their wives and families and retire to Mudŭng Valley on White Moon Mountain (Paegwŏlsan), which is in the vicinity of the present-day city of Ch'angwŏn in South Kyŏngsang Province. There they established crude hermitages as their residences. In essence they became śramaṇa, renouncers of the world who strive for enlightenment. Pudŭk diligently sought after Maitreya *(kŭn'gu Mirŭk)* and Pakpak religiously recollected Amitābha *(yenyŏm Mit'a)*.

According to the narrative, one night in the spring of 709, just before dark, a beautiful and alluring young woman arrived at Pakpak's residence and requested to spend the night there. Pakpak, fearing that his physical attraction to the woman might cause him to break the monastic rule of celibacy, not to mention the rule prohibiting monks from residing in the same room with a woman, turned her away rudely. She then went to Pudŭk's residence and begged for shelter. Her sincere request for his compassion caused him to submit to her request. Pudŭk chanted in the corner of his cell while the woman prepared herself to rest. Though her mere presence in his hermitage was a violation of the precepts, she made a further appeal that shocked Pudŭk. After announcing that she would give birth that evening, she asked him to lay some straw for her, an even more severe violation of the monastic code of discipline. Furthermore, after bearing the child she further importuned Pudŭk to prepare a bath for her. When the beautiful woman got into the bath, the bath water turned into a fragrant, beautiful, gold-colored elixir. She invited the astonished Pudŭk to join her in the bath, wherein his bodily passions were cooled and his mortal hull was transformed into a gold color. The beautiful woman revealed herself as Avalokiteśvara, who had come to help him achieve *mahābodhi* (great enlightenment), and disappeared.

The next morning Pakpak hurried to his friend's residence, certain that Pudŭk had violated the precepts by having sexual relations with the woman. He saw his friend instead seated on a lotus throne in the fashion of a golden image of Maitreya. Pakpak lamented his lack of spiritual attainment, but Pudŭk informed him that there was some liquid remaining in the bath. Pakpak bathed himself in the golden water and was also transformed into the image of Amitābha. The people of the settlement nearby flocked to see the miraculous beings. Eventually, the story goes, they rose up on clouds and flew away while preaching the Dharma.

This story, despite its fantastic elements, implies that, like Pudŭk, common people could obtain powerful spiritual experiences through "diligently seeking after Maitreya." By saying that these two commoners attained buddhahood in this very body, the author of the tale, who is obviously influenced by the doctrine that all beings inherently possess buddha-nature, asserts that single-minded devotion to a Buddhist deity is a viable and efficacious path of practice that not only causes the aspirant to acquire merit but enables him to access his full spiritual potential.

Whereas commoners such as Pudŭk worshipped the bodhisattva, it appears that aristocrats and social elites such as the Silla king monopolized the commissioning of images. Even though this miraculous event took place in 709, it took at least thirty years for the government to recognize the eminence of these monks and more than fifty years to build the royally sponsored Southern Monastery of White Moon Mountain (on the site of Pudŭk's former hermitage). Silla king Kyŏngdŏk (r. 742–765) began construction in 757. He also commissioned images of Maitreya and Amitābha, which were enshrined in the golden and lecture halls (whose titles alluded to Pudŭk's and Pakpak's attainment of buddhahood) in 764. That Maitreya was enshrined in the Golden Hall (the main image hall) indicates the continued importance of the Maitreya cult in Silla in the middle of the eighth century. In the narrative, the remaining liquid gold from the bath was used to color the clay images.[35] In this story, the cults of Maitreya, Amitābha, and Avalokiteśvara are all combined. There is no hierarchy in the worship of Maitreya and Amitābha; both are respectable objects of Buddhist practice and piety.

Perceived Similarity between Sukhāvatī and Tuṣita

There is even more evidence that the Silla aristocracy did not differentiate between rebirth in Maitreya's Tuṣita Heaven and rebirth in Amitābha's Sukhāvatī, the world system of Extreme Bliss in the West. The perceived similarity between Sukhāvatī and Tuṣita may be demonstrated by the fact that aristocrats commissioned images of both Maitreya and Amitābha to adorn monasteries they commissioned. Kim Chisŏng was a true-bone aristocrat and protégé of the Silla prince and chief state minister Kaewŏn (d. 706). After having served in the expanding Silla bureaucracy and as an emissary to China in 705, he built Kamsan Monastery about twenty *li* southeast of the capital city of Kyŏngju and commissioned images of Maitreya and Amitābha in 719 for the benefit of his deceased parents. Fortunately, both of these images exist, and they are among the few extant Silla images with inscriptions. Edited versions of the inscriptions on these images are contained in Iryŏn's *Memorabilia of the Three Kingdoms*.

After briefly announcing the purpose for building Kamsan Monastery and commissioning the stone image of Maitreya, the inscription first treats Kim's father Injang, suggesting that he achieved enlightenment and encouraged his sons to complete the bodhisattva path. The inscription then details Kim Chisŏng's intellectual and religious pursuits. It says that Kim formally studied and was examined in *The Way and Its Power*

(*Daode jing*), but later turned to studying arcane teachings such as the "Dharma Approaches of the Seventeen Stages," a list of the stages of the bodhisattva path described in Mahāyāna literature.[36] The account then says that no expense was spared in building this monastery on behalf of his deceased parents. All surviving family members, both legitimate and illegitimate, are named with their titles with a prayer and a vow that they will all escape from the six destinies in the cycle of rebirth and death by developing wholesome roots.[37]

There is nothing extraordinary about this inscription. Inscriptions in East Asia are fundamentally formulaic and do not necessarily express the heartfelt religious insights of the person who commissioned the image and the inscription thereon. An account of Kim Chisŏng's philosophical pursuits and accomplishments is presented, which indicates that he was well read in what we presently consider to be "Buddhist" and "Daoist" literature, respectively. However, his knowledge of *The Way and Its Power* more accurately implies that he was familiar with texts that were commonly studied by the learned elite of his time. Kim is not presented as a particularly pious Buddhist with regard to every day religious observances. His commissioning of the images, however, confirms a desire on his part to acquire merit for himself and his deceased parents. The edited version found in *Memorabilia of the Three Kingdoms* says that the image of Maitreya was placed in the Golden Hall, attesting once again to the preeminence of Maitreya worship vis-à-vis Amitābha worship among the elite in their monasteries during the early decades of the eighth century.

Besides synthesis with the worship of Amitābha, the cult of Maitreya may have expanded to combine with the cult of the Bodhisattva Kṣitigarbha (Ch. Dizang, Kor. Chijang)—a bodhisattva that assists Amitābha by entering hell to ferry the souls of the dead to Amitābha's Western Paradise. Kṣitigarbha's cult began to flourish in Silla during the middle of the eighth century, although the bodhisattva was probably introduced to the peninsula earlier. Practitioners of the cult of Kṣitigarbha, like the cult of Maitreya and all other cults of the time for that matter, became preoccupied with repentance rituals and with Buddhist divination ceremonies that predicted one's karmic status, often as a prerequisite to receiving the Buddhist precepts.[38]

Chinp'yo's Repentance Rituals and the Worship of Maitreya

The monk Chinp'yo (fl. eighth century) was probably a head-rank six elite, since he hailed from the former Paekche territory and was acknowledged as a monk of Paekche in the *Lives of Eminent Monks Compiled in the Song (Song gaoseng zhuan)*. Furthermore, the name of his father, Chinnaemal, in the thirteenth-century *Memorabilia of the Three Kingdoms*, appears to be a corruption of the Silla title of *naemal* or *namal*, which was the highest rank that an individual of head-rank six status could attain. The names of his parents are not recorded in the earlier tenth-century Chinese source.

The connection between Chinp'yo and the cult of Maitreya is intriguing because there are essentially three different versions of the same basic story of Chinp'yo's receiving a visitation from Maitreya and Kṣitigarbha as a result of his sincere repentance and desire to receive the Buddhist precepts: (1) "The Biography of Chinp'yo of Kŭmsan Monastery in the Tang Dominion of Paekche" in the *Lives of Eminent Monks Compiled in the Song*, from which are derived "Chinp'yo" in the *Biographies of Divine Monks (Shenseng zhuan)* and the "Biography of Chinp'yo" in the *Newly Edited and Compiled Biographies of Monks of the Six Learnings (Xinxiu kefen luxue seng zhuan)* by the Yuan-dynasty monk Tane (1285–1373);[39] (2) "Chinp'yo Transmits the Divination Sticks" in *Memorabilia of the Three Kingdoms;*[40] and (3) the "Account of the Stele at Paryŏn Monastery on Maple Peak (P'ungak) in Kwandong," preserved in *Memorabilia of the Three Kingdoms.*[41] The actual inscription from the stele dating to 1199 has survived mostly intact.[42]

In the first account, preserved in the *Lives of Eminent Monks Compiled in the Song*, Maitreya appeared to Chinp'yo after he had been tested sufficiently, in response to his sincere and extreme method of repentance and observation of the precepts. During the Kaiyuan period (713–742) Chinp'yo was raised as a hunter but had a life-transforming experience after he wantonly killed some frogs. His sudden remorse caused him to reject the householder life, cut off his hair, and seek the precepts through miraculous means in the mountains by performing intense repentance rituals such as knocking his head on the rocky ground for a period of seven days and nights. At dawn after the seventh day he saw golden symbols dangling from the hand of the Bodhisattva Kṣitigarbha, who instructed him in the precepts. After being tested further by spirits and ghosts of the local area, Maitreya appeared and gave Chinp'yo two special divination sticks inscribed with the characters *ku* (nine) and *p'al* (eight). Maitreya commanded Chinp'yo to make 108 divination sticks and to inscribe the names of the 108 defilements on the sticks. He then instructed Chinp'yo concerning the method of divining whether someone is able to receive the precepts and what level of precepts they can receive. A postulant must perform penance for ninety days, forty days, or thirty-seven days and then combine the special divination sticks with the 108. The postulant casts them in the air before an image of the Buddha on an altar, and how the sticks fall to the ground on the consecrated space foretells whether the person's sins have been eradicated or not. If he throws the sticks and only the special sticks inscribed nine and eight remain on the altar, then he will receive the precepts of the highest order of the highest class. If he casts the sticks and there are sticks touching the sticks nine and eight, these are the postulant's defilements. After repenting of these he receives the precepts of the middle class; however, if the two special sticks are buried by the other sticks, the postulant's sins have not been eradicated, he must repent in excess of ninety days, and he will obtain the precepts of the lowest class. This practice of divining whether one's repentance has been successful or if one has defilements he needs to repent of is presented without any scriptural support.

Let me digress for a moment to discuss the significance of the two divining sticks named nine and eight. These two numbers are specifically related to a man's destiny in traditional Chinese divination practices associated with the *Book of Changes (Yijing)*. The number nine is a potent yang number, but it also enumerates the rites a man passes through in his life. These rites are said to symbolize the five permutations of matter, such as the changes between the five elements (fire, water, wood, metal, and earth). Nine is also symbolic of heaven and earth: there are nine fields of heaven, nine regions in the earth, and so forth. The number eight is an important yin number and plays a vital role in mystical numerology connected with a man's life. There are eight trigrams in the *Book of Changes*, and the life of a man is ruled by the number eight. At eight months he gets his milk teeth; at eight years he loses them; at two times eight years he becomes an adult man; and at eight times eight years he is said to be incapable of procreation, and so on. Eight here is also probably related to the eight characters associated with the time of one's birth, the "four pillars and eight characters" for the year, month, day, and hour of one's birth *(saju p'alcha)*, which were believed to play a role in the fortune or destiny of a person.

The two other accounts from the *Memorabilia of the Three Kingdoms* suggest instead that Chinp'yo, who was active during the reign of Silla king Kyŏngdŏk, received the *Book of Divining the Requital of Wholesome and Unwholesome Actions (Zhancha shane yebao jing)* along with the two special divination sticks. The context of the story implies that the divination sūtra and the divination sticks go together. The problem with this combination is that the *Book of Divining the Requital of Wholesome and Unwholesome Actions* does not teach the practice of casting sticks to divine one's karmic status. It instead teaches a method of spinning tops to predict one's possible fate. The divination ritual taught in this sūtra—by the mouth of Kṣitigarbha and not at all related Maitreya—contains a list of 189 possible fates.[43] Perhaps this explains the peculiar appearance of Kṣitigarbha in the accounts where he seems to function merely as an attendant to Maitreya.[44]

Through austere repentance practices performed in conjunction with a divination ritual, in this account Chinp'yo ultimately received a prophecy of his future buddhahood from Maitreya in 760 (or 752). Afterward, he rebuilt Kŭmsan Monastery and commissioned an image of Maitreya, which was cast in 764 and enshrined at the site in 766.[45] Chinp'yo was revered by Silla kings and traveled widely on pilgrimage throughout Silla and to spread his cultic practice. His initial vision of Maitreya was said to have taken place at a hermitage called the Room of Inconceivable Meaning (Pulsaŭibang), which is on Mount Pyŏn in Poan district, presently Puan County, a peninsula jutting off the west side of North Ch'ungch'ŏng Province. The Paryŏn Monastery, on Maitreya Peak (Mirŭkpong) in the Diamond Mountains (Kŭmgangsan) on the North Korean side of Kangwŏn Province, was established by Chinp'yo about 770 and preserves a stele marking the former location of his ashes. The inscription lauds Chinp'yo's promotion of the worship of Maitreya in that region. Other sites mentioned in the various Chinp'yo narratives have continued to be connected to Maitreya worship to this day. Kŭmsan Monastery, which is on Mount Moak in North Chŏlla Province in southwestern Korea, is where Chinp'yo became a monk under Sunje, who putatively studied under the Tang Pure Land master Shandao (613–681) and encountered Maitreya on China's Mount Wutai. The monastery boasts a large Maitreya Hall (Mirŭkchŏn) putatively rebuilt by Chinp'yo in 766, although the current hall dates from 1635.[46] Chinp'yo's disciples were instrumental in spreading the worship of Maitreya to the Mount Songni region, which now plays host to Pŏpchu Monastery in the Poŭn District of North Ch'ungch'ŏng Province and currently features a gilt-bronze image of Maitreya thirty-three meters tall.[47] Chinp'yo's efforts must have made the cult of Maitreya more accessible to ordinary people, though there is little textual or archeological evidence remaining from Silla times.

Ch'ungdam's Offerings of Tea to Maitreya

The image of Maitreya enshrined on Samhwa Ridge of South Mountain in the Silla capital by Saengŭi in 643 continued as a significant center for the cult of Maitreya well into the eighth century. Monks made pilgrimages to the image and made offerings on holidays. The following account describes the cultic practice of the monk Ch'ungdam (fl. 742–765), who was probably a head-rank six elite. He was a talented composer of native songs *(hyangga)*, a skill he may have developed as a member of a *hwarang* band as a youth, and a pious adherent to the Maitreya cult.

On the third day of the third month, King Kyŏngdŏk rode in his palanquin out to the Kwijŏng Gate of the Silla capital, ascended its tower, and told his attendants to fetch a splendidly clothed monk from the road and to present the monk before him. After a few failures, they saw a man who wore the robes of a monk and carried a barrel made of cherry wood on his back. The king was pleased at the sight of this monk, greeted him, and had him ascend the tower. Looking inside the barrel the king found it was full of tea-making supplies. The king became more curious about this monk, learned that his name was Ch'ungdam and that every year on the third day of the third month and the ninth day of the ninth month (*chungsam chunggu*) he brewed tea and presented it as an offering to Maitreya on Samhwa Ridge on South Mountain.

The king was duly impressed and requested that the monk make him a bowl of tea. The monk then brewed some tea and offered it to him. The aroma and taste of the tea were extraordinary, and the strange fragrance in the bowl left an elegant sensation. The king had Ch'ungdam sing the *saenae norae* (another name for a *hyangga* or native song of Silla) he had heard him singing as he walked along the road and ordered the monk to compose another song about his peaceful rule. The king so admired it that he offered to raise Ch'ungdam to the rank of Royal Preceptor (*wangsa*), but, bowing to take his leave, the monk politely and firmly declined the title.[48]

Ch'ungdam made offerings of tea to Maitreya on the third day of the third month and the ninth day of the ninth month. These two days have no clear Buddhist reference. "Maitreya's birthday" was traditionally celebrated in China and the rest of East Asia on the first day of the first lunar month.[49] These days do have significance, however, in the Chinese calendar, and refer to the most auspicious days in spring and autumn. The story also provides evidence that the people of Silla were becoming more accustomed to the sexigesimal calendar adopted from China. Ch'ungdam's offering tea to Maitreya also indicates that he may have received training in China or been trained by a monk who had inasmuch as drinking tea and making offerings of tea became significant characteristics of Chinese elite society during this period. Before the mid-eighth century, according to Lu Yu's *Book of Tea (Cha jing)*, which was composed about 760, tea was associated with Daoists and Confucians in southern China during the period of disunion (ca. 220–589). Buddhist monks, particularly Chan meditation monks and thaumaturges, however, played a vital role in the dissemination of tea drinking and its associated aesthetics throughout northern China.[50] A poem by the monk Jiaoran (730–799) called "Drinking Tea with the Recluse Lu Yu on the Double Ninth," which alludes to the poet Tao Qian (Tao Yuanming, 372–427), supports the association of tea and Buddhism in the mid-eighth century in Silla.

> On the day of the Double Ninth, in a mountain monastery,
> By the Eastern fence, chrysanthemums bloom yellow.
> Common folk float them in their wine,
> But who can explain how they would improve the flavor of tea?[51]

Although the connection between monks making offerings of tea and the cult of Maitreya seems a little tenuous, texts found at the Silk Road town of Dunhuang report that tea was an appropriate offering for Maitreya in medieval China.

The cult of Maitreya is well attested in the "transformation tales" of Dunhuang *(Dunhuang bianhua)*. Though the dating remains tentative for many of these writings preserved at this remote Chinese outpost beyond the Jade Gate (Yumenguan) at the crossroads of the Silk Road in the Gobi desert, the manuscripts probably reflect currents developing in Chinese Buddhism from the seventh century. We know that monks actively encouraged people to believe in Maitreya and pursue rebirth in Tuṣita Heaven because of the preservation of a monk's notes for a sermon on the *Sūtra on Maitreya's Rebirth Above in Tuṣita Heaven*.[52] The figure of Maitreya also appears in many other stories, such as in a few individual manuscript copies of sermon notes on the *Vimalakīrtinirdeśa Sūtra (Weimojie jing)*.[53] A short essay titled "Treatise on Tea and Wine" *(Chajiu lun)*, however, preserves an interesting reference to the cult of Maitreya. The essay is told from the perspective of personified Tea and Wine arguing their merits vis-à-vis the other. In one passage, Tea argues that he is used to do good things such as to "make offerings to Maitreya and Avalokiteśvara" *(gongyang Mile, fengxian Guanyin)*. He then goes on to vilify wine, asserting that it breaks up homes and leads to licentious behavior.[54] Because direct information on how to worship Maitreya or how Maitreya was worshipped is limited in the Dunhuang materials, it seems probable that the cult of Maitreya was not as commonly practiced among ordinary individuals during the mid- and late Tang periods when these writings were composed. The anecdote on Ch'ungdam also suggests that Silla Buddhists were aware of common Buddhist cultic practices in China and actively spread them in their homeland.

The commissioning of large images of Maitreya in China continued well into the eighth century. The monk Huiyun (d. ca. 712–713) built an eighteen-foot image of Maitreya at Xiangguo Monastery in Luoyang, the Eastern Capital.[55] This makes perfect sense for the time since the usurper, Empress Wu, had previously announced her connections to Maitreya by briefly claiming the title Cishi, the Chinese translation of Maitreya, in 694–695. Later, during the reign of Xuanzong (712–756), however, the monk Haitong constructed a 360-foot image of Maitreya on the edge of a river bank in Jiazhou, present-day Mount Shengmei in Sichuan. He also restored a nine-story pavilion and established Lingyun Monastery on the site.[56] If the cult of Maitreya was truly in decline, it seems unlikely that such large images would have been constructed in China. Furthermore, an iron image of Maitreya was made at Mount Shibi in Taiyuan in 738, and during the Yuanhe period (806–820), the monk

Faxing built a three-story, 915-foot-tall Great Pavilion of Maitreya (Mile dage) on Mount Wutai, which is said to have housed a large image of Maitreya.[57] Academic interest in Maitreya may have decreased slightly, but iconographic indications of the cult of Maitreya are still abundant for the case of China. The cult of Maitreya probably did not decline during the eighth century as some scholars have supposed. The lack of exegetical information probably reflects the paucity of sources because of the destruction of the An Lushan rebellion (755–763) and the chaos of the post–An Lushan period.

South Mountain in Kyŏngju was the most conspicuous cultic site for the worship of Maitreya during the Silla period. Besides the image of Maitreya installed on Samhwa Ridge, there was a valley named after the bodhisattva on the northeastern area of the mountain. Also, a large sixteen-foot image of the bodhisattva was erected at Yongjang Monastery, the ruins of which are on the western side of the mountain.[58] Iryŏn reports that "the founder of the Yogācāra school, the venerable T'aehyŏn, resided in Yongjang Monastery on South Mountain. There he would circumambulate the sixteen-foot stone image of Maitreya, whereupon the story says that image would turn its face toward him."[59]

T'aehyŏn (or Taehyŏn, fl. 742–765) was also known as the Śramaṇa of the Blue Hills (Ch'ŏnggu saman) and was the third-most-prolific composer of extant exegetical literature of the Silla period. Some modern scholars, following Iryŏn's hagiographical account above, consider him to be the founder of the Yogācāra school since his *Study Notes to the Treatise on the Completion of Consciousness-Only (Sŏng yusing-non hakki)*, ten sections in six rolls, demonstrated his deep understanding of this doctrine.[60] In support, others conjecture that he was a disciple of Xuanzang in the line of Wŏnch'uk (613–696) through Tojŭng (d.u.). T'aehyŏn's adoration of Maitreya and his circumambulation of his image could be expected at this level.[61] However, since he composed two commentaries on the *Book of Brahmā's Net (Fanwang jing)*, which demonstrate his comprehensive knowledge of the bodhisattva precepts, and commentarial compositions dealing with Bhaiṣajyaguru's vows and the *Awakening of Faith*, he was really an exegete with broad intellectual interests. T'aehyŏn is also said to have lectured on the *Sūtra of Golden Light (Jinguang jing, Suvarṇaprabhāsa Sūtra)* at the Silla palace during a drought in 752 to pray for sweet rain, a prayer that, according to tradition, immediately engendered a compassionate response by nature.[62]

Most of the accounts we have discussed highlight conventional forms of worshipping Maitreya. Worship of Maitreya has included making images, circumambulating images, making offerings to images, and religiously chanting the name of Maitreya. All of these practices are commonly found throughout East Asia. However, this final hagiographical account presents an example of a monk offering a powerful song in the Korean vernacular to Maitreya. The song functioned much like a dhāraṇī. The *hwarang* learned to compose native songs, perhaps for use in state-sponsored rituals and while on pilgrimages to Silla's sacred mountains. The study of Indic languages was an important stimulus in Silla elites' recognition of the importance of their own native tongue and in the development of Silla's systems of clerical readings (*idu*) and poetic readings (*hyangch'al,* lit. "local letters") of Chinese characters.[63] The former were used in official documents and on inscriptions to transliterate native words whereas the latter seems to be the term used to describe the method of using some Chinese characters for their sound and some for their meaning in transcribing native Korean songs. The peace and prosperity of King Kyŏngdŏk's reign, in conjunction with the growing belief in the propaganda propounding a supposed ancient Buddhist heritage of the Silla lands and its important position as a special Buddhaland, may have caused the elites of Silla to value their own cultural accomplishments at the same level as those of India and China. One of the ways in which Silla elites recognized a high level of cultural distinction was in their appreciation of the thaumaturgic power associated with native songs composed in their own vernacular, as opposed to Indic languages, such as Prākṛit or Sanskrit, or Chinese, the lingua franca of East Asia. An example of a native composition that was efficacious appears in a narrative regarding a postman named Chigwi, who turned into a fire spirit because of his lust for Queen Sŏndŏk. Her magicians composed a spell that banished Chigwi's spirit across the sea. The version of the spell that has been preserved is in Chinese, but it is impossible to be certain whether the spell was originally chanted in the vernacular.[64]

The monk Wŏlmyŏng was formerly a *hwarang* noted for his skill in creating native songs. He was probably a head-rank six elite. The following anecdote describes how a native song honoring Maitreya was just as efficacious as a Sanskrit dhāraṇī in rectifying an anomaly in the sky.

In the spring of 760, two suns appeared in the sky for ten days and caused great disturbance among the people. One of King Kyŏngdŏk's astrologers recommended that a monk destined by karma (*yŏnsŭng*) be invited to compose a song on the topic of scattering flowers that would end this disturbing celestial phenomenon. A special altar was constructed at Chowŏn Hall, and the king went to Ch'ŏngyang Tower to await the coming of the monk. Right at that time the monk Wŏlmyŏng came walking southward on the levee path. The king had his attendants bring the monk to him. The king asked the monk to prepare a platform and compose a song. Wŏlmyŏng said that as a *hwarang* he had learned the skill of composing vernacular songs but did not know Sanksrit dhāraṇīs.

The king commanded the monk to proceed since he was the "chosen one." Wŏlmyŏng then composed the "Song of Tuṣita Heaven" in the vernacular:

> I sing of flowers scattered here today:
> O you strewn flowers
> Since you adhere to the commands of my upright heart
> Serve the lord of Maitreya's seat![65]

The calamity in the sky soon vanished. The king then offered Wŏlmyŏng a package of fine tea and a rosary of 108 crystal beads. Suddenly a handsome young man appeared from a small gate to the west of the Silla palace bearing the tea and the rosary. Wŏlmyŏng thought he was a page of the queen and the king thought he was a follower of the monk. Both were wrong. The king sent a servant to follow the youth, but he vanished into a stūpa in the inner chambers, and the tea and rosary were found in front of the southern painting of Maitreya.

That Wŏlmyŏng would choose to invoke Maitreya in his song, which was composed to get rid of a calamity in the sky, demonstrates that the cult of Maitreya was still strong in Silla. It also shows that the connection between the *hwarang* and Maitreya was still a potent religious force in Silla culture. As a result of Wŏlmyŏng's song, Maitreya himself is said to have appeared again as a youth in order to bear away the offerings and to place them in front of his image in the king's personal chapel. That the Maitreya-youth left tea and rosary beads in front of a painting of Maitreya in the palace chapel suggests the continued royal patronage of the Maitreya cult and that the practices performed by the Kims residing therein included making offerings of tea and chanting the name of Maitreya, using the rosary beads to count the recitations. The gift of tea is significant because it further attests to the practice of offering tea to Maitreya, which was performed by Ch'ungdam and by monks in China. The 108 rosary beads imply a connection with the repentance practice of chanting the name of Maitreya to get rid of bad karma, the number 108 representing the standard number of defilements just as in the list referred to in the narratives on Chinp'yo. Wŏlmyŏng was not exclusive in his worship of Maitreya, however; he also invoked the vows of Amitābha on behalf of his sister who died before him, composing a native song alluding to their future reunion in Amitābha's *kṣetra (Mit'a ch'al)*, the Pure Land Sukhāvatī. Thus we see that even though Wŏlmyŏng participated in the cult of Maitreya, he evidently desired to be reborn in Sukhāvatī. This is yet another example of the connections between the cults of Maitreya and Amitābha.

Changes in the Context of Belief

By the late Silla period (780–935), the symbolic ties between the aristocratic *hwarang* and Maitreya had deteriorated. The cult of Maitreya was gradually subsumed into the expansive Hwaŏm approach of conceptualizing the Buddhist universe. Although veneration of Maitreya must have continued among Koreans in all areas, there is not much anecdotal evidence from which to derive an image of how it was practiced. Nevertheless, as Buddhist culture in Silla continued to mature and the ideology of the age of the decline of the Dharma reemerged, it appears that worship of Maitreya transformed. There is little contemporary evidence of the commissioning of images of Maitreya by the Silla royalty in the ninth and tenth centuries, as compared to the eighth century. It seems reasonable, however, that Silla's worship of Maitreya passed through an important new stage of domestication on the Korean peninsula during this time. As with the case of ninth- and tenth-century China, the context of belief in Maitreya changed. In Korea, however, there is no evidence that it developed in the direction it went in China with the veneration of what has become known as the Laughing Buddha or Hemp-bag Bonze, the *Upadhyāya* Budai as an incarnation of Maitreya.

An inscription fragment remains on an image of a standing buddha carved into the face of a rock wall *(maaebul)* in present-day Chinju County in North Ch'ungch'ŏng Province in central Korea. Aside from the date, "the second day of the third month of *kyŏngsul*, the fourth year of the Taihe reign period" (29 March 830), all that remains is the phrase "The Buddha Maitreya" *(Mirŭk pul)*, strongly suggesting that the outlined image is of Maitreya, venerated in his guise as the future Buddha.[66] Though the patron who commissioned the image is unknown, the image provides evidence that Maitreya continued to be worshipped in Silla in the early ninth century.

The Silla scholar Ch'oe Ch'iwŏn, whose life and connections to Hwaŏm Buddhism will be treated in greater detail in chapter 4, composed an ornate stele inscription for the pagoda preserving the remains of "the Great *Upadhyāya* Nanghye," which is the posthumous name of the monk Muyŏm (800–888), an important early figure in the development of Korean Sŏn traditions and who achieved renown in Korea because of his studies in China. Ch'oe concludes the long inscription, believed to have been composed about 890, with nine poems praising the achievements of Muyŏm. The ninth poem is as follows:

> The lord's grace [runs] a thousand years deep;
> The master's transformations [inspire] ten thousand generations'
>   adoration.
> Who will grasp an axe with a handle?

Who will tune a zither without strings?
Even though the dhyāna-sphere lacks protection,
How is the clinging dust [of defilements] able to invade?
Waiting for Maitreya on Cock Peak (Kukuṭapada, Kyejoksan)
He will reside in Cock Grove (Kyerim, Silla) in the east.[67]

The reference to Maitreya in the final couplet alludes to the story, famous in medieval East Asian Buddhist culture, of the Buddha Śākyamuni's assigning his disciple Kāśyapa the responsibility to carry on the work of spreading the Dharma when the Buddha dies and enters *parinirvāṇa*. At this time Śākyamuni also is said to have entrusted him with his gold embroidered *kaṣāya* (cassock) to be passed down until Maitreya comes. Kāśyapa, the first Chan monk, is believed to be waiting absorbed in samādhi, in this case a meditative type of cryostasis, on Mount Kukuṭapada for the coming of the future Buddha Maitreya in the distant future.[68] Silla Buddhists, such as Ch'oe, did not hesitate to emphasize tacit linguistic connections between sacred Buddhist sites in India and in the Silla homeland—the Cock Peak in India and Cock Grove in Silla—for these provided further evidence that Silla was Buddha-land and had a great role to play in the future of Buddhism. Ch'oe would also have been familiar with the stories circulating in Silla regarding Maitreya's appearance as a *hwarang*.

In another literary document, Ch'oe Ch'iwŏn recorded the history surrounding the building of an eight-sided lamp tower at the State Protection Fortress in Such'ang Commandery (in present-day Susŏnggu in Taegu in south-central Korea). The lamp tower was erected by a local official named Ijae, a *chungalch'an* (the lowest head-rank six title), in supplication for a happy event for the country and to remove the sins and excesses of warfare. According to Ch'oe, Ijae was a "householder bodhisattva" and a loyal servant of the state who maintained peace in the region for ten years. On the night of the *kyŏngsin*-day of the sixth month of *mujin*-year (7 July 908), he had a dream while spending the night at Majŏnggye Monastery, which was on the northern side of Talbul (Achieving Buddhahood) Fortress. Ijae dreamed that he saw a buddha image seated on a lotus throne reaching high into the heavens with an attendant bodhisattva of similar height on its left. Walking to the south he encountered a brook, where he saw a woman. He asked her the reason for the buddha image. This woman was a lay believer, an *upāsikā*, who said the area occupied by the fortress had been designated as sacred space. In a vision Ijae saw seven images of Maitreya stacked one on top of the other on Buddha Mountain (Pulsan) on the south side of the fortress. They stood facing northward, their feet standing on shoulders, their height like a pillar soaring into the sky. Days later, he dreamed of arhats on the east side of the fortress on Deer Mountain (Changsan). Ijae built the lamp tower because of these dreams. Work on the tower began immediately and was carried out during the tenth month of the same year (28 October–26 November 908).[69]

Ijae's vision of seven Maitreyas stacked one atop the other indicates that Maitreya was still important in late Silla Buddhism. However, it is obvious that direct veneration of Maitreya is not the focus of this story. The appearance of the Maitreya images in the dream merely serves to demonstrate that the land where the lamp tower was built was an ideal site for a building because it manifested numinous traces of the future Buddha.

The Maitreya Cult in the Silla-Koryŏ Transition: Maitreya as Messianic Leader

The idea that Maitreya would incarnate among the people in the age of the decline of the Dharma was prevalent in medieval China, and after first being deployed by the Northern Wei hegemons to legitimate their rule in the late fifth century, the Maitreya myth was used frequently by rebels and dissidents. During the chaos that ensued as the Sui dynasty came apart at the seams—as well as during the rise of the Tang—Buddhist monks and laymen justified some of their rebellions by drawing upon the imagery and beliefs common to the cult of Maitreya.[70] In the year 613 alone, two unsuccessful uprisings were led by men who claimed to be Maitreya incarnate. The first was led by Song Zixian, a reputed thaumaturge, who claimed to be an incarnation of Maitreya and planned to recruit Buddhist laymen at religious services for an attack on the emperor; however, when the plot leaked and was discovered by the authorities, he was killed, along with many of his followers. The second was led by a monk, Xiang Haiming, who also claimed to be an earthly manifestation of Maitreya. Attracting several tens of thousands of adherents, the sources say, he declared himself emperor before being exterminated by the imperial forces.[71] Later, Empress Wu attempted to legitimate her usurpation of the Tang throne and her declaration of her Zhou dynasty (690–705) by identifying herself with Maitreya, based upon an interpretation of the apocryphal *Great Cloud Sūtra (Dayun jing; *Mahāmegha Sūtra)*.[72] Although she gave up the title after only three and a half months (694–695), her actions demonstrate that veneration of Maitreya was still a very powerful tool that could be deployed by power seekers. Despite Empress Wu's short-lived imperial adoption of Maitreya cult imagery to legitimate her rule, scholars have shown that either followers of Maitreya rebelled frequently through the Song period or that rebels drew upon Maitreya cult imagery to lend authority and religious fervor to their uprisings.[73]

The first Silla rebel to draw upon the imagery of the cult of Maitreya's descent to legitimate political insurrection was Kim Kungye (fl. 891–918), an illegitimate son of either Silla king Hŏnan (r. 857–861) or Kyŏngmun (r. 861–875), who had also spent time as a Buddhist monk. Taking power as a rebel leader in Silla's northern border areas, he appropriated the title of king in 901. Although scholars typically refer to the state he founded as Later Koguryŏ, it was originally called Majin in 904. In 911 he renamed his kingdom T'aebong and declared himself to be Maitreya and two of his general-sons to be bodhisattvas.[74] He is said to have composed twenty rolls of scriptures to support his claim to be Maitreya. Kungye grew increasingly despotic and ordered the deaths of many underlings: in particular, the monk Sŏkch'ong, who denounced the validity of Kungye's scriptural compositions, and his wife Lady Kang and their sons. His tyranny and meglomania as Maitreya, his official biography suggests, were important factors that contributed to his being deposed by his subordinates in 918 and replaced by Wang Kŏn (877–943), the founder of the Koryŏ kingdom that succeeded Silla in 935.

The assumption of the status of Maitreya by a rebel leader was not a common characteristic of the cult of Maitreya in Silla. That it emerged at the end of the Silla period demonstrates increasing Korean familiarity with the potent legacy of Maitreya symbolism in medieval China, which circulated among the people by word of mouth, and a firm belief that assuming the name and status of Maitreya would provide needed legitimacy among a large cross-section of the population, particularly in the old Paekche lands in the southwestern section of the peninsula, as well as in Manchuria. Kungye began to appropriate Maitreya imagery long before he claimed to be Maitreya. The first name he selected for his kingdom, Majin, refers to Mahācīnasthāna (Mahajindan, Ch. Mohezhendan), the Indian name for China, the great country of the eastern region. More important, as recorded in the *Ratnamegha Sūtra (Baoyu jing)*, it is the name of the place where "Prince Moonlight" (Yueguang), an important forerunner to Maitreya, will be born in the final age of the Buddhadharma.[75] Kungye may have been familiar with some of the teachings of this sūtra, or perhaps the *Great Cloud Sūtra*, because it claims that Maitreya will be born in Mahācīna, which is in the northeastern region of Jambudvīpa, the name for our world system. The evidence indicates that Kungye was familiar with developments in Tang China and was probably influenced by the Empress Wu's deployment of Maitreya symbolism to provide legitimacy for the expansion of his state among the masses of people (Koreans, Chinese, and other tribal peoples) who anticipated the coming of Maitreya and the establishment of peace and prosperity.[76]

Furthermore, Kyŏnhwŏn (r. 892–936), the founder of the Later Paekche kingdom, attempted to resurrect the worship of Maitreya at the Miruk Monastery in Iksan, which had been built in the early seventh century by the Paekche kings Pŏp and Mu. We know from earthenware bearing the date 858 (Dazhong 12) discovered during modern excavations at the site that the monastery was in use during the Unified Silla period. Having wrested this region back briefly from the young Koryŏ state, Kyŏnhwŏn built a pagoda and performed other votive activities at the monastery in the summer of 922.[77]

Wang Kŏn, the Koryŏ founder, built several monasteries at the end of 936, when he had finally achieved peace on the peninsula. Among these was a Mirŭk Monastery that he constructed in his capital Songak, present-day Kaesŏng.[78] That he would build a monastery with this name suggests that Maitreya occupied an important symbolic role in the early Koryŏ court and that Kungye had not worn out the efficacy of the Maitreya cult. Obviously Wang and his political and religious advisers felt he had much to gain from demonstrating a link to the future Buddha by constructing a physical structure in his honor and bearing his name. The court's adoption of Maitreya imagery, however, should be seen instead as one aspect of its deployment of Hwaŏm symbolism to provide the new court with legitimacy.[79] Mirŭksa was never among the most important monasteries to the Koryŏ royal family, though it contained a hall for the propitiation of the merit subjects, served as a site for special vegetarian feasts and assemblies to pray for victory over the Khitans, and later served as a place where Yogācāra monks of Koryŏ sat for their religious exams.[80] Wang probably built it in recognition of the future Buddha's prominence among the Hwaŏm Divine Assembly of buddhas, bodhisattvas, and gods, which symbolically had enabled him to restore peace among the peoples of the Korean peninsula.

At the same time he founded his Mirŭk Monastery in the capital, Wang began work on Kaet'ae Monastery at Yŏnsan, in Paekche territory, present-day South Ch'ungch'ŏng Province. It was completed in 940.[81] As evidence of the assimilation of the Maitreya cult into the Hwaŏm tradition, Kaet'ae Monastery contained a Hwaŏm Enlightenment Site (Hwaŏm toryang) and a Maitreya Enlightenment Site (Mirŭk toryang). Since an enlightenment site (Skt. *bodhimaṇḍa*, Ch. *daochang*) refers to a place where Buddhist ritual observances are carried out,[82] the two special halls built at this monastery suggest that the Buddhist deities associated with the *Avataṃsaka Sūtra* and Maitreya were propitiated with their own rituals in the early Koryŏ period and that Maitreya held a special place in the Hwaŏm Divine Assembly.[83]

Since the cult of Maitreya flourished in Silla long before the introduction of the Hwaŏm tradition, it took time for the all-encompassing Buddhist system based on the *Avataṃsaka Sūtra* to assimilate it. Other cults entered Silla much later and were more quickly absorbed into the Hwaŏm synthesis of cultic practices because they were promoted by monks associated with the Hwaŏm tradition. The rich literature that exists describing various methods and procedures used by practitioners to invoke the saving power of Avalokiteśvara shows that such a cult was important in Silla. Because many adherents to the Avalokiteśvara cult were intellectual proponents of Hwaŏm, they indirectly paved the way for the dominance of Hwaŏm Buddhism.

CHAPTER THREE
The Cult of Avalokiteśvara

Worship of the Bodhisattva Avalokiteśvara (Kwanseŭm, Kwanŭm) is the most widespread devotional practice of Buddhism in East Asia. Venerated as the goddess of mercy in China and manifest in human form as the Dalai Lama in Tibet, Avalokiteśvara is the most beloved of all Buddhist deities. When the cult of the bodhisattva of compassion was first introduced to Korea, the role of this versatile deity had not yet expanded to its current rich form. The story of Avalokiteśvara's transformation into the ultimate savior being is indelibly linked to an abundant group of ritual observances that continued to grow during Silla times. Anecdotes and narrative literature imply that, during the seventh century, the participants in the cult of Avalokiteśvara in Silla were principally nobles of true-bone status. By the first half of the eighth century, the conditions were right for ritual practices, spells, and ideas that had spread throughout mainland China in earlier centuries to flourish in Silla with the rise of Hwaŏm Buddhism and infiltrate downward from elite society into the lives of ordinary people. Worship of Avalokiteśvara expanded as a corollary to the cult of Amitābha since the bodhisattva is said to appear to individuals who will be reborn in the Pure Land to welcome them. By the ninth and tenth centuries, invocation of Avalokiteśvara was a common component of mainstream Mahāyāna Buddhism in Silla Korea.

The Worship of Avalokiteśvara in Medieval Sinitic Buddhism

In medieval China, the cult of Avalokiteśvara developed from murky beginnings into a religious force embraced by all strata of Chinese society. Avalokiteśvara (Ch. Guanshiyin or Guanyin) is the bodily manifestation of the Buddhist concept of compassion *(chabi,* Ch. *cibei)*, which acts as the Mahāyāna counterbalance to the Buddhist pursuit of wisdom *(chihye,* Ch. *zhihui)*. Avalokiteśvara was accessible through supplication anytime or anyplace, particularly when one was in danger, and recollection of Avalokiteśvara's characteristics and recitation of his name were the basic practices of the cult. As with the cults of Maitreya and Amitābha, aristocratic monks and laity commissioned images of Avalokiteśvara to generate merit and serve as objects of worship. The cult of Avalokiteśvara flourished throughout the Northern and Southern dynasties period and entered the Korean peninsula, where Silla aristocrats made images and supplicated Avalokiteśvara for temporal blessings.

The process by which Avalokiteśvara transformed into the Chinese Guanyin is closely linked to representations of Avalokiteśvara in Buddhist literature that circulated in medieval China.[1] The most important is the well-known chapter on the bodhisattva in the *Lotus Sūtra*, "The Gateway to Everywhere of the Bodhisattva He Who Observes the Sounds of the World" *(Guanshiyin pusa pumen pin)*.[2] This chapter, which circulated separately as the *Avalokiteśvara Sūtra (Guanshiyin jing)*, outlines the situations and methods for praying for the aid of Avalokiteśvara by intoning the bodhisattva's name. The bodhisattva also appears in a prominent place in the Pure Land sūtras as an attendant of Amitābha. In the *Lotus Sūtra*'s chapter on Avalokiteśvara, the bodhisattva is said to appear in the world to save beings in thirty-three different apparitional forms according to the needs of the people to whom he manifests.[3] A similar list of thirty-two transformation bodies is found in the *Śūraṃgama Sūtra*.[4] Also germane to the development of the cult are indigenous Chinese scriptures, such as *King Gao's Sūtra of Avalokiteśvara (Gaowang Guanshiyin jing)*, which are closely associated with the cultic practices of making images of Avalokiteśvara, sūtra chanting, and dhāraṇīs.[5] Typically, scholars have asserted that the role of the bodhisattva in several esoteric sūtras, in which the bodhisattva is depicted in various esoteric forms, caused the worship of Avalokiteśvara to skyrocket because these forms were linked to rituals and procedures invoking the bodhisattva by means of dhāraṇīs. These so-called esoteric forms include the eleven-headed form (Skt. Ekadaśamukha, Ch. Shiyimian), the white-clad or white-robed form (Skt. Pāṇḍaravāsinī, Ch. Baiyi), the thousand-armed or thousand-handed form (Skt. Sahasrabhuja, Ch. Qianshou), and the thousand-eyed, thousand-armed form (Ch. Qianyan qianbi). Although modern scholars classify these forms of Avalokiteśvara as esoteric or tantric Buddhist, Chinese Buddhists who invoked the bodhisattva in these forms did not think of themselves as participating in a separate tradition of esoteric Buddhism.[6] Calling upon the name of Avalokiteśvara, intoning or chanting his name, became one of the most powerful and widespread dhāraṇīs in medieval Sinitic Buddhism. Avalokiteśvara, in the bodhisattva's various forms, was propitiated and invoked for protection, wish fulfillment, and absolution of sins in nonesoteric and nontantric Buddhism rituals long before putatively orthodox tantric Buddhism entered China during the eighth century.[7]

Unlike the cults of Maitreya and Amitābha in China, the origins of which can be traced back historically to the Buddhist figures Daoan (312–385) and Lushan Huiyuan (334–417), respectively, scholars are unable to link the cult of Avalokiteśvara to any particular early monastic figure. Faxian (d. after 423), the famous Chinese Buddhist pilgrim, encountered monks in Mathurā who made offerings to the bodhisattva, and he himself directed his mind toward the bodhisattva for protection when caught in a tempest at sea on his way home from his travels in India during the years 399–414,[8] but general East Asian exposure to this bodhisattva stems from two sources: the *Lotus Sūtra* and the *Pure Land Sūtra*. Various versions of the *Pure Land Sūtra* and a partial translation of the *Lotus Sūtra* were available in the third century, but the Chinese origins of this cult, and of the Maitreya and Amitābha cults, seem to be manifest in the carvings of the bodhisattva made in the Yungang caves during the Northern Wei during the fifth century.[9] The cult of Avalokiteśvara was stimulated greatly through the dissemination of miracle tales on the wondrous powers of the bodhisattva.[10]

Adoration of Avalokiteśvara in Paekche

Granted Paekche's cultural contacts and affinity with several southern Chinese states, it is not surprising that tales exist of Paekche monks who sought Buddhist training in China south of the Yangzi River. The earliest of these accounts concerns the monk Palchŏng (Ch. Fazheng), who is said to have studied in the state of Liang during the Tianjian reign period (502–520). The tale of Palchŏng was originally contained in what was probably an early Tang addendum to a Southern dynasties' collection titled *Record of Marvelous Experiences Enacted by Avalokiteśvara (Guanshiyin yingyan ji)*.[11] A similar rendition of this tale is also contained in *Tales of the Lotus Sūtra (Fahua zhuanji)*, by the seventh-century Tang monk Sengxiang (also known as Huixiang).[12] Palchŏng, a śramaṇa, is said to have studied in China for thirty years but missed his homeland so much that he decided to return to Paekche. Having heard from a fellow monk about an enlightenment site (Ch. *daochang*, Kor. *toryang*) dedicated to Avalokiteśvara on Mount Jie in Yuezhou (most probably near present-day Hangzhou in Zhejiang Province), he decided to visit it before catching a boat to return home. Palchŏng intended to visit the site to pay homage to Avalokiteśvara and the *Lotus Sūtra* for the miracles performed there. The tale then proceeds to give the background story regarding the sanctuary, which had been established by two unnamed Southern Qi (479–502) monks who were attempting to memorize and chant the entire *Avataṃsaka* and *Lotus* sūtras, respectively. The crux of the miracle tale is that the monk who struggled to memorize and recite only the *Avalokiteśvara Sūtra* portion of the *Lotus*, with great difficulty, was rewarded by witnessing flowers rain down from heaven and by recognizing that Avalokiteśvara had manifested himself to him as an old man who had regularly brought him provisions. The tale emphasizes that Palchŏng was able to witness himself the very walls of the enlightenment site in which the bodhisattva had appeared. Palchŏng is the earliest Paekche monk known to have studied abroad, and the earliest person of Paekche to have traveled to China other than members of diplomatic missions. Because he returned to his homeland it seems probable that he promoted the cult of Avalokiteśvara in Paekche. The account of Palchŏng also shows an early connection between the *Avataṃsaka Sūtra* and the *Lotus Sūtra,* though the story emphasizes the superiority of the *Lotus*.[13]

Although Buddhism supposedly came to Paekche relatively early, of the more than thirty extant images thought to be of Paekche composition, nearly all date from the late sixth and seventh centuries.[14] The earliest works were mainly small, gilt-bronze images, some of which portray a bodhisattva holding a pearl in both hands—perhaps Avalokiteśvara holding a wish-fulfilling gem *(cintāmaṇi,* Ch. *ruyi baozhu,* Kor. *yŏŭi poju).* This type of image was widespread in Paekche and may have influenced Buddhist images in Japan during the Asuka period, such as the Yumedono Kannon (Dream Chamber Avalokiteśvara).[15]

Although the textual information on the worship of Avalokiteśvara in Paekche is limited, Paekche immigrant sculptors in early Japan fashioned some of their most beautiful creations when depicting this bodhisattva, which strongly implies the popularity of the bodhisattva among Paekche's elite and royalty. The graceful lines and expression of the Kudara Kannon (Paekche Avalokiteśvara) bear witness to the talents of the Paekche artists in the late sixth and early seventh centuries or, at least, the influence of these immigrant Paekche artists on their Japanese students.

Furthermore, in his study of the influence of Sui regional substyle on early Korean bronze images, Jonathan Best deals in depth with several images of Avalokiteśvara dating to the middle of the seventh century. Some images show distinct characteristics of southern Chinese styles, which is not surprising in light of Paekche's history of diplomatic and cultural ties to the southern coast of China. Others show influence from the Hebei and Shandong regions due to geographic proximity. The founding of the Sui dynasty, the subsequent unification of China, and the subsequent diplomatic missions sent by the Korean kingdoms to Chang'an, however, show the influence of the image styles of the Shanxi region on Paekche images of Avalokiteśvara.[16] Because these images were produced primarily for wealthy donors and the royal family, it seems apparent that in Paekche, at least, the cult of Avalokiteśvara existed in some form among the elite, but was poised to flourish among the general population.

Extant sculptural evidence indicates that ancient Koreans mainly revered the two bodhisattvas Maitreya and Avalokiteśvara. Furthermore, evidence also suggests that the cult of Avalokiteśvara gradually surpassed the cult of Maitreya following Silla's conquest and forced unification of the Three Kingdoms. It continued to prosper and remains, at present, one of the most dynamic and persistent forms of Buddhist devotion performed by both monks and laity. The numbers of identifiable images of this bodhisattva remaining from the Three Kingdoms and Unified Silla periods demonstrate the high regard and great appeal that Avalokiteśvara enjoyed among early Korean Buddhists. A published collection of Korean Buddhist images identifies five statues of the bodhisattva from the Three Kingdoms period, two of which are of Silla manufacture, and seven from the Unified Silla period, out of a total of 184 images. Roughly three times as many images of Maitreya were produced during the Three Kingdoms period, but images of Avalokiteśvara were more than double those of Maitreya during the Unified Silla period.[17]

The cult of Avalokiteśvara in Silla was often centered on monasteries in which an image of the bodhisattva was enshrined in commemoration of a manifestation of the bodhisattva. Worship of the bodhisattva appears to have been conducted by individuals supplicating the bodhisattva by themselves for specific needs related to their own family circumstances or social or temporal condition, regardless of whether the suppliant was a monk or a lay believer. According to the available sources, people who supplicated Avalokiteśvara did so primarily for the reasons expressed in the chapter dealing with this bodhisattva found in the *Lotus Sūtra,* such as for the birth of a son. However, one significant difference is that often individuals supplicated the bodhisattva not for themselves but for a relative who was in a precarious situation, such as one captive in a hostile country or one lost at sea. Another important aspect of the cult of Avalokiteśvara is its interrelationship with the cults of Maitreya and Amitābha. In many of the accounts treated below, an incarnation of Avalokiteśvara appears in order to help a suppliant succeed in both his worldly and spiritual endeavors—whether it be curing the individual from illness, rescuing him from an unfortunate situation, or testing a monk's understanding of nonduality—and mediates the encounter between the monk's primary object of his devotion (usually either Maitreya or Amitābha).

Supplication for Obtaining Sons and Destroying Bad Karma

The earliest account of the supplication of Avalokiteśvara in Silla is found in Daoxuan's (596–667) *Further Lives of Eminent Monks* and is further developed by a Korean version of the same tale in Iryŏn's *Memorabilia of the Three Kingdoms*. The story demonstrates that the cult of Avalokiteśvara first flourished under aristocratic patronage. Although the account proper is a treatment of the life of Chajang (b. ca. 600–d. ca. 650–655), the section we are most concerned with deals with Chajang's father, Kim Murim. He was a true-bone aristocrat related to the ruling family of Silla, and under the variant name Duke Horim, he is remembered one of six honored advisers of Silla queen Sŏndŏk.[18]

Kim Murim did not have an heir and became very depressed over the prospect of dying without a son. Because he was a lay Buddhist, he exercised his faith by giving alms generously and by praying earnestly about the Buddhadharma. Daoxuan's record says that Murim commissioned a thousand-armed, thousand-eyed image of Avalokiteśvara (Ch. Qianbu Guanyin, Kor. Ch'ŏnbu Kwanŭm) to express his hope for a son. Iryŏn's account does not say that Murim made an image of Avalokiteśvara but says that Murim supplicated before a thousand-armed, thousand-eyed image of Avalokiteśvara vowing, "If I beget a son, I will release him from family life so that he may become a ford across the sea of the Dharma." His wife dreamed of a falling star that entered her bosom just before she conceived. A son, who eventually became the monk Chajang, was born at dawn on the eighth day of the fourth month—the Buddha's birthday.[19]

We may draw some conclusions about the nature of the Avalokiteśvara cult from this account. First, the doctrine that Avalokiteśvara will bless people who are unable to have children was known among the elites of Silla society in and near the capital, present-day Kyŏngju. It is unclear whether the dissemination of this doctrine was oral or written, although the literate members of the Silla aristocracy were probably familiar with the chapter on Avalokiteśvara in the *Lotus Sūtra;* however, the sūtra specifically encourages women who desire children to worship Avalokiteśvara; it says nothing of men.[20] Murim appears to have been praying for a son on behalf of his wife. He supplicated the bodhisattva not because they did not have any children, but because they did not have a son. Murim had a daughter, Lady Namgan, whose son was the monk Myŏngnang.[21] Furthermore, while the Silla nobility practiced levirate marriage, it is unclear whether Murim's wife's inability to bear a son was viewed as her fault—as it would be centuries later because of the influence of neo-Confucian moral thought.[22]

The concept of praying to Avalokiteśvara on behalf of a family member is a striking characteristic of the cult in Silla. Second, Murim's inclination to commission a thousand-armed, thousand-eyed image of Avalokiteśvara may indicate that he (or his artist) was familiar with the most recent manner of representing the bodhisattva. This story concerning Chajang's birth is the only reference to a thousand-armed, thousand-eyed image of Avalokiteśvara found in the *Further Lives of Eminent Monks*.[23] Third, this account implies that the practices of commissioning images of Avalokiteśvara and supplicating those images were done for specific purposes, in this case, so that the worshipper could obtain a son.

Earlier, we briefly discussed how images of Maitreya were buried by Silla elites in hopes that sons would be born to them who would become *hwarang* and protect the country through ritual and martial arts. Kim Murim would have been familiar with this native custom but instead chose to perform a practice that would ensure that his son would pursue a religious path. Although not developed during the early stage of the cult in Silla, the doctrine of the Bodhisattva Avalokiteśvara's providing protection and support would soon become more prominent as Silla elites and royalty entered into tributary relations with their powerful neighbor, Tang China.

Silla-Tang relations grew very strong under the guiding hand of Kim Ch'unch'u (King Muyŏl), who traveled to China in the 640s to secure an alliance with the Tang court for protection against the other Korean states of Koguryŏ and Paekche. Silla's most dangerous enemy was Paekche, while the Tang desired to reduce the power of Koguryŏ. Although the terms and details of the alliance have not been preserved in either Chinese or Korean documents, Silla adopted Tang official dress and the Tang calendar to signify their dependent, tributary relationship on the Tang and their participation in China's cosmopolitan world order.[24] Several years after Ch'unch'u ascended the throne of Silla, the Silla and Tang alliance for the conquest of Paekche and Koguryŏ began. Paekche was subdued in 660, Koguryŏ in 668. After the wars were over, however, the Tang generals were given orders to incorporate these conquered territories into the Tang administrative structure. Kim Ch'unch'u's son Kim Pŏmmin (King Munmu) began harassing the Tang forces with guerrilla tactics and making special arrangements with the remnants of the Paekche and Koguryŏ forces to expel the Chinese from the peninsula. At this time King Munmu's younger brother Kim Inmun (629–694), the second of six sons of Kim Ch'unch'u, served as the Silla envoy in Chang'an and a general in the unification wars.[25] The Tang court threatened King Munmu on several occasions for insubordination and even warned that they would dethrone him and replace him with Inmun. Concern for Inmun's safety and welfare is addressed in conjunction with faith in Amitābha, as recorded an anecdote preserved in *Memorabilia of the Three Kingdoms:*

When [Kim] Inmun was in captivity, the people of the country took a monastery that was originally called Inyong Monastery, rebuilt it, and renamed it the Avalokiteśvara Enlightenment Site (Kwanŭm toryang). Then, when Inmun died at sea while returning home, they renamed it Amitābha Enlightenment Site (Mi'ta toryang).[26]

The renaming of Inyong Monastery as Avalokiteśvara Enlightenment Site is significant because it demonstrates that the Silla royalty and aristocracy understood Avalokiteśvara's primary function as a savior-being as found in the *Lotus Sūtra*. There undoubtedly would have been an image of the bodhisattva enshrined in the main hall of the monastery where royally sponsored monks and family prayed to Avalokiteśvara for Kim Inmun's safe return to Silla. Even though supplication of Avalokiteśvara could be performed at any monastery where there was an image of the bodhisattva to adore, by specifically naming the site after Avalokiteśvara it probably became consecrated solely for the performance of rituals invoking Avalokiteśvara to save people from danger. One problem with the story, however, is that according to the *History of the Three Kingdoms*, Inmun did not die at sea, even though he made the dangerous trip to Tang China seven times. He died in Chang'an in 694 after serving as a respected member of the Tang emperor's night guard for twenty-two years. He was honored by the Tang court, and his spirit and coffin were escorted back to Silla by Chinese dignitaries in 695. It was probably at this time—instead of during the height of tension between Silla and Tang in the 670s—that the monastery was again renamed, this time as Amitābha Enlightenment Site.[27] Rituals and prayers were probably performed on his behalf so that he might be reborn in Sukhāvatī. According to the information available, this site appears to have been a private monastery where family and close friends prayed specifically for Kim Inmun and for no one else. Furthermore, the images contained therein were probably commissioned in Inmun's name so that the merit would benefit him directly.

The term "enlightenment site" was a common term for "monastery" during the seventh century. It was originally a translation of *bodhimaṇḍa*, the place under the bodhi tree where Śākyamuni became enlightened. During the Northern Wei period it came to mean a place where Buddhist ritual and ceremonies, such as ordinations and special assemblies, were performed. Sui emperor Yang (r. 604–617) then changed the name for all monasteries in China to "enlightenment site" in 613. It is also likely that during the period of Empress Wu's influence and reign (ca. 660–705) the term was again substituted for the ordinary term for monastery (*si*) given that the imperial temples in the eastern and western palaces bore the designation interior enlightenment site (*neidaochang*).[28]

The implication of the foregoing account is that during the late seventh century, the Silla monarchy and aristocracy viewed the cult of Avalokiteśvara as viable for people's protection or salvation while alive and the cult of Amitābha for salvation postmortem. Because Avalokiteśvara is the bodhisattva that personifies the Mahāyāna ideal of compassion, his mercy toward beings is demonstrated by his using his powers to succor people in their weaknesses by granting their desires for safety, prosperity, and protection. This seems to be the best explanation for the Silla royalty's renaming Inyong Monastery first after Avalokiteśvara while Kim Inmun was still alive and then after Amitābha when he passed away. This account further highlights the close relationship between the cults of Avalokiteśvara and Amitābha. In the Pure Land scriptural tradition, Avalokiteśvara serves as an attendant bodhisattva to Amitābha and appears to faithful suppliants prior to their rebirth in Sukhāvatī.[29] Thus, in a sense, suppliants of Avalokiteśvara are turned over to Amitābha when they pass from this life. Avalokiteśvara protects them in this world and delivers them to Amitābha's Land of Extreme Bliss, where the faithful are reborn in the calyx of a lotus flower.

Circumstantial relationships between the cults of Avalokiteśvara and Amitābha, based on the names of monasteries, are also found in the only exegetical evidence that mentions practices of the cult of Avalokiteśvara in Silla. Several methods of worshipping Avalokiteśvara are discussed in the "Vow Made at the White Lotus Enlightenment Site" *(Paekhwa toryang parwŏn mun)*, which was composed by Ŭisang, a true-bone aristocrat and founder of the Hwaŏm tradition in Korea. The document is regarded as a "Pure Land document" by scholars of Korean Pure Land Buddhism,[30] presumably because the vow was made at White Lotus Enlightenment Site. The term "White Lotus" usually refers to the lotus flower into which an aspirant is born in the Pure Land. The prose of the vow-text, however, is clearly associated with the Avalokiteśvara cult. Avalokiteśvara's mercy is the focus of the vow, whereas Maitreya is mentioned only once in the document. The practices that the aspirants vowed to cultivate include chanting the Great Compassion Spell *(taebi chu,* Ch. *dabei zhou)*, recollecting the name of the Bodhisattva Avalokiteśvara *(yŏm posal myŏng)*, and taking refuge in Avalokiteśvara.[31]

The Great Compassion Spell

The Great Compassion Spell is the focus of the *Nīlakaṇṭha (Qianyan qianbi Guanshiyin pusa tuoluoni shenzhou jing)*, which was translated into Chinese a few times during the early Tang by Zhitong in Luoyang in the Zhenguan reign period (627–649) and also by Bhagavaddharma (Qiefandamo), perhaps during the Yonghui or Xianqing reign periods (650–661).[32] Ŭisang would have had access to these translations and to the dhāraṇīs contained therein, and he probably disseminated them in Silla. Although it was undated, this vow-text was probably composed after Ŭisang's return from Tang in 676 as he preached and established monasteries oriented toward the Hwaŏm teaching throughout Silla's newly conquered domain.

The power of this dhāraṇī, which is also called the spell invoking the thousand-armed Avaloktieśvara *(chŏnsu chu,* Ch. *qianshou zhou),* was believed to be extremely potent, and a whole range of cultic practices was associated with chanting it. According to Zhitong's translation of the sūtra, if people are able to maintain the Great Compassion Spell in their minds day and night six times, all their karmic hindrances will be eliminated, and they will attain all dhāraṇīs. If a person reads aloud or chants this dhāraṇī, all of that person's defilements and karma will be eliminated. If a person chants the dhāraṇī at daybreak, he will be protected by Avalokiteśvara continually, and all that he thinks about will come to pass. If someone chants the dhāraṇī seven times, there is no vow or wish that will not come to fruition. The sūtra also promises those who chant the Great Compassion Spell that they will not fall into the evil destinies (beasts, hungry ghosts, denizens of hell) and that they will destroy bad karma, obtain the merit of a thousand cakravartins, always be reborn with Avalokiteśvara, and always be reborn into noble families. If one takes a handful of incense and flowers, scatters them in front of an image of Avalokiteśvara, and chants this dhāraṇī seven times, he will obtain the merit of a great chiliocosm *(daqian,* a Buddhist world system) and the characteristic of great compassion. If someone looks at the face of an image of Avalokiteśvara and chants this dhāraṇī, he will be able to see the mark of Avalokiteśvara's subtle smile. The sūtra encourages believers to put on white clothes to hold a Feast of the Eight Prohibitions *(baguanzhai)* on the fifteenth day of every month and to make stūpas containing *buddhaśarīra* (relics of the Buddha) and altars in front of these stūpas. They are to scatter all kinds of flowers on the altar and burn incense and light lanterns in front of the Buddha (i.e., the stūpa). The sūtra says that if they produce a thought of reverence before the Buddha, Avalokiteśvara will come and enter the altar. When they chant the dhāraṇī 108 times, all the sins and hindrances of each person, as well as the unwholesome karma of the five heinous crimes[33] and heavy sins, will be eradicated. The sūtra also teaches people to inscribe the Great Compassion Spell on banners *(chuang)* as a means of protecting against calamities.[34]

During the eighth century this spell was recited daily in ritual observances performed by five virtuous monks on Mount Odae, where it probably served as a means of protecting Silla from calamities and eradicating the king's bad karma. Ŭisang's religious community, on the other hand, probably chanted this spell in repentance rituals to eliminate the karma of their sins and defilements so that they could be reborn in the Sukhāvatī, which is also one of the specific benefits of chanting the Great Compassion Spell in Bhagavaddharma's translation of the *Nīlakaṇṭha*.[35] As part of the *Thousand Hands Sūtra* (Ch. *Qianshou jing*, Kor. *Ch'ŏnsu kyŏng*), the Great Compassion Spell continues to play an important role in modern Korean Buddhist liturgy.[36] Dhāraṇīs associated with the myriad forms of Avalokiteśvara continued to be an important characteristic of Sino-Indian Buddhist practice. New spells and dhāraṇī procedures associated with Avalokiteśvara arrived frequently in Silla throughout the eighth century.

Silla's Mount Potalaka

Ŭisang was a student of the voluminous *Avataṃsaka Sūtra*, the last chapter of which, "Entry into the Dharma Realm" *(Ru fajie pin)*, tells the story of a monk named Sudhana who is sent on a spiritual quest by the Bodhisattva Mañjuśrī to learn all the techniques taught by all the bodhisattvas in the world. Avalokiteśvara is the twenty-seventh such bodhisattva Sudhana meets, and he is directed to find him in the south on a mountain called Potalaka. There Avalokiteśvara instructed Sudhana in his practice of great compassion.[37] The popularity of this bodhisattva may have inspired Ŭisang, or another like-minded monk, to find places reminiscent of Mount Potalaka in their home countries.

If the following account from Iryŏn's thirteenth-century *Memorabilia of the Three Kingdoms* is authentic, the Silla exegete Ŭisang ushered in a cult of the earthly abode of Avalokiteśvara in Silla a few centuries before the cult of Mount Putuo in China began to emerge as a pilgrimage center in the tenth century.[38] Korea's Mount Potalaka, presently called Mount Obong, is on the eastern coast of the peninsula in Yangyang County, in Kangwŏn Province.[39] No physical evidence datable conclusively to the seventh century remains at the site of Naksan Monastery, where the events in the following and upcoming tale are said to have occurred during the Silla period. According to tradition, the invading Mongols destroyed the shrines and monastic buildings that were said to have been erected by Ŭisang and subsequent monks. All the existing structures dating from the Chosŏn period (1392–1910) and modern renovations were destroyed recently in a great natural wildfire in 2005.[40]

The story goes that when Ŭisang returned from Tang China he heard a rumor that the Dharma body, or true form, of the Bodhisattva of Great Compassion (Taebi, Avalokiteśvara) could be found in a cave on Silla's northeastern coast. He named the place Naksan after Avalokiteśvara's home on Mount Potalaka, which is said to be an island. The place was also called Small White Blossom (Sobaekhwa) because the form of Avalokiteśvara that commonly appeared at this site wore white clothing.

Ŭisang performed purification rituals lasting for seven-day periods while at this site and worshipped Avalokiteśvara in a cave where the dragon of the East Sea gave him a crystal rosary and a fabulous jewel. After another seven-day period of purification he entered the cave and beheld the true features of the bodhisattva. He was instructed to found a monastery on a site where two bamboo shoots were growing. The main hall of Naksan Monastery was built on this spot. A lifelike image of Avalokiteśvara was enshrined therein, into which the jewel and rosary were deposited.

The famous Buddhist scholar Wŏnhyo, who was also an important proponent of the Hwaŏm teachings, is also said to have encountered an emanation of Avalokiteśvara in female form in the vicinity of the cave as he made a pilgrimage to worship there. A woman wearing sandals was washing her menstrual napkin in a clear stream running to the sea. When Wŏnhyo asked her for a drink of water, she scooped up filthy water and offered it to him. He threw it away and scooped his own water. The woman disappeared as a blue bird cried "O Monk," and all that was left was a pair of sandals by a tree. Later, when Wŏnhyo reached the monastery he found the same sandals under the seat of the image of Avalokiteśvara. Only then did he realize that he had seen a true body of the bodhisattva. He wanted to enter the cave to see the true form of Avalokiteśvara, but a storm prevented him from doing so.[41]

The apparitional form of Avalokiteśvara alluded to in this tale is commonly known as the White-robed Guanyin (Baiyi Guanyin). From the tenth century on, when the bodhisattva was featured in this fashion it was almost exclusively regarded as feminine. Furthermore, the White-robed Guanyin has been the most popular form of the bodhisattva in sculpture, painting, poetry, and other media since the tenth century in China. There has also been much scholarly debate on the identification of this bodhisattva. Some have asserted that she is either the tantric goddess Pāṇḍaravāsinī (clad in white) or the Chinese White Tārā, the consort of the male Avalokiteśvara, both of which are found in the Tibetan pantheon and thought to have been first introduced into China during the eighth century. All of these versions of the bodhisattva would have arrived in Korea too late for our story. Common sense dictates that the appearance of White-robed Guanyin strongly suggests that the story dates from the Koryŏ period. Nevertheless, there is some literary evidence that another White-robed Guanyin was known as early as the sixth century. Dhāraṇī ritual procedures for accomplishing vows and for curing all manner of illnesses deploy images of apparitional manifestations of Avalokiteśvara wearing white robes. Such images of the bodhisattva are described meticulously in the sixth-century *Dhāraṇī Miscellany (Tuoluoni zaji)*. Although the translator of this collection of Buddhist spells and their ritual procedures is unknown, it is listed in the *Liang Register (Liang lu*, comp. ca. 502–557). In this text, the bodhisattva Avalokiteśvara, whose sex is not specified, is depicted as wearing white clothes *(baiyi)*, sitting on a lotus throne, and holding a lotus flower in one hand, a vase or bottle *(kuṇḍika)* in the other.[42] Although the depiction of Avalokiteśvara in this story of Ŭisang and Wŏnhyo probably dates from a later time, other elements of the story are instructive, nevertheless.

Ŭisang's worship of Avalokiteśvara apparently involved strict observance of the monastic precepts and fasting for purification for seven days *(chaegye ch'iril)* to behold the true form of the bodhisattva. (Such seven-day rituals were common during the seventh century, especially when the practitioner desired some kind of guidance.)[43] For doing this Ŭisang is rewarded with an audience with the bodhisattva, who directed him where to build the monastery and to enshrine an image of the white-clad Avalokiteśvara. Wŏnhyo, on the other hand, encounters the bodhisattva unwittingly and botches his chance to demonstrate that he understands the nonduality of phenomena—that there is no difference between purity and impurity—when he refuses the water mixed with menstrual fluid offered by the disguised bodhisattva. Avalokiteśvara is plainly associated with the notion of nonduality in the *Heart Sūtra*, in which Avalokiteśvara teaches that the ultimate Buddhist truth is that there is no difference between emptiness and form.[44] This Buddhist scripture was particularly prominent in East Asia in the seventh century because of the Chinese monk Xuanzang. Wŏnhyo is not associated with any particular practice but is said to have traveled to Naksan on pilgrimage following in the footsteps of Ŭisang to catch a glimpse of the bodhisattva. According to tradition, fires destroyed many of the shrines first built by Ŭisang, but these were rebuilt by the monk Pŏmil (810–899) when he returned to Silla from Tang in 847 after the suppression of Buddhism during the Huichang period (840–846).[45]

Worship of the Bodhisattva Avalokiteśvara was widespread among the elites by the end of the seventh century. The main practice of the cult was supplication before an image of the bodhisattva. In the following narrative, Taehyŏn *salch'an* and his wife, Lady Yongbo, pray sincerely before an image of Avalokiteśvara for several days *(in'gi rusŏk)* on behalf of their son Puryerang, the state sylph, the ritual leader of the *hwarang*, who had been captured by the northern barbarians. Although their surname is not stated, they must have been of true-bone status inasmuch as Taehyŏn was raised to the rank of *t'aedae kakkan*, an honorary post held by or posthumous title granted to eminent statesmen and true-bone nobles who had performed a great service for the state, such as General Kim Yusin and the diplomat Kim Inmun. I surmise that their family name was Kim because of the titles held by family members, though no surname is mentioned.

On the sunny side of Diamond Ridge (Kŭmgangnyŏng) north of Silla's heartland was Paengnyul Monastery. Enshrined in the monastery was an image of the Bodhisattva of Great Compassion. In 693, King Hyoso (r. 692–702) made Puryerang the *kuksŏn*. Of his thousands of followers, Puryerang's favorite was Ansang. In the spring of 694, Puryerang led an excursion up to the northern borders of Silla's domain where the party was attacked by northern barbarians. Those who were not captured left their belongings and fled home. Puryerang was captured, but his faithful friend Ansang tracked the barbarians northward. Meanwhile, back in the Silla capital, a mysterious cloud appeared over the treasury in which Silla's prized zither and flute were stored. When the king dispatched some men to investigate, they were shocked to find the treasured instruments missing. The king, saddened by the loss of his *hwarang* leader, became even more distressed and offered a great reward for the return of the musical instruments. Puryerang's parents went before the image of Avalokiteśvara at Paengnyul Monastery and prayed sincerely for several nights. Suddenly, the two treasures appeared on top of the incense table, and Puryerang and Ansang emerged from behind the image.

When asked to relate his story, Puryerang said that he had been put to work as a shepherd in the northern steppes. Soon thereafter a monk appeared and consoled him. The monk was carrying the zither and flute in his hand. Puryerang knelt down before the monk, confessing great attachment to his parents and to his king. The monk invited Puryerang to follow him. When they arrived at the edges of the sea they also met Ansang. The monk flew them back to Silla on the zither and flute. When the details of this story were made known to the king, all those involved were rewarded, and great emoluments were given to Paengnyul Monastery.[46]

Extant evidence indicates that, prior to and during the reign of King Hyoso, the participants in the cult of Avalokiteśvara in Silla were all nobles of true-bone rank. Puryerang's parents pray to the image of Avalokiteśvara at Paengnyul Monastery for several nights on his behalf. It seems obvious that they were praying for the safety and protection of their son, although they may also have been praying for the return of the treasured zither and flute. The narrative suggests only that a dark, ominous power stole these cultural objects of Silla. Did Avalokiteśvara take them on purpose? Did the bodhisattva need them to save Puryerang and Ansang? It is perhaps not fruitful to seek a logical answer. What this narrative does demonstrate is that Sillans probably believed that the country's human and material assets were protected by Avalokiteśvara and that steadfast propitiation of the bodhisattva could lead to protection from enemies and social and material benefits for the faithful.

In many cases that have been examined above, worship of Avalokiteśvara in Silla seems to conform to practices described in the

Lotus Sūtra. There is, however, one major difference. The *Lotus Sūtra* teaches that individuals who are themselves in danger, who suffer from unwholesome sexual desires, or who are barren should call upon Avalokiteśvara, chanting the bodhisattva's name, and they will be saved, freed from carnal passions, or enabled to conceive handsome sons and beautiful daughters. In the cases we have examined, however, it is typically a different party—a spouse, parents, or family member—who calls upon Avalokiteśvara for help. We have no idea whether Chajang's mother, Kim Inmun, or Puryerang invoked the name of Avalokiteśvara. Nevertheless, we may conclude that Silla nobles clearly understood the Mahāyāna concept of the transfer of merit *(hoehyang,* Skt. *pariṇāmanā)* in their religious practices and aspirations. In other words, they understood that the wholesome karma deriving from their cult worship could be directed toward another individual. The efficacy of rituals and dhāraṇī procedures associated with Avalokiteśvara further bolstered the claims made by the *Lotus Sūtra* about the power of the bodhisattva. The introduction of new forms of Avalokiteśvara and their concomitant dhāraṇīs became more prominent in succeeding centuries.

Spells, Songs, and New Compassionate Forms

During the eighth century, several new translations of spell sūtras, some of which depicted new iconographic representations of the Bodhisattva Avalokiteśvara, entered Silla from Tang China. Even though the Korean sources on the cult of Avalokiteśvara mostly date from the thirteenth century, the wide dissemination and domestication of this cult throughout all social strata in pan–East Asian society, and therefore in Silla Korea, can be demonstrated by reference to the general contours of this cult in contemporary China and Japan.[47] By the early Tang, the cult of Avalokiteśvara was widespread throughout China, and the worship of this bodhisattva was common among elites and nonelites alike. For example, the famous Chinese pilgrim Xuanzang chanted the name Avalokiteśvara for protection and guidance with great success throughout his journey to the west (629–645) when he was threatened by potential robbers or assassins and for worship of the bodhisattva when he encountered massive images of him in Central Asia and India.[48] Also, during the late seventh and eighth centuries a number of ritual texts referring to various new forms of Avalokiteśvara were translated into Chinese and then transmitted to Korea and Japan. But perhaps more important, innumerable images were made of the bodhisattva. The proliferation of images of Avalokiteśvara, featuring the thousand-armed form and Amoghapāśa (Ch. Bukong juansuo Guanyin, Kor. Pulgong kyŏnsak Kwanŭm),[49] which flourished during the eighth century, have been treated in detail by Yü

Chün-fang and Kobayashi Taichirō.[50] These new forms of Avalokiteśvara are often labeled tantric or esoteric. There is, however, little evidence that actual practitioners in China and Korea viewed them as anything other than mainstream Mahāyāna Buddhism.

The *Catalog of Buddhist Scriptures Compiled in the Kaiyuan Reign Period (Kaiyuan shijiao lu)* records an account of an otherwise-unknown monk from Silla named Myŏnghyo, who prompted the translation of the *Amoghapāśa Dhāraṇī (Bukong juansuo tuoluoni jing)*.[51] Amoghapāśa is one of the six forms of the Bodhisattva Avalokiteśvara, who snatches up beings like fish in his unerring net of mental emptiness in the great sea of rebirth and death (saṃsāra) and carries them to the shore of nirvāṇa.[52] The translators apparently consulted a handwritten manuscript in an Indic language (*fanben*) that had been circulating widely in China before they executed their translation.

> During the third month of *gengzi,* the third year of the Shengli reign period of the age of Empress Wu Zetian [25 March–23 April 700], the monk Myŏnghyo from the country of Silla had traveled far to see the "Tang transformation" and was about to bestow alms on the road. In front of the Zongchi [Dhāraṇī] Gate he remained mindful. Subsequently, with respect and resolve he firmly requested [the imperial sūtra-translation committee] to translate this dhāraṇī (*zhenyan*) to enable that border territory [viz. Silla] to share in hearing the secret teaching (*mijiao*). Thereupon [the dhāraṇī] was translated as the *Amoghapāśa Dhāraṇī* in one section at the Sūtra-Translation Bureau (Fanjingyuan) at Foshouji Monastery. . . . It was completed in the eighth month of the first year of the Jiushi reign period [17 September–16 October 700].[53]

This "secret teaching" Myŏnghyo sought was not "secret" or "esoteric" in the sense that it was intended for only a few initiates: it was a "secret teaching" because the Mahāyāna itself was widely regarded as the "esoteric teaching" (*mijiao*). The Mahāyāna acquired this epithet because only those with the aspirations of the bodhisattva would appreciate the Mahāyāna teachings and because only the Mahāyāna preserves the ultimate truth of emptiness and the nonproduction of dharmas. The Hīnayāna, in contrast, was widely regarded in medieval Sinitic Buddhism as the "exoteric teaching" (*xianjiao*). These rhetorical views are fundamentally different from the way the concepts of "esoteric" and "exoteric" were deployed in the sectarian milieu of Heian Japan (794–1185) and succeeding periods.[54]

Given that Myŏnghyo had the means to travel to Tang and the social prestige to request the translation of this dhāraṇī, it is probable that he was a monk of true-bone status. Since the translation of this Buddhist spell was completed quickly, it was possibly carried out on commission by the Silla monk who requested that it be done. This notice deploys "dhāraṇī" *(tuoluoni)* and "mantra" *(zhenyan)* interchangeably, which I and other scholars have demonstrated was a common practice in translations made during the seventh and eighth centuries.[55]

Veneration of the eleven-headed version of Avalokiteśvara (Skt. Ekadaśamukha) also makes its appearance in Silla in the early eighth century. Probably sometime during the first quarter of the century, the scholar-monk Kyŏnghŭng, who served as the State Elder of Silla's Buddhist church for King Sinmun lay bedridden once for about a month. One day a nun came to pay him a visit and waited upon him. She paraphrased the *Avataṃsaka Sūtra (Huayan jing)* saying that, because his present illness was caused by anxiety and toil, joy and laughter would cure him. She made eleven masks with hilarious faces, each of which had a removable chin.[56] Kyŏnghŭng was so pleased by the masks that he forgot about his illness and was cured. The nun subsequently left his room and entered Namhang Nunnery. When he pursued her all he found was the walking stick she had used placed against a hanging scroll painting of the eleven-headed Avalokiteśvara *(Sibilmyŏn Wŏnt'ong sang)*.[57]

The cult of Avalokiteśvara in the Silla capital included veneration of various forms of the bodhisattva. Not only was it patronized for a while by the royalty (as we can infer because they built the Avalokiteśvara Enlightenment Site), but the cult is also seen in this story at Namhang Nunnery in the form of a miracle-working scroll painting. That the eleven-headed version of Avalokiteśvara would be found in Silla at this time is also highly probable considering that texts referring to this incarnation of the bodhisattva entered China a century before, during the Northern Zhou dynasty (557–581).[58] It seems likely that the nuns who inhabited the nunnery near the leader's own monastic residence had been ordered to supplicate the bodhisattva on behalf of the monk who had been the State Elder and that some of them might have visited and administered to the religious leader. The eleven-headed version of the bodhisattva must have been prominent among the Silla elite: a stone icon of this form of Avalokiteśvara occupies a prominent position directly behind the main Buddha image in the Sŏkkuram grotto built by the aristocrat Kim Taesŏng between the years 751 and 775.

Also during the eighth century, evidence indicates that the cult of Avalokiteśvara had spread among the common people of Silla by the reign of King Kyŏngdŏk. The commoners worshipped the bodhisattva the same way as the nobles during the previous century. They prostrated themselves before images of Avalokiteśvara for salvation from earthly dangers and made special offerings to the bodhisattva for healings.

Avalokiteśvara worship also expanded in accordance with the success of the cult of Amitābha. According to Pure Land scriptures, Avalokiteśvara will appear to people seeking rebirth in the Pure Land to welcome them.[59] The idea that Avalokiteśvara will appear to people pursuing rebirth in the Pure Land is given an interesting twist in the narrative of the commoners Nohil Pudŭk and Taltal Pakpak, discussed previously within the context of the cult of Maitreya.

Although Pudŭk worshipped Maitreya and Pakpak supplicated Amitābha, they were visited by the Bodhisattva Avalokiteśvara, apparently, as the ultimate test of their resolve and their understanding of the Mahāyāna principle of nonduality. My point is not that the initial failure of Pakpak and the success of Pudŭk implies any inherent superiority of the cult of Maitreya or its practitioners over the cult of Amitābha. Rather, this story illustrates belief in the secondary role of Avalokiteśvara as a bodhisattva that facilitates an individual's completion of the path or achievement of buddhahood in this very body (*hyŏnsin sŏngdo*). Before these ordinary men can achieve buddhahood in this very body, becoming incarnations of the very buddhas that they worship, Avalokiteśvara must make them understand that there is no fundamental difference between the notions of purity and impurity. For this reason they are subject to a situation in which they are forced to break one monastic precept after another to comply with—or perhaps better "to perfect"—the Mahāyāna "perfection" (Skt. *pāramitā*) of wisdom, the understanding that all dharmas are empty of self-nature, and of compassion, the ideal personified in Avalokiteśvara. This is the same test Wŏnhyo failed in his putative encounter with the bodhisattva near Naksan Monastery.

In the tales preserved in *Memorabilia of the Three Kingdoms*, commoners were the main recipients of Avalokiteśvara's compassionate power to save, protect, and heal during the eighth century. We can assume that the supplicant of Avalokiteśvara described in the following story, Pogae, was probably a commoner since she and her son Changch'un were indigent and did not have surnames. Changch'un signed on as a boat hand in a trading venture over the Yellow Sea to China to earn some money for his destitute family, who lived in Ugŭm Village in the vicinity of the Silla capital. Time passed, and by 745 Pogae had heard no news of her son. She probably feared that he had been shipwrecked or had perished at sea. She went to Minjang Monastery, which had been converted from the residence of a noble named Minjang, and prayed before the image of Avalokiteśvara for seven days. Her son then suddenly appeared and told his story: His ship had been caught in a storm, and he was shipwrecked on the Chinese shore in the Wu region, the vicinity of present-day Shanghai. After being enslaved by the locals who found him, he was sent to work in the fields. One day a monk, who seemed to be a man of Silla, visited him in the paddies and offered to help him get home. They left Wu around sunset and traveled for what seemed a long time to Changch'un. The young man was emotionally distraught when they reached a great ditch and, being exhausted physically, began to cry. The monk grabbed Changch'un by the armpits and jumped over the ditch. In the meantime Changch'un passed out and did not revive until he heard people speaking in his native tongue. When they arrived in Silla it was late evening. Miraculously, they had traveled the whole distance from China to Korea in a matter of hours.[60]

As in the foregoing story concerning Puryerang's parents, Pogae offered worship in front of an image of the Avalokiteśvara for seven days before the bodhisattva acted. The text does not say that she prayed for her son Changch'un's safe return, but it does assert that she wished to hear news of him. This is not included on the list of circumstances included in the *Lotus Sūtra* in which one should invoke the power of Avalokiteśvara. So far as we know, Changch'un did not pray to the bodhisattva to be saved or returned to Silla. The story of Pogae, however, provides more circumstantial evidence supporting my supposition that praying to the bodhisattva on behalf of a family member is a distinct characteristic of the cult of Avalokiteśvara in Silla. The final account of Avaloktieśvara worship in Silla in the eighth century, however, shows an individual praying and making an offering to the bodhisattva for himself.

As with the foregoing account, we can infer that the main characters, Hŭimyŏng and her son, like Pogae and Changch'un, were probably commoners inasmuch as they were impoverished and did not have surnames. This story takes place at Punhwang Monastery, which is in the heart of Kyŏngju due north of Hwangnyong Monastery, the main hub of Buddhist rituals sponsored by the Silla court. The eminent monks Chajang and Wŏnhyo resided at Punhwang Monastery for a time during their respective careers. Little remains of the once proud monastery founded in the third year of the reign of Queen Sŏndŏk (634): three stories of what was once a nine-story brick stūpa, which is a national treasure, and a Hall of Bhaiṣajyaguru, the Medicine Buddha (Yaksajŏn).[61]

During the reign of King Kyŏngdŏk, Hŭimyŏng lived in Han'gi Village, which was probably in the vicinity of the Silla capital. She found herself in dire straits when her son went blind at age five. They supplicated a painting of the thousand-armed, thousand-eyed form of Avalokiteśvara, which was on the northern wall of the Left Hall of Punhwang Monastery. Hŭimyŏng had her blind son sing a song to Avalokiteśvara in which he asked the bodhisattva to bestow upon him one of his thousand eyes. Over time the child's eyesight returned. The song composed by the boy was recorded in the form of a native song:

The Cult of Avalokiteśvara

> Falling to my knees,
> Pressing my hands together,
> Thousand-armed Bodhisattva
> I send this prayer of supplication.
> Of your thousand hands and thousand eyes
> Please send one down to me
> And lessen yours by one.
> As for me, who does not have two,
> Please give me one to cure me by your mystery, O Compassionate One.
> If you grant me this boon
> How great will be the bounty of your compassion.[62]

The cultic practices performed in this account were a combination of worshipping a painting of the thousand-armed, thousand-eyed version of Avalokiteśvara and the composition of a song as an offering to the bodhisattva. Like the verses composed by the monk Myŏngwŏl, who participated in the cult of Maitreya, this native song was deployed just like a dhāraṇī to invoke the saving power of the bodhisattva. In a sense, a case is being made that the efficacy of the native songs of Silla is equal to that of dhāraṇīs.

Supplication for Wish-Fulfillment and Protection

During the ninth and tenth centuries, the cult of Avalokiteśvara began to resemble the general contours of the form it would maintain for much of the succeeding millennium on the Korean peninsula. The late Silla period is also punctuated by the rise of Sŏn traditions throughout the Korean peninsula. Although Sŏn Buddhist literature dealing with this period makes no reference to the cult of Avalokiteśvara, the importance of the *Diamond Sūtra* in Chinese Chan Buddhist hagiography, and its close relationship to the *Heart Sūtra,* attributed to Avalokiteśvara, gave new life to the veneration of Avalokiteśvara in monastic circles. In particular, the spell at the end of the *Heart Sūtra,* along with the Great Compassion Spell, became the two most important dhāraṇīs deployed by monks of the Chan tradition in East Asia.[63] Both spells have continued to be part of Korean Sŏn liturgy to the present.[64] Korean literary materials preserve only a few narratives describing supplicants of Avalokiteśvara during this period, and these stories demonstrate that the bodhisattva was propitiated for protection and for the acquisition of worldly desires. Furthermore, although female forms of the bodhisattva have appeared in numerous Korean tales, they become more prominent in these stories from late Silla.

We have previously seen how an aristocrat worshipped Avalokiteśvara to obtain a son and how the Silla royalty propitiated the bodhisattva to protect a Silla prince and envoy. The *Lotus Sūtra* teaches that people fearful of giving in to carnal desires should call upon Avalokiteśvara to overcome these physical passions. This idea is twisted in the following story of an otherwise unknown monk named Chosin. Since he was appointed as manorial overseer *(changsang)* of a small, local monastery in Silla's northeastern province of Myŏngju (roughly present-day Kangwŏn Province), we may safely assume that he was of elite background, perhaps a head-rank six elite. Furthermore, we may also take his aspiration to the hand of the daughter of the provincial lord, as the following story describes, as circumstantial evidence of his being of elite status, because it is unlikely that he would have considered the match remotely possible if the gap between their social positions had been great.

Probably sometime during the reign of Silla king Munsŏng (839–857), Segyu Monastery, which was in the Nalli Commandery of Myŏngju (in present-day Kangwŏn Province), dispatched the monk Chosin to serve as overseer to a manor belonging to the monastery. When Chosin arrived in the area he was deeply attracted to the daughter of the governor, Duke Kim Hŭn (803–849).[65] He frequently went before the image of the Bodhisattva of Great Compassion at Naksan, secretly supplicating to obtain its favor, though the girl had been betrothed to another man for several years. When he learned this information he went before the image, angry at the bodhisattva's not accomplishing his desires. He sobbed before the image until nightfall, emotionally worn out.

Chosin seemed to fall asleep, and he immediately dreamed that Duke Kim's daughter had entered the gate of his residence. She told him that she had also fallen in love with him at first sight, but until now had submitted to her parents' wishes. Finally realizing that she preferred a love match to following her parents' orders, she said that she wished to elope with him. Chosin was overcome with joy, and they returned to his hometown where they lived for many years in happiness, during which time five children were born to them. As in other such dream narratives,[66] the family then fell on hard times and was reduced to begging on the roads. Their eldest child, a fifteen-year-old boy, died and was buried at Hyehyŏn Ridge. When they arrived in Ugok District they made a thatch hut. Their remaining four children begged for them and suffered much. Eventually Chosin's wife addressed her husband, saying that their lives together had been full of joy and sensual pleasure early on, but now they were full of suffering. She suggested that they each take two children and go in opposite directions. Chosin was relieved when she said this. The moment that he and his wife separated on the road Chosin awoke from his dream.

It was just before dawn when he awoke. When it was light he found that his whiskers and hair had turned completely white and that he had no more desire for the sensual pleasures of women and the world. He humbly prostrated himself before the image of Avalokiteśvara to repent and cleanse himself. He then returned to Hyehŏn Ridge, where he had buried his son in a dream, and exhumed an image of Maitreya. He returned to the Silla capital, gave up his post as manorial overseer, and spent his personal fortune to build Ch'ŏngt'o (Pure Land) Monastery.[67]

There are several interesting facets to this story, not the least of which is Chosin's purpose in and method of supplicating the image of Avalokiteśvara. The story also introduces a number of contradictions. A point that we might have taken for granted is that Chosin is indeed a monk. It would seem natural for a head monastery to dispatch a monk as a manorial overseer and also that a monk would struggle with his vow of celibacy when bewitched by a beautiful woman. When Chosin prays before the image of Avalokiteśvara that he might have the girl, however, he makes no reference to monastic vows of celibacy. The only fact we know is that she had been betrothed to another for many years. Was Chosin actually a monk at this time? After the bodhisattva responded to his emotional predicament in a dream, Chosin gained the resolve to give up worldly pursuits, relinquish his appointment, and use his personal wealth to commission a monastery. Perhaps Chosin was not a monk at the time of this story, but became one soon afterward. If this is the case, it would reflect the type of practice an elite might have performed at that time to obtain blessings for himself, such as Chajang's father Kim Murim, discussed above. If Chosin really was a monk, this account vividly portrays the mental and physical struggles common to many Buddhist monks. Their vows of celibacy did not completely free them from carnal thoughts or lustful desires. Even if Chosin was a monk at this time, that he kept his personal fortune and was able to use it to build a monastery also conforms to evidence compiled by Gregory Schopen for the case of Indian monks of the same period.[68]

Another point made clear by this tale is the relationship between the three cults of Maitreya, Avalokiteśvara, and Amitābha. In his dream, Chosin's son is buried on Hyehyŏn Ridge, and when he goes to that spot afterward he finds an image of Maitreya, which he promptly enshrines. After his conviction in the Buddhist faith is made certain, though, he exhausted his family fortune in building Chŏngt'o Monastery, which implies a link with the cult of Amitābha. Regardless of his social or monastic status, Chosin participated in the cults of Maitreya, Avalokiteśvara, and Amitābha freely, a fact that certainly reflects the synthetic nature of Buddhist worship during this time in Silla.

In *Memorabilia of the Three Kingdoms,* Iryŏn preserves an account of the rise of a particularly efficacious cultic site for the propitiation of

Avalokiteśvara during the final years of Silla. This new center for the worship of the Bodhisattva of Great Compassion was Chungsaeng (Living Beings) Monastery, which was on Wolf Mountain (Nangsan) in the Silla capital. On display at the monastery were three paintings of different emanations of Avalokiteśvara purportedly painted by an émigré Chinese painter whose skill in capturing minute details almost resulted in his being executed at the hands of the Chinese emperor. After narrowly escaping with his life by being able to portray the elegant beauty of the eleven-headed version of Avalokiteśvara, which the emperor had seen in a dream, the painter had relocated himself permanently to Silla, apparently as penance. Regardless of whatever else in the story might be true, in reality the painter was probably exiled. The people of the Silla capital, nevertheless, admired the skill displayed in these depictions and invoked the power of the bodhisattva to fulfill their hopes and desires.

During the Tiancheng period (926–929) the Silla elite Ch'oe Ŭnham (d.u.) prayed before the paintings of the bodhisattva at Chungsaeng Monastery to provide him with a son and heir. His supplication was heard and his wife conceived and bore a son. Before the child had been alive for three months, the armies of Kyŏnhwŏn of Later Paekche (ca. 892–935) stormed the Silla capital, putting any who opposed them to the sword. Carrying his infant son in his arms, Ŭnham sought refuge in the monastery, where he tearfully entrusted the baby to the care of Avalokiteśvara. He implored the bodhisattva tearfully three times with the following statement: "Troops from a neighboring country have stormed the city. The situation is urgent. This newborn is a heavy burden. I may not be able to escape. If he was really bestowed upon us by thee, O great saint, I humbly request that thou wouldst watch over and nourish him by the power of thy great mercy and cause us, father and son, to see each other again." The father covered the child in swaddling clothes and concealed him under the lion seat, the high seat of the monastery, entrusting him to the bodhisattva's power.

According to the narrative, two weeks later the invading forces retreated from the Silla capital, and Ŭnham returned for his son. The baby's skin was soft and clean, and the smell of milk was still present in his mouth, attesting to the miraculous power of the bodhisattva. This child eventually grew into a man of surpassing intellect and wisdom: Ch'oe Sŭngno (927–989), the architect of Koryŏ's governmental system.[69]

Iryŏn emphasizes the bodhisattva's responsiveness to the devotion of Ch'oe Ŭnham and the power of the bodhisattva to nourish the child entrusted to its care. This is also the first case in which the diction of the text implies that the image of the bodhisattva that was supplicated was in female form. In previous stories we have considered, incarnations of Avalokiteśvara have appeared female form, a canonical possibility inherent in the *Lotus Sūtra*. In China, there is little evidence of Avalokiteśvara in female form prior to the Song period (960–1279). If we are to judge from extant images, until the end of the Tang period, the iconography of the bodhisattva most often featured male and in some cases androgynous forms. The earliest extant female forms are found in Dazu in Sichuan and date to the early Song.[70] The image of the eleven-headed version of Avalokiteśvara in Sŏkkuram, which dates to the mid-eighth century, may be seen as an androgynous representation of the bodhisattva of the kind that became widespread in the Tang. Newer and more feminine representations of the bodhisattva, as the tale describes, could have come as a result of immigration and other forms of cultural exchange.

One aspect of the cult of Avalokiteśvara in China that is striking for its absence in Korea is the Miaoshan myth, which provides a Chinese context for the origin of Avalokiteśvara as a female. This myth, the basis of which may trace back to the late Tang, was deployed in the Song in 1104 to promote the worship of Avalokiteśvara at the Upper Tianzhu Monastery in Hangzhou.[71] From the Song onward Avalokiteśvara had transformed completely into the Chinese goddess Guanyin. Still, although Korean paintings of the bodhisattva emulated Song forms, sculptural representations retained the older male and androgynous forms of the Silla period.

I shall now turn to the Hwaŏm tradition of Silla, which has lurked in the background in several of the anecdotes I have treated thus far. Ŭisang, the founder of the Hwaŏm tradition in Silla, was among the most important monastic proponents of the worship of Avalokiteśvara. Not only did he identify Naksan as the earthly abode of Avalokiteśvara in Silla, but he also promoted the practice of chanting the Great Compassion Spell. This spell invoking the Thousand-armed Avalokiteśvara is one of the most popular dhāraṇīs in East Asian Buddhism. In Silla it was also deployed as part of detailed cult procedures to venerate Avalokiteśvara within the context of a grand Hwaŏm-inspired Buddhist ritual context.

CHAPTER FOUR

The Rise of Hwaŏm Buddhism in Silla

The *Avataṃsaka Sūtra* (*Buddhāvataṃsaka Sūtra*, Ch. *Dafangguang fo huayan jing*) provides a compelling vision of reality and a comprehensive Buddhist worldview. This Mahāyāna scripture was regarded as the first sermon preached by the Buddha Śākyamuni in the Lotus Storehouse World System after his enlightenment. Because it was delivered to a vast assembly of gods, spiritual beings, and bodhisattvas, but understood only by beings with advanced spiritual capacity, the scripture was conceptualized as an esoteric teaching (Kor. *milgyo*, Ch. *mijiao*) by medieval Buddhists. The sūtra presents a unified vision of reality tied to a detailed description of the bodhisattva path and incorporates the cults of several of the most prominent buddhas, bodhisattvas, gods, and other related beings of power believed to reside or be accessible in the phenomenal world. Buddhist intellectuals in Silla from the seventh century onward increasingly understood the scripture as unassailable, being at once the initial and consummate Buddhist teaching. Differences are overcome in this sūtra and shown to be integral parts of a transcendent whole.

When the scripture was deployed ritually and institutionally, its emphasis on the ultimate interdependence and interfusion of all things was useful in producing politico-religious symbolism that could be systematized by the Silla royalty, aristocracy, and Buddhist intellectuals to promote a vision of unity amid diversity in order to protect and maintain the Silla state. The whole of the preexisting Buddhist intellectual tradition, Mahāyāna and non-Mahāyāna, was subsumed into one stratified and inclusive system just as the Silla elites hoped to incorporate the subjugated peoples of Paekche and Koguryŏ into their sociopolitical order. In Silla from the eighth century onward, adherence to the *Avataṃsaka Sūtra*'s conceptualization of the Buddhist universe gradually replaced the earlier promotion of individual cults of buddhas and bodhisattvas by providing a system in which all the earlier cult figures could be venerated. This and the next chapter will describe this gradual process by emphasizing developments in what we may call provisionally the Hwaŏm tradition of Silla, which assimilated preexisting cults of buddhas and bodhisattvas and synthesized new cultic practices. The tradition combined and unified Buddhist doctrines and cultic practices into one coherent whole that could be deployed by the Silla state to promote its purposes and protect the privileges of its elites. Previously, scholars have examined aspects of the rise of what they call "Hwaŏm faith" *(Hwaŏm sinang)*, which comprises various cultic developments: reverence for the *Avataṃsaka Sūtra*, a cult of the Divine Assembly described in the sūtra, veneration of the abodes of bodhisattvas depicted in the scripture, the development of Hwaŏm communities, the worship of the founder of the Hwaŏm school in Silla, and special dharma assemblies associated with the *Avataṃsaka Sūtra*.[1] In this chapter, for the sake of context, I review the basic contours of the tradition in China and Japan. The bulk of the chapter is devoted to describing the literary and material evidence of the growing interest in Hwaŏm Buddhism among Buddhist intellectuals and the royalty of Silla, the formation of a Hwaŏm tradition in Silla focused on Ŭisang but popularized by his disciples, and the observances of Hwaŏm societies.

The East Asian Context to the Rise of Hwaŏm in Silla

The Hwaŏm/Huayan tradition (Hwaŏmjong) was one of several Buddhist movements that began to develop during the Sui-Tang period in medieval China. Among the other movements arising at this time, the most influential were Tiantai, Chinese Yogācāra (Ch. Faxiang, Weishi, or Cien after the name of Kuiji [632–682]), Chan, and tantric Buddhism.[2] The received tradition of Chinese Huayan Buddhism traces its origins to the monk Dushun (557–640, officially called Fashun). Dushun is said to have built upon the foundations laid by the masters of the *Daśabhūmika Śāstra* (Treatise on the *Sūtra on the Ten Stages,* Ch. *Shidi jing lun;* usually simply *Di lun*), which was a commentary describing the ten stages of a bodhisattva. The *Daśabhūmika* itself became roll eight of Buddhabhadra's translation of the *Avataṃsaka Sūtra* in sixty rolls (trans. 418–420). As a youth Dushun joined the service battalions of the army, performing such menial labor as carrying water and gathering firewood. At age eighteen, however, he left the householder lifestyle to pursue a religious life and cultivate his meditative skills. Many miraculous occurrences were said to have attended his religious perambulations, and he became known as the Dunhuang Bodhisattva, after his place of origin. His fame became so great that Emperor Wen of the Sui dynasty (r. 581–604) conferred on him the title Imperial Heart and awarded him with a monthly stipend for his personal maintenance. Dushun was succeeded by Zhiyan (602–668), who was also known as Yunhua because he often preached the *Avataṃsaka Sūtra* at Yunhua Monastery. The monks Ŭisang and Fazang (643–712) were both disciples of Zhiyan. Fazang is often considered to be the "true" founder of the Huayan tradition because his synthesis of its doctrines, as set forth in the *Treatise on the Golden Lion (Jinshizi zhang)*, became widespread in East Asia. Nevertheless, Robert Gimello has demonstrated that because the primary doctrinal innovations of Huayan thought may be found in the writings of Zhiyan, he should not be overlooked as the first major synthesizer of Huayan Buddhism. Gimello has also shown that Zhiyan was more concerned with practice than with doctrinal speculations.[3] Zhiyan's practice-oriented Huayan Buddhism was transmitted to Korea by Ŭisang. Even though other eminent Korean monks, such as Chajang, were said to have lectured on the *Avataṃsaka Sūtra*,[4] Ŭisang is unquestionably regarded as the founder of the Hwaŏm tradition in Silla Korea. He maintained some contact with Fazang through his student Sŭngjŏn (fl. ca. 670–700), who studied in China and returned to Silla with copies of the latest exegeses of and a personal letter from Fazang.[5]

Fazang was of Sogdian ancestry, though he was born in Chang'an and was completely Sinicized. He was also known as Master Xianshou (Worthy Head), and as a result the Huayan tradition is sometimes called the Xianshou tradition. As a youth he assisted Xuanzang as a member of the imperial translation bureau, but following the beliefs of Zhiyan, with whom he later studied, he disagreed with Xuanzang regarding the doctrine that there were some people who did not possess buddha-nature (Skt. *icchantika,* Ch. *wuming*) and that a novice must pass through various stages gradually before finally attaining the final goal of liberation (nirvāṇa). It is also said that he later assisted in the translation activities of Yijing (635–713) and that during the years 695–704 he was a spiritual adviser to Empress Wu Zetian. She importuned Fazang to assist the monk Śikṣānanda (652–710) in his eighty-roll version of the *Avataṃsaka Sūtra* (trans. 695–699), which was based on the previous translation.

Fazang and his Huayan metaphysics briefly gained particular prominence during Empress Wu's brief Tang interregnum. His Huayan tradition, though, was not the exclusive recipient of imperial favors at this time: many other monk-exegetes, translators, and devotional specialists in the cult of Amitābha, as well as Chan meditation masters, also received imperial sponsorship. Scholars generally conclude that Empress Wu singled out Huayan as particularly representative of the religious aspirations of her Zhou dynasty vis-à-vis the Tang because the central doctrines of the Huayan tradition coincided with her political goals.[6] The doctrines of the oneness or totality of all things, the complete interpenetration of all phenomena *(shishi wuai),* and of all truth emanating from one cosmic Buddha (Vairocana) served her political goals of creating a centralized bureaucracy to break the power of the great aristocratic families of Hebei and other northern provinces, enhancing imperial prestige, and seizing totalitarian power. Although this theory is persuasive, Richard Guisso suggests that at best it is only a partial explanation of Empress Wu's patronage of Huayan inasmuch as she showed genuine interest in Huayan as early as 670, probably long before she contemplated usurping the Tang throne. She also supported other nascent traditions such as Chan. Furthermore, the altruistic nature of Huayan doctrine hardly seems conducive to creating and maintaining totalitarian power. Thus, Guisso surmises that Empress Wu's fondness for Huayan may have come as a "product of sincere faith and of a metaphysical sophistication" seldom found among Tang emperors.[7]

The *Avataṃsaka Sūtra* outlines the most complex description of the bodhisattva path found in Buddhist literature: a grand scheme of fifty-two stages that emphasizes the ten stages of the *Daśabhūmika*.[8] Huayan doctrine explains that the bodhisattva reaches enlightenment by passing through ten stages and acquires thaumaturgic powers along the way so that he can bring the cosmos together in order to deliver beings from suffering in the mundane realm; however, because the whole universe is interconnected, all ten of these stages (as well as the master list of fifty-two) are part and parcel of each other, and the completion of any one stage implies completion of the entire path. For this reason, setting out on the path and completing the path of practice are essentially indistinguishable and, therefore, from the standpoint of traditional schemes of practice (Skt. *mārga*), irrelevant. The point of Buddhist practice is to arouse the *bodhicitta* or thought of enlightenment *(fa puti xin)* and to be enlightened immediately thereby. This teaching of the suddenness of Huayan practice and its rewards lends hope to those desiring to become enlightened immediately as opposed to traversing countless eons of rebirths to develop the bodhisattva traits necessary to become enlightened like the Buddha. That Empress Wu probably appreciated this manner of doctrine, which could consider her to be such a bodhisattva that unifies all things, cannot be denied. For instance, she had herself depicted as such a bodhisattva in the commentary on the *Great Cloud Sūtra (Dayun jing)* and even as Vairocana himself in the great stone-relief carved in the Fengxian Monastery at the Longmen caves between 655 and 675.[9]

After Fazang, however, there were no major intellectual figures until after the An Lushan rebellion had severely weakened the centralized authority of the Tang empire. Nevertheless, veneration of the *Avataṃsaka Sūtra* in China continued during the first half of the eighth century, and Koreans participated in the development of China's Huayan tradition. For instance, the Korean monk Wŏnp'yo went to Tang during the Tianbao reign period (742–755) searching for traces of the Western region.

He went to Lingfu on Mount Zhiti carrying a copy of the eighty-roll translation of the *Avataṃsaka Sūtra* on his back and placed it in a stone cave on the mountain.[10]

The final seminal figure in Chinese Huayan that must be mentioned is Chengguan (ca. 720/38–837/38). In later conceptualizations of the "Huayan school," he is the next in line after Fazang and is known as Master Qingliang, who was invited by Tang emperor Dezong (r. 779–804) to participate in another new translation of the scripture: the forty-roll version of the *Avataṃsaka Sūtra* by Prajña in 796. He wrote many commentaries on the *Avataṃsaka* and unabashedly sought imperial support and to link Huayan doctrine with the imperial court. For example, buried in one of his commentaries he explained that as the mind *(xin)* unifies all the dharmas and yet is the most excellent of dharmas, the monarch *(wang)* presides over all within the "four seas" and yet is most excellent of monarchs—signifying that the emperor and his empire are one and the smaller unit (the emperor) embodies the larger (the empire) and vice versa.[11] This suggests that Chengguan may have hoped that Tang emperors would utilize Huayan philosophy to restore symbolic order to their fragmented empire dominated by regional warlords. Huayan adherents in China considered him to be an incarnation of Mañjuśrī and called him the Huayan Bodhisattva. He was a teacher of Zongmi (780–841), the late Tang Buddhist syncretist who may have been the first thinker to combine Huayan and Chan.[12] Iryŏn records that the Silla monk Pŏmsu (d.u.) introduced Chengguan's teachings to the Korean peninsula in 799 in the form of a commentary on the forty-roll new translation of the *Avataṃsaka*.[13]

Huayan Buddhism (Kegon in Japanese) enjoyed a brief period of efflorescence in Nara Japan during the eighth century. Granted that Japanese Buddhism developed sectarian characteristics from a very early stage—the most compelling case being Saichō's (767–822) establishment of separate "bodhisattva ordinations" for his Tendai sect in 818 (although approved by the government only after his death in 822)—the Kegon tradition was merely one of the six academic Buddhist traditions of Japan's Nara period (710–794): Sanron, Jōjitsu, Hossō, Kusha, Kegon, and Ritsu. The high point of the tradition came with the construction of Nara's great Tōdaiji and its enormous bronze image of Vairocana, which was finally cast, despite great difficulty, by virtue of the skill of imported craftsmen from Silla in 752. The Japanese ruler demonstrated his patronage of Kegon doctrines by his binding himself to the great image to show his subservience to Vairocana during the eye-opening *(kaigen)* ceremony.[14] Scholars also suggest that Kegon ideology is connected to the propagation of Kokubunji monasteries in the major centers of the Japanese domain. In fact, a Silla monk, Simsang (Jpn. Shinjō, d. 742), is purported to have been the first monk to preach the *Avataṃsaka Sūtra* in Japan in 740.[15] The Korean monks Wǒnhyo and Ŭisang (Jpn. Gangyo and Gishō) are revered and immortalized as among the founders of the sect or tradition in a beautiful scroll painting by the Japanese Kegon monk Myōe (1173?–1232) known as the *Scroll Painting on the Origins of Kegon (Kegon engi emaki)*, dating from the twelfth century.[16] After the eighth century the Kegon tradition was more or less marginal in Japanese history because of the rise of the Tendai and Shingon schools beginning in the early ninth century.[17] Nevertheless, Tōdaiji was and is still recognized as the main Kegon monastery in Japan.

Hwaǒm Doctrine, the State, and the Aristocracy

Like many Mahāyāna sūtras, the *Avataṃsaka Sūtra* is a synthesis of discussions of a variety of topics regarding the nature of Buddhist practice, such as the ten stages a bodhisattva must traverse before becoming a fully awakened buddha and the doctrine of the Tathāgatagarbha (Kor. *yŏrae chang*, Ch. *rulai zang*) or the innate potential of all beings, no matter how low the present level of their spiritual capacities may be, to achieve buddhahood. One of the most striking features of Hwaǒm Buddhism in Silla is that the textual materials tend to be oriented toward practices rather than philosophy. This feature suggests that Ŭisang was more like his teacher Zhiyan than like his colleague Fazang, who was consumed by metaphysical speculation. For example, Ŭisang's *Seal-diagram of the Dharmadhātu According to the One Vehicle (Hwaǒm ilsŭng pŏpkye to)*, which he composed in China in 668, before he returned to Silla in 670, is a brilliant encapsulation of Ŭisang's understanding of Zhiyan's doctrinal innovations and practical application of Huayan thought.[18]

The text of the seal-shaped diagram meanders along as people often do in the course of their lives. The end of the text returns to the starting point. The reader is encouraged to arouse the *bodhicitta (pal pori-sim)* and practice, while knowing that the mere act of producing the thought of enlightenment has put him on the path to buddhahood. On the way he acquires dhāraṇīs that give him thaumaturgic power to work wonders in the mundane world. Because the stages he must transverse are all interconnected, however, the beginning of the path and the end of the path are one and the same: therefore, he is a buddha. Whereas the Hwaǒm cosmological principle of "the one containing the many" and "the many being contained in the one" is repeated here, Hwaǒm thought here is devoid of the political affiliation observed in the cases of either Fazang or Chengguan.[19]

Many Korean scholars, beginning with the eminent historian Lee Kibaik, have maintained that this is indicative of the Silla royalty's grand design of the late seventh and eighth centuries to fashion a centralized government in which the king wielded autocratic power like the Tang Chinese emperors. Kim Sang-hyun, by contrast, has argued convincingly that, unlike the case of China, there is no written historical or exegetical material precisely linking Hwaŏm doctrine to the attempted establishment of an autocratic, centralized bureaucracy in Silla by the kings of Kim Ch'unch'u's direct line (654–780).[20] Furthermore, Kim finds little evidence to suggest that the Hwaŏm tradition was particularly interested in capturing the attention and support of any strata of Silla's highly graduated social order. He cites a passage from the account of Ŭisang in the *Lives of Eminent Monks Compiled in the Song* that suggests that Ŭisang may have eschewed the royalty and wealthy aristocracy upon his return from Tang:

> The king of the country venerated [Ŭisang] and bestowed paddy lands and slave workers on him. [However,] [Ŭi]sang spoke to the king saying, "My dharma is neutral, the high and low are both equal, and the noble and abased are rated the same. The *Nirvāṇa Sūtra* [speaks of] eight impure possessions;[21] what need do I have for paddy lands or use for slave workers? The poor ascetic *(pindao)* regards the dharma realm (*fajie;* Skt. Dharmadhātu) as his home, farms, and waits for the harvest. The wise monk *(huiming)* [who seeks to acquire] the dharma body (*fashen;* Skt. Dharmakāya) takes this into account during his life."[22]

Kim uses this passage to reassess Lee Ki-baik's assertion that Ŭisang's Hwaŏm thought was the central ideology of unification for the ruling elite. Kim then goes on to briefly discuss what has already been noted in foregoing chapters: how the monk Ŭisang was also closely associated with practical religious issues relating to the cult of Avalokiteśvara and Amitābha.[23] Nevertheless, the foregoing account of Ŭisang's apparent rejection of financial support from the Silla king contradicts other evidence, which will be treated below, that shows that Ŭisang constructed monasteries under royal order. Though it seems unlikely that Ŭisang could completely shun the wealthy elite, my point is that the foregoing statement better reflects the way in which Zanning, the author of the *Lives of Eminent Monks Compiled under the Song,* sought to present Ŭisang's stance on maintaining himself as a Buddhist practitioner first and foremost and not being bogged down in the mundane task of the economic functions of a monastery. Ŭisang may have been attributed such a statement because titled clerical positions in Silla were probably the social prerogative, responsibility, and preoccupation of monks who came from elite families.

Although I believe it is probable that Ŭisang considered the practices he cultivated correct for people of any social group, the evidence suggests that most of the people associated with lecturing on Hwaŏm thought, those who combined cultic practices under the Hwaŏm banner in Silla, and those who commissioned monasteries associated with the Hwaŏm tradition were initially either aristocrats or royalty.

The Rise of Hwaŏm in Seventh- and Eighth-Century Silla

Sillan interest in the *Avataṃsaka Sūtra* derives from the gradual maturation of its exegetical tradition and the utility of Hwaŏm-inspired imagery to promote unity. It is well known that the Huayan tradition was one of several Buddhist movements that began to develop during the Sui-Tang period. Although the received tradition of Huayan Buddhism traces its origins to the monks Dushun and Zhiyan, scholastic interest in the sūtra's doctrine was common among many influential Buddhist scholiasts of the late sixth and early seventh centuries, such as Jingying Huiyuan (523–592), Tanqian (542–607), and Fachang (567–645). The Silla monk Chajang, who may have been a mentor to Wŏnhyo, studied with Fachang and Wŏnhyo and was greatly inspired by the exegeses composed by Jingying Huiyuan on various topics. Iryŏn's *Memorabilia of the Three Kingdoms* reports that when Chajang returned to Silla in 643 after his trip to Tang China, he lectured on the myriad gāthās (poetic verses) of the *Avataṃsaka Sūtra,* and in response fifty-two female transformation bodies appeared attesting to the power of the sūtra and the wholesomeness of the lecturer.[24] This is the first account of a dharma assembly in which the *Avataṃsaka Sūtra* was either lectured on or chanted. Iryŏn also preserves several other brief anecdotes of Hwaŏm-inspired dharma assemblies. The next convocation was presided over by Ŭisang in 671. Ŭisang led his disciples to a place called Awl Grotto (Ch'udong) on Mount Sobaek, where they constructed grass huts. To an audience of three thousand gathered followers, Ŭisang lectured on the *Avataṃsaka Sūtra* for ninety days, during which time his student Chit'ong (b. 655) culled the main points discussed by the eminent monk, wrote them down, and crafted a two-roll book entitled the *Record of Awl Grotto (Ch'udong ki)* in commemoration of the event. The commemorative record apparently still existed in Iryŏn's day.[25]

The monk Wŏnhyo has figured in several aspects of the cultic Buddhism of Silla, so it should be no surprise that this exegete par excellence is also regarded as one of the premiere figures in the Huayan/Hwaŏm tradition in East Asia. Wŏnhyo resided at Punhwang Monastery in the Silla capital, which was also the sometime residence of the monk Chajang. While he resided at this monastery during the second half of the seventh century, he not only instructed lay Buddhists and other practitioners, such as Kwangdŏk and Ŏmjang (fl. 661–681) in the correct visualizations leading to rebirth in the Pure Land, but also prepared a work of exegesis on the *Avataṃsaka* that would have been his magnum opus.

According to *Memorabilia of the Three Kingdoms*, when Wŏnhyo reached the fourth roll of his *Commentary on the Avataṃsaka Sūtra (Hwaŏm-gyŏng so)*, on the "Ten Transferences Chapter" *(Shi huixiang pin)*, he simply laid down his brush and did not continue when he had completed it.[26] The chronology of Wŏnhyo's life has been an enduring dilemma for students of Korean Buddhism because none of Wŏnhyo's several extant commentaries are dated. Robert Buswell suggests that after Wŏnhyo completed the *Commentary on the Avataṃsaka Sūtra* he retired from his work as a textual exegete around 676 and began proselytizing among the people from 677 to 685. Before his death in 686, Wŏnhyo returned to scholarship and wrote his *Commentary on the Vajrasamādhi Sūtra (Kŭmgang sammaegyŏng non)*, which is the subject of his biography in the *Lives of Eminent Monks Compiled in the Song*.[27] Iryŏn portrays his connection to the Hwaŏm tradition as follows:

> By chance one day, he came upon an actor who was dancing with a large gourd [mask], the appearance of which was bizarre and strange. He made his own religious instrument in the same shape, and ordered that it be named Muae [Unhindered] after a [passage in] the *Avataṃsaka Sūtra:* "All unhindered men leave birth and death along a single path."[28] He then composed a song that circulated throughout the land. He used to take up this [gourd] and sing and dance his way through thousands of villages and myriad hamlets, touring while proselytizing in song. He prompted all classes of "mulberry doorposts and jar windows" [the destitute] and even "gibbons and macaques" [youth and country bumpkins] to recognize the name "Buddha," and recite together the invocation "Homage." [Wŏn]hyo's proselytizing was great indeed![29]

The song that Wŏnhyo sang that circulated throughout the land of Silla is commonly referred to as the "Song of No Hindrance" *(Muae ka)*. Although there is no evidence regarding what points of doctrine the song may have taught to the people, some scholars have speculated that the song encouraged people to chant and take refuge in the name of Amitābha. Wŏnhyo's close association with Hwaŏm teachings, nevertheless, continued after his death. A badly damaged stele with a partially readable inscription commemorating Wŏnhyo's accomplishments was discovered in 1968 at the ruins of a small monastery north of Punhwang Monastery. Scholars have dated the stele to the reign of Silla king Aejang (r. 800–809), because a fragment of the stele was discovered bearing reference to the Tang reign period Zhenyuan (785–804). The stele mentions the names of two of Wŏnhyo's works: the *Reconciliation of Disputes in Ten Approaches (Simmun hwajaeng non)* and *Thematic Essentials of the Avataṃsaka Sūtra (Hwaŏm chongyo)*.[30] Selected passages have been preserved from the former, but the latter has been lost completely, though portions of his commentary on the *Avataṃsaka* do exist.[31]

Iryŏn also preserves an interesting tale concerning Ŭisang's disciple Sŭngjŏn, who founded a monastery on the borders of Kaenyŏng Commandery, which was within the passes of Sangju. About the year 680, Sŭngjŏn lectured on the *Avataṃsaka Sūtra* to an audience of stone skeletons that represented government officials. The śramaṇa Kagwi, Sŭngjŏn's successor, composed an essay titled *The Mainspring of the Mind (Simwŏn chang)* in which he described his mentor's teaching and discussions during these dharma lectures and other events that transpired at this religious site, which later became known as Kalgyŏng Monastery. Iryŏn then says that Sŭngjŏn's stele inscription supports the information contained in Kagwi's essay and that it is identical with another account preserved in the now-lost veritable records *(sillok)* of the Koryŏ monk Ŭich'ŏn (1055–1101).[32] Ha Tae-Hung speculates that Sŭngjŏn's preaching before stone skeletons symbolically represented his lecturing before the royal court because "it was the custom to place inscribed stone tablets in lines before the audience hall of a royal palace to mark the places where officials were to stand during court ceremonies."[33] There is far too little evidence to be certain whether these stone skeletons represent government officials or some other group, but what is undeniable is that lecturing on the *Avataṃsaka Sūtra* was believed to be beneficial and to generate merit for those in attendance.

According to a contemporaneous account, just after the construction of Pulguk Monastery and Sŏkkuram began on Mount T'oham in 751, an otherwise unknown monk named Pŏphae lectured on the *Avataṃsaka Sūtra* at the main monastic complex of the Silla capital, Hwangnyong Monastery. Although one purpose of this chapter is to show that the Hwaŏm tradition of Silla received both royal and aristocratic patronage, I do not mean to infer that Silla kings did not sponsor lectures, dharma assemblies, and convocations not associated with the *Avataṃsaka*. On the contrary, Silla kings, such as King Kyŏngdŏk, sponsored lectures on various sūtras (since merit and spiritual manifestations could be obtained thereby) to aid in the legitimation of their rule and to stimulate support for their policies.

> In the summer of the next year, the *kabo* year [754], the king also requested Pŏphae, a [monk] of great virtue at Hwangnyong Monastery, to lecture on the *Avataṃsaka Sūtra*. [The king] made a royal excursion by palanquin to offer incense and spoke gently saying, "The previous summer Dharma

Master Taehyŏn [= T'aehyŏn] lectured on the *Suvarṇaprabhāsa Sūtra (Jinguang jing)* and from the wells water sprung up seventy feet. What is your dharma technique like?" Pŏphae replied, "That is pretty small stuff. What would be more suitable? I will straightaway overturn the azure sea and have it flow in the capital city. And to top it off it will be no trouble." The king could not believe it and thought he was kidding him.

He lectured when it reached noon. The drawn [incense] burner went silent, and, for a moment, within the forbidden inner chamber [of the palace] there was the sound of weeping and wailing. The palace valet ran and made a report saying, "The East Moat has already overflowed and has washed away more than fifty *k'an/kan* ["pillar-spaces"] of the inner halls. The king was beside himself and lost it. [Pŏp]hae smiled and addressed him saying, "Since the East Sea is about to overturn, the water veins initially overflow in [their courses]." The king, unaware [of himself], offered worship. The next day a missive arrived from Kamŭn Monastery [stating] that at noon time the previous day seawater overflowed and went as far as before the stairway in front of the Buddha hall. It returned [to normal] at evening time. The king believed and revered [Pŏphae and the power of the *Avataṃsaka*] even more.[34]

This narrative demonstrates the superiority of the *Avataṃsaka Sūtra* to all other sūtras, even the famed *Suvarṇaprabhāsa Sūtra,* or the *Sūtra of Golden Light,* which is renowned for being chanted during Buddhist rituals for the protection of the state *(hoguk pulgyo)* and political legitimation in China and Japan.[35] While in one sense this story seems to say that the *Avataṃsaka* would have been revered by King Kyŏngdŏk, the account specifically states that the king's reverence was reserved for the monk Pŏphae himself. This may then suggest that what matters is not the sūtra as much as the internal spiritual power of the monk-cum-thaumaturge who lectures on it. Nevertheless, within the context of all the other material regarding the Hwaŏm tradition and the *Avataṃsaka Sūtra* in Silla, it is safe to assert that this sūtra was singled out for particular importance during the reign of King Kyŏngdŏk.

The last anecdote preserved by Iryŏn about Silla kings holding Hwaŏm-inspired dharma assemblies deals with King Wŏnsŏng (r. 785–798). Sometime during his reign, perhaps as late as 795, he invited the famous monk Chihae of Hwangnyong Monastery to the palace to lecture on the *Avataṃsaka Sūtra.* The monk intoned the sūtra for fifty days for the benefit of the king and country.[36] Wŏnsŏng was a descendant of the early Silla ruler Naemul (r. 356–402), who came to the throne five years after the hereditary elites of Silla's aristocracy deposed King Hyegong, the son and hapless successor to King Kyŏngdŏk, and committed regicide in 780. Most scholars agree that the Silla elites discontinued the rule of Kim Ch'unch'u's line because they tried to empower the throne at the expense of the aristocrats' hereditary privileges. Apparently the new kings of Silla did not associate the Hwaŏm assemblies as symbolically representative of the centralizing tendencies of the kings in Kim Ch'unch'u's line or as threatening to the prerogatives of the aristocrats because Silla kings continued to enjoy recitals of and lectures on the *Avataṃsaka Sūtra* during the ninth century.

Silla king Aejang began building Haein Monastery for the monk Sunŭng (d. after 804) on Mount Kaya in 802, the third year of his reign.[37] This monastery is in the northwestern region of present-day South Kyŏngsang Province south of Taegu. Sunŭng had traveled to Tang China with his friend Ijŏng (d.u.) to study the Buddhadharma and, according to tradition, achieved some renown by healing the Tang queen of an illness.[38] The name of the monastery is an allusion to the famous "ocean-seal samādhi" (Ch. *haiyin sanmei*, Kor. *haein sammae*) of the *Avataṃsaka Sūtra*.[39] In this powerful state of mental absorption the practitioner's mind becomes like a calm ocean that is able to reflect all things like a mirror, thereby gaining penetrating insight into the true nature of things. In other words, the practitioner sees and experiences things as they really are. This type of insight, which allows him to understand the interpenetration of things, or how all things in the world are mutually dependent, develops into wisdom: the type of wisdom leading to buddhahood. The founding of this monastery suggests the Silla king's hope to harness the great powers associated with this absorption for the benefit of the Silla state. As the name of this monastery is directly connected to the *Avataṃsaka Sūtra*, it became an important intellectual center for Hwaŏm monks in the late Silla period and continued in this capacity throughout the succeeding Koryŏ period.[40]

Material evidence of the importance of the sūtra during the reign of King Kyŏngdŏk was discovered in 1979 at Hwaŏm Monastery, which is on the southern peak of Mount Chiri in South Chŏlla Province: several rolls of an illustrated edition of the eighty-roll translation of the *Avataṃsaka Sūtra*, as well as a postface, written in black ink on white paper during the thirteenth and fourteenth years of Kyŏngdŏk's rule (754–755). The postface says that the monk Yŏn'gi (d.u.) of Hwangnyong Monastery swore a vow to copy the sūtra to make merit for his parents—he says "to repay the love of his parents"—and for all living beings to attain buddhahood. The copying of the sūtra took almost a year to complete.[41] This hand-copied sūtra is known as National Treasure number 196. A Korean gazetteer first compiled in the fifteenth century records Yŏn'gi as the founder of Hwaŏmsa, but mentions that it is not known when the monk lived.[42] Combining this information places the building of the monastery during the mid-eighth century during the reign of King Kyŏngdŏk, despite the fact that monastery records compiled much later during the late Chosŏn and Japanese colonial periods attempt to place its founding as early as the mid-sixth century.

Another piece of evidence that serves as in important indicator of the importance of the Hwaŏm tradition in Silla is the existence of roughly two hundred pieces of the *Avataṃsaka Sūtra* carved in stone preserved in the Hall of the Thearch of Awakening (Kakhwangjŏn) at this same Hwaŏm Monastery. Eleven pieces have enough text that they can be identified reliably. All eleven pieces contains fragments of passages from the *Avataṃsaka Sūtra* in sixty rolls, the first full translation of the text made in the first quarter of the fifth century.[43] The Japanese colonial-period editors of the *Comprehensive Collection of Korean Epigraphy (Chōsen kinseki sōran)* first estimated 680, during the reign of King Munmu, as the date of the carvings.[44] They probably decided that if such a project had been prepared later it would have used the translation in eighty rolls executed between 695 and 699. An account of the creation of the stone tablets recorded in the *Historical Traces of Great Hwaŏm Monastery (Tae Hwaŏmsa sajŏk)*, which was written in 1936, seems to support this thesis. The monastic record preserves a brief narrative from the *Record of Pongsŏng (Pongsŏng chi)*, which says, "During the reign of Silla King Munmu, Ŭisang, under orders from the king, carved the *Avataṃsaka Sūtra* in eighty rolls on stone tablets, which remain in Hwaŏm Monastery. In the *dingyou* year of Wanli [reign period] (1597–1598) [the tablets] were burned by fire and the pieces came to their present state of being strewn in a pile." There is, however, a fundamental problem with this passage: the eighty-roll translation of the *Avataṃsaka* did not exist in Munmu's time; the translation was not complete until 699. Furthermore, the tablets are definitely from the earlier sixty-roll version. The same monastic record from Hwaŏm Monastery says, "The Great King Kyŏngdŏk built a new hall. Four texts of the *Avataṃsaka Sūtra* in Indic (lit. "Brahmic") and Chinese [script] were carved at Mount Chii [= Mount Chiri]. He requested that the stone [tablets] be placed in the four facing walls of the Hall of the Sixteen Foot [Buddha Image] (Changnyukchŏn)."[45] Master Chin Chinŭng, a Buddhist lecturer at Hwaŏm Monastery during the colonial period, however, suggests that they were carved at the close of the Silla period sometime between the reigns of kings Chŏnggang (886–887) and Kyŏngsun (927–935). Both Hwang Suyŏng and Kamata Shigeo are comfortable with this late Silla date for the carved tablets.[46]

There is no reason to doubt the idea that the stone tablets were damaged during the time of the Hideyoshi invasion of Korea (1592–1598), for the whole monastic complex was burned to the ground in the warfare. But when were the stone tablets made? The form of the Chinese characters is the Kaishu calligraphy style common during the Sui and Tang periods as well as during the Nara period in Japan during the eighth century. Monks in China carved the Buddhist scriptures in stone in an effort to protect the Buddhadharma in times of chaos, such as the lithic canon *(shijing)* discovered at Fangshan in northern China begun at the end of the Sui.[47] The *Avataṃsaka* may have been carved in stone in order to invoke the Buddha to protect the Silla state, but why do it in a monastery deep in the heart of the old Paekche country? Perhaps the Silla king commissioned the carving of these stone tablets as an expedient to pacify the discontented people in the territory of its old enemy. If this is so, the Silla king probably ordered them before the late ninth century because by that time Hwaŏm Monastery was no longer under the safe jurisdiction of Silla, and it was soon under the control of the rebel founder of Later Paekche, the hegemon Kyŏnhwŏn (fl. 892–936). Hence, I suggest that the carving of the *Avataṃsaka* in stone probably took place during the middle of the eighth century. At least some buildings at Hwaŏm Monastery may have been built by King Kyŏngdŏk to house the stone tablets.

Hwaŏmsa may have been built on the remains of an earlier monastic settlement, but it is improbable that the stone sūtra tablets were at the site prior to the second half of the eighth century. There may have been tablets carved of the translation in eighty rolls as well. That only examples of the sixty-roll version of the *Avataṃsaka* remain merely demonstrates that that version continued to be venerated in Silla even after the eighty-roll translation was completed. The importance of the sixty-roll version in Silla is supported by evidence from Silla's cult of the Divine Assembly of the *Avataṃsaka Sūtra,* which is treated in the next chapter.

Ŭisang's Ten Disciples

The Hwaŏm tradition founded by Ŭisang is the only religious tradition mentioned in *Memorabilia of the Three Kingdoms* that actually lists unambiguous names of disciples and their residence at some monasteries that over time became associated specifically with the Hwaŏm tradition. Some scholars have been able to trace the development of Silla's Hwaŏm monks throughout the Silla period;[48] nevertheless, here I will merely focus on Ŭisang's immediate disciples.

> [Ŭisang's] disciples were Ojin, Chit'ong, P'yohun, Chinjŏng, Chinjang, Toyung, Yangwŏn, Sangwŏn, Nŭngin, Ŭijŏk, and so forth, ten [monks] of great virtue *(taedŏk,* Skt. *bhadanta)* who became spiritual leaders. All were secondary saints and each has his own biography. [O]jin, from early on, resided at Koram Monastery on Mount Haga. Every night he extended his fingers to light the chamber lantern of Pusŏk [Monastery]. [Chi]t'ong authored the *Record of Awl Grotto (Ch'udong ki)* and, for the most part, in-

herited the personal instructions [of Ŭisang]. For this reason, his words are profuse and his attainments are sublime. [P'yo]hun, from early on, dwelt at Pulguk Monastery and frequently visited the Heavenly Palace *(ch'ŏn'gung)*.[49]

When [Ŭi]sang dwelt at Hwangbok Monastery he circumambulated the stūpa with his followers. Every step he took up in the air came down as on a measured staircase. For this reason, that stūpa was not outfitted with a measured stone walkway. His followers set back the walkway three feet, and the shoe tread revolved in the air. [Ŭi]sang, at this point, turned and said, "When people of the mundane world see this, they will, of necessity, regard it as strange—[but] we are not able to instruct the mundane world [about it]." The remainder are compiled in the *Basic Biography (Ponjŏn)* by Marquis Ch'oe [Ch'iwŏn].[50]

Hwangbok Monastery was where Ŭisang was ordained a monk and where, apparently, he spent years of practice before and between his and Wŏnhyo's attempts at crossing over to China to study with the great masters of the Tang capital. The story about the miraculous occurrence in response to Ŭisang's disciples following their master in circumambulating the stūpa at that monastery probably corresponds to the time after he returned from Tang China. What is important about this story is that it provides more detail into the religious observances and practices of the early Hwaŏm tradition in Silla. That the monks circumambulated a stūpa confirms Ŭisang's focus on religious practice and corresponds well with the other stories associated with his personal observances including participation in penance practices and in the cults of Avalokiteśvara and Amitābha. Another interesting point to which this miraculous account alludes is the association of the late Silla literatus Ch'oe Ch'iwŏn to the Hwaŏm tradition. The relationship between Ch'oe and the Hwaŏm tradition is corroborated by other textual evidence.

Ch'oe Ch'iwŏn, like most government officials in China and Korea of the late ninth and early tenth centuries, maintained extensive contacts with the Buddhist community. In 868, as a youth, he had traveled to China to study and sit for the civil service examination, which he passed in 874. Eventually he secured a succession of posts in the sprawling Chinese government during the Tang dynasty's steady decline in the late ninth century. He returned to Silla in 885 in hopes of serving the Silla government. However, since his lack of social status—he was a head-rank six elite in a society dominated by true-bone aristocrats—barred him from significant political advancement in the capital, he retired to secluded regions and kept company with intellectual Buddhist monks and opted to study arcane teachings. Many scholars have demonstrated Ch'oe's Buddhist ties with the Sŏn traditions sponsored by regional strongmen.⁵¹ Nevertheless, his extant writings also evince connections to Hwaŏm Buddhism. Ch'oe composed the detailed biography of the eminent Chinese Huayan exegete Fazang that is presently preserved in the Buddhist canon and composed several poems at monasteries associated with the Hwaŏm tradition.⁵² Furthermore, in the preface to his *Life of Kyunyŏ (Kyunyŏ chŏn)*,⁵³ which was composed in 1075, Hyŏngnyŏn Chŏng (fl. 1074–1105) wrote, "Duke Ch'iwŏn of the Ch'ŏngha [Ch'oe descent group]⁵⁴ wrote the *Life of Master [Ŭi]sang (Sangsa chŏn)*."⁵⁵ The evidence suggests that the scholar Ch'oe Ch'iwŏn was intimately associated with Hwaŏm communities in both China and Korea: he not only wrote biographies on Ŭisang and Fazang, important founders of Hwaŏm Buddhism in Silla and Tang respectively, but composed other documents associated with the tradition. Subsequently, he retired to Haein Monastery with his friends the monk Hyŏnjun (d.u.) and Master Chŏnghyŏn (d.u.) after his failure to influence late Silla politics.⁵⁶

Hwaŏm Societies and the Veneration of the Hwaŏm Founders in Late Silla

In the waning years of Silla in the late ninth and early tenth centuries, Ch'oe Ch'iwŏn composed a number of vow-texts associated with the veneration of the founders of Hwaŏm Buddhism in China and Korea. These writings, along with many other poetic compositions on topics associated with the Huayan/Hwaŏm tradition in the Chinese and Korean kingdoms, were collected and preserved by the Koryŏ monk Ŭich'ŏn in a work titled *Literature of the Perfect [Hwaŏm] Tradition (Wŏnjong mullyu)*, of which only a few rolls remain. Kamata Shigeo, in his study of Huayan Buddhism in China, alludes to a few of these vow-texts written by Ch'oe to describe the nature of Huayan societies in China during the late Tang period, but they may more aptly illustrate the characteristics of religious communities in the late Silla period.⁵⁷

The oldest datable vow-text, titled "Vow-Text of the Society for Recompensing Grace to the *Upadhyāya* Zhiyan on old Mount Zhongnan" *(Kosu Namsan ŏm hwasang poŭn sahoe wŏnmun)*, was probably written in 884 in China for a Chinese audience, since Ch'oe was still in Tang. Ch'oe refers to the *Avataṃsaka Sūtra* as "that which came from the Esoteric Storehouse *(milchang)* in the Dragon Palace." Ch'oe reports that the society consisted of a group of monks of great virtue led by the Korean Hwaŏm monks Kyŏrŏn and Hyŏnjun (perhaps the same person as the Hyŏnjun mentioned earlier), whom Ch'oe praises as being renowned for their preservation and explication of wisdom. The members of this society swore a vow that every year during the first ten-day period *(maengsun)* of the eighth lunar month, they would gather to venerate Zhiyan, the Indian monks who made the various translations of the *Avataṃsaka Sūtra*, and the Chinese masters who composed gāthās and songs praising it. Fazang is also mentioned specifically. Ch'oe reports that they held a convocation in which they lectured upon and discussed the holy teaching in a noble manner in order to repay the grace of the Buddhadharma.[58] Although the ritual took place in China, it was led by Silla monks and so probably followed Silla procedures.

The first Hwaŏm community in Silla was instituted on Mount Odae probably during the first half of the eighth century and was an integral part of the royally sponsored cult established on that mountain to promote the health and welfare of the Silla king and the prosperity of the state. I will treat this community more fully in the following chapter. Hwaŏm societies flourished in Silla during the late ninth century when Ch'oe Ch'iwŏn composed "Vow-Text Commemorating the Death Day of the First Founder of Hwaŏm in Silla" *(Haedong Hwaŏm ch'ojo kisin wŏnmun).* It was probably composed sometime between 885 and 900, after Ch'oe's return to Silla and before his self-exile to Haein Monastery. The following brief excerpt comes from the end of the text:

> We desire, O Founding Monk of Great Virtue [Ŭisang], [that thou wouldst] draw all living beings up into Tuṣita Heaven and brightly approach Magadha. The ocean is interfused with wisdom and the clouds are obscured by compassion. Transmitting the Buddha mind, we take complete pleasure in the *Miscellaneous Flowers [Avataṃsaka Sūtra];* raising your jeweled hand, we climb the long path to the holy fruit [of buddhahood]. Although the kalpa-ashes[59] enervate [all things], incense-burning [worship] will not be exhausted.[60]

What is important here is that Ch'oe relates a belief that was probably prevalent among monks associated with the Hwaŏm tradition during the late ninth and tenth centuries: the desire to be reborn in Tuṣita Heaven and to have all living beings reborn there as well. In this respect, these Hwaŏm monks preserve certain beliefs held by many earlier monks and laypeople associated with the cult of Maitreya. Also, in the last sentence of the passage Ch'oe hints at the idea that veneration of Ŭisang and of the *Avataṃsaka* will endure beyond the destruction of the world. It also seems apparent that Ch'oe believed he was writing during a time generally conceived as being close to the time of the decline of the Buddhadharma, or the period of the Final Dharma *(malbŏp).*

Ch'oe repeats this last sentiment in another vow-text he composed for a Hwaŏm community that was centered on the Silla capital. Ch'oe reports that a number of eminent monks and monks of great virtue made a religious society *(hyangsa)* and prepared a special lecture mat during the time of the Semblance Dharma and the Final Dharma *(sangmal)*. Ch'oe explains that the Hwaŏm society follows in the tradition of Lushan Huiyuan's (334–417) White Lotus Society (Bailian she), in which the members vowed to be reborn in Amitābha's Pure Land in the West. If someone in the society passed away, the remaining members would gather together at Hwangbok Monastery and lecture on the *Avataṃsaka Sūtra* for one day, and seek their happiness in the other world.[61] Hwangbok Monastery would have been significant to people associated with the Hwaŏm tradition in Silla because it was the monastery where Ŭisang became a monk and where miracles associated with Ŭisang and the Hwaŏm tradition occurred. In later years the monastery, like many other monastic complexes in Silla, must have developed an association with the Hwaŏm tradition.

In 886, Ch'oe composed a vow-text for a Hwaŏm society led by King Chŏnggang. The king held a Hwaŏm dharma assembly to pray for a blessing upon his deceased brother, the late King Hŏn'gang (r. 875–886). During the assembly he had the distinguished monk of great virtue Hyŏnjun lecture on the *Avataṃsaka Sūtra*.[62] Thus we can see that veneration of the *Avataṃsaka* was a common component of Buddhist ritual and communal practice during the late Silla period. By representing the consummate interfusion of all Buddhist teaching, the *Avataṃsaka Sūtra* could invoke all the blessings one might desire for the next life, rebirth in Amitābha's Pure Land in the West or in Tuṣita Heaven to be with Maitreya, and venerating it could replace venerating individual texts because it contains the fullness of the Mahāyāna.

The Spread of Hwaŏm Imagery to Silla's Northern Regions

In connection with the increased promotion of the *Avataṃsaka Sūtra* and its teachings among the Silla people, representations of Vairocana also began to appear in monasteries on the edges of the Silla domain. Inscriptions carved on the backs of three statues of Vairocana demonstrate the extent to which Hwaŏm symbolism and ideology had penetrated Silla's northern areas and mixed with another seminal Buddhist theme: the decline of the Buddhadharma and the anticipation of Maitreya's descent alluded to above.

The first inscription comes from Top'ian Monastery, which was in Ch'ŏrwŏn Commandery in Silla's northwestern Hanju Province. The monastery is on present-day Mount Hwagae, in Ch'ŏrwŏn County in Kangwon Province. The inscription records the completion of an iron image of Vairocana (fig. 2) in the first lunar month (31 January–28 February) of the year 865, made to solemnize a collective vow made by more than fifteen hundred householders who felt themselves bound by karmic

FIGURE 2. Iron image of Vairocana, Top'ian Monastery, Ch'ŏrwŏn.

connections. The collective donors of this iron image report that it has been 1,806 years since the Buddha's passing and that they made this iron image of Vairocana since they both lamented his passing and were unsettled by the fact that he no longer illuminates the universe. They also vowed "to abase their family names and homes" and "beat themselves with spears and mallets"—a euphemism for becoming śramaṇas and performing ascetic practices—so that they might awake from their long stupors and remove their simple, rustic wills and dedicate themselves to the origin of the truth. They recognized that although they are consumed by forms, there is nothing of substance to observe or see in the mundane world.[63]

On the basis of sketchy circumstantial evidence, some scholars suggest that Top'ian Monastery was associated with Silla's Yogācāra intellectual tradition and attempt to demonstrate how this inscription depicts a Yogācāra-style lamentation of the decline of the Dharma.[64] The importance of the Ch'ŏrwŏn region is undeniable though; the fortress there was an important stronghold of Kungye and eventually served as his capital in the early tenth century.

By the late medieval period, Buddhists in East Asia generally ascribed to the view that the Buddha Śākyamuni entered *parinirvāṇa* in 949 B.C.E., though some Chinese and Korean texts give even earlier dates for the Buddha's life and others later.[65] Drawing on the prophecies of the ultimate disappearance of the Buddhadharma in a number of scriptures translated into Chinese, medieval Sinitic Buddhist thinkers eventually codified a tripartite approach to the decline of the Dharma in which successive 500-year periods of the True Dharma *(zhengfa,* Kor. *chŏngbŏp),* the Semblance Dharma *(xiangfa,* Kor. *sangbŏp),* and the Final Dharma demarcate the process of the steady demise of the Buddha's teaching.[66] According to the calculations of those who made this image in question, however, the Buddha would have passed away in roughly 941 B.C.E. Regardless, the significance of this particular inscription is that the donators recognize that they are living well into the period of the Final Dharma. Their recording their vows on a Vairocana image is interesting because Vairocana, being an anthropomorphic representation of the Buddha as reality itself, suggests a medium that is ultimately indestructible because it symbolizes the Buddha's body of the truth: the Dharmakāya.

The transcendent role of Vairocana during the period of the Final Dharma is also a theme in the second inscription, found on the back of an iron buddha image at Samhwa Monastery. This monastery, situated on Mount Tut'a in Tonghae City, also in Kangwŏn Province, was putatively first established by the Korean Sŏn monk Pŏmil with the name Samgong Monastery.[67] The inscription, however, also reports that a Hwaŏm community was behind the donation of this image. The supreme heads of this community were "the eminent monk Kyŏrŏn,[68] who was skilled in the Hwaŏm" *(Hwaŏmŏp Kyŏrŏn taet'ae[dŏk]),* as well as the *dānapatis* (lay almsgivers) Sŭnggŏ and Ch'ŏngmuk of the Sŏk family and their kinsman the monk Toch'o. Although the surname Sŏk usually refers to fully ordained monks, Sŭnggŏ is specifically referred to as a *"dānapati* who has aroused the *bodhicitta" (palsim tanwŏl).* Ferreting out the lay or monastic state of these men is beyond the scope of my discussion here, but there does seem to be some similarity to the kind of Buddhist community that produced Nohil Pudŏk and Taltal Pakpak, whose cultic practices were treated in chapter 2. Nonetheless, the members of the community were inspired to make this image and to promote the Buddhist teaching in accordance with a vow made by the Silla king and "completed this buddha about three hundred years after the age of the Final Dharma," which suggests about the year 860. The connection between Vairocana and Maitreya is made more explicit in the following passage: "The *dānapatis* of the ten directions [the members of the community] were of the same mind and made the same vow due to the accomplishment of the great will of the Buddha Vairocana and due to the power of the great vow of Vairocana. Hence, Maitreya, who will descend in the future, will preach the *Avataṃsaka Sūtra* in this place [Silla] and this will come to pass due to the great workings of causes and conditions." The inscription also reports that those who apprehend the *Avataṃsaka Sūtra* as taught by the Buddha who manifests in a future kalpa will also become "*dānapatis* who have aroused the *bodhicitta*."[69]

Inasmuch as all buddhas preach the *Avataṃsaka Sūtra* once they have achieved enlightenment, the donators of this iron image of the Buddha make the teaching of the scripture the point that binds the anticipation of Maitreya's descent in the future to the current hope for their awakening to wisdom in the present. The scripture is important not only because it claims to be the first sūtra taught by a buddha, according to Mahāyāna lore, but also because it describes in detailed fashion all the practices of bodhisattvas. In the final chapter of the *Avataṃsaka Sūtra*, the voluminous "Entry into the Dharma Realm"—also known as the *Gaṇḍavyūha Sūtra*—the intrepid Sudhana (Shancai, Kor. Sŏnjae), following the instructions of the Bodhisattva Mañjuśrī, perambulates the universe in search of spiritual mentors in order to learn their strategies or expedient means *(upāya, fangbian)* of liberating beings. Maitreya is the fifty-first of fifty-three bodhisattvas he encounters in this chapter. In Maitreya's presence Sudhana learns the true nature of reality inside the great tower of the adornments of Vairocana *(Piluzhena zhuangyan da louge)*. Inside the tower Sudhana sees in a vision a complex and intertwined panorama of the life and ministry of Maitreya in which the future Buddha does what all bodhisattvas do in promoting the Buddhadharma and teaching all beings, and he sees that Maitreya will follow the archetypal pattern of all the buddhas in his achievement of buddhahood in one lifetime. The point of this, however, is that Maitreya wants Sudhana to learn that all these wondrous manifestations he has just witnessed have neither come from nor gone anywhere. They are emanations of the fundamental state of quiescence enjoyed by all the buddhas, which is the nature of the true reality of things: in other words, that which Vairocana represents.[70]

The third inscription was carved on the back of a stone image of Vairocana at Changan Monastery, which is at the base of Changgyŏng Peak in the Diamond Mountains of Kangwŏn Province in present-day North Korea. Since the monastery was inhabited by Sŏn monks during the early Koryŏ period, some scholars suggest that it was a Sŏn monastery from the outset and that the inscription is influenced by Sŏn ideas.[71] I am not convinced, however, because the diction selected by the author and the activities promoted by the members of the community all suggest a mainstream Mahāyāna approach.

> Since the Dharma-body is devoid of marks, it responds to things and hands down forms. Since prajñā is originally void [of self], it observes [karmic] connections by their radiance. For this reason, those who see visages transcend to the Great Path [the Mahāyāna] and those who choose the Dharma assemble with the birthless.
>
> However, being right at the end of the Semblance Dharma [period spoken of by] our Buddha Śākyamuni, the śramaṇa Kakhyŏn devoted his attention to his plan for the non-severed inheritance of the life-force of wisdom.[72] The former Dharma masters, relying on acts of the begging bowl and people with all manner of [karmic] connections, respectfully cast [this image of the] Buddha Vairocana on the eleventh day of the fourth month of the next *inu* year, the third year of the Xiantong reign period [13 May 862].
>
> We respectfully vow that the Buddha Sun will increase in brightness and that the wheel of the Dharma will always turn. We humbly vow that through acts of sincerity in which are donated [even so little as] a single kernel of grain or a half strand of thread, we will turn the land and revolve the stones and that the breed of those who turn their minds [to the Dharma] will be pointed together to the Lotus Storehouse [Realm] and at the same time will receive prophecies of their future buddhahood.
>
> Furthermore, we also vow that those who worship and praise will eradicate everlastingly their karmic hindrances from the past and will suddenly manifest the Dharma-body and that those who have disbelieved and slandered [the Dharma] will be freed from their vainly grasping at clouds and will obtain the purity of the Dharma eye [viz. enlightenment].
>
> We universally vow that the restrained spirits who have consciousness will be liberated speedily in the Dharma Realm of Emptiness *(hŏgong pŏpkye)* from the bonds of their desires and ascend to the fruit of buddhahood.
>
> We respectfully make [this] true buddha so that all meritorious virtues may extend universally and the Dharma realm may be exhausted infinitely. The foregoing recompenses the four graces[73] and to conscious beings, benefactors, and the flocks of beings gives evidence of their practice of awakening.

Composed by Pŏpp'il on a day in the eighth month of *inu* [29 August–27 September 862].[74]

The śramaṇa Kakhyŏn and the monk Pŏpp'il are otherwise unknown, though they were probably local leaders of the lay community at Changan Monastery. Kakhyŏn may have lived during an earlier time, but there is not enough information for any further precision. There is nothing particularly unusual about this inscription, and that is what makes it an important piece of evidence of how the Hwaŏm approach to the Buddhadharma seamlessly absorbed and synthesized the preexisting Buddhist traditions. The aspirations set forth in the inscription are conventional Mahāyāna-style vows made by monks and laity who would be bodhisattvas. As with the first inscription, Maitreya is not mentioned by name, though the idea of the approaching decline of the Dharma lingers in the background. One important difference from the foregoing two inscriptions is its referral to the end of the Semblance Dharma period instead of the Final Dharma; however, the writer seems to imply that the Final Dharma period has now started. Nevertheless, there is no hint of sadness at this prospect because the aspirants have access to the Dharmakāya Buddha Vairocana. The end result is that those who commissioned the stone image of Vairocana still make the same sorts of vows to liberate all beings caught in saṃsāra and still seek after complete and total enlightenment. In this way, the cult of Vairocana in the Hwaŏm tradition can be seen as subsuming the cult of Maitreya and providing a comprehensive approach to Buddhist practice for aspirants seeking enlightenment by entering upon the bodhisattva path in the age of the Final Dharma.

The influence of the *Avataṃsaka Sūtra* began to disseminate in Silla during the late seventh century even before the return of Ŭisang from Tang and his founding of the Hwaŏm tradition in Silla. During the eighth century, the traditions associated with this sūtra reached high peaks of influence in China, Korea, and Japan. Although some direct evidence for the influence of Hwaŏm doctrine on the development of a centralized, autocratic government may be found in China and to a lesser extent in Japan, it is much more difficult to discover it for the case of Korea. Nevertheless, Silla kings venerated the *Avataṃsaka Sūtra* to a much greater extent and more consistently than rulers in other East Asian kingdoms. They established monasteries named to symbolically link to the *Avataṃsaka Sūtra,* they commissioned copies of the sūtra in paper and stone, and they provided the impetus for other Silla elites and regional notables to make bodhisattva vows to achieve enlightenment and to save all beings, as well as to cast images of Vairocana. The next chapter treats more specific examples of the Hwaŏm tradition's promotion of the synthesis of Buddhist cults in Silla.

CHAPTER FIVE

The Hwaŏm Synthesis of Buddhist Cults

The Hwaŏm tradition succeeded in becoming the most powerful and influential Buddhist organization in Silla during the eighth century and continued as such until the end of the dynasty because it was the only intellectual tradition to incorporate cultic practices successfully and to develop an institutional apparatus based on royal and aristocratic support to the point that it was able to operate some of its own monasteries. Some monasteries, such as Pusŏk Monastery, were initiated by Ŭisang, the purported founder of Hwaŏm in Korea; others, such as Pulguk Monastery, were founded by aristocrats; and later, others, such as Haein Monastery, were commissioned by the royal family. Unlike the other Buddhist exegetical traditions founded during the Silla period, in the Hwaŏm tradition we find names of masters, disciples, and other monastic adherents. Although Hwaŏm thought, which teaches the interpenetration of all things, may have been ideal for Silla's kings, who were seeking to unify their newly expanded state culturally and religiously, there is little direct evidence to support this supposition. Monasteries associated with the Hwaŏm tradition, however, were constructed on the five sacred mountains, which were associated with the symbolic unification of the peninsula. The figurative relationship between the state and the Buddhist church became close as Buddhist practices and rituals were institutionalized under the umbrella of the Hwaŏm tradition. Furthermore, because Hwaŏm doctrine presents a unified vision of the cosmos peopled with stratified orders of deities, the Divine Assembly that makes up the audience of the *Avataṃsaka Sūtra* was invoked for the protection of the state and was a convenient way of integrating native gods of Silla into the expansive Buddhist pantheon. In this chapter, I will explore the evidence demonstrating the combined attempt of Silla's aristocratic government and the Buddhist church to order Buddhist cults under the symbolic and ritual apparati of the Hwaŏm tradition and to deploy cults for the protection of the state.

The Royal Hwaŏm Cult on Mount Odae

The association of the Silla royalty and aristocracy with the *Avataṃsaka Sūtra* and Hwaŏm symbolism can be traced back to Chinese models dating from the later Northern dynasties through the Sui-Tang period. Korean monks related to the royal family of Silla were associated specifically with the importation and indigenization of the Chinese cult of Mount Wutai. During the war, bloodshed, and uncertainty of the Chinese interregnum (ca. 220–589), Buddhism gained a foothold in the hearts and minds of the Chinese people. Whereas the cults of Śākyamuni, Maitreya, and later Avalokiteśvara and Amitābha flourished among communities of the faithful and at such sites as the Buddhist caves at Dunhuang, Yun'gang, and Longmen, a tradition linking Mañjuśrī (Wenshu, Kor. Munsu), the bodhisattva of wisdom, to Mount Wutai gained prominence and cosmopolitan fame in Shanxi Province. When the *Avataṃsaka Sūtra* was translated into Chinese in the early fifth century, Mount Wutai was equated to the Mount Qingliang (Mount Clear and Cool) mentioned in the text as the dwelling place of Mañjuśrī and situated northeast of India.[1] By the early Tang period, several monks and lay believers reported sightings of Mañjuśrī and other bodhisattvas on Mount Wutai. These stories eventually entered the local traditions as well as the commentaries on the *Avataṃsaka Sūtra* by Chinese Huayan monks. Thereafter, the mountain was regarded as the earthly abode of Mañjuśrī, and altars, shrines, and monasteries were established there to honor him. Furthermore, several monasteries, hermitages, and terraces were built by means of royal and aristocratic patronage during the Northern dynasties and Sui-Tang periods. Monks from Korea and Japan thought of China as the home away from home of Buddhism, and inasmuch as China was much closer than India and the route far less dangerous to travel, China became a major attraction for monks and laity.[2] The Silla monk Chajang, encountered previously, was one such pilgrim.

In the late 640s, after Chajang returned to Silla from Tang after his experience of meeting Mañjuśrī on China's northern hinterland of Mount Wutai, he also encountered this same bodhisattva on a mountain in Silla's northern borderland of Myŏngju (in present-day Kangwŏn Province); that mountain soon became known as Mount Odae. Although called "Mount" Odae, like Mount Wutai in China, the mountain in fact comprises a range of peaks or terraces that have been codified into five peaks corresponding to the five directions—in other words, the four cardinal directions and the center—hence, the name Mountain of Five Terraces.

Iryŏn's *Memorabilia of the Three Kingdoms* preserves an anecdote about two sons of King Sinmun, the crown prince Poch'ŏn and his younger brother Hyomyŏng, who would later succeed his father as King Hyoso.

The Hwaŏm Synthesis of Buddhist Cults 111

As young men the brothers went on an excursion up to Hasŏ Protectorate with their bands of a thousand followers each.³ After lodging for the night at the estate of the local vassal lord Sehŏn *kakkan,* they passed into the hinterland and amused themselves on the Sŏngo Plains for several days. Suddenly, however, the brothers made a secret pact to abandon their princely lifestyle and pursue the Buddhist path. Without letting any of their followers know, they fled secretly and hid on Mount Odae. Having no idea where their lords had gone, the followers had no choice but to return to the Silla capital. The brothers built a humble dwelling, which became known as Poch'ŏn Hermitage, and encountered all sorts of spiritual manifestations on the five peaks of the mountain as they attended to their worship and religious cultivation.

The narrative reports that ten thousand dharma-bodies of Avalokiteśvara appeared to them on Mount Manwŏl, the eastern terrace. Ten thousand dharma-bodies of Kṣitigarbha, led by eight great bodhisattvas, manifested themselves on Mount Kirin, the southern terrace. Ten thousand dharma-bodies of Mahāsthāmaprāpta, led by the Tathāgata Amitāyus (Amitābha), became visible on Mount Changnyŏng, the western terrace. Five hundred great arhats, led by the Tathāgata Śākyamuni, came into view on Mount Sangwang, the northern terrace. And finally, ten thousand dharma-bodies of Mañjuśrī, led by Vairocana, revealed themselves on Mount P'ungno (also called Mount Chiro), the central terrace. The brothers offered worship to each of these thousands of spiritual manifestations. Every morning at the break of dawn thirty-six forms of Mañjuśrī would appear in Chinyŏ (True Suchness) Cloister (called the Upper Cloister in the Koryŏ period).

The narrative says that the two brothers would always gather water from a cavern spring from which they made tea for offerings, and at night they would perform religious observances in their own hermitages. When King Sinmun passed away in 691, royal commissioners were dispatched to search out the crown prince to solve the succession dispute in the capital. When the brothers were found, auspicious five-colored clouds marked the site for seven days so that the representatives of the Silla court could find them. They begged Poch'ŏn, the crown prince, to return with them, but he tearfully declined. His younger brother Hyomyŏng, on the other hand, accepted the call to the throne and returned to the capital. A direct translation of the *Memorabilia of the Three Kingdoms'* account will be more beneficial from this point since important aspects of the royal cult of Mount Odae are treated specifically.

> In the first year of the Shenlong reign period, on the fourth day, the beginning third month of *ŭlsa* [1 April 705], [the royalty] first began reconstructing Chinyŏ Cloister. The Great King [Sŏngdŏk] personally led

100 officials to the mountain. They built a hall and a shrine and placed a molded clay image of the Great Saint Mañjuśrī in the shrine. They had the spiritual master Yŏngbyŏn and five other acolytes *(wŏn)* course in the *Avataṃsaka Sūtra (chŏn Hwaŏm kyŏng)* and, furthermore, they organized a Hwaŏm Community *(kyŏl wi Hwaŏmsa)*.

[To provide for] the expenses for offerings made throughout the long year, every year in spring and autumn, from the storehouses of each district in the region near the mountain 100 straw sacks of tax rice and a barrel of pure oil were given [to the community], which became a regular custom. They traveled 6,000 paces west from the cloister, arriving on the outskirts of Moni Steeps and Koi Slope, [where there are] fifteen plots *(kyŏl)* of brush land, six plots of chestnut trees, and two plots of idle arable land on which they constructed a manor house.

Poch'ŏn always drew and consumed water from his numinous cave. For this reason, in his declining years his flesh body flew in the air and landed beyond the Flowing Sand River (Yusagang) and stopped for a time in the Heaven-in-a-Palm Grotto (Changch'ŏn'gul) in the Country of Flourishing Treasures (Ulchin'guk),[4] where he chanted the *Mahāpratisarā Dhāraṇī (Suiqiu tuoluoni)*[5] as his task both day and night. The god of the grotto appeared in bodily [form] and addressed him saying, "I have been the god of this cave for 2,000 years. Today was the first time I heard the true explanation of the *Mahāpratisarā [Dhāraṇī]*." He requested to receive the bodhisattva precepts, and after he had received them, the next day there was, moreover, no [supernatural] entity in the grotto. Poch'ŏn was startled and [thought it was] strange. He remained twenty days and then returned to the Divine Saint Grotto (Sinsŏng'gul) on [Mount] Odae, where he further cultivated the true [path] for fifty years. The gods of Trayastriṃśas Heaven (Torich'ŏn) [came] to hear the Dharma three times [a day]; the heavenly throng of the Pure Abodes *(chŏnggŏ ch'ŏnjung)* [in the fourth Dhyāna Heaven] boiled tea and offered it to him. Forty saints ascended ten feet into the air and protected him at all times. The tin staff that he carried made a sound three times a day, so he would circumambulate the chamber three times and use this as the bell sound [to inform the monks] that it was time for the work of [religious] cultivation. Mañjuśrī once anointed Poch'ŏn's head with consecrated water and gave him written certification of his attainment of the Path (i.e., buddhahood). On the day when Poch'ŏn was about to enter complete quiescence, he left behind a record instructing those who would later come to the mountain in rituals for assisting and benefiting the state *(puik pangga chi sa)*. It says:

> This mountain is of the same great range as Mount Paektu. Each terrace is a constant abode of the True Bodies *(chinsin)* [of buddhas and bodhisattvas]. Green ones reside beneath the northern peak of

the eastern terrace and at the end of the southern foot of the northern terrace. [On the eastern terrace] you should establish a dwelling for Avalokiteśvara, within which you should enshrine a full image of Avalokiteśvara and a portrait of ten thousand Avalokiteśvaras against a green background. Five virtuous monastic acolytes[6] should read aloud the *Sūtra of Golden Light (Suvarṇaprabhāsa)* in eight rolls,[7] the *Perfection of Wisdom Sūtra for Benevolent Kings*,[8] and the spell [invoking] the thousand-armed Avalokiteśvara *(ch'ŏnsu chu)* by day and at night they should recite ritual confessions to Avalokiteśvara. You shall call it the Perfectly Pervasive Shrine (Wŏnt'ongsa).

For the red one on the southern face of the southern terrace, you should establish a dwelling for Kṣitigarbha, wherein you should enshrine a full image of Kṣitigarbha and a portrait of ten thousand Kṣitigarbhas headed by the eight great bodhisattvas against a red background. Five virtuous monastic acolytes should read aloud the *Kṣitigarbha Sūtra* and the *Diamond Sūtra* by day and at night they should recite a ritual confession based on the *Book of Divining [the Requital of Good and Evil Actions] (Zhancha jing)*. You shall call it the Diamond Shrine (Kŭmgangsa).

For the white one on the southern face of the western terrace, you should establish a dwelling for Amitābha, wherein you should enshrine a full image of Amitāyus and a portrait of ten thousand Mahāsthāmaprāptas headed by the Tathāgata Amitāyus against a white background. Five virtuous monastic acolytes should read aloud the *Lotus Sūtra* in eight rolls by day and at night recite ritual confessions to Amitābha. You shall call it the Crystal Shrine (Sujŏngsa).

For the black one on the southern face of the northern terrace, you should establish a shrine for the arhats and within it enshrine a full image of Śākyamuni and a portrait of the five hundred arhats headed by the Tathāgata Śākyamuni against a black background. Five virtuous acolytes should read aloud the *Sūtra of the Buddha's Recompense of Kindness* and the *Nirvāṇa Sūtra* by day and at night they should recite a ritual confession based on the *Nirvāṇa Sūtra*. You shall call it the White Lotus Shrine (Paengnyŏnsa).

The yellow one is to be enshrined in the True Suchness Cloister (Chinyŏwŏn) on the central terrace. In it you should enshrine clay images of Mañjuśrī and Acala. Against the back wall are to be thirty-six portraits of transformational forms *(hwahyŏng)* headed by Vairocana against a yellow background. Five virtuous monastic acolytes should read aloud the *Avataṃsaka Sūtra* and the *Perfection of Wisdom* in 600 rolls by day and at night they should recite a ritual confession to Mañjuśrī. You shall call it the Flower Garland Shrine (Hwaŏmsa).

You shall also renovate Poch'ŏn's hermitage and call it the Flower

Treasury Monastery (Hwajangsa). Within it you should enshrine a full image of the Vairocana triad and a complete Buddhist canon. Five virtuous monastic acolytes should store the scriptures by the long gate and at night they should recite [the names of the gods of] the Divine Assembly of the *Avataṃsaka Sūtra*. Every year you should observe a Flower Garland Convocation (Hwaŏmhoe), which is to last one hundred days. You should call this place the Dharma Wheel Shrine (Pŏmnyunsa). This Flower Garland Monastery is to be the main monastic headquarters of the shrines on the five terraces [of Mount Odae]. If you observe [these instructions] resolutely, commanding the fields of merit [monks] to perform pure practices and preserve and foster the flames of incense, the king of our country will reign a thousand years, his people shall be peaceful and prosperous, the civil and the military shall be harmonious and just, and the hundred grains shall be rich and abundant. Furthermore, Munsugap Monastery, in the lower court, is to become the nexus of the shrine complex. Seven virtuous monastic acolytes should continuously, day and night, perform ritual confession to the Divine Assembly of the *Avataṃsaka Sūtra*. For the thirty-seven acolytes mentioned above if food, clothing, and expenses are provided for from the taxes of the eight regions within the circuit of Hasŏ Protectorate [roughly present-day Kangnŭng], there will be a fullness of the means to furnish them with the four necessities,[9] and if lords and kings throughout the ages neither forget nor neglect to do these things, it shall be fortunate for them.[10]

There is no apparent relationship between the royal Buddhist cult on Mount Odae and the Hwaŏm tradition founded by Ŭisang about the same time, but both deploy the inclusive structure of Hwaŏm cosmology to systematize cultic practices associated with the worship of buddhas and bodhisattvas. This cult harkens back to the strand of the Hwaŏm cult promoted by Chajang, which emphasizes rituals for the benefit of the state and royal family. This was accomplished by invoking the names of the gods of the Divine Assembly *(sinjung)*.

Poch'ŏn and his younger brother Hyomyŏng seem to act like leaders of *hwarang* divisions at the beginning of the story as they guide their groups of a thousand followers into the mountains of Myŏngju, which at that time was the dangerous borderland between Silla and the state of Parhae (Ch. Bohai, 698–926). This Sinified state was founded by a former Koguryŏ general and aristocrats, with a substratum of the tribal Malgal. Parhae comprised the former territory of Koguryŏ in Manchuria and the northern part of the Korean peninsula. Perhaps in the same way that Mount Wutai created a powerful religious buffer zone between the tribes of the Turko-Mongol barbarians in northern China with its association with Mañjuśrī, Mount Odae in Silla symbolically protected the kingdom from a northern invasion. This scenario seems to be supported by the description of the royally commissioned construction of a Buddhist religious complex, the personal organization of a Hwaŏm community by King Sŏngdŏk in 705, and ritual readings of the *Sūtra for Benevolent Kings* and the *Sūtra of Golden Light*. The monks there would "course *(chŏn)* in the *Avataṃsaka Sūtra*." "Coursing" in a sūtra combines a few aspects of the Buddhist cult of the book: the rolls of the sūtra would be unrolled and rolled up again; the "coursers" would perhaps chant some lines or sections of the sūtra or even lecture on a few particular points; the whole thing would be done to generate merit for the one who commissioned the coursing.[11] In this case, the coursing and other activities of the Hwaŏm community, such as the hundred-day-long Flower Garland Convocation, were to be done for the benefit of the state: the long life of the king, the peace and security of the people, the harmonious relationship between the civil and military branches of government, and prosperity in agricultural pursuits. Provision was made for taxes from the local districts to be funneled to the mountain regularly to provide for the monks and their regular observances. The royal monk Poch'ŏn, son of King Sinmun, presided over the Hwaŏm community during his lifetime and held the responsibility for ensuring that rituals for the protection of the state were performed on the mountain. That Poch'ŏn was also a master of dhāraṇīs suggests that dhāraṇī rituals and procedures were common in all monastic traditions in Silla as they were in medieval China.[12] Although left unstated, further royally commissioned construction on the five peaks of the mountain must have continued for many years, since Poch'ŏn's account of seasonal observances to be performed by the monks refers to separate shrines and detailed rituals to be held on each of these peaks. There is another version of this tale, which is similar in most respects but is awkward in its dating.[13] Both accounts demonstrate the central role of the *Avataṃsaka Sūtra* in the cultic practices performed on Mount Odae and reveal as well how the cults of Avalokiteśvara and Amitābha, specifically, as well as dhāraṇī, more generally, can be ordered or harnessed into a unified cultic structure.

Repentance rituals or ritual confessions *(yech'am,* Ch. *lichan)* are other essential cultic practices found in the composition of official liturgy at Mount Odae. We have encountered them previously with regard to Chinp'yo's quest to encounter Maitreya and Ŭisang's seeking to see Avalokiteśvara at Naksan. Repentance rituals were a seminal characteristic of Buddhist practice in China from the Northern and Southern dynasties through the Sui-Tang period.[14] Tiantai Zhiyi (538–592), Daoxuan, Shandao, and Daoshi all promoted various types of repentance rituals in their writings.[15] Repentance rituals were so popular a practice in medieval China that the famous cataloger Zhisheng (fl. 700–740) made a compilation of the procedures found in all the confessional texts he could find in the scriptures.[16] Monks participating in the royal Hwaŏm cult on Mount Odae nightly chanted ritual confessions to Avalokiteśvara on the eastern peak; Kṣitigarbha, by way of the *Book of Divining the Requital of Good and Evil Actions,* on the southern peak; Amitābha on the western peak; Śākyamuni, by way of the *Nirvāṇa Sūtra,* on the northern peak; and Mañjuśrī on the central peak.

The founding and promotion of the royally sponsored Buddhist cult at Mount Odae in some sense represents the apex or consummation of Silla's Buddha-land propaganda with its assimilation of Hwaŏm cosmology in which all things are interconnected. As will be seen below, many more developments in eighth- and ninth-century Silla Buddhism are connected to Hwaŏm thought, Hwaŏm cosmology, or the Hwaŏm tradition. These were either supported or directly commissioned by the royalty, but they were only able to flourish with the blessing of Silla's hereditary aristocracy.

Pusŏk Monastery and the Syncretism of Buddhist Cults

Pusŏk Monastery, the first headquarters of the Hwaŏm tradition in Silla, is midway up Mount Ponghwang in Yŏngju. It is nestled in between the two ranges of Mount T'aebaek and Mount Sobaek in present-day North Kyŏngsang Province. The monastery was established by the royal command of King Munmu in 676 under the direction of the eminent monk Ŭisang upon his return from Tang China.[17]

The *Lives of Eminent Monks Compiled in the Song* preserves the story of the founding of this monastery. When Ŭisang was about twenty years old (ca. 650), he and Wŏnhyo attempted to travel to Tang to study Huayan and Yogācāra philosophy in Chang'an with Xuanzang and the other masters in the Chinese capital. They were detained by a rainstorm before embarking on a boat to cross the Yellow Sea and spent the night in what they thought was a cave. Wŏnhyo woke up thirsty during the night and found what he thought was a bowl, drank water from it, and was refreshed. The next morning, however, they discovered that they had in fact spent the night in an open tomb. When the storm did not desist, they were forced to spend the night there again. This time Wŏnhyo was beset by demons and apparitions. This experience served as a spiritual catalyst for Wŏnhyo, who realized that all dharmas arise from the mind. Thus, according to tradition, Wŏnhyo decided that there was no need for him to go to China because he could ascertain all truth in his own mind without the expedient of studying under the great masters of the Tang capital.¹⁸ Another version of this anecdote, which was current in China at the end of the Northern Song period (960–1127), suggests that Wŏnhyo had this experience alone in China and that it was the precursor to his writing his commentary on the *Avataṃsaka Sūtra*.¹⁹

Ŭisang, on the other hand, caught a boat and landed at Dengzhou, on the northern side of the Shandong peninsula. There, he stayed in the home of a lay believer while his papers were being processed by the imperial authorities. The lay householder had a beautiful daughter named Shanmiao, who fell in love with Ŭisang at first sight. As the story goes, though the ingénue was very attractive and persistent, Ŭisang, "making his heart as a stone," withstood her advances and remained unmoved. Sensing Ŭisang's firm resolve to comply with the precept of chastity, Shanmiao suddenly aroused the *bodhicitta* and vowed to convert to Buddhism under his guidance from rebirth to rebirth through all generations of time and further vowed that, as his disciple, she would offer her life up to aid Ŭisang in his times of need and accomplish great deeds as she became acquainted with the teachings of Mahāyāna Buddhism.

Ŭisang then proceeded on to Chang'an, where he studied the teachings of Huayan Buddhism under Zhiyan and became friends with Fazang. After many years, Ŭisang completed his studies and felt that he needed to return to his homeland to preach the Buddhadharma. (Korean sources suggest that he also desired to warn King Munmu of an impending invasion by the Tang, the Silla-Tang alliance having broken down following the victory of the erstwhile allies after the conquest of Koguryŏ around 670.)²⁰ When Ŭisang arrived back at Dengzhou, he found that Shanmiao had prepared some new monastic robes for him and several kinds of Buddhist ritual implements. She was not there when he arrived, and Ŭisang hurriedly caught a boat and headed back to Silla. When she arrived back in Dengzhou, Shanmiao chanted a Buddhist spell *(zhouwen)* and vowed to turn herself into a large dragon to protect Ŭisang on the dangerous voyage across the Yellow Sea and to aid him in his teaching the Dharma back in Silla. She then cast herself into the sea and, touching the hearts of the gods of the mundane world, was transformed into a dragon by the power of her vow. As a dragon, she caught up with Ŭisang's boat, placed herself underneath it, and carried it on her back until it landed safely.

Upon his return to Silla, Ŭisang preached the Dharma throughout Silla's newly acquired domain "in the dust of Koguryŏ and in the winds of Paekche." Though he obtained some measure of success, in his heart he desired an auspicious place where he could expound the wondrous teachings of Hwaŏm Buddhism. Shanmiao, who accompanied the monk always in her dragon form, then accomplished another great transformation, turning herself into an immense rock floating in the air. The floating rock measured nearly one *li* in width, and people wondered whether it would descend on the roof of some monastery building *(saṃghārāma)* and crush it. As the story goes, the rock began to descend at a place where a flock of monastic adherents of the Lesser Vehicle (Hīnayāna) had gathered, but when they saw it they scattered to the four directions. Ŭisang entered the now deserted monastery and lectured on the *Avataṃsaka Sūtra* during the winter and summer retreats. Although he did not make any special effort to call for students, many people flocked to hear him and to study under his tutelage.[21]

According to tradition, the remnants of the floating rock are on the west side of (behind) the Hall of Amitāyus (Muryangsujŏn), the oldest remaining building of Pusŏk Monastery. The construction of this hall suggests the close relationship between the Hwaŏm tradition and the cult of Amitābha in Korea. If the existence of such a building could be traced to the Silla period, it could serve as evidence demonstrating the link between Hwaŏm and the cult of Amitābha. Unfortunately, the earliest documentary evidence regarding the structure suggests that although the Hall of Amitāyus is the oldest remaining wooden structure in Korea, reconstructed in and dating to 1376, it probably was not constructed prior to the Koryŏ period.[22]

However, there is some evidence that demonstrates that Ŭisang recognized the importance of the cults of Amitābha and Avalokiteśvara. In the chapter on the cult of Avalokiteśvara I noted Ŭisang's encounter with Avalokiteśvara and his founding of Naksan Monastery. Furthermore, an inscription on the Stele of State Preceptor Wŏnyung [Consummate Interfusion] at Pusŏk Monastery *(Pusŏksa Wŏnyung kuksa pi)* appears to preserve some views of Amitābha that Ŭisang remembered from his teacher Zhiyan. The stele was erected in 1054, the eighth year of Koryŏ king Munjong (r. 1046–1083), in memory of the monk Kyŏrŭng (964–1053), an important exponent of Hwaŏm in the early Koryŏ period.

> Ŭisang said that his master, Zhiyan, held that, with respect to the One Vehicle, Amitābha did not enter nirvāṇa, [but that] he took the Pure Lands of the Ten Directions as his form *(ch'e)*; and that there are no marks of rebirth and extinction. For this reason, the "Entering into the Dharma Realm" chapter *(Ru fajie pin)* of the *Avataṃsaka Sūtra* says: "Those who see Amitābha and the Bodhisattva Avalokiteśvara are consecrated and receive prophecies of their future attainment of Buddhahood fill up the whole dharma realm."[23] Succeeding bodhisattvas *(poch'ŏ)*[24] fill in the vacancies. The Buddha did not [pass away into] nirvāṇa and there is no time in which the world has been without [the Buddha]. For this reason, . . . [two characters missing] and succeeding bodhisattvas did not set up portraits and stūpas. This is the deep meaning of the One Vehicle.[25]

If this passage indeed reflects Ŭisang's (and Zhiyan's) views, it suggests that Ŭisang considered the worship of Amitābha to be contained within the One Vehicle, or Buddhayāna, the comprehensive vehicle of the Buddha. It is entirely plausible that Ŭisang would have positive impressions of the cult of Amitābha since his experience in Tang China would have predisposed him to the rise of Amitābha worship through the endeavors of such contemporary monks as Daochuo (562–645) and Shandao. He would have recognized the trend in Chinese Buddhism whereby the cults of Śākyamuni and Maitreya were replaced with the cults of Amitābha and, later, Avalokiteśvara. The reference to the passage in the *Avataṃsaka Sūtra* is significant as well because it is apparently the only place in Buddhabhadra's translation of the sūtra that mentions the name of Amitābha.

Furthermore, one of the few pieces of exegetical evidence that discusses the syncretism between the cults of Maitreya, Avalokiteśvara, and Amitābha by the Hwaŏm tradition in Silla is the "Vow Made at the White Lotus Enlightenment Site" *(Paekhwa toryang parwŏn mun)*, which was composed by Ŭisang. Although undated, I think this vow-text was probably composed after Ŭisang's return from Tang in 676 as he preached and established monasteries throughout Silla's newly conquered domain. The text is commonly regarded as a "Pure Land document" by scholars of Korean Pure Land Buddhism,[26] presumably because the vow was made at White Lotus Enlightenment Site—the term "White Lotus" usually referring to the lotus flower an aspirant is born into in the Pure Land; however, if the vow-text is classified by its content alone, it would undoubtedly be a record of the Avalokiteśvara cult because neither Amitābha nor his Pure Land in the west is mentioned directly.

Avalokiteśvara's mercy is the focus of the vow, and veneration of Maitreya is mentioned but once in the document. The practices that the aspirants vowed to cultivate include chanting the Great Compassion Spell,[27] recollecting the name of the Bodhisattva Avalokiteśvara, and taking refuge in Avalokiteśvara.[28] Nevertheless, the sūtras associated with the Great Compassion Spell promote the dual worship of Amitābha and Avalokiteśvara. Bhagavaddharma's translation of the *Nīlakaṇṭha (Qianshou qianyan Guanshiyin pusa guangda yuanman wuai dabeixin tuoluoni)* has Avalokiteśvara instruct people who would learn the Great Compassion Spell to abide by the following procedures: recollect the name of Avalokiteśvara with a sincere mind *(zhixin)* and also solely recollect *(zhuannian)* the Tathāgata Amitābha prior to chanting the Great Compassion Spell. The bodhisattva further teaches that if people chant the dhāraṇī a full five times in one night, they will eliminate the karma of heavy sins committed in the body over hundreds of thousands of myriad kalpas. If men and gods chant this verse of great compassion, when they die, all the buddhas of the ten directions will come take their hands so that they will be reborn with the buddhas, and, according to their desires, they will obtain rebirth in the Pure Land *(wangsheng)*.[29] This vow-text shows that verbal recollection of the name of Avalokiteśvara and recitation of the Great Compassion Spell may have been common practices in religious communities established by Ŭisang or associated with Ŭisang's Hwaŏm tradition. More important, however, the ritual procedures associated with these practices incorporated the cult of Amitābha for rebirth in Sukhāvatī. Thus, this document attests to the syncretism between Buddhist cults in Silla under Hwaŏm Buddhism. While the name of the monastery suggests the cult of Amitābha, the vow-text composed for the lay community at that site prescribed practices associated with the cults of Avalokiteśvara, Maitreya, and Amitābha.

Pulguk Monastery and Sŏkkuram

According to Iryŏn's *Memorabilia of the Three Kingdoms,* the aristocrat Kim Taesŏng (d. 775) was responsible for initiating construction of Pulguk Monastery and the stone Buddhist grotto Sŏkkuram, both of which are on Mount T'oham to the east of the Silla capital. Among the monastery records of Pulguk Monastery is a handwritten document titled *Foundation Record of Pulguk Monastery Past and Present (Pulguksa kogŭm ch'anggi).* No author or date of completion is mentioned, but since the final entries of the manuscript list the Chinese Jiaqing reign period (1796–1820), I maintain that it is probably a mid-nineteenth-century document. This document purports that the monastery was originally established as a nunnery in 528, that reconstruction work took place there in 574, and that new construction occurred again in 670, prior to Kim Taesŏng's construction and restoration effort of 751.[30]

Although I agree that Kim Taesŏng probably did not begin building a monastery at a site that was not previously inhabited by Buddhist monks, I am very skeptical of the *Foundation Record*'s position that the monastery was first founded in 528. According to the *History of the Three Kingdoms,* Hŭngnyun Monastery was the first Buddhist complex undertaken by the Silla government, and work on this monastery did not begin until 535, concerning which point I have suggested that this date, rather than 527, marks the official acceptance of Buddhism by the aristocratic government of Silla. I am even suspicious of the reference to the construction of the lecture hall in 670 because Ŭisang did not return from Tang China until 671, and it is highly unlikely that his important disciples would have been stationed there until the early eighth century. I am willing to concede that the now-lost *Record of Conduct of Master Wŏnhyo (Hyosa haengjang),* by Ch'oe Ch'iwŏn, might have contained a reference to a lecture hall's being built on that site, but the insinuation that Ŭisang's disciples were stationed there as early as the late seventh century is far-fetched.³¹

The traditional narrative of the true-bone aristocrat Kim Taesŏng's building of Pulguk Monastery and Sŏkkuram brings together threads of a few of the cultic practices mentioned in the preceding chapters on the cults of Maitreya and Avalokiteśvara. According to the *Memorabilia of the Three Kingdoms'* account, during the reign of King Sinmun, in Moryang Village (also called Puyun settlement) there was a poor woman named Kyŏngjo, who had a son. Because the boy's forehead was big and flat, like a city wall, she called him Taesŏng (Big Wall). Since his family was indigent, he sold his labor to the wealthy farmer Pogan to make a living tending to the rich man's fields. One day a monk named Chŏmgae came to Pogan's land begging for money so that he could hold a special dharma assembly at Hŭngnyun Monastery. Pogan made a large donation of hemp cloth, and Taesŏng overhead the monk promise that since he made generous offerings he would be rewarded ten-thousand-fold and would enjoy peace and long life. Upon hearing this he returned home to his mother and told her that their family had fallen on such hard times because they had never made offerings to the Buddhist church and that their family would continue to be poor in their next cycle of lives as well. He was determined to make an offering for the dharma assembly to break the cycle and obtain merit and reward for his actions.

Taesŏng died not long afterward and, on the night of his death, a voice from heaven was heard at the estate of the chief minister, Kim Mullyang, saying that Taesŏng of Moryang Village was going to be reborn into Minister Kim's house. Servants from the household were dispatched to Moryang Village to find out about Taesŏng and verify his death. Minister Kim's wife conceived at the moment the voice was heard from heaven and in due time delivered a son. The baby held his left hand clenched for seven days; when he finally opened his hand, all saw that the characters for "Taesŏng" were inscribed on his hand. For this reason he was named Taesŏng, and the chief minister brought Taesŏng's mother from his previous life into their home and took care of her. A few scholars have likened this scenario to stories suggesting that there was a cult whereby Silla aristocrats worshipped images of Maitreya so that beautiful sons would be born into their families and that these children were seen as emanations of Maitreya, if not as Maitreya himself.³²

Taesŏng liked to hunt as he was growing up and was once lodging in a little village at the base of Mount T'oham after catching a bear. He dreamed that the bear changed into a ghost who threatened that in his next life he would catch and eat Taesŏng if Taesŏng killed him. Taesŏng then asked for forgiveness in the dream and the ghost-bear asked him to build a monastery in his behalf. Taesŏng vowed to do just that, and when he woke up he discovered that he had been perspiring profusely. Taesŏng then gave up hunting and built Changsu (Long Life) Monastery on the site where he caught the bear. His mind and heart were by now completely turned to Buddhism. He then built Pulguk Monastery for his parents in his present life (Kim Moryang and his wife) and Sŏkpul Monastery (viz. Sŏkkuram) for his parents in his previous life (Kyŏngjo), both of which are on Mount T'oham. The account also adds that two Buddhist monks, the otherwise unknown Sillim and the previously mentioned P'yohun, were made to reside there. Construction on Pulguk Monastery began in 751; it had not yet been completed, however, when Kim Taesŏng passed away on the second day of the twelfth month of *kabin,* the ninth year of the Dali reign period (8 January 775). The Silla government then stepped in and completed it.[33]

At the end of this account Iryŏn also suggests that Pulguk Monastery was first the abode of eminent Yogācāra (Yuga) monks and that to his day (ca. 1285) the monastery had been passed down in their hands. For example, the Yogācāra exegete Haewŏn (1262–1340), who gained a measure of fame in northern China under the Mongols, originally lived at Pulguk Monastery.[34] Nevertheless, the following sentence says that another "old account" *(kojŏn)* disagrees (apparently with the supposition that Pulguk Monastery was controlled by Yogācāra monks). Although Iryŏn does not include what this other tradition might be, he concluded the account by admitting that he does not know which tradition is right.[35] Circumstantial architectural evidence suggests that Pulguk Monastery was probably associated with the Hwaŏm tradition rather than Yogācāra since the layout of the monastery and extant poetry about the monastery, which purportedly dates from that period, are related to Hwaŏm cosmology.

Pulguksa literally means "Monastery of the Buddha's Country," and the layout of the monastery suggests that Kim Taesŏng sought to imbue the monastery with imagery alluded to in the *Lotus Sūtra* and also to present an idealized vision of the transcendent realm of the buddhas as found in the *Avataṃsaka Sūtra*. The monastery was rebuilt by the South Korean government in 1973, and the present reconstruction attempts to approximate the appearance of the basic structure of the earliest layout of the monastery in the period immediately following Kim Taesŏng's day. Below I will briefly summarize the significant structures in this monastic complex that demonstrate how the cults of Vairocana, Avalokiteśvara, and Amitābha were combined in this one monastic complex. Traditionally, when people entered Pulguk Monastery, they would first ascend two exquisitely carved stone bridges, White Cloud Bridge (Paegun'gyo) and Blue Cloud Bridge (Ch'ŏngun'gyo), and pass through Purple Mist Gate (Chahamun) into the courtyard of the main hall or golden hall *(kŭmdang)*, the Hall of the Great Hero (Taeungjŏn). In this courtyard are two stone stūpas (pagodas): the Stūpa of Many Treasures (Tabot'ap) to the east and the Śākyamuni Stūpa (Sŏkkat'ap) to the west. For our purposes here, the Stūpa of Many Treasures is significant because the name of the stūpa is a direct reference to a chapter of the *Lotus Sūtra* that mentions the Stūpa of Many Treasures—the abode of the Tathāgata Prabūtaratna (Duobao rulai)—which appears when the Buddha begins to preach the *Lotus Sūtra* to verify the truthfulness of the sermon that will be taught.[36] Because the Śākyamuni Stūpa suggests the presence of the Buddha Śākyamuni, in one sense, the construction of the courtyard attempts to recreate the cosmic setting in which the *Lotus Sūtra* was taught. The lecture hall, the Hall of No Talking mentioned previously, is directly behind the Hall of the Great Hero, which houses an image of Śākyamuni.

The Vairocana Hall (Pirojŏn) is behind the Hall of the Great Hero and the Hall of No Talking on a slightly raised terrace. In Hwaŏm cosmology, Vairocana is the original essence (Ch. *benti;* Kor. *ponch'e*) of all the buddhas, the body of truth, or the cosmic Buddha from whence all other buddhas spring. Vairocana is also the main Buddha of tantric Buddhism, and most tantric sūtras refer to him as the Great Sun Buddha (Ch. Dari rulai; Kor. Taeil yŏrae; Jpn. Dainichi Nyorai). From this ideological point of view or frame of reference, the hall may be considered the point farthest into the interior of the monastery. As with the Stūpa of Many Treasures, the inclusion of this Vairocana Hall suggests an allusion to Vairocana, in a few chapters in the *Avataṃsaka Sūtra*.[37] A gilt-bronze image of Vairocana that dates to the mid-eighth century is enshrined therein. To the east of this hall, on a mound and platform raised higher than the Vairocana Hall, is the Avalokiteśvara Hall (Kwanŭmjŏn). The mound is said to represent Mount Potalaka. This hall is also a counterpart to the cultic site at Naksan Monastery, founded by Ŭisang, discussed in chapter 4. I do not think that there is any direct connection between these two places for worshipping Avalokiteśvara, but it is significant that halls dedicated to these important bodhisattvas and buddhas are all brought together in the Pulguk Monastery complex.

The Amitābha Hall, or Hall of Extreme Bliss (Kŭngnakchŏn), is particularly important with regard to religious symbolism and ties to Hwaŏm cosmology. It has its own courtyard to the west of the Hall of the Great Hero courtyard. One ascends into this mundane Pure Land by means of two finely carved stone bridges, the Seven Treasures Bridge (Ch'ilpogyo) and Lotus Bridge (Yŏnhwagyo), and enters through the Gate of Peace and Nurturance (Anyangmun). All three of these are direct references to Sukhāvatī. The Pure Land is filled with the seven treasures or seven jewels, and those who are reborn in Sukhāvatī are reborn in the calyx of lotus flowers that will eventually open, the speed of which depends on their merit, sincerity, and spiritual capacity. The Land of Peace and Nurturance is merely another name for Sukhāvatī, as is the Land of Extreme Bliss. A curious construction of three flights of stone stairs leads from the empty courtyard behind the Hall of Extreme Bliss to the courtyard of the Hall of the Great Hero. Each of the flights contains sixteen steps, forty-eight steps in total. The number forty-eight refers to the number of vows made by Amitābha, which enabled him to create his Pure Land, as contained in the *Larger Pure Land Sūtra* (Skt. *Sukhāvatīvyūha Sūtra;* Ch. *Wuliangshou jing*). The number sixteen refers to the number of visualizations one may perform to enable oneself to be reborn in Sukhāvatī, as contained in the *Book on the Visualization of the Buddha Amitāyus (Guan Wuliangshou jing)*. Although I am skeptical of the connection, I may add here that Pulguk Monastery's official Web site suggests that these forty-eight steps refer to the "pure land" of Gṛdhrakūṭa (Lingjiu shan), otherwise known as Vulture Peak, the place where the Buddha preached the *Lotus Sūtra*.[38] The number three suggests the three grades or classes of rebirth available to those who seek rebirth in Sukhāvatī, according to their spiritual capacities and the sincerity of their vows, as spoken of in both sūtras. A gilt-bronze image of Amitābha dating to the mid-eighth century is enshrined in the Hall of Extreme Bliss; it is a companion to the image of Vairocana mentioned above. The scholar Ch'oe Ch'iwŏn wrote a poem about this image, which suggests that Korean Buddhists of the tenth century probably considered Pulguk Monastery to be associated with the Hwaŏm tradition. The poem is preserved in the *Collected Works of Koun Ch'oe Ch'iwŏn (Koun chip)* and *Foundation Record of Pulguk Monastery Past and Present*. A slightly different version of this same poem is found in Uich'ŏn's *Literature of the Perfect [Hwaŏm] Tradition*.[39] The poem is curious because it explicitly refers to a Hwaŏm cosmology that has completely absorbed the imagery of the cult of Amitābha.

> On the eastern mountain of Tonghae (Silla), there is a beautiful monastery,
> "Hwaŏm Pulguk" is its name.
> A high-ranking official of the royal clan personally established it—
> The four words of the monastery's name have deep meaning.
> Fixing your eyes on the Flower Garland brings to mind the Lotus Storehouse,
> In the Buddha's country, the racing mind is brought to Peace and Nurturance.
> [If you] desire to command Devil Mountain and control Poison Peak,
> In the end you will rule over the Sea of Pain without making waves.
> A lovable "monk" is made to explain the principles [of Buddhism],
> And is able to guide a *dānapati* (alms-giver) when he hopes to offer his mind.

> Dwelling in the east and imagining the west is the appearance of the wild-goose form,
> Visualizing myself in the darkening landscape, I point to [Mount] Yanzi.
> In each and every one of their countries they give blessings and benefits,
> The Tathāgata Akṣobhya [the Buddha of the East] is also peculiar and strange.
> Sage advice does not necessarily distinguish my course bearings,
> In the end it points to the mind, causing it to possess a ground.
> Absurd arising and absurd action—emptiness faces emptiness,
> Self-cultivation for floating generations consists of scrupulous consideration.
> Having been able to live peacefully I rely on first-birthday guests,
> Who is said "to face the wall" and not have thaumaturgic powers?
> Great practices sustain the lords and also keep the lords at a distance,
> Existing in nothing, all dwell in the country of the Buddha.[40]

This poem explicitly refers to Pulguk Monastery as being associated with the Hwaŏm tradition and alludes to the Lotus Storehouse World System where the *Avataṃsaka Sūtra* was preached. As I mentioned previously, "Peace and Nurturance" is merely another name for Amitābha's Sukhāvatī. Furthermore, according to the *Expanded Rhyming Dictionary (Guangyun)*, Mount Yanzi is a literary reference to the place where the sun goes when it descends in the western sky.[41] This is certainly another metaphor for Sukhāvatī. If this poem may be attributed genuinely to Ch'oe, which I am inclined to believe because of its inclusion in Ŭich'ŏn's collection of Hwaŏm literature, it suggests that during the late ninth and early tenth centuries Pulguk Monastery was associated with the Hwaŏm tradition and that the Hwaŏm tradition of Silla had subsumed the Amitābha cult. This should not be a surprise. In fact, it is to be expected because there was never a separate Pure Land tradition in Silla. If this was so, then Pulguk Monastery's association with the Hwaŏm tradition may have existed as early as its construction in the mid-eighth century.

I think that same association with Hwaŏm cosmology holds true for Sŏkkuram, which was originally called Sŏkpul Monastery when, as mentioned above, Kim Taesŏng began constructing it for his parents of his previous life about 751. Sŏkkuram was constructed facing the East Sea (Tonghae; Sea of Japan) high up on Mount T'oham. Kim's grotto design utilized two styles of Buddhist architecture and is a unique structure in East Asia. He merged the barrel design of the caitya-halls of India with the cave-temple design of Central Asia and China, as seen along the Silk Road and in Dunhuang, Yun'gang, and Longmen. In contrast to such caves, which the Indians, Serindians, and Chinese cut into living rock, Sŏkkuram simply looks like a cave-temple cut into living stone; the hard, rocky mountains of Korea precluded such excavation. There are essentially three parts to the grotto shrine: an antechamber to the shrine *(chŏndang)* featuring stone reliefs of the eight groups of gods *(p'albusin)*,[42] such as dragons, titans *(asura)*, and devas; a hallway *(pido)* adorned with stone carvings of the four heavenly kings *(sach'ŏnwang)*; and the circular chamber *(wŏnsil)*, which features images of the major Indian gods, the Buddha's major disciples *(śrāvaka)*, and the major bodhisattvas surrounding a central seated image of the Buddha *(ponjon pul)*.

The greatest mystery concerning this stone grotto is the identity of the central Buddha image. There are three theories: the most compelling explanation is that the image is Śākyamuni; an old, and generally discredited, theory holds that the image is Amitābha; and an interesting, if fanciful, argument alleges that the image is the tantric Vairocana.

That the image exhibits the mudrā commonly referred to as the Buddha's "calling the earth to witness" (Skt. *māratarjanabhūmisparśa mudrā;* Ch. *xiangmo chudi yin;* Kor. *hangma ch'okchi in*) supports the theory that the main image is Śākyamuni. When Māra, the Lord of Illusion, disputes Śākyamuni's attaining of enlightenment, the Tathāgata touches the earth, which then quakes, to signal that the Buddha has spoken the truth. Kang Woo-bang suggests that the designers of this stone image attempted to make it the same size as the image of Śākyamuni enshrined at the Mahābodhi Monastery at Bodhgāya, traditionally believed to be the exact site of the Buddha's enlightenment, the size of which was described by Xuanzang in his *Record of the Western Regions during the Mighty Tang (Da Tang xiyu ji)*.[43] Although the measurements in the book do not match perfectly those of the Sŏkkuram image, Kang asserts that there is probably a connection. Kang also suggests that Sŏkkuram may be interpreted according to either the *Lotus Sūtra* or the *Avataṃsaka Sūtra.* When seen from the perspective of the *Lotus,* the situation of the central Buddha image combines with the surrounding images to suggest a representation of the Buddha on Vulture Peak about to teach the sūtra. From the perspective of the *Avataṃsaka,* however, when Śākyamuni attained enlightenment, he became both a Tathāgata and the Buddha Vairocana simultaneously—because, according to Hwaŏm thought, a nondualistic relationship exists between Śākyamuni and Vairocana. Sŏkkuram's architectural space is a manifestation of Vairocana's Lotus Storehouse Realm, where the *Avataṃsaka Sūtra* was expounded. Thus, the main purpose of Sŏkkuram is to express the idea of enlightenment.[44] In correlation with the foregoing remarks on enlightenment, Kang also suggests that the image spoken of in Xuanzang's travel record was based on the *Lalitavistara (Fangguang da zhuangyan jing)*. He demonstrates how certain passages in the eighth and ninth rolls of this sūtra—which describe in great detail the account of the Buddha's going to the place of enlightenment (*Zhi putichang pin* in roll 8), quelling Māra (*Xiangmo pin* in roll 9), and attaining complete enlightenment (*Cheng zhengjue pin* in roll 9)—mirror the imagery seen at Sŏkkuram.[45] Kang then goes on to say that Sŏkkuram's purpose of promoting enlightenment supported a few prevalent ideas in Silla Buddhism of this time: promoting the idea that Silla was a Buddha-land and being an iconographic representation of "comprehensive Buddhism" *(t'ong Pulgyo),* a concept or viewpoint, attributed to Wŏnhyo, in which all of the different and sometimes seemingly contradictory strands of Buddhist thought and practice are harmonized under the head of one prevailing concept. Kang suggests that this concept was *enlightenment.*[46]

Hwang Suyŏng is the main proponent of the theory that the central seated image may be Amitābha. When in 1967 Hwang discovered the underwater tomb of King Munmu, known as the Tomb of the Great King (Taewangam), which he demonstrated was linearly connected to the grotto shrine, the standard theory that the seated Buddha image inside was Śākyamuni was called into question. According to Hwang, since the "dragon spirit" of the underwater tomb faces west toward Mount T'oham, and since Amitābha is the Buddha of the Western Paradise, the image on the inside of the grotto may be of Amitābha.

The writings of the Japanese colonial-period Buddhologist Ōno Genmyō seemingly support this theory. He purportedly had access to monastic records of the grotto (now lost) that were kept at a nearby hermitage. These records stated that there was a wooden plaque before the hall that read Hall of Life and Light (Sugwangjŏn), a possible reference to Amitābha/Amitāyus, the Buddha of Infinite Light and Life, and before the cave was a plaque that read Amitābha Cave (Amit'agul).

This wooden plaque had been made by Cho Sunsang, a military official posted at Ulsan (north of Kyŏngju on the east coast of Korea) at the end of the nineteenth century. The narrative concerning this plaque stated that one night while he was en route to Kyŏngju, he had a dream of a magnificent cave image on the slopes of Mount T'oham. The image was crying out in desperation to him. The next morning he asked the local villagers whether there was a Buddhist grotto up in the mountains. After being told there was, he sought out the cave and found it to be the same one he had seen in his dream. Feeling that he had received a divine commission to restore the grotto, he carried out this work, made a wooden plaque by his own hand, and recorded his work in the monastic records.

Although the plaque was lost, Hwang purportedly found a small piece of it in 1964, and this piece is now preserved in the Dongguk University Museum.[47] Ko Ikchin suggests that if Sŏkkuram and the underwater tomb are viewed from a Hwaŏm doctrinal perspective, which he believes was dominant at the time of its construction, the main image could be Amitābha.[48] The theory that the central seated image is Amitābha, though interesting, is not ultimately compelling. Images of Amitābha never feature the "calling the earth to witness" mudrā, and the linear connection with the Tomb of the Great King, while intriguing, has not convinced many scholars that the image must be Amitābha because the other physical or circumstantial evidence—the plaques that are no longer extant, in particular—is just too muddled to be conclusive. Furthermore, like Pulguk Monastery, the iconographical construction of the grotto lends itself more fully to canonical representations of either the *Lotus Sūtra* or the *Avataṃsaka Sūtra*.

Finally, other scholars suggest that the main image of Sŏkkuram may be Vairocana. In an essay that attempts to flesh out connections between ancient Korean shamanism and Buddhism, James Huntley Grayson conjectures that Sŏkkuram was a royal shrine where the shaman-kings of Silla would perform religious rituals on the sacred Mount T'oham. He indicates what he perceives as connections between shamanism and "Esoteric Buddhism" in Silla, and opines that the iconography of Sŏkkuram, specifically the domed chamber and the main image surrounded by gods, disciples, and bodhisattvas, is actually a maṇḍala of the Buddhist cosmos. This being the case, the main image should be Vairocana.[49] Unfortunately, there is little proof to support Grayson's thesis. There is no evidence that Sŏkkuram was ever the exclusive domain of the Silla royal family. The only circumstantial evidence to support his theory that the grotto presents esoteric Buddhist views is the stone relief of eleven-headed Avalokiteśvara (Skt. Ekadaśamukha), which is directly behind the main image underneath the circular halo stone or mandorla. In chapter 3 I have argued against the representation of this version of Avalokiteśvara as being exclusively esoteric or tantric. None of the other imagery would demand that the grotto be interpreted according to esoteric Buddhist doctrines. According to art historians, the iconography of Sŏkkuram supports interpretations from the *Lotus, Avataṃsaka,* and other sutras, so it does not matter whether the central Buddha is Śākyamuni or Vairocana.[50] If seen within the all-inclusive Hwaŏm context, the image may be either. In fact, it may be both, because, according to the *Avataṃsaka Sūtra,* Śākyamuni is an emanation of Vairocana, and Śākyamuni *became* Vairocana at the moment of enlightenment.

The Five Sacred Mountains and Ten Hwaŏm Monasteries

Since the Hwaŏm tradition received royal and aristocratic support, it eventually became associated inextricably with the ruling ideology and propaganda of the Silla kingdom during the eighth, ninth, and tenth centuries. This point may be clarified by demonstrating the relationship between Hwaŏm monasteries and the five sacred mountains of Silla. During the eighth century, the Silla government, both royalty and aristocracy, selected five mountains in the country to serve as ritual sites for the protection and prosperity of the country. This new system of five sacred mountains was modeled on the Chinese five marchmount (*wuyue*) system and replaced an earlier ritual system based on the worship of three mountains, all of which were in or around the Kyŏngju plain, so as to be inclusive of the major symbolic areas of mountain forces under Silla's hegemony.[51] The five sacred mountains of Silla were

>Eastern Peak: T'ohamsan in modern Kyŏngju
>Western Peak: Kyeryongsan in modern Kongju
>Southern Peak: Chiisan (more commonly known as Mount Chiri) on the border of the modern South Kyŏngsang Province and North Chŏlla Province
>Northern Peak: T'aebaeksan in modern Kangwŏn Province
>Central Peak: P'algongsan (then known as Puak) in modern Taegu

The eminent Silla literatus Ch'oe Ch'iwŏn, while writing his *Biography of the Eminent Tang Upadhyāya Fazang of Dajianfu Monastery (Tang Taech'ŏnboksa kosaju pŏn'gyŏng Taedŏk Pŏpchang hwasang chŏn)* at the beginning of the tenth century, listed ten monasteries associated with the Hwaŏm tradition in Silla during his day in an interlinear note.

>There are ten mountains [associated with] the great learning of Hwaŏm in Haedong. On the Central Peak, Mount Kong (Mount P'algong), is Miri Monastery. On the Southern Peak, Mount Chii, is Hwaŏm Monastery. On the Northern Peak is Pusŏk Monastery. On Mount Kaya in Kangju is Haein Monastery and Pogwang Monastery. In Kaya Ravine in Ungju is Powŏn Monastery. On Mount Kyeryong is Su Monastery. (According to the *Comprehensive Monograph on Geography [Kwalchiji]* on Mount Kyeram is Hwasan Monastery in Sakchu.) On Mount Kŭmjŏng in Yangju is Pŏmŏ Monastery. On Mount Pisŭl is Okch'ŏn Monastery. On Mount Mo in Chŏnju is Kuksin Monastery. [And] on Mount Pua in Hanju is Ch'ŏngdam Monastery.[52]

Later, the Koryŏ monk Iryŏn included a similar yet incomplete list in his biography of Ŭisang contained in *Memorabilia of the Three Kingdoms:* "[Ŭi]sang thereafter caused the teaching to be disseminated in ten monasteries: Pusŏk Monastery on Mount T'aebaek, Pimara [Monastery] in Wŏnju, Haein [Monastery] on [Mount] Kaya, Okch'ŏn [Monastery] on [Mount] Pisŭl, Pŏmŏ [Monastery] on [Mount] Kŭmjŏng, Hwaŏm Monastery on the Southern Peak, and so forth."[53]

If we combine the information from these two excerpts with my foregoing argument regarding the relationship between Pulguk Monastery and the Hwaŏm tradition, we find that each of the five sacred mountains of Silla had a monastery associated with the Hwaŏm tradition.

Eastern Peak: Pulguk Monastery
Western Peak: Su Monastery
Southern Peak: Hwaŏm Monastery
Northern Peak: Pusŏk Monastery
Central Peak: Miri Monastery

These data suggest that the Hwaŏm tradition was a vehicle used by the Silla government to promote unity and state protection during the late Silla period. It was the only Buddhist "institution" in Silla in the sense that specific monasteries were associated with the tradition, and that they may have received some level of financial support from the government to carry out their operations can be inferred from their location on Silla's sacred mountains. Although the association between Hwaŏm monasteries and Silla's five sacred mountains is significant and seems to support my supposition that the Buddhist cults of Silla and various strands of Buddhist practice were brought together under the aegis of the Hwaŏm tradition, a few questions remain: Why did Ch'oe Ch'iwŏn consciously omit Pulguk Monastery and the Eastern Peak from his list of Hwaŏm monasteries? Are we making too much of the relationship between the ten Hwaŏm monasteries and the five sacred mountains?

Lee Ki-baik disregards the idea that Pulguk Monastery was the Hwaŏm monastery associated with the Eastern Peak yet thinks it is significant that four of the five sacred mountains of Silla had Hwaŏm monasteries. Accordingly, he theorizes that the Hwaŏm tradition fulfilled a moral role of supporting the Silla monarchy's bid to develop a centralized, autocratic monarchy by placing monasteries on the five sacred mountains. To bolster this claim he indicates that aristocrat-officials who were loyal to Silla kings often retired to the five mountains when their service to the state had ended.[54] Lee's theory has been accepted generally by most Korean scholars.

Kim Sang-hyun, on the other hand, suggests that Lee's selected focus on a few monasteries and their associated mountains misses the true significance of the Hwaŏm tradition in Silla. Even setting aside Pulguk Monastery, by focusing on the four monasteries linked to the five sacred mountains, we disregard the fact that six other mountains of Silla housed Hwaŏm monasteries. Furthermore, Kim lists ten other monasteries that are not included on either list of the ten monasteries yet bear sufficient association with Ŭisang, his disciples, and the Hwaŏm tradition to be considered "Hwaŏm monasteries." These include Naksan

Monastery and Pulguk Monastery—the former because it was founded by Ŭisang, and the latter because it is mentioned as a place where the *Avataṃsaka Sūtra* was preached and Ŭisang's disciples resided.[55] Some scholars have offered the opinion that the ten monasteries listed by Ch'oe Ch'iwŏn perhaps represent monasteries in the direct lineage of Ŭisang, while the other Hwaŏm monasteries represent the general influence of Hwaŏm learning in Silla.[56] Kim challenges this view by demonstrating that since Ch'oe's list comes in the context of his biography of Fazang, it would rather represent the influence of "Fazang's lineage" in Korea.[57] Although I am not convinced by Kim's interpretation, because the names of all these Silla monasteries are presented in a minor interlinear note, the potential associations are something to consider. Furthermore, Kim's most significant disagreement with Lee's theory has to do with the Hwaŏm monasteries' support of autocratic government. I am more persuaded by Kim's contention of the importance of Hwaŏm Buddhism in Silla than by Lee's theory of its supposed connection with the great project of the royal scions of Kim Ch'unch'u's line (which ruled Silla from 654 to 780), who strove to turn Silla into a centralized, autocratic bureaucracy following the Chinese model over a roughly hundred-year period by systematically attempting to restrict and remove aristocratic privileges enjoyed by the hereditary elites. The most blatant and final attempt to centralize monarchical power came during the reign of King Kyŏngdŏk, when he rearranged and renamed governmental institutions to accord with the Tang model. The royal enterprise to centralize power, however, culminated in an aristocratic coup and the eventual regicide of his son King Hyegong. Ch'unch'u's descendants were thus removed from the Silla throne. The aristocratic power broker, the chief minister *(sangdaedŭng)*, then replaced them with rulers who were amenable to the hereditary privileges of Silla's true-bone aristocrats. Kim, furthermore, proposes that the great period of expansion and building of Hwaŏm monasteries did not begin until the reign of King Aejang, when construction of Haein Monastery began in the Kaya Mountains and Silla kings and the aristocrats once again shared the putatively common goal of maintaining their hereditary privileges. This would suggest that there must be another reason for the Silla monarchy and aristocracy's support of Hwaŏm Buddhism, since the power of Lee's theory of the strong relationship between the five sacred mountains and the Hwaŏm tradition diminishes when we consider that the monarchy no longer pursued a policy of attempting to centralize autocratic power and curb hereditary prerogatives after 780.[58]

I suggest that Silla nobles continued to support the Hwaŏm tradition because it had synthesized the Sillan approach to devotional practice and had assimilated all the cults of Buddhist deities that were popular among the Silla people. Almost all aspects of Buddhism on the ground on the Korean peninsula in the late Silla period are best interpreted through the lens of Hwaŏm cosmology. Although beyond our discussion here, Rhi Ki-yong constructed a compelling argument that artistic representations of the buddhas of the four directions *(sabangbul)* carved on stones and stone stūpas in the vicinity of the Silla capital adhere to the Hwaŏm model better than the descriptions in any other sūtra do.[59] Also, aside from the Hwaŏm cultic sites on Mount Odae and the ten other mountains introduced previously, the ethereal Diamond Mountain was recognized and renamed by Buddhists as the abode of the Bodhisattva Dharmodgata, or Dharma Arouser (Pŏpki, Ch. Faqi), mentioned in the eighty-roll translation of the *Avataṃsaka Sūtra:* "In the midst of the ocean [in the northeast region] there is a place called Diamond Mountain. Since days of yore all the bodhisattvas have stopped to dwell [there for a time]. The Bodhisattva Dharma Arouser and his entourage is an assembly of all the bodhisattvas, one thousand two hundred personages in all. They reside there constantly expounding the Dharma."[60] The location of Diamond Mountain was not mentioned in the sixty-roll *Avataṃsaka Sūtra*. The eighty-roll translation was completed at the end of the seventh century, but this mountain was not yet called Diamond Mountain. The early Huayan master Fazang regarded this stunningly beautiful mountain in Silla's territory in his *Record of Searching for the Arcane in the* Avataṃsaka Sūtra *(Huayan jing tanxuan ji)* as "Zhidan," the earthly abode of a bodhisattva named Dharmodgata (Tanwujie, Kor. Tammugal), who is mentioned in the sixty-roll sūtra as having an entourage of twelve thousand bodhisattvas somewhere in the middle of the four great seas of the world.[61] Before one hundred years had passed, however, in a commentary on the *Avataṃsaka,* his intellectual successor Chengguan unambiguously reports that the place in Silla that had been called the abode of Dharmodgata has now been recognized as Diamond Mountain:

> Diamond Mountain is a mountain called "Jingang" [Kor. Kŭmgang, diamond, adamantine] located in the east of Haidong [Silla]. Although it is not made wholly of gold *(jin),* up, down, all around, and when you go into the mountain's precincts it is all gold in the midst of the sand of the flowing waters. When you look at it from a distance the whole thing is golden. Furthermore, the people of Haidong [Silla] have told each other from ancient times that this mountain has long been a place where saintly beings *(shengren,* vis. bodhisattvas) are manifest.
>
> Nevertheless, in the Jin [sixty-roll] translation this location is listed as the ninth because, like the tenth Zhuangyan Cave, they are both located in the middle of the sea. And those who dwell here now think it is within the eight directions because it is attached to the northeastern region. If

this is not so, why would something clearly explained as being in the eight directions suddenly be said to be in the sea?

Furthermore, in the Jin translation, in the middle of the sea there are two dwelling places. One is called Zhidanna, on which a bodhisattva named Dharmodgata manifests. There are twelve thousand bodhisattvas in his entourage. What is called Zhidan is more fully called Nizhiduo, which means "gushing" *(yongchu)*. "Diamond" refers to its essence, and "gushing" refers to its condition. As for Dharmodgata, it is said to mean "dharma producing" *(fasheng)*, "dharma gushing" *(fayong)*, and also "dharma stillness" *(fashang)*. Now he is called "Dharma Arouser" *(faqi)*, the meaning of which is the same as "producing" or "gushing"; namely, it is akin to "Ever Weeping" *(changti,* Skt. Sadāprarudita).[62] The entourage of the bodhisattva is ten times [as large] in this sūtra or perhaps the previous translation is in error.[63]

Because Chengguan was active on China's sacred mounts Wutai, Emei, and Zhongnan during the period between 776 and 833, it seems plausible that the mountain was renamed by Buddhists sometime during the eighth century. Later Korean geographical works report that Ŭisang's disciples P'yohun, Nŭngin, and Sillim actively founded new monasteries and restored old monasteries in the vicinity of Diamond Mountain during the last quarter of the seventh and early eighth centuries, which suggests that Hwaŏm adherents had special claim on this area.[64] The development of such cultic sites aided in the accommodation of Hwaŏm Buddhism in Silla and in the state's presentation of itself as a bona fide Buddha-land rather than a marginal country on the edge of the civilized world.

The Hwaŏm Cult of the Divine Assembly in Late Silla

The Hwaŏm cult of the Divine Assembly *(sinjung,* Ch. *shenzhong)*, like the royal Hwaŏm cult on Mount Odae, is another example of the ritual deployment of the *Avataṃsaka Sūtra* by monks and aristocrats for the protection of the state. This cult flourished at the royally sponsored Haein Monastery during the late Silla period and provided a means whereby not only Silla's indigenous gods and spirits could be incorporated into the framework of the Buddhist pantheon, but also all the Buddhist deities could become accessible in Silla. Although its origins may trace back to the beginnings of Hwaŏm in Silla, the cult assumed a more concrete shape in Silla during the ninth and tenth centuries. The Divine Assembly cult is associated with both the sixty-roll and eighty-roll versions of the *Avataṃsaka Sūtra*. The Divine Assembly refers to the bodhisattvas, gods, and supernatural beings that were in attendance when

FIGURE 3. Painting of the Divine Assembly, Mangwŏl Monastery, Namsan, Kyŏngju.

the Buddha taught the *Avataṃsaka Sūtra* (fig. 3). The sixty-roll version of the *Avataṃsaka* provides a list of thirty-four classes of divine beings (see appendix 1); the eighty-roll version produces classifications for forty types of deities (see appendix 2).[65] The cult that matured during the late Silla period presented these divine protectors of the Buddhadharma as guardians of monks and laity who cultivated the "Avataṃsaka samādhi"

(*Hwaŏm sammae*). These deities could also be deployed to protect monastic precincts and states.

The Divine Assembly appeared previously in our discussion of the royal Hwaŏm cult of Mount Odae. Iryŏn's *Memorabilia of the Three Kingdoms* preserves instructions for the performance of state-protection rituals left by the royal monk Poch'ŏn before his death in the first half of the eighth century. Among the prescriptions for ritual activities on the monastery on the central peak of the mountain are the following: five acolytes are to recite the names of the Divine Assembly of the *Avataṃsaka Sūtra* at night *(ya yŏm Hwaŏm sinjung)* and seven acolytes are to perform a yearly ritual confession to the Divine Assembly of the *Avataṃsaka Sūtra (Hwaŏm sinjung yech'am)*.[66] Iryŏn's work also preserves a reference to a representation of the Divine Assembly that was enshrined along with an image of Amitābha at Mujang Monastery in the Silla capital. At Mujang Monastery is a stele inscription pertaining to the Amitābha image that scholars have dated to the year 801, but it does not contain a direct reference to the Divine Assembly.[67]

One of the legends of the founding of Pŏmŏ Monastery on Mount Kŭmjŏng alludes to the Hwaŏm cult of the Divine Assembly and projects its practice back to Ŭisang. This monastery, which was founded by Silla king Hŭngdŏk (r. 826–836) in the first half of the ninth century, is one of the previously mentioned ten mountain monasteries of the Hwaŏm tradition and is in the vicinity of present-day Pusan in South Kyŏngsang Province. The legend is preserved in the *Record of Historical Traces at Pŏmŏ Monastery (Pŏmŏsa sajŏk ki):* In 678, in response to learning that the Japanese were mounting an invasion of Silla with a hundred thousand warships, Ŭisang traveled to Mount Kŭmjŏng, where single-mindedly he chanted sūtras for seven days and seven nights. In response to his act of religious piety there was an earthquake and a great flash of light. All of the buddhas, the kings of heaven, and the Divine Assembly, including the attendants of the Bodhisattva Mañjuśrī, appeared, brandishing weapons. These divine protectors loosed their weapons on the Japanese invaders, and the gods of the wind roused a black wind that caused the Japanese ships to crash into each other, killing all the soldiers and sailors.[68] The site of Ŭisang's chanting sūtras—probably the *Avataṃsaka*—would become Pŏmŏ Monastery. Although the story is obviously spurious—there is no evidence from either the *History of the Three Kingdoms* or the *History of Japan (Nihon shoki)* that there was an invasion in that year—it shows how Koreans of a later time, probably the ninth century, continued to reinterpret the reimagined history to provide legitimacy for their ever-changing religious and cultural landscape.

In his *Record of Mount Ch'ŏn'gwan (Ch'ŏn'gwansan ki)*, the Koryŏ monk Ch'ŏnin (1205–1248) records a story about how the Divine Assembly was supplicated to preserve the royal line of Silla during the tumultuous ninth century. When King Sinmu (r. 839) of Silla was crown prince, he was once reprimanded by the king and exiled to Wando, south of Mount Ch'ŏn'gwan in present-day South Chŏlla Province. The local Hwaŏm master, Hongjin, had long liked the crown prince. When he heard that the crown prince had been exiled and his succession was in question, he went to this monastery, worshipped, and sang praises to the Divine Assembly of the *Avataṃsaka Sūtra* diligently day and night. The whole Divine Assembly subsequently responded by singing and surrounding the peak to the south of the monastery, which was thereafter known as Divine Assembly Cliff (Sinjung'ak) in the Koryŏ period.[69] The Hwaŏm Master Hongjin is otherwise unknown, but the story suggests that the Hwaŏm cult of the Divine Assembly was known in southwestern Korea, deep in the former territory of Paekche, which was then under the control of the merchant prince Chang Pogo (d. 846). Furthermore, the main thrust of the story is that the cult of the Divine Assembly was invoked for the protection of the royal line of succession in Silla.

The cult also flourished at Haein Monastery from the late ninth century through the tenth century. This monastery was another of the ten Hwaŏm monasteries mentioned previously. It was first built in the early years of the ninth century by King Aejang and rose to prominence as an intellectual center of Hwaŏm learning by the end of the century. The Silla literatus Ch'oe Ch'iwŏn retired there and developed a close relationship with Saṃgha Overseer Hŭirang (fl. 875–927).

A stele record dating to 895, which was discovered inside a stone stūpa at a small mountain monastery on Mount Paeksŏng in the vicinity of Haein Monastery, provides evidence that the Divine Assembly was conceptualized as a distinct unit in the late ninth century. It does this by referring to various lists of names that in turn allude to the constituent parts of the *Avataṃsaka Sūtra*. For instance, after listing the titles of several sūtras that have been placed as relics in the stūpa, the record notes "the names of the two buddhas of the *Avataṃsaka*" *(Hwaŏm ibul myŏngho)*. The two buddhas, both of which are transliterations of Vairocana, are Nosana of the translation in sixty rolls and Pirojana of the translation in eighty rolls. Immediately afterward it notes "the names of the forty classes of the Divine Assembly" *(simnyu sinjung yŏlmyŏng)*, alluding to the opening section of the eighty-roll edition. The record goes on to refer to the names of the fifty-five spiritual mentors encountered by Sudhana, the names of the fifty-three buddhas, the names of the ten great disciples, and the names of the seven locations, nine assemblies, and thirty-nine sections or chapters of the sūtra (Kor. *p'um*, Ch. *pin*). This is followed by the titles of several other sūtras.[70] Hence, it is probable that the portion dealing with the Divine Assembly, like other sections of the *Avataṃsaka*

Sūtra, circulated separately and was the focus of its own cult in the late ninth century.[71] In this sense it was probably like the chapter of the *Lotus Sūtra* that circulated separately as the *Avalokiteśvara Sūtra.*

A narrative preserved in the *Old Monastic Records of Haein Monastery on Mount Kaya (Kayasan Haeinsa kojŏk)* suggests that Saṃgha Overseer Hŭirang was a practitioner of the cult of the Divine Assembly. At the end of the Silla period in the early tenth century, Hŭirang was the head monk at Haein Monastery and obtained the samādhi of the Divine Assembly of the *Avataṃsaka Sūtra (Hwaŏm sinjung sammae).* At that time, the account reports, Koryŏ king T'aejo (Wang Kŏn) fought with Wŏlgwang, a prince of Paekche.[72] Wŏlgwang held Mount Misung with plenty of provisions and stout soldiers. The king of Koryŏ, however, could not be subdued. He entered Haein Monastery and received instruction from Hŭirang. Having entered the powerful samādhi, the Hwaŏm master dispatched a large army of intrepid spiritual troops under the direction of the gods of the Divine Assembly to assist him. When Wŏlgwang saw their golden armor filling the sky he knew that they were divine warriors and surrendered immediately. The Koryŏ king became a disciple of Hŭirang and donated five hundred plots *(kyŏl)* of dry fields and rebuilt the buildings of the old mountain monastery.[73] As above, the gods of the Divine Assembly are deployed by a monastic adept in order to protect the person who will be the rightful ruler of the Korean peninsula.

The Hwaŏm cult of the Divine Assembly continued to flourish well into the early Koryŏ period. The *History of Koryŏ (Koryŏsa)* records that Wang Kŏn established a Divine Assembly Cloister (Sinjungwŏn) in Songdo (present-day Kaesŏng), the Koryŏ capital, in the year 924.[74] Furthermore, Hyŏngnyŏn Chŏng (fl. 1074–1105) reports not only that the early-Koryŏ-period monk Kyunyŏ (923–973) was well versed in the *Sūtra on the Divine Assembly (Sinjung kyŏng)* but that his own interest in Kyunyŏ, which led to his composing the *Life of Kyunyŏ (Kyunyŏ chŏn),* resulted from his fortuitous encountering of a certain Ch'angun in 1074, who was a master commentator on the same *Sūtra on the Divine Assembly.*[75] Although the evidence is circumstantial at best, the *Sūtra on the Divine Assembly* was not a new sūtra but was probably the portion of the first roll of the eighty-roll version of the *Avataṃsaka Sūtra* describing the forty classes of divine beings and probably circulated separately since the late ninth century.

The cult of the Divine Assembly assimilated the worship of the indigenous gods of mountains and rivers to the veneration of the buddhas and bodhisattvas. It brought to fruition a process begun soon after Buddhism was accepted as a state cult in Silla: the Buddhist transformation of ancient Silla's sacred sites by the building of monasteries and shrines within their precincts. The building of Hwaŏm monasteries on the five sacred mountains of Silla's conquest state are further evidence of the religion's domestication. By this means, the native gods and spirits of Silla's mountains were converted to Buddhism, and Silla was recognized as a once and future Buddha-land. By being defined geographically in terms of the *Avataṃsaka Sūtra,* Silla was thus endowed with all the limitless gods, spirits, buddhas, and bodhisattvas spoken of in Mahāyāna Buddhist scriptures, and these deities were responsive to adept monks and practitioners through cultic practices.

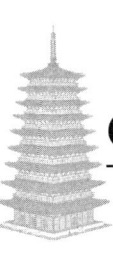

Concluding Reflections

Scholarship in East Asia and the West has hitherto described the process of the accommodation of Buddhism in Korea in terms of its assimilation of Sino-Indian and Chinese intellectual traditions, or schools. Since the colonial period, when Japanese Buddhologists portrayed their country as the most Buddhist country in the world by claiming, for polemical purposes, that "Japanese Buddhism"—the idea of this itself was a newly emerging concept—preserves all of the intellectual and practice-oriented traditions of Eastern Buddhism,[1] it has been a matter of necessity and pride for Korean Buddhologists to demonstrate that most of these traditions also flourished in ancient Korea, particularly during the Unified Silla period and, more important, that certain brilliant Koreans developed native intellectual traditions that emphasized uniquely Korean approaches to the Buddhadharma so that they might match up favorably with their Japanese neighbors.[2]

The problem with this is not only that it forces an arbitrary teleology onto and retroactively interprets Korean Buddhist history according to a model developed to serve a now-outdated agenda set by polemicists in a different country, but that the theoretical model itself compels adherents to make specious interpretations about the nature and goals of the ministries of influential historical Buddhists and to construct speculative schemata to prove that "Korean Buddhism" was no less endowed than "Chinese Buddhism" and "Japanese Buddhism." All of these ideas project arbitrary distinctions that limit our ability to see overarching connections in the process of the indigenization of Buddhism in Korea, not to mention unity among all the Buddhist traditions in East Asia.

For instance, the received tradition of five major schools of intellectual Buddhism in Silla comprises a Vinaya school (Kyeyulchong) founded by Chajang, a Nirvāṇa school (Yŏlbanjong) founded by Podŏk (fl. 650), a Dharma Nature school (Pŏpsŏngjong) founded by Wŏnhyo, a Hwaŏm school (Wŏnyungjong) founded by Ŭisang, and a Yogācāra school (Pŏpsangjong) founded by Chinp'yo.[3] Recently scholars have begun to question the assignation of these individuals as founders of particular schools.[4] Still more important, these arbitrary designations for the most part collapse when we approach these figures from the standpoint of the Buddhist cults in which they participated and the practical teachings they promoted. In the foregoing chapters we have seen the eminent monks Chajang, Wŏnhyo, and Ŭisang not only as important purveyors of cultic practices but also as key advocates of the *Avataṃsaka Sūtra* and Hwaŏm Buddhism. Even Chinp'yo's promotion of repentance rituals and his worship of Maitreya share much common ground with the penance practices observed in the Hwaŏm cult on Mount Odae.

Podŏk, a Koguryŏ monk who emigrated to Paekche prior to the unification wars in the seventh century, may be an exception. He is a cipher of a figure, and that a school is attributed to him is representative of what is wrong with this theory. The sole evidence for his being the "founder" of the Nirvāṇa school is a brief anecdote in *Memorabilia of the Three Kingdoms* reporting that he lectured on the *Nirvāṇa Sūtra* in forty rolls.[5] His school is presumed to have carried over to Silla after the conquest and unification of the Three Kingdoms. The historicity of Podŏk, however, is less important than the need for the historical existence of his school so that Korean Buddhism can have as many schools as Chinese and Japanese Buddhism.

Buddhist cults played a seminal role in the domestication of the Buddhadharma in Silla and in the development of Korean Buddhist culture. The approach of cults is more fruitful than focusing on schools because it tells us about what people did, were remembered as doing, or encouraged others to do; how Buddhist practices were deployed by people in different social strata; how the process of domestication was dominated by elites; and how Hwaŏm thought was translated into reality on the ground and became the most powerful Buddhist tradition in Silla. Hwaŏm, more than any other intellectual Buddhist tradition, provides the basis for understanding Korean Buddhism. This does not belittle the importance of Sŏn because it is the combination of these two that constitutes an important pillar of Chinul's (1158–1210) compelling and enduring Korean approach to Zen.[6]

As Buddhist cults spread throughout Silla, they embraced and subsumed preexisting religious practices and local cults. Furthermore, since Buddhism was a cosmopolitan religion that linked India, Central Asia, China, Korea, and Japan, the people of Silla needed to demonstrate the significance of their conversion to Buddhism to their Asian religious colleagues. This is best seen in the spiritual remapping of Silla. We have covered many examples of this phenomenon: the prophecy concerning

Concluding Reflections

seven future sites of Buddhist monasteries in Silla; the Buddha-land propaganda associating the site of Hwangnyong Monastery with the former Buddha Kāśyapa; the transplantation of Mount Wutai to Silla and the institution of the Hwaŏm-inspired state cult at Mount Odae; the location of Avalokiteśvara's Mount Potalaka at Naksan on Silla's east coast; the association of Silla's five peaks with monasteries of the Hwaŏm tradition; and the connection of other sacred mountains and monasteries with teachings or places mentioned in the *Avataṃsaka Sūtra,* such as Diamond Mountain and Haein Monastery.

Ŭisang's introduction of the Hwaŏm tradition to Korea provided for a Buddhist cosmology that contained several characteristics like those that are usually ascribed to tantric or esoteric Buddhism. The Hwaŏm practice Ŭisang introduced embraced the cultic worship of several deities—buddhas and bodhisattvas, such as Vairocana, Avalokiteśvara, and Amitābha—in its cosmology, as seen in the layout of monasteries such as Pulguksa. Its practices included the chanting of dhāraṇīs, the circumambulation of stūpas, repentance rituals, and the cultic worship of Maitreya, Avalokiteśvara, and Amitābha. Ŭisang received royal support to build monasteries, and the royalty used Hwaŏm cosmology in the formation of a state cult at Mount Odae that would perform rituals on behalf of the state and invoke the deities of the *Avataṃsaka Sūtra,* the Divine Assembly, to protect the state. Also, the major monasteries constructed in the eighth and ninth centuries were all associated with the Hwaŏm tradition and signal this Buddhist school's ascendancy on the Korean peninsula during the mid-Silla period. Furthermore, the doctrine of Tathāgatagarbha, emphasizing the inherent Buddha-nature or spiritual potential in all beings, which is central to Hwaŏm thought, rendered unnecessary the performance of tantric rituals that cause immediate enlightenment because, according to the Hwaŏm understanding of the Buddhist mārga, based on the concept of the interpenetration of all things (Ch. *shishi wuai,* Kor. *sasa muae*), beginning on the path to enlightenment by arousing the *bodhicitta* is ultimately the same as achieving total enlightenment.

Focusing on cults demonstrates that Korean Buddhism became centered upon the expansive vision of the *Avataṃsaka Sūtra* as the ultimate expression of Buddhist teaching. While the *Avataṃsaka* emphasizes the role of the Buddha Vairocana as the most profound expression of reality, it advocates the veneration of all buddhas and bodhisattvas as manifestations of Vairocana and intentionally encapsulates the whole of the Buddhist message and promotes universal participation on the bodhisattva path. The success of the synthesis of various Buddhist cults and ritual observances in Hwaŏm monasteries illustrates how Hwaŏm symbolism appealed to Silla's elites; and as we have seen, it was the only tradition to approach institutional status. The extant evidence about these cults, prior to their synthesis in the Hwaŏm tradition, suggests that they were instigated and promoted by aristocrats and social elites, both monks and laypeople, long before they became widespread among the common people.

Silla aristocrats and royalty built lavish monasteries and commissioned impressive icons of Maitreya and Avalokiteśvara during the sixth and seventh centuries. Royal and aristocratic devotion to the Dharma soon transferred to the vision of Buddhism promoted by the Hwaŏm tradition. They chanted dhāraṇīs and performed myriad other mainstream Buddhist practices invoking buddhas, bodhisattvas, and deities as a means of warding off evil influences and gaining protection from evil or danger. For the most part it was not until the eighth century that common people began to participate in these cults. My conclusions resonate with the findings of Peter Brown with respect to the development of Latin Christianity in early medieval Europe that religious and social elites were the main promulgators and supporters of religious cults. The evidence also shows that the cults of buddhas and bodhisattvas are interrelated and cannot be understood in Silla as separate traditions of religious devotion. In several anecdotes we have observed Avalokiteśvara playing an important intermediary role in the cults of Maitreya and Amitābha by facilitating and acknowledging people's attainment of enlightenment.

Buddhist cults and their synthesis in the Hwaŏm tradition were particularly suited to Silla's highly stratified society because they provided a means for expressing deep religious aspirations, they constituted methods for aristocrats and elites to ensure the continuation of their social ascendancy, and they were acceptable ways to display wealth and opulence. Silla's aristocratic elite first imported and assimilated the Buddhist culture of the Chinese Northern dynasties, with its emphasis on the close relationship between the state (royal family and aristocracy) and the church (saṃgha) and concomitant focus on Buddhist cults, particularly the cult of Maitreya. The cult of Maitreya was associated with many mainstream Buddhist practices that generate merit, such as sūtra recitation, stūpa circumambulation, meditative absorption, the making of images, and the personal observance of Buddhist precepts. All possible merit-making practices were included within the cult of Maitreya. In other words, to worship Maitreya was to be Buddhist. Vowing to be reborn in Tuṣita Heaven or to be reborn on the earth in the future when Maitreya comes was what pious Buddhists did, monastics and laypeople alike. Furthermore, chanting the name of Avalokiteśvara and reciting the Great Compassion Spell associated with him were encouraged by practice-oriented monks such as Ŭisang. An individual need not leave home to become a monk or immerse himself

Concluding Reflections 143

in intellectual learning to be assured the accumulation of great merit and a better rebirth.

The promotion of Buddhism by social elites in Silla set the stage for the universalization of Buddhism in Korea during the succeeding Koryŏ period. The predominance of anecdotes about elites reaffirms observations from later Korean history that Korean society has long been dominated by a small privileged population. These people were the trendsetters and the advocates of cosmopolitan and Buddhist culture on the Korean peninsula. In a world system defined, in the Buddhist way, ethically and socially in terms of causes and conditions based on karma acquired over previous lifetimes, Silla's elites were justified in their hereditary ascendancy by the very nature of their (re)birth into such a position in society. This belief provided support for the long-term stability of Silla's social order and encouraged emulation of the religious observances of the elites among the lower social strata, who sought to acquire the spiritual and material benefits enjoyed by the elites by making merit to become elites themselves in future lifetimes.[7] In this way the elites influenced the Buddhist beliefs and observances of the ordinary people in later generations.

Silla's cultural and religious leaders transplanted and domesticated Chinese Buddhist cults, specifically those of Maitreya, Avalokiteśvara, and Amitābha. Each of these cults first flourished because of aristocratic and royal patronage and devotion. These influential people alone possessed the hereditary privileges necessary to provide the economic means to make the Buddhist church viable in Silla. Although there is some evidence of lay Buddhist communities in Silla, modeled roughly after those found in China, even these were dominated by the privileged aristocrats. The dominant role played by elites in Silla reaffirms the general trends of later developments in Korean culture, such as the promotion of Zhu Xi's (1130–1200) revision of Confucianism during the late Koryŏ and early Chosŏn periods.[8] The promotion of Buddhist cults served to preserve social status and provide spiritual legitimation and symbolic resources that supplemented more visible economic and political resources.

The evidence I have presented in this book suggests that cult-oriented Buddhist practices ordinarily typified as "popular Buddhism" were performances first promoted by the social and religious elite of Silla, following the example set by their colleagues in China. Consequently, we need to reconsider what we mean when we deploy such terms as "elite" or "popular" religion, particularly for the case of Buddhism in East Asia. The promotion of cults by elites and aristocrats not only jibes with the conclusions of recent scholarship on the nature of early Latin and medieval Christianity but should cause us to rethink what we consider to be mainstream Sinitic Buddhism. By amplifying the study of Buddhism "on the ground"—to use Gregory Schopen's wording—we are better able to see how people understood and actually put into practice the doctrines found in sūtras and in exegetical literature. An emphasis on cults allows us to more fully appreciate the rich tapestry of Buddhist practices observed by Silla Buddhists. The predominance and overwhelming popularity of Buddhist cults and cultic activities also help explain why they continued to flourish in later times, despite the rhetoric denying their efficacy as deployed by certain advocates of the Chan/Sŏn tradition. The affirmation of cults as the way Buddhism looks on the ground may also help explain why other cults—such as the veneration of Chan masters and the worship of the Ten Kings (Ch. *shiwang*, Kor. *siwang*) and arhats (Ch. *luohan*, Kor. *nahan*)—were deployed later by Chan/Sŏn masters. The cults of Maitreya, Avalokiteśvara, and Amitābha, as well as the Divine Assembly of the *Avataṃsaka Sūtra*, were accommodated as mainstream Buddhism in Korea from the earliest times and have remained seminal aspects of Buddhist faith and culture until the present. By focusing on Buddhist cults and their associated practices, scholars will be able to develop a more nuanced understanding of Buddhist culture in the Sinitic world.

The approach of focusing on cults and cultic practices provides a useful and functional counterbalance to the traditional emphasis on intellectual traditions in the study of religion. It enables us to look at exegetes, religious elites, and aristocrats as religious practitioners first and tempers our understanding of their scholastic productions and political actions. To cite some of my favorite examples from the Western tradition, the focus on cults permits us to accept that Augustine, besides being a philosopher of tremendous capability, truly did believe in the miraculous power of Saint Martin of Tours manifest through his holy relics at various sites in Europe and that this faith may have provided the basis for his intellectual discourses contained in the *City of God*. It also allows us to accept that the great patronage King Henry VIII of England bestowed on the Catholic Church early in his reign, earning him the title Protector of the Faith, was definitely more than mere lip service to the Holy See and that the rituals he sponsored religiously demonstrate deep heartfelt beliefs that were discarded reluctantly and with great personal struggle when they collided with his overpowering obsession to father a son to be his heir to the English throne.

The cults and cultic practices contained in all religious traditions indicate religious observances that are shared across broad social and intellectual boundaries within particular cultures or religious communities. They show how people put scriptural pronouncements and prescriptions into practice on the ground and, in some cases, how scriptures themselves were venerated as objects of worship. The aspects of patronage, ritual procedures, and devotional display also hint at overarching similarities between distinct and diverse religious traditions. The study of religion cannot be divorced from social, political, and cultural history. A richer and more nuanced image of religion appears when devotional practice is not subordinated to doctrine and philosophy.

Appendix 1

The Divine Assembly from the *Avataṃsaka Sūtra* in Sixty Rolls

	NAME	SYNOPSIS OF ACCOMPLISHMENTS AND ACTIVITIES
1.	great bodhisattvas *(tae posal)*	All were spiritual mentors of Vairocana in previous lifetimes. They all cultivate a great ocean of meritorious virtue and all of the *pāramitās*. All acquire self-existence in the ocean of living beings. All acquire the universally worthy vow to satisfy the true bodies of all living beings.
2.	vajra-wielding warriors *(kŭmgang yŏksa)*	All make great vows to protect all the buddhas for limitless kalpas. They obtain immeasurable meritorious virtue and purity.
3.	enlightenment-site gods *(toryangsin)*	All make vows to practice in the presence of a buddha.
4.	dragon gods *(yongsin)*	All constantly adorn the dharma halls of the Tathāgatas for inconceivable kalpas in the past.
5.	Earth gods *(chisin)*	All arise from the same virtuous origin. They cultivate the vows and practices of the past buddhas.
6.	tree gods *(susin)*	All achieve the universal radiance of great happiness.
7.	medicinal-herb gods *(yakch'osin)*	All achieve the universal radiance of great compassion.
8.	grain gods *(koksin)*	All achieve the completion of great happiness.
9.	river gods *(hasin)*	All are able to benefit living beings with seminal diligence.
10.	ocean gods *(haesin)*	All are completely full of oceans of the Buddha's immeasurable meritorious virtue.
11.	fire gods *(hwasin)*	All radiate and remove darkness for living beings.
12.	wind gods *(p'ungsin)*	All are able to harmonize with living beings causing beings to not dissipate and scatter.
13.	gods of empty space *(hŏgongsin)*	All of their minds are without blemish, firm, pure, and sublime.
14.	gods who rule the directions *(chubangsin)*	All are able to provide wholesome radiance to all living beings.
15.	gods who rule the night *(chuyasin)*	All are discreet and love music in aiding the religious teaching (Dharma of the Path, *tobŏp*).
16.	gods who rule the day *(chujusin)*	All have confidence in the ornamentation of the pleasurable True Dharma *(chŏngbŏp)*.
17.	asura gods *(asurasin)*	All are able to subdue pride and debauchery.
18.	garuḍa kings *(karurawang)*	All have achieved expedient means to enrich living beings.
19.	kinnara kings *(kinnarawang)*	All are seminally diligent in encouraging living beings and are able to cause them to take pleasure in the Dharma.

	NAME	SYNOPSIS OF ACCOMPLISHMENTS AND ACTIVITIES
20.	mahoraga kings *(mahoragawang)*	All remove the net of ignorance for living beings.
21.	kumbhāṇḍa kings *(kubanch'awang)*	All habitually cultivate unhindered dharma approaches.
22.	kings of ghosts and spirits *(kwisinwang)*	All are able to provide diligent protection for all living beings.
23.	deities of the moon's body *(wŏlsin ch'ŏnja)*	All diligently use wisdom and universally arouse unsurpassed jeweled thoughts in living beings.
24.	deities of the sun *(ilch'ŏnja)*	All complete clean and pure wholesome roots and desire constantly to indulge and benefit living beings.
25.	kings of the heaven of the thirty-three gods *(samsipsamch'ŏnwang)*	All prepare clean and pure wholesome roots and are able to cause living beings to be reborn in pure and sublime places.
26.	kings of Yama's heaven *(Yamach'ŏnwang)*	All diligently cultivate and produce joy and contentment.
27.	kings of Tuṣita Heaven *(Tosolt'ach'ŏnwang)*	All achieve the dharma approaches to quiescence and subdue living beings.
28.	kings of the heaven of the pleasure of transformations *(hwarakch'ŏnwang)*	All complete the samādhi on recollecting the Buddha *(yŏmbul sammae)*.
29.	kings of the heaven of the self-existence of others' transformations *(t'ahwajajaech'ŏnwang)*	All diligently cultivate the True Dharma of self-existence.
30.	kings of the heaven of great Brahmā *(taebŏmch'ŏnwang)*	All are full of great mercy to ferry and liberate living beings, and they radiantly remove defilements. They are clear and cool, soft and pliant.
31.	kings of the heaven of light and sound *(kwangŭmch'ŏnwang)*	All peacefully dwell in dharma approaches of the light of happiness and expansive bliss.
32.	kings of the heaven of universal purity *(p'yŏnjŏngch'ŏnwang)*	All constantly cause living beings to dwell peacefully in expansive bliss.
33.	deities of the heaven of results and reality *(kwasil ch'ŏnja)*	All dwell wholesomely in mental approaches to quiescence.
34.	deities of immeasurable pure abodes *(muryang chŏnggŏch'ŏn)*	All have cultivated dharma realms of the signless and equanimity.

Source: From *Dafangguang fo huayan jing* 1, T 278, 9.395b–397a.

Appendix 2

The Divine Assembly from the *Avataṃsaka Sūtra* in Eighty Rolls

	NAME	SUMMARY OF ACCOMPLISHMENTS AND ACTIVITIES
1.	bodhisattva-mahāsattvas (*posal mahasal*)	They cultivate good roots with Vairocana and, by means of their vow, seek to help all beings obtain a wisdom body.
2.	vajra-wielding gods (*kŭmgangsin*)	They guard the places where buddhas dwell by means of their spiritual powers.
3.	multiple-body gods (*sinjungsin*)	They fulfill great vows made in the presence of past buddhas and serve them with offerings.
4.	footstep-following gods (*chokhaengsin*)	They are close associates with past buddhas, constantly following them.
5.	enlightenment-site gods (*toryangsin*)	They make extensive offerings to past buddhas, perfecting their mental capacities.
6.	city gods (*chusŏngsin*)	They adorn the palaces in which past buddhas stayed.
7.	Earth gods (*chujisin*)	They make solemn vows to always associate with buddhas and to always cultivate virtuous actions.
8.	mountain gods (*chusansin*)	They obtain pure eyes regarding all dharmas.
9.	forest gods (*churimsin*)	They preserve infinite lovable and pleasing glows.
10.	medicine gods (*chuyaksin*)	They help beings with kindness and compassion, being free from defilement.
11.	crop gods (*chugasin*)	They attain to the perfection of great happiness.
12.	river gods (*chuhasin*)	They concentrate on benefiting living beings.
13.	ocean gods (*chuhaesin*)	They fill their bodies with the great ocean of the virtues of the buddhas.
14.	water gods (*chususin*)	They strive diligently to rescue and protect all beings.
15.	fire gods (*chuhwasin*)	They manifest various kinds of light to destroy irritations to living beings.
16.	wind gods (*chup'ungsin*)	They work to dispel prideful thoughts.
17.	gods of empty space (*chugongsin*)	They possess minds that are flawless, vast, and pure.
18.	gods of the directions (*chubangsin*)	They continuously illuminate the ten directions.
19.	gods of the night (*chuyasin*)	They practice diligently, delighting in the True Dharma.
20.	gods of the day (*chujusin*)	They have faith in the sublime Dharma and work together to adorn the palace.
21.	asura [titan] kings (*asurawang*)	They strive to conquer pride and the other defilements.
22.	garuḍa kings (*karura wang*)	They perfect their skills in expedient means of liberation and are able to rescue all beings.

	NAME	SUMMARY OF ACCOMPLISHMENTS AND ACTIVITIES
23.	kinnara kings *(kinnarawang)*	They diligently contemplate all things with minds that are always blissful and that roam freely.
24.	mahoraga kings *(mahoragawang)*	They cultivate expedient means that cause living beings to tear apart the net of ignorance.
25.	yakṣa kings *(yach'awang)*	They strive to guard and protect all living beings.
26.	dragon kings *(yongwang)*	They work hard making clouds and spreading rain to cause the heat and afflictions of beings to dissipate.
27.	kumbhāṇḍa kings *(kubanch'awang)*	They study and practice the teachings of freedom from impediments and emit great light.
28.	gandharva kings *(kŏndalp'awang)*	They have deep faith in the great teaching and practice it diligently without lassitude.
29.	moon deities *(wŏlch'ŏnja)*	They strive to bring the light of the mind-jewel to living beings.
30.	sun deities *(ilch'ŏnja)*	They diligently learn and practice to benefit all beings and increase their wholesome roots.
31.	kings of the heaven of the thirty-three gods *(samsipsamch'ŏnwang)*	They strive to produce great works in all worlds.
32.	kings of Yama's Heaven *(Yamach'ŏnwang)*	They diligently cultivate wholesome roots, and their minds are always joyful and content.
33.	kings of Tuṣita Heaven *(Tosolt'ach'ŏnwang)*	They diligently recollect the names of all the buddhas.
34.	kings of the heaven of the pleasure of transformations *(hwarakch'ŏnwang)*	They work diligently to train living beings to enable them to obtain liberation.
35.	kings of the heaven of the self-existence of others' transformations *(t'ahwajajaech'ŏnwang)*	They diligently practice the vast dharma approaches of independent expedient means.
36.	kings of the heaven of great Brahmā *(taebŏmch'ŏn wang)*	They have great compassion for living beings, illuminate all things everywhere, and cause beings to be joyful and blissful.
37.	kings of the heaven of light and sound *(kwangŭmch'ŏnwang)*	They dwell in a state of unhindered peace, tranquility, joy, and bliss.
38.	kings of the heaven of universal purity *(p'yŏnjŏngch'ŏnwang)*	They abide securely in the great teaching and work diligently to benefit all realms of existence.
39.	kings of the heaven of vast results *(kwanggwach'ŏnwang)*	They dwell in peace in the palace of tranquility.
40.	kings of the heaven of great self-existence *(taejajaech'ŏnwang)*	They diligently contemplate the signless Dharma, and their actions are equanimous and impartial.

Sources: From *Dafangguangfo huayan jing* 1, T 279, 10.2a–5a. See also Thomas Cleary, trans., *The Flower Ornament Scripture,* 56–64.

Notes

Introduction

1. *Samguk yusa* 4, T 2039, 49.1005a–b; SYKY 4:340–341. Iryŏn's interlinear notes have been removed. For more discussion on this anecdote see Richard McBride, "The Vision-Quest Motif in Narrative Literature on the Buddhist Traditions of Silla," 28–31.

2. The traditional dates for Silla are 57 B.C.E –935 C.E. Kim Pusik defines Silla's three periods as the ancient period (*sangdae,* 57 B.C.E.–654 C.E.), the middle period (*chungdae,* 654–780), and the late period (*hadae,* 780–935) (*Samguk sagi* 12:127 [Kyŏngmun 9]). Following the dynastic chronology *(wangnyŏk)* attached to the front of the *Samguk yusa,* wherein Silla's three periods are defined as high antiquity (*sanggo,* 57 B.C.E.–514 C.E.), middle antiquity (*chunggo,* 514–654), late antiquity (*hago,* 654–935) (*Samguk yusa* 1, T 2039, 49.958b, 959c; SYKY 1:16, 20), scholars of Korean history typically consider the Silla epoch to belong to ancient Korea. However, since the Silla period also corresponds to what scholars refer to as China's medieval period (ca. 317–907), and since ancient Silla society corresponds well in many ways, I refer to it as early medieval and medieval in this book.

3. Peter Brown, *The Cult of the Saints,* 12–22.

4. See Brown, *The Cult of the Saints;* Gregory Schopen, *Bones, Stones, and Buddhist Monks;* and Michel Strickmann, "The *Consecration Sūtra:* A Buddhist Book of Spells," *Mantras et Mandarins,* and *Chinese Magical Medicine.*

5. Catherine Bell, *Ritual Theory, Ritual Practice,* 185. Although the ideas expressed by Bell are in the context discussing Hinduism, the same may well be said for Buddhism. See Erik Zürcher, *The Buddhist Conquest of China,* "Buddhist Influence on Early Taoism," and "Prince Moonlight: Messianism and Eschatology in Early Medieval Chinese Buddhism"; Tsukamoto Zenryū, *Shina Bukkyōshi kenkyū.*

6. Michel Strickmann, "India in the Chinese Looking-Glass," 59.

7. Bell, *Ritual Theory, Ritual Practice,* 124.

8. *Samguk sagi* 18:166 (Sosurim 2–5); cf. *Samguk yusa* 3, T 2039, 49.986a; SYKY 3:203–204. According to the *Lives of Eminent Monks (Gaoseng zhuan),* the Eastern

Jin monk Zhi Dun (Daolin, 314–366) sent a letter to an unnamed Koguryŏ monk speaking highly of another Chinese monk named Zhu Qian (Fashen, 268–374). See *Gaoseng zhuan* 4, T 2059, 50.348a12–15; Ahn Kye-hyŏn, "Koguryŏ Pulgyo ŭi chŏn'gae," 65–66.

9. *Samguk sagi* 24:222 (Ch'imnyu 2); *Samguk yusa* 3, T 2039, 49.986a; SYKY 3:204.

10. *Sam Mirŭk-kyŏng so,* T 1774, 38.317b21–24; HPC 2.99a13–17. Kyŏnghŭng's list is actually derived from a list developed by the Chinese Yogācāra monk Kuiji (632–682). See *Guan Mile shangsheng Doushuaitian jing zan* 2, T 1772, 38.295b22–29; Ahn Kye-hyŏn, *Silla chŏngt'o sasang yŏn'gu,* 90n38.

11. *Sam Mirŭk-kyŏng so,* T 1774, 38.317b24–29; HPC 2.99a17–23.

12. Schopen, *Bones, Stones, and Buddhist Monks,* 252.

13. See Arthur Whaley, *The Real Tripitaka,* 17, 21, 29, 37, 39, 40–41, 47, 93, 98, 113, 129; Sally Hovey Wriggins, *Xuanzang: A Buddhist Pilgrim on the Silk Road,* 96, 64, 86, 131; Richard McBride, "Dhāraṇī and Spells in Medieval Sinitic Buddhism," 101–102.

14. For discussion on Daoshi's dates see Chen Jinhua, *Monks and Monarchs, Kinship and Kingship,* 24–25n39. For more on the *Fayuan zhulin,* see Stephen F. Teiser, "T'ang Buddhist Encyclopedias"; Chen Yuzhen, "Daoshi yu *Fayuan zhulin.*"

15. See, for instance, Stephen F. Teiser, *The Ghost Festival in Medieval China,* 43–112; and Yü Chün-fang, *Kuan-yin: The Chinese Transformation of Avalokiteśvara.*

16. See Richard McBride, "A Koreanist's Musings on the Chinese *Yishi* Genre."

17. Henrik Sørensen, "Problems with Using the *Samguk yusa* as a Source for the History of Korean Buddhism," 271–288; see also Sørensen, "On the Sinin and Ch'ongji Schools and the Nature of Esoteric Buddhist Practice under the Koryŏ," 49–61.

18. See Richard McBride, "Is the *Samguk yusa* reliable?"

Chapter 1: Buddhism and the State in Silla

1. *Samguk sagi* 12:123–124 (Kyŏngmyŏng 5, *non*); *Samguk yusa* 1, T 2039, 49.968b; SYKY 1:79–80; *Koryŏsa* 2:12b–13a.

2. *Samguk yusa* 3, T 2039, 49.986a–b; SYKY 3:205–206.

3. *Samguk yusa* 3, T 2039, 49.986b; SYKY 3:205.

4. *Samguk yusa* 3, T 2039, 49.986a–987b; SYKY 3:205–210

5. Ahn Kye-hyŏn, "A Short History of Ancient Korean Buddhism," 3.

6. For an overview of ancient Silla religion see Richard McBride, "What is the ancient Korean religion?"

7. *Samguk yusa* 3, T 2039, 49.987b–988b; SYKY 3:212–219.

8. Ahn, "Koguryŏ Pulgyo ŭi chŏn'gae"; Kodama Daian, "Serindia and Paekche Culture," 118–120.

9. *Samguk sagi* 4:35–36 (Pŏphŭng 4, 7, 8).

10. The *Samguk sagi* version says nothing about Pak's head flying away to Mount Kŭmgang; however, this accretion to the story is found in both of the later versions preserved in the *Samguk yusa*. See note 11 below. This Kŭmgangsan, not the one in present-day North Korea, is also presumed to have been one of the three sacred mountains of Silla, so it makes sense that Pak's head would fly there as a symbolic representation of the mountain god's protection or reception of Buddhism. On the theories concerning the location of Kŭmgangsan, see Yi Pyŏngdo, *Kugyŏk Samguk sagi*, 499n5.

11. *Samguk sagi* 4:36 (Pŏphŭng 15); *Samguk yusa* 3, T 2039, 49.987b–988b; SYKY 3:212–219. There are essentially three versions of the tale of Ich'adon and King Pŏphŭng. I have followed the *Samguk sagi* account here for the most part, which Kim Pusik says is based on an account recorded in Kim Taemun's (fl. 704) *Miscellaneous Tales of Cock Grove (Kyerim chapchŏn)*. In the *Samguk yusa*, Iryŏn copies, because of its great detail, the "Community Compact for Burning Incense before the Tomb of [Pak Yŏm]ch'ok and Worshipping the Buddha" *(Ch'ok hyangbun yebul kyŏlsa mun)*, which was composed by Illyŏm (fl. 806–821), a monk of Namgan Monastery. Iryŏn preserves a third version of the story by alluding to a "local chronicle" *(hyangjŏn)* several times in interlinear notes because it contained other variations on the story not found in both his master narrative and the version found in the *Samguk sagi*.

12. Lee Ki-baik, *Silla sasangsa yŏn'gu*, 12, 76.

13. *Samguk sagi* 4:37 (Pŏphŭng 27).

14. *Samguk sagi* 4:37 (Pŏphŭng 18, 21).

15. Lee Ki-baik, *Silla sasangsa yŏn'gu*, 76–78.

16. *Samguk sagi* 4:37 (Pŏphŭng 23).

17. Lee Ki-baik, *Silla sasangsa yŏn'gu*, 79–80.

18. Narendra M. Pankaj, "The Life and Times of the Silla King Chinhŭng," 12–23.

19. *Apidamo jushe lun (AbhidarmakoŚabhāṣya)* 12, T 1558, 29.64b28–c9.

20. *Samguk sagi* 4:40 (Chinhŭng 33, Chinji). Kim Ch'ŏlchun suggests that the *sa* of Saryun is probably a transliteration of *soe*, meaning "iron." Since the older brother of the crown prince represents the copper wheel, it is appropriate to refer to the younger brother as the iron wheel. See Kim's "Silla sangdae sahoe ŭi Dual Organization (ha)," 91. See also Lee Ki-baik, *Silla sasangsa yŏn'gu*, 81n12.

21. *Samguk sagi* 4:38–39 (Chinhŭng 12, 19).

22. *Samguk sagi* 4:40 (Chinhŭng 37).

23. *Samguk sagi* 4:38 (Chinhŭng 5, 10).

24. *Samguk sagi* 4:39 (Chinhŭng 26).

25. *Samguk sagi* 4:38–39 (Chinhŭng 14, 27).

26. *Samguk sagi* 4:40 (Chinhŭng 33).

27. *Samguk sagi* 4:40 (Chinhŭng 35, 36).

28. See Kim Young-tai, "Mirŭk sŏnhwa ko," 145; Lee Ki-baik, *Silla sasangsa yŏn'gu*, 80–83.

29. The Buddhist scriptures strongly advise that monks should not bow to their parents or rulers, but one of the Buddhist leaders of the time, Faguo (fl. 396–398), promoted the revolutionary doctrinal concept that the Northern Wei Emperor Taizu, Daowu (r. 386–409), was not a mere earthly ruler but actually a living Buddha, a Tathāgata; therefore, it was proper for monks to bow to him. The Northern Wei rulers capitalized on this situation by making Faguo an imperial official over Buddhism, the "Buddhist Overseer" *(daoren tong)*, and thus causing Buddhism and the imperial state to be inseparably linked. See Tsukamoto Zenryū, "The Śramaṇa Superintendent T'an-yao and His Time," 371.

30. *Samguk sagi* 4:41 (Chinp'yŏng 1). See Kim Ch'ŏlchun, "Silla sangdae sahoe ŭi Dual Organization ha," 92; Lee Ki-baik, *Silla sasangsa yŏn'gu*, 81.

31. Lee Ki-baik, *Silla sasangsa yŏn'gu*, 81–82.

32. Kim Ch'ŏlchun, "Silla sangdae sahoe ŭi Dual Organization ha," 92.

33. *Samguk yusa* 3, T 2039, 49.990c5–6; SYKY 3:236–237; Lee Ki-baik, *Silla sasangsa yŏn'gu*, 82.

34. *Mile xiasheng jing*, T 453, 14.421a–423c; *Guan Mile shangsheng jing*, T 452, 14.418b–420c; Richard Rutt, "The Flower Boys of Silla," 1–66; Kim Young-tai, "Mirŭk sŏnhwa ko," 135–149. See Lee Ki-baik, *Silla sasangsa yŏn'gu*, 83n18.

35. Lee Kidong, *Silla kolp'umje sahoe wa hwarangdo*, 330–358; Lee Jong-Wook, *Silla kolp'umje yŏn'gu*, 372–373, 390.

36. Mishina Shōei, *Shiragi karō no kenkyū;* Lee Kidong, *Silla kolp'umje sahoe wa hwarangdo*, 32–33.

37. Kim Young-tai, "Sŭngnyŏ Nangdo ko," 255–274.

38. Richard McBride, "The *Hwarang segi* Manuscripts," 242–248; see also Peter H. Lee, *Lives of Eminent Korean Monks*, 67–68n314.

39. Lee Kidong, "Silla sahoe wa hwarangdo," 32–33; Lee Kidong, "Hwarangsang ŭi pyŏnch'ŏn e kwanhan kaksŏ," 105–109; Kim Sang-hyun, *Silla ŭi sasang kwa munhwa*, 521–523.

40. *Samguk yusa* 3, T 2039, 49.994c–995b; SYKY 3:266–270.

41. *Samguk sagi* 41:393–398; *Samguk yusa* 1, T 2039, 49.969a–b; SYKY 1:84–87.

42. *Samguk yusa* 2, T 2039.49, 973b–974b; SYKY 2:116–119.

43. *Chang ahan jing (Dīrghāgama)* 6, T 1, 1.41c29.

44. Lee Ki-baik, *Silla sasangsa yŏn'gu*, 83.

45. See Rhi Ki-yong, "Sangjingjŏk p'yohyŏn ŭl t'onghaesŏ pon 7–8 segi Silla mit Ilbon ŭi Pulgukto sasang," 507–534; also Rhi, "Shōchōteki hyōgen o tōshite mitaru shichi hasseki Shiragi oyobi Nihon no Bukkokuto shisō," 1–44. See also McBride, "What is the ancient Korean religion?" An example of the rapprochement between pre-Buddhist Korean religion and Buddhism is found in the tale of the "Holy Mother of Mount Fairy Peach." The goddess of the mountain appeared to a nun in a dream and told her where to find money with which to commission images of buddhas, supernatural beings, the gods of heaven, and the gods of the five sacred mountains of Silla to be enshrined in a monastery on the mountain.

The images were to be used in a special divination dharma assembly to benefit all people. See *Samguk yusa* 5, T 2039, 49.1011c–1012a; SYKY 5:387–389; for a translation see Peter H. Lee, *Sourcebook of Korean Civilization*, 94–95.

46. The system of worship at the sacred three mountains *(samsan)* of Silla is not well understood, and the identity of the three mountains is open to conjecture. Scholars, however, propose that the three mountains were on the Kyŏngju plain and correspond to Nangsan, which was roughly east of Kyŏngju; Kŭmgangsan, which was just north of the Silla heartland; and Orisan, southwest of the Silla capital. There was also a cult in Paekche centered on the worship of three mountains in Puyŏ Commandery: Paeksan, Osan, and Pusan. When Paekche flourished, gods were said to live on each of them and fly between them constantly. There must have been some interaction between the ancient Koreans and Japanese because, in the Nara area, where the early culture of Paekche and Silla was most influential, there was also a Japanese cult of three mountains. Three mountains in the vicinity of the Asuka capital—Unebi, Miminashi, and Kaguyama—were worshipped as the "three mountains of Yamato" *(Daiwa sansan)* and considered to be the dwelling place of the gods who founded Japan. *Samguk yusa* 2:98; T 2039, 49, 979b6–8; SYKY 2:157; see also Rhi Ki-yong, "Brief Remarks on the Buddha-land Ideology in Silla during the Seventh and Eighth Centuries," 165–166.

47. Rhi Ki-yong, *Han'guk Pulgyo yŏn'gu*, 509.
48. *Samguk yusa* 3, T 2039, 49.986b; SYKY 3:205–206.
49. Rhi, *Han'guk Pulgyo yŏn'gu*, 510–511.
50. *Samguk yusa* 3, T 2039, 49.989a–b; SYKY 3:226–228.
51. *Samguk yusa* 3, T 2039, 49.990a–b; SYKY 3:233–236. See also Rhi, "Brief Remarks," 168–169.
52. *Samguk yusa* 3, T 2039, 49.990b20–23; SYKY 3:235.
53. *Samguk yusa* 3, T 2039, 49.990b; SYKY 3:235–236.
54. For Chinese approaches to solving the problem of being a borderland to the homeland of Buddhism see Tansen Sen, *Buddhism, Diplomacy, and Trade*, 55–101.
55. Rhi, *Han'guk Pulgyo yŏn'gu*, 513; Rhi, "Brief Remarks," 170.
56. See Tsukamoto, "The Śramaṇa Superintendent T'an-yao and His Time," 371; James R. Ware, "Wei Shou on Buddhism," 127–128; see also Kenneth Ch'en, *Buddhism in China*, 146.
57. Kenneth Ch'en, *Buddhism in China*, 168–169. See also R. E. Emmerick, *The Sūtra of Golden Light*, 23–43.
58. *Samguk sagi* 4:40 (Chinhŭng 33).
59. *Guan Mile pusa shangsheng Doushuaitian jing*, T 452, 14.420a15; *Mile xiasheng jing*, T 453, 14.422c27; *Mile dachengfo jing*, T 456, 14.432a8–9.
60. Rhi, *Han'guk Pulgyo yŏn'gu*, 221. See also Kim Jongmyung, "Buddhist Rituals in Medieval Korea (918–1392)," 98–102.
61. *Samguk yusa* 3, T 2039, 49.990c18–19; SYKY 3:237; see also Ahn, "P'al-

gwanhoe ko." For the *p'algwanhoe* as practiced during the Koryŏ period, see Kim Jongmyung, "Buddhist Rituals," 170–192.

62. *Renwang bore boluomi jing*, T 246, 8.840a11–19; see also Chou Yi-liang, "Tantrism in China," 296n10; Mochizuki Shinkō, *Bukkyō kyōten seiritsu shiron*, 425–485; Rhi, *Han'guk Pulgyo yŏn'gu*, 163–193; Robert Buswell, *The Formation of Ch'an Ideology in China and Korea*, 44n8. For research on the function of this sūtra in sixth-, seventh-, and eighth-century China and an English translation, see Charles D. Orzech, *Politics and Transcendent Wisdom*, 207–288. It was held for the first time in Japan in 660 C.E.; see Marimus Willem de Visser, *Ancient Buddhism in Japan*, 1:116.

63. *Samguk sagi* 4:43 (Chinp'yŏng 35); 5:47 (Sŏndŏk 5). The mid-seventh-century *Xu gaoseng zhuan* biography of Wŏn'gwang says that he died in 630 (Iryŏn amends it 640 in an interlinear note), but since the *Samguk sagi* says he was alive in 636, modern scholars have attempted to amend his dates to roughly 555 to 638. Zanning's biography of Wŏnhyo contains a reference to another convocation that, if it indeed really occurred, must have taken place during the reign of either King Munmu (r. 661–681) or King Sinmun (r. 681–691). See *Song gaoseng zhuan* 4, T 2061, 50.730a6–b29; Rhi, *Han'guk Pulgyo yŏn'gu*, 185; and Robert Buswell, "Hagiographies of the Korean Monk Wŏnhyo." Although this and other assemblies were quite common during the succeeding Koryŏ (918–1392) as well, Buswell suggests that the allusion to the *Renwang jing* convocation in the *Song gaoseng zhuan* is probably only a legend since the date is unknown and no other historical evidence is extant. See his *Formation of Ch'an Ideology in China and Korea*, 44–47, especially 46n12.

64. *Samguk yusa* 2, T 2039, 49.974a8–9; SYKY 2:119.

65. *Samguk sagi* 9:97 (Hyegong 15), 11:117 (Hŏngang 2), 11:118 (Hŏngang 12), 11:119 (Chŏnggang 2), 11:119 (Chinsŏng 1); *Samguk yusa* 2:91, T 2039, 49.977b25–27; SYKY 2:145.

66. *Samguk sagi* 4:38 (Chinhŭng 14), 5:49 (Sŏndŏk 14).

67. Lee Ki-baik, *Silla sasangsa yŏn'gu*, 51–74; Han'guk Pulgyo Yŏn'guwŏn, *Silla ŭi p'yesa I*, 15–27.

68. "Hwangnyongsa kuch'ŭngt'ap ch'alchu pon'gi," in *Samguk Silla sidae Pulgyo kŭmsŏngmun kojŭng*, 180.

69. *Samguk yusa* 3, T 2039, 49.990c–991a; SYKY 3:236–240; see also Peter Lee, *Sourcebook*, 87–89.

70. See *Luoyang qielan ji* 1, T 2092, 51.999b–1000a; see also Yang Chŏngsŏk, "Silla Hwangnyongsa, Puk Wi Yŏngnyŏngsa kurigo Ilbon Taegwan Taesasa," 9–56.

71. See *Nihon shoki* 23:233–235 (Jomei 11); William Aston, *Nihongi*, 2:169; see also Yang Chŏngsŏk, *Hwangnyongsa ŭi choyŏng kwa wanggwŏn*, 153–170; Park Youngbok, "The Monastery Hwangnyongsa and Buddhism of the Early Silla Period," 140–153.

72. For a brief discussion of this ritual see Sørensen, "On the Sinin and Ch'ongji Schools," 55–60.

73. *Samguk yusa* 2, T 2039, 49, 972a–b; SYKY 2:107–108; Peter Lee, *Sourcebook*, 93; Han'guk Pulgyo Yŏn'guwŏn, *Silla ŭi p'yesa I*, 28–35.

74. *Samguk sagi* 38:362 (Sach'ŏnwangsa sŏngjŏn); *Samguk yusa* 2, T 2039, 49.963a–b; SYKY 2:113–116; Han'guk Pulgyo Yŏn'guwŏn, *Silla ŭi p'yesa I*, 41–48.

75. See Yi Hongjik, "Silla sŭnggwanje wa Pulgyo chŏngch'aek ŭi chemunje," 661–679; Nakai Shinkō, "Shiragi ni okeru Bukkyō tōsei kikan ni tsuite," 1–21; and Hŏ Hŭngsik, *Koryŏ Pulgyosa yŏn'gu*, 391–395; Han'guk Pulgyo Yŏn'guwŏn, *T'ongdosa*, 15–23.

76. *Samguk yusa* 5, T 2039, 49.1012c–1013a; SYKY 5:395–397; Hŏ Hŭngsik, *Koryŏ Pulgyosa yŏn'gu*, 392–395.

77. *Samguk yusa* 5, T 2039, 49.1010c–1011b; SYKY 5:380–384.

Chapter 2: The Cult of Maitreya

1. Tamura Enchō, *Kodai Chōsen Bukkyō to Nihon Bukkyō*, 68–97; Tamura, *Bukkyō denrai to kodai Nihon*, 84–173.

2. Suh Yoon-kil, "Silla Mit'a sasang," 287–304; Cho Aegi, "Shiragi ni okeru Miroku shinkō no kenkyū," 236–281; Tamura Enchō, "Kodai Chōsen no Miroku shinkō," 1–28.

3. Lee Yu-Min, "Ketumati Maitreya and Tuṣita Maitreya in Early China," part 1, 1–11, part 2, 1–11.

4. Jan Nattier, "The Meanings of the Maitreya Myth," 23–32.

5. Tsukamoto Zenryū, *A History of Early Chinese Buddhism*, 2:753–755; see also Hayami Tasuku, *Miroku shinkō*, 34–36; and *Fangguang bore jing*, 20 rolls, T 221, 8.1a–146c.

6. Arthur E. Link, "Biography of Shih Tao-an," 21, 36–37.

7. Tsukamoto, *Shina Bukkyōshi kenkyū*, 228–233, 368–369, 375–376, 377–382, 513; Hayami Tasuku, *Miroku shinkō*, 37–39.

8. See Jacques H. Kamstra, *Encounter or Syncretism: The Initial Growth of Japanese Buddhism*; and McBride, "The Vision-Quest Motif," 16–47.

9. Tsukamoto, *Shina Bukkyōshi kenkyū*, 564–594, 605–609.

10. Tsukamoto, *A History of Early Chinese Buddhism*, 2:756.

11. *Samguk Silla sidae Pulgyo kŭmsŏngmun kojŭng*, 13–14; Hwang Suyŏng et al., *Han'guk pulsang sambaeksŏn*, 33.

12. Ahn, "Short History," 7.

13. *Samguk Silla sidae Pulgyo kŭmsŏngmun kojŭng*, 15–16. The dating of this image is problematic. The first line of the inscription reads "the seventh year of the Yŏnggang reign period" and then adds the strange phrase "the year was the next *kap*" (*yŏnggang ch'illyŏn se ch'a kap*), but no such Koguryŏ reign period exists. Scholars have suggested that it might refer to the Yŏngnak reign period of King Kwanggaet'o, but that would place it about the year 396, a bit too early (p. 16).

14. *Samguk Silla sidae Pulgyo kŭmsŏngmun kojŭng*, 20–21.

15. Hwang Suyŏng et al., *Han'guk pulsang sambaeksŏn*, 24, 27, 36.

16. *Nihon shoki* 20:149 (Bidatsu 13); Aston, *Nihongi*, 101.

17. Yun Changsŏp, *Han'guk kŏnch'uksa*, 81–86; Ahn, "Short History," 11–12.

18. *Samguk sagi* 27:240, 241 (Pŏp 2, Mu 35); *Samguk yusa* 2, T 2039, 49, 978a. See also Jonathan Best, "Buddhism in Paekche," 75–78, 233n56.

19. *Samguk yusa* 2, T 2039, 49.979b–c; SYKY 2:158–160; translation adapted from Ahn, "Short History," 11.

20. Jonathan W. Best, "Imagery, Iconography and Belief in Early Korean Buddhism," 31–32; Hwang Suyŏng et al., *Han'guk pulsang sambaeksŏn*, 81–89 (nos. 60–68), 96 (no. 75), 140 (no. 42), 143 (no. 45), 150 (no. 51).

21. See Lewis R. Lancaster, "Maitreya in Korea," 135–153; and Kim Samyong, *Han'guk Mirŭk sinang ŭi yŏn'gu*.

22. Korean scholars have presented an argument for reading the name "Misi" as "Miri," which is a closer cognate to "Maitreya." For a discussion of "Miri" see Kim Sanggi, "Hwarang kwa Mirŭk sinang e taehayŏ," 3–12.

23. *Samguk yusa* 3:153–155, T 2039, 49.994c–995b; for an English translation of this story see McBride, "Vision-Quest Motif," 25–27.

24. Suh, "Silla Mirŭk sasang," 297.

25. *Samguk yusa* 2, T 2039, 49.973b–974b; SYKY 2:117–118.

26. For a more detailed discussion of Kim Yusin and his significance as a historical figure see Richard McBride, "Hidden Agendas in the Life Writings of Kim Yusin," 101–142.

27. *Mile xiasheng jing* 1, T 453, 14.421a–423b; *Mile xiasheng chengfo jing* 1, T 454, 14.423c–425c.

28. *Samguk sagi* 41:394.

29. *Samguk sagi* 41:394; McBride, "Hidden Agendas," 110–113. Yi Pyŏngdo suggests instead that because the story takes place before the Silla unification, the Central Peak mentioned in the Kim Yusin story must be one of the three sacred mountains of Silla: Naeryŏk, Korhwa, and Hyŏllye. If one accepts the position that Korhwa refers to Mount Kŭmgang and is the Northern Peak (Pugak), Yi says that Hyŏllye, which he equates to Mount Orye in Ch'ŏngdo County, is the best candidate for the Central Peak. See Yi, *Kugyŏk Samguk sagi*, 615n4. Kim Sayŏp follows Yi in suggesting Mount Orye as the Central Peak. See Kim, *Sankoku shiki: kan'yaku*, 716n3. I think that Mount P'algong in the vicinity of Taegu may be the Central Peak mentioned here because Silla's three sacred mountains are never referred to this way in the text of the *Samguk sagi*. The Central Peak mentioned in the story may just as well be an anachronistic reference to the central peak of the five-peak system *(oak)* of Unified Silla, which is Mount P'algong. See *Samguk sagi* 32:314 (Taesa, Chungsa).

30. *Samguk yusa* 3, T 2039, 49.991c; SYKY 3:244–245.

31. See Han'guk Pulgyo Yŏn'guwŏn, *Silla ŭi p'yesa II*, 25–26, 74–78.

32. *Samguk sagi* 6:59 (Munmu 2); 6:62 (Munmu 7), ranked as *taeach'an;* 6:65 (Munmu 9, 10), ranked as *p'ajinch'an;* 42:400–401 (Kim Yusin 2); 44:414 (Kim Inmun), ranked as *haech'an;* 46:429 (Kangsu). See John Jamieson, "The *Samguk Sagi* and the Unification Wars," 180, 186.

33. *Samguk yusa* 5, T 2039, 49.1010b–c.

34. For the names of Maitreya's parents see the *Mile xiasheng jing* 1, T 453, 14.421b29–c3; and for the names of Amitābha's parents see the *Amituo guyin shengwang tuoluoni jing* 1, T 370, 12.352b24–25. See Kim Young-tai, "Silla Paegwŏlsan isŏng sŏrhwa ŭi yŏn'gu," 34n2; Cho Aegi, "Shiragi ni okeru Miroku shinkō no kenkyū," 258n18; and Suh Yoon-kil, "Silla ŭi Mit'a sasang," 302n71.

35. *Samguk yusa* 3, T 2039, 49.995b–996b; SYKY 3:270–277.

36. For a quick list of the seventeen stages see *Yuga shidi lun* (*Yogācārabhūmi*, Treatise on the stages of the Yogācāra) 1, T 1579, 30.279a. They are described in the "Section on Basic Stages" *(bendi fen)*, *Yuga shidi lun*, T 1579, 30.279a–577c.

37. *Samguk Silla sidae Pulgyo kŭmsŏngmun kojŭng*, 68–69; *Samguk yusa* 3, T 2039, 49.1000b; SYKY 3:304–305.

38. These rituals and divination ceremonies have been studied in detail by Kim Young-tai, "Silla chŏmch'al pŏphoe wa Chinp'yo ŭi kyobŏp yŏn'gu," 99–136; Chŏng Pyŏngjo, "Silla sidae Chijang sinhaeng ŭi yŏn'gu," 327–344; and Ch'ae Inhwan, *Shiragi Bukkyō kairitsu shisō kenkyū*, 505–629.

39. *Song gaseng zhuan* 14, T 2061, 50.793c29–794c14; cf. *Shenseng zhuan* 7, T 2064, 50.997b–998a; cf. *Xinxiu kefen luxue seng zhuan* 28, X 133.465a–c.

40. *Samguk yusa* 4, T 2039, 49.1007b–1008a; SYKY 4:356–361.

41. *Samguk yusa* 4, T 2039, 49.1008a–1009a; SYKY 4:361–367.

42. See *Samguk Silla sidae Pulgyo kŭmsŏngmun kojŭng*, 93–109; *Chōsen kinseki sōran* 1:426–430; and *Han'guk kŭmsŏk chŏnmun*, 925–930.

43. For a detailed description of the sūtra's teaching see Whalen Lai, "The *Chan-ch'a ching*: Religion and Magic in Medieval China," 179–182. For the 189 fates see *Zhancha shane yebao jing* 1, T 939, 17.905b–906c.

44. For other studies on this divination repentance ritual see Kim Young-tai, "Chŏmch'al pŏphoe wa Chinp'yo ŭi kyobŏp sasang" and "Silla chŏmch'al pŏphoe wa Chinp'yo ŭi kyobŏp yŏn'gu."

45. See *Samguk yusa* 4, T 2039, 49.1008a–1009a; SYKY 4:361–367; Kim Samyong is mistaken in suggesting that he received the prophecy of his future buddhahood in 766; see Kim, *Han'guk Mirŭk sinang ŭi yŏn'gu*, 150–151.

46. Han'guk Pulgyo Yŏn'guwŏn, *Kŭmsansa*, 67.

47. Han'guk Pulgyo Yŏn'guwŏn, *Pŏpchusa*, 20–21, 85–90.

48. *Samguk yusa* 2, T 2039, 49.974b–c; SYKY 2:122–126.

49. See Joseph Edkins, *Chinese Buddhism*, 208.

50. See James A. Benn, "Temperance Tracts and Teetotalers under the T'ang," 43. The Chinese pilgrim Yijing (fl. 635–713) also mentions the practice of boiling tea for offerings in his travels; see *Nanhai jigui neifa zhuan* 2, T 2125, 54.218a15.

51. Benn, "Temperance Tracts and Teetotalers," 12–13. See *Quan Tang shi* 8017:9211.

52. See *Foshuo guan Mile pusa shangsheng Doushuaitian jing jiangjing wen*, in *Dunhuang bianwen jiaozhu* 5:960–968.

53. Seven distinct manuscripts of sermon notes on this sūtra exist, but the character of Maitreya appears to play an important role in only three. See *Weimo-*

jie jing jiangjing wen 4, 6, and 7, in *Dunhuang bianwen jiaozhu* 5:857–883 (4), 5:903–912 (6), 5:913–923 (7).

54. See *Chajiu lun*, in *Dunhuang bianwen jiaozhu* 3:423.
55. *Song gaoseng zhuan* 26, T 2061, 50.874b25–26.
56. *Fozu tongji* 14, T 2035, 49.374c10–12.
57. Han'guk Pulgyo Yŏn'guwŏn, *Kŭmsansa*, 43.
58. See Han'guk Pulgyo Yŏn'guwŏn, *Silla ŭi p'yesa II*, 45–50.
59. *Samguk yusa* 4, T 2039, 49.1009c; SYKY 4:373; translation following Peter Lee, *Sourcebook*, 186.
60. See *Sŏng yusing-non hakki*, X 80.1a–3a; HPC 3.483b–690c; Peter Lee, *Sourcebook*, 186–191.
61. Ch'ae Inhwan, *Shiragi Bukkyō kairitsu shisō kenkyū*, 353–354.
62. *Samguk yusa* 4, T 2039, 49.1009c–1010a; SYKY 4:373–375. See also Ch'ae, *Shiragi Bukkyō kairitsu shisō kenkyū*, 353–361.
63. Inoue Hideo, "The Reception of Buddhism in Korea and Its Impact on Indigenous Culture," 30–41.
64. *Silla sui chŏn*, "Sinhwa yot'ap," 173. The story is preserved in the Chosŏn-period encyclopedia dictionary of Korean words, *Taedong unbu kunok* 20:625a9–10; see also Yi Kŏmguk and Ch'oe Hwan, *Silla sui chŏn chipkyo wa yŏkchu*, 44.
65. *Samguk yusa* 5, T 2039, 49.1013a–b; SYKY 5:399–401. For alternative translations of the poem see Peter H. Lee, *Studies in the Saenaenorae*, 66–67, or Lee, *Sourcebook*, 1:207. He also composed another impromptu piece called "Song of Scattering Flowers," which has not been presented.
66. *Samguk Silla sidae Pulgyo kŭmsŏngmun kojŭng*, 137; *Han'guk kŭmsŏk chŏnmun* 1:165.
67. *Samguk Silla sidae Pulgyo kŭmsŏngmun kojŭng*, 244–245; see "Yu Tang Sillagukko yangjo kuksa kyoik tae Nanghye hwasang paegwŏl pogwang chi t'appimyŏng pyŏngsŏ," in Ch'oe Yŏngsŏng, *Yŏkchu Ch'oe Ch'iwŏn chŏnjip*, 1:97–98.
68. *Da Tang xiyu ji* 9, T 2087, 51.919b. See also Kwak Sŭnghun, *T'ongil Silla sidae ŭi chŏngch'i pyŏndong kwa Pulgyo*, 240–241, for a brief review of Korean scholarship on the significance of this story.
69. "Silla Such'anggun hoguksŏng p'algak tŭngnu ki" (The record on the eight-sided lamp tower at the state protection fortress in Sunch'ang Commandery), in *Tongmunsŏn* 64:10b–13a (esp. 12a); see also Ch'oe Yŏngsŏng, *Yŏkchu Ch'oe Ch'iwŏn chŏnjip*, 2:295–306.
70. Kegasawa Yasunori, "Zuimatsu Mirokukyō no ran o meguru ichikōsatsu," 15–32.
71. *Zizhi tongjian* 182:5686–5687; Stanley Weinstein, *Buddhism under the T'ang*, 154–155n1.
72. Weinstein, *Buddhism under the T'ang*, 41–43, and 162–164nn15–30. See also Antonino Forte, *Political Propaganda and Ideology in China at the End of the Seventh Century*.
73. Kanaoka Shoko, "Donkō bunken yori mitaru Miroku shinkō no ichishokumen," 38.

74. *Samguk sagi* 50:453.

75. *Baoyu jing,* T 660, 16.284a–c; Zürcher, "Prince Moonlight," 26–27.

76. For a more detailed discussion of these issues see Yi Yŏngja, "Namal Hu Samguk Mirŭk sinang ŭi sŏngkyŏk"; and McBride, "Why did Kungye claim to be the Buddha Maitreya?"

77. Kim Samyong, *Han'guk Mirŭk sinang ŭi yŏn'gu,* 150n1; Hŏ Hŭngsik, *Koryŏ Pulgyosa yŏn'gu,* 586, 592.

78. *Koryŏsa* 2:12b.

79. For the importance of Hwaŏm symbolism in the Silla-Koryŏ transition see Kim Tujin, *Kyunyŏ Hwaŏm sasang yŏn'gu,* and Cho Insŏng, "Kungye ŭi seryŏk hyŏngsŏng kwa Mirŭk sinyang," 23–52.

80. See Han Kimun, *Koryŏ sawŏn ŭi kujo wa kinŭng,* 40–48, 311; Hŏ Hŭngsik, *Koryŏ Pulgyosa yŏn'gu,* 75, 85, 94, 220, 300; and Yi Chŏng, *Han'guk Pulgyo sach'al sajŏn,* 179.

81. *Koryŏsa* 2:12b, 14a; *Sinjŭng Tongguk yŏji sŭngnam* 18:16a–b.

82. Chen Jinhua, "The Tang Buddhist Palace Chapels," 101–102.

83. Han Kimun, *Koryŏ sawŏn ŭi kujo wa kinŭng,* 40–48; Hŏ Hŭngsik, *Koryŏ Pulgyosa yŏn'gu,* 14–15, 298, 301.

Chapter 3: The Cult of Avalokiteśvara

1. Yü, *Kuan-yin,* 31–149.

2. *Miaofa lianhua jing* 7, T 262, 9.56c–58b; Leon Hurvitz, *Scripture of the Lotus Blossom of the Fine Dharma,* 311–319.

3. *Miaofa lianhua jing* 7, T 262, 9.57a–c; see also Hurvitz, *Scripture,* 314–315.

4. *Shoulengyan jing* 6, T 945, 19.128b–129a; see also Charles Luk, *The Śūraṃgama Sūtra,* 136–139.

5. Also called the *Sūtra of Life-saving Avalokiteśvara (Jiusheng Guanshiyin jing);* see *Fayuan zhulin* 17, T 2122, 53.411b24–c5. A sūtra roll has been preserved in Japan with this title. See *Gaowang Guanshiyin jing,* one roll, T 2895, 85.1425b–1426a.

6. See Richard McBride, "Is there really 'esoteric' Buddhism?" and McBride, "Dhāraṇī and Spells in Medieval Sinitic Buddhism"; see also Robert H. Sharf, *Coming to Terms with Chinese Buddhism,* 263–278. That esoteric Buddhism was not (yet) recognized as a category, Abé suggests, is punctuated by the fact that in Nara Japan (710–794), the thousand-armed Avalokiteśvara was not yet understood or appreciated in its true "esoteric" form. See Abé Ryūichi, *The Weaving of Mantra,* 157–163.

7. See *Fayuan zhulin* 60, T 2122, 53.736c10–737c10; McBride, "Dhāraṇī and Spells."

8. *Gaoseng Faxian zhuan,* T 2085, 51.859b27–28, 866a3–4, 866a18–19; see also James Legge, *A Record of Buddhistic Kingdoms,* 46, 112, and 113.

9. Kenneth Ch'en, *Buddhism in China,* 341; Hayami Tasuku, *Kannon shinkō,* 3–17.

10. Yü Chün-fang notes that of the three earliest collections of miracle tales

concerning Avalokiteśvara, which were completed by the end of the fifth century, fifty stories take place in northern China as opposed to thirty in southern China; see Yü, *Kuan-yin*, 162. See also Makita Tairyō, *Rikuchō koitsu Kanzeon ōikenki no kenkyū*; Hayami Tasuku, *Kannon shinkō*, 17–38.

11. Makita, *Rikuchō koitsu Kanzeon ōken-ki no kenkyū*, 3–108, esp. 58–60. The text—which was discovered earlier this century in a Japanese monastery—is divided into three sections, each compiled by a different person. The tale of Palchŏng and an account of a Paekche monastery built on royal command that was destroyed by lightning in 639 are appended to the third section, which was composed by a Southern Qi official, Lu Gao (459–532). See also Jonathan W. Best, "Tales of Three Paekche Monks Who Traveled Afar in Search of the Law," 148n20.

12. *Fahua zhuanji* 6, T 2068, 51.72a–72c.

13. See Best, "Tales of Three Paekche Monks," 148–152.

14. Hwang et al., *Han'guk pulsang sambaeksŏn*, 40–71.

15. Ahn, "Short History," 12. On the Paekche connection to the Yumedono Kannon see Jonathan W. Best, "Early Korea's Role in the Stylistic Formulation of the Yumedono Kannon, a Major Monument of Seventh-Century Japanese Buddhist Sculpture," 13–26.

16. Jonathan W. Best, "Early Korean Buddhist Bronzes and Sui Regional Substyles," 492–501.

17. Best, "Imagery, Iconography and Belief," 32–33; Hwang Suyŏng et al., *Han'guk pulsang sambaeksŏn* 77–78 (nos. 56, 57), 124–126 (nos. 26, 27, 28), 138 (no. 40), and 142 (no. 44).

18. *Samguk sagi* 1:59; Sin Chongwŏn, *Silla ch'ogi Pulgyosa yŏn'gu*, 252. The change from Murim to Horim is probably the result of Iryŏn's deploying the tiger-*ho* logograph in place of the martial-*mu* logograph for reasons of taboo.

19. *Xu gaoseng zhuan* 24, T 2060, 50.639a8–17; *Samguk yusa* 4, T 2039, 49.1005a17–18; SYKY 4:339.

20. *Miaofa lianhua jing* 7, T 262, 9.56c–57a; Hurvitz, *Scripture*, 313.

21. Sin, *Silla ch'ogi Pulgyosa yŏn'gu*, 254.

22. On the levirate custom in Silla see *Samguk sagi* 16:152–154; translated in Peter Lee, *Sourcebook*, 1:53–55. For neo-Confucian influences on Korean marriage practices in the Chosŏn period (1392–1910) see Martina Deuchler, *The Confucian Transformation of Korea*, 231–281.

23. See Makita Tairyō and Suwa Gijun, *Tō kosōden sakuin*, 4:923.

24. In Buddhist sources, the monk Chajang is seen as the influential aristocratic monk who encouraged the Silla government to replace the indigenous apparel and customs of Silla with Tang Chinese dress, rites, and calendar. See *Xu gaoseng zhuan* 24, T 2060, 50.639c26–29; *Samguk yusa* 4, T 2039, 49.1005c9–13. However, in the official Korean histories, this honor is attributed to Kim Ch'unch'u (King T'aejong Muyŏl, r. 654–661), the first king of Unified Silla. See *Samguk sagi* 5:51; and *Tongguk t'onggam* 7, 1:191.

25. For Kim Inmun's official biography see *Samguk sagi* 44:412–414; for a translation see Jamieson, "The *Samguk Sagi* and the Unification Wars," 174–180.
26. *Samguk yusa* 2, T 2039, 49.972c; SYKY 2:109.
27. *Samguk sagi* 44:413–414; see also Jamieson, "The *Samguk Sagi* and the Unification Wars," 179–180.
28. See Chou, "Tantrism in China," 309–310; see also Chen Jinhua, "The Tang Buddhist Palace Chapels," 101–102.
29. *Guan Wuliangshou jing* 1, T 365, 12.344c–345a; Inagaki Hisao, *The Three Pure Land Sūtras*, 109–111.
30. See Pulgyo Munhwa Yŏn'guwŏn, *Han'guk Chŏngt'o sasang yŏn'gu*, 453.
31. *Paekhwa toryang parwŏn mun*, HPC 2:9a.
32. Great Compassion Spell (Ch. *dabei zhou*), in *Qianyan qianbi Guanshiyin pusa tuoluoni shenzhou jing* 1, T 1057, 20.84a–c, 90b–91a; *Qianshou qianyan Guanshiyin pusa guangda yuanman wuai dabeixin tuoluoni jing* 1, T 1060, 20.107b–c; Lewis R. Lancaster, *The Korean Buddhist Canon*, 108–109 (c.v. K 292, K 294). See also Maria Reis-Habito, "The Great Compassion Dhāraṇī."
33. The five heinous crimes (Ch. *wuni*) are patricide, matricide, killing an arhat, shedding the blood of a buddha, and destroying the harmony of the saṃgha. See *Apidamo jushe lun* (*Abhidharmakośabhāṣya*) 17, T 1558, 29.926b27–29.
34. *Qianyan qianbi Guanshiyin pusa tuoluoni shenzhou jing* 1, T 1057, 20.84c–85b.
35. *Qianshou qianyan Guanshiyin pusa guangda yuanman wuai dabeixin tuoluoni jing* 1, T 1060, 20.107a.
36. The *Thousand Hands Sūtra* is the principal chant used in all offering ceremonies and funeral observances in Korean monasteries today. In this text, the Great Compassion Spell is called the Great Dhāraṇī of Spiritually Sublime Phrases (*Sinmyo changgu tae tarani*). Cf. *Qianshou qianyan Guanshiyin pusa guangda yuanman wuai dabeixin tuoluoni jing* 1, T 1060, 20.107b24. For a Sino-Korean transliteration of the dhāraṇī see Robert Buswell, *The Zen Monastic Experience*, 229, 238–239.
37. *Huayan jing* 50, T 278, 9.717c28–29; roll 51, T 278, 9.718a–19a (Avalokiteśvara is called Guanshiyin); *Huayan jing* 68, T 279, 10.366c–67b (Avalokiteśvara is called Guanzizai). See also Thomas Cleary, *The Flower Ornament Scripture*, 1275–1280.
38. See Yü Chün-fang, "P'u-t'o Shan: Pilgrimage and the Creation of the Chinese Potalaka," 191.
39. *Sinjŭng Tongguk yŏji sŭngnam* 44:39a1.
40. Han'guk Pulgyo Yŏn'guwŏn, *Naksansa*, 13–40.
41. *Samguk yusa* 3, T 2039, 49.996c–997c; SYKY 3:278–280.
42. See Yü Chün-fang, "Guanyin: The Chinese Transformation of Avalokiteśvara," 169–172; Rolf A. Stein, "Avalokiteśvara/Kouan-yin: un exemple de transformation d'un dieu en deesse," 28; *Tuoluoni zaji* 6, T 1336, 21.612b17–20; and *Tuoluoni zaji* 10, T 1336, 21.635a22–24.

43. See, for instance, Daniel B. Stevenson, "Pure Land Buddhist Worship and Meditation in China," 377–379.
44. *Bore boluomiduo xin jing* 1, T 251, 8.848c.
45. *Samguk yusa* 3, T 2039, 49.996a; SYKY 3:281.
46. *Samguk yusa* 4, T 2039, 49.992c–993a; SYKY 4:250–254.
47. See Hayami Tasuku, "Narachō no Kannon shinkō ni tsuite," 155–156. See also Kyoko Motomochi Nakamura, *Miraculous Stories from the Japanese Buddhist Tradition*, 84–87; and George J. Tanabe, Jr., and Willa Jane Tanabe, *The Lotus Sutra in Japanese Culture*.
48. See Waley, *The Real Tripitaka*, 17, 29, and 98; and Kenneth Ch'en, *Buddhism in China*, 235.
49. Amoghapāśa is one of the six forms of Avalokiteśvara who snatches up beings, like fish, in his unerring net of mental emptiness *(bukong juansuo)* in the great sea of rebirth and death and carries them to the shore of nirvāṇa. For more on the myriad manifestations and activities of this bodhisattva see *Bukong juansuo shenbian zhenyan jing (Amoghapāśakalparāja)* 1, T 1092, 20.227b20–29; and 228b23–29a10.
50. Yü, "Guanyin," 151–181, esp. 152–155; Kobayashi Taichirō, "Tōdai no Daihi Kannon," 43–68.
51. *Bukong juansuo tuoluoni jing* 1, T 1096, 20.409a–421b.
52. For a descriptive account of Amoghapāśa's myriad forms and expedients see *Bukong juansuo shenbian zhenyan jing* 1, T 1092, 20.227b20–29; 228b23–229a10.
53. *Kaiyuan shijiao lu* 9, T 2154, 55.566b16–24.
54. See McBride, "Is there really 'esoteric' Buddhism?"
55. See McBride, "Dhāraṇī and Spells."
56. The masks made by the bodhisattva, which are described in the text, bear a striking resemblance to some of the masks used in traditional Korean mask dance, a type of folk drama featuring stock characters and social situations. The basic materials of these masks were dried gourds, paper, wood, and pine bark. Some of these masks have removable chins. The most prominent examples come from the Hahŏe masks *(Hahŏe pyŏlsin kamyŏn)* used in the town's mask dance exorcism *(Hahŏe pyŏlsin kut)*. Six of the nine remaining masks (originally there were twelve) have removable chins: the Aristocrat *(yangban)*, the Scholar *(sŏnbi)*, the Depraved Monk *(chung)*, the Foolish Servant *(ime)*, and the Butcher *(paekchŏng)*. Each of the masks displays a hilarious expression. Some scholars suggest that some of these masks date from the Koryŏ period (918–1392), but no document has been found to support this claim. Cho Oh-kon proposes some influence from both Buddhist and Confucian art; however, to my knowledge, no scholar has suggested the existence of any link between the tale and this activity of nonelite social strata during the Chosŏn period. See Cho Oh-kon, *Traditional Korean Theatre*, 116–119.
57. *Samguk yusa* 5, T 2039, 49.1012c–13a; SYKY 5:395–397.

58. See Yü, "Guanyin," 154–155.

59. *Guan Wuliangshou jing* 1, T 365, 12.344c9–46a25; Inagaki, *The Three Pure Land Sūtras*, 110–117; Takakusu Junjirō, *Amitāyur-dhyāna-sūtra: The Sūtra on the Meditation of Amitāyus*, 188–198.

60. *Samguk yusa* 3, T 2039, 49.993a; SYKY 3:254.

61. See Han'guk Pulgyo Yŏn'guwŏn, *Silla ŭi pyesa I*, 92–99.

62. *Samguk yusa* 3, T 2039, 49.996b–c; SYKY 3:277–228. For an alternate translation of the *hyangga* see Peter H. Lee, *Studies in the Saenaenorae*, 75.

63. Kimura Toshihiko and Takenaka Chitai, *Zen no darani*.

64. Buswell, *The Zen Monastic Experience*, 232–233, 237–239.

65. *Samguk sagi* 44:414–415. Kim Hŭn, who is also known as Kim Yang (style: Wihŭn), was a ninth-generation descendant of King T'aejong Muyŏl (Kim Ch'unch'u, 604–661).

66. See, for instance, the story of Narada, who asks the god Viṣṇu to show him the power of the gods to make people believe in illusion *(maya)*. The god and Narada walk in a desert and come across some huts. The god commands Narada to fetch him some water. Narada is blinded by the "almond eyes" of a nubile maiden he meets in the village, marries her, and raises a family. Years pass in bliss, but then the family is torn from him by a flood and he laments. When he wakes up from the dream put upon him by the god Viṣṇu, he ultimately comprehends the power of illusion. See Heinrich Robert Zimmer, *Myths and Symbols in Indian Art and Civilization*, 32–34.

67. *Samguk yusa* 3, T 2039, 49.997a–c; SYKY 3:281–286.

68. Gregory Schopen, *Buddhist Monks and Business Matters*, 1–18.

69. *Samguk yusa* 3, T 2039, 49.992a–c; SYKY 3:246–250.

70. Angela Howard, "Tang and Song Images of Guanyin from Sichuan," 49–57.

71. See Yü, *Kuan-yin*, 293–351; and Richard von Glahn, *The Sinister Way*, 150–151.

Chapter 4: The Rise of Hwaŏm Buddhism in Silla

1. Kim Sang-hyun, "T'ongil Silla sidae ŭi Hwaŏm sinang," 65–88; Yi Haenggu, "Kankoku Bukkyō ni okeru Kegon shinkō no tenkai," 77–119; Hong Yunsik, "Silla sidae Hwaŏm sinang ŭi sŏngkyŏk kwa kŭ yŏnghyang," 109–129.

2. Tantric Buddhism is often erroneously called esoteric Buddhism *(mijiao)*, a term commonly deployed to promote the superiority of the Mahāyāna. See McBride, "Is there really 'esoteric' Buddhism?"

3. Robert M. Gimello, "Chih-yen (602–668) and the Foundations of Hua-yen Buddhism," 415–445.

4. *Samguk yusa* 4, T 2039, 49.1005b28; SYKY 4:343.

5. *Samguk yusa* 4, T 2039, 49.1009a–b; SYKY 4:367–369. For the letter, see X 103.422a–b; or for a translation see Peter Lee, *Sourcebook*, 165–166. For a differ-

ent interpretation and study of this letter, see Antonino Forte, "Un gioiello della rete di Indra," 35–83; and also Forte, *A Jewel of Indra's Net*.

6. Chen Jinhua has also demonstrated that Fazang used Empress Wu to accomplish his agenda and abandoned her when her political power waned; see Chen's "More Than a Philosopher," 320–358.

7. R. W. L. Guisso, *Wu Tse-t'ien and the Politics of Legitimation in T'ang China*, 48–49.

8. The fifty-two stages of the bodhisattva path are conceptualized as follows (the citations are to lists): the ten faiths *(shixin)*, see *Renwang bore boluomi jing* 1, T 245, 8.826b26–27; the ten abodes *(shizhu)*, see *Huayan jing* 8, T 278, 9.444c29–45a1; the ten practices *(shixing)*, see *Huayan jing* 11, T 278, 9.466b27–c2; the ten transferences *(shi huixiang)*, see *Huayan jing* 14, T 278, 9.488b26–c4; the ten stages (Skt. *bhūmis*, Ch. *shidi*), see *Huayan jing* 23, T 278, 9.542c27–c4; equal enlightenment *(dengjue*, or *dengzhengjue)*, see *Huayan jing* 53, T 278, 9.736a, and wonderful enlightenment *(miaojue*, or *miaojuezhe wushangdi)*, see *Pusa yingluo benye jing* 1, T 1485, 24.1011b8–24 (here, the final forty-two stages are described and the Sanskrit names given).

9. Guisso, *Wu Tse-t'ien*, 48–49. See also Kamata Shigeo, *Chūgoku Kegon shisōshi no kenkyū*, 107–128. For more on the commentary of the *Dayun jing* see Forte, *Political Propaganda and Ideology*.

10. *Song gaoseng zhuan* 30, T 2061, 50.895b7–10.

11. *Dafangguang fo huayan jing suishu yanyi chao* 76, T 1736, 36.599b16–17. I owe this reference to Kim Sang-hyun; see his "Silla chungdae chŏnje wanggwŏn kwa Hwaŏmjong," 63n15.

12. See Peter N. Gregory, *Tsung-mi and the Sinification of Buddhism*.

13. *Samguk yusa* 4, T 2039, 49.1009a23; SYKY 4:368; see also Kamata Shigeo, *Kegon no shisō*, 244–245.

14. Kamata, *Kegon no shisō*, 14–18.

15. See Nakamura Hajime, Kasahara Kazuo, and Kanaoke Shuyu, *Ajia Bukkyōshi Nihon hen I*, 202–205; Kasahara Kazuo, *Nihon shūkyōshi*, 1:57–58; and Rhi, "Shōchōteki hyōgen o tōshite mitaru shichi hasseki Shiragi oyobi Nihon no Bukkokuto shisō," 38–39.

16. See George J. Tanabe, Jr., *Myōe the Dreamkeeper*, 131–136; Komatsu Shigemi, *Kegonshū soshi eden (Kegon engi);* and Karen Brock, "Tales of Gishō and Gangyō." The *Kegon engi* depicts the stories of Wŏnhyo and Ŭisang as they are described in the *Song gaoseng zhuan*. These stories will be retold below.

17. See Sueki Fumihiko, *Nihon Bukkyōshi*, 83–124.

18. *Hwaŏm ilsŭng pŏpkye to*, T 1887A, 45.711a; HPC 2.1a. Some recent scholarship on the Fangshan lithic canon suggests that this seal-diagram may have been composed by Zhiyan and not Ŭisang. See Yao Chang-shou, "Bōzan sekikyō ni okeru Kegon tenseki ni tsuite," 411–437.

19. In the exegetical community of Silla, however, there was some opposition to Ŭisang's vision of the world as explicated in the seal-diagram. An other-

wise unknown monk named Myŏnghyo' composed another seal-diagram, called the *Treatise on the Ocean-Seal Samādhi (Haein sammae ron)* (X 103.299c–301b; HPC 2.397b–399b), which seems to critique Ŭisang's diagram. While Rhi Ki-yŏng demonstrated that Myŏnghyo seems to depend on Wŏnhyo's view of *The Awakening of Faith (Qixin lun)*, Walter Lew has suggested that Myŏnghyo may merely be a pseudonym for Wŏnhyo. See Rhi, *Han'guk Pulgyo yŏn'gu*, 535–543; and Walter Kyu-sung Lew, "Against Counting Up the Verses," 49–61.

20. Kim Sang-hyun quotes several Korean scholars who have uncritically accepted Lee Ki-baik's assertion of the relationship between the Hwaŏm tradition and the central government in his "Silla chungdae chŏnje wanggwŏn kwa Hwaŏmjong," 60–65.

21. The eight impure possessions *(ba bujingcai,* Kor. *p'al pujŏngjae;* also *ba bujingwu,* Kor. *p'al puljŏngmul)* are gold, silver, male slaves, female slaves, livestock (lit. "oxen and sheep"), storehouses, shops and stores, and land for cultivation; see *Daban Niepan jing* 6, T 374, 12.399c–400a.

22. *Song gaoseng zhuan* 4, T 2061, 50.729b15–19.

23. Kim Sang-hyun, "Silla chungdae chŏnje wanggwŏn kwa Hwaŏm-jong," 65–71.

24. *Samguk yusa* 4, T 2039, 49.1005b; SYKY 4:343.

25. *Samguk yusa* 5, T 2039, 49.1017c; SYKY 5:430.

26. Only the preface and third roll are extant; see *Hwaŏm-gyŏng so*, T 2757, 85.234c–236a; HPC 1.495c–498b.

27. See Robert Buswell, "The Chronology of Wŏnhyo's Life and Works," 940; Buswell, "Hagiographies," 553–562; *Song gaoseng zhuan* 4, T 2061, 50.730a6–b29.

28. *Huayan jing* 5, T 278, 9.429a19; Buswell, "Chronology," 960n28.

29. *Samguk yusa* 4, T 2039.49.1006b; SYKY 4:348–349; translation slightly amending Buswell, "Hagiographies," 561.

30. See *Samguk Silla sidae Pulgyo kŭmsŏngmun kojŭng*, 47–52; *Han'guk kŭmsŏk yumun*, 72–74.

31. For the selected passages of the *Simmun hwajaeng non* see HPC 1:838a–40c. Only the preface and a portion of roll three have been preserved from his *Hwaŏm-gyŏng so;* see HPC 1:495a–497c.

32. *Samguk yusa* 4, T 2039, 49.1009a–b; SYKY 4:368–369.

33. Tae-Hung Ha and Grafton K. Mintz, *Samguk Yusa: Legends and History of the Three Kingdoms of Ancient Korea*, 323.

34. *Samguk yusa* 4, T 2039.49.1010a; SYKY 4:373–375.

35. Kenneth Ch'en, *Buddhism in China*, 199; Daigan and Alicia Matsunaga, *Foundation of Japanese Buddhism*, 1:23, 78, 112, 120. For a translation of the sūtra see Emmerick, *The Sūtra of Golden Light*.

36. *Samguk yusa* 2, T 2039, 49.975b; SYKY 2:130–131.

37. *Samguk sagi* 10:103 (Aejang 3).

38. *Chōsen jisatsu shiryō* 1:495–496; Ch'oe Wŏnsik, "Silla hadae ŭi Haeinsa wa Hwaŏmjong," 5–9.

39. *Huayan jing* 6, T 278, 9.434c6; 26, T 278, 9.571c12; 34, T 278, 9.620c27.
40. See, for instance, Kim Tujin, *Silla Hwaŏmsasangsa yŏn'gu*.
41. Hwang Suyŏng, "Silla Kyŏngdŏk wangdae ŭi paekchi hŭksŏ Hwaŏm kyŏng," 121–126; Lee Ki-baik, "Silla Kyŏngdŏk wangdae Hwaŏm kyŏng sagyŏng kwanyŏja e taehan koch'al," 133; Mun Myŏngdae, "Silla Hwaŏm kyŏng sagyŏng kwa kŭ pyŏnsangdo ŭi yŏn'gu," 27–64; for a translation of the postface see Peter Lee, *Sourcebook*, 201–202.
42. *Sinjung Tongguk yŏji sŭngnam* 39:8a4–6.
43. The tablets include fragmented passages from rolls 10, 12, 13 [two], 19, 24, 35, 46, 54, and 55 [two]. See *Samguk Silla sidae Pulgyo kŭmsŏngmun kojŭng*, 77–82; *Han'guk kŭmsŏk chŏnmun* 1:88–93.
44. See *Chōsen kinseki sōran* 1:27–34.
45. The two passages from the *Hwaŏm-sa chŏk* are quoted in *Samguk Silla sidae Pulgyo kŭmsŏngmun kojŭng*, 83.
46. Han'guk Pulgyo Yŏn'guwŏn, *Hwaŏmsa*, 24–25, 100–102; Kamata, *Kegon no shisō*, 245.
47. The first carvings of Buddhist scriptures in stone were made during the Northern Qi period (550–577) around the capital at Ye. A grand project of preserving the Buddhist scriptures was begun during the end of the Sui period (581–618) at Yunju Monastery on Fangshan, in northern China southwest of present-day Beijing. In dread of the impending decline of the Dharma and the corruption and loss of the Buddhist religion, the monk Jingwan (d. 639) vowed to carve the entire canon of Buddhist scriptures onto stone as a means of preserving them for all time. The stone tablets were stored in mountain caves and underground caches near the monastery at Shijing shan (Stone Scripture Mountain). With both imperial and local support, the project continued through the Tang (618–907), Liao (907–1125), and Jin (1125–1234) dynasties. More than four thousand stone tablets from nine caves and ten thousand buried tablets of the Fangshan lithic canon have been identified. See Lewis R. Lancaster, "The Rock Cut Canon in China," and Lothar Ledderose, "Ein Programm für den Weltuntergang," 15–33.
48. For more on Silla's Hwaŏm monks see Kim Sang-hyun, "Silla Hwaŏm haksŭng ŭi kyebo wa kŭ hwaltong," 43–86.
49. This may be an allusion to either the royal palace or, perhaps, the heavens of the deva-kings.
50. *Samguk yusa* 4, T 2039.49.1007b–c; SYKY 4:353–354.
51. See, for example, Han Chongman, "Koun ŭi Pulgyogwan," 87–120.
52. For more information on Ch'oe's relationship to the Hwaŏm tradition and his biography of Fazang, see Kim Poksun, *Silla Hwaŏmjong yŏn'gu*, 147–212. For Ch'oe's biography of Fazang see *Tang Taech'ŏnboksa kosaji pŏn'gyŏng Taedŏk Pŏpchang hwasang chŏn*, one roll, T 2054, 50.280a–289c. For more on Ch'oe's Buddhist thought see Han Chongman, "Koun ŭi Pulgyogwan," 87–120.
53. Kyunyŏ (923–973) was a monk of the early Koryŏ period who wrote a

commentary on Ŭisang's seal-diagram; see his *Ilsŭng pŏpkye to wŏnt'ong ki*, two rolls, HPC 4:1a–39a.

54. Here Hyŏngnyŏn Chŏng is probably attempting to connect Ch'oe Ch'iwŏn to the powerful Chinese Qinghe Cui lineage that was famous for the intellectuals it produced during the medieval period. Kim Pusik's *Samguk sagi* says that he was a native of the Saryang region of the Silla capital, Kyŏngju, and makes no mention of any Ch'ŏngha Ch'oe descent group. See *Samguk sagi* 46:429–431; see also Peter Lee, *Sourcebook*, 126–127.

55. *Tae hwaŏm sujwa Wŏnt'ong yangjung taesa Kyunyŏ chŏn pyŏngsŏ* 1, K 47.259c4–5; HPC 4.511a10–11; see also Adrian Buzo and Tony Prince, *Kyunyŏ-jŏn*, 23 (for information on Hyŏngnyŏn Chŏng see 3–5).

56. *Samguk sagi* 46:431.

57. Kamata, *Chūgoku Kegon shisōshi no kenkyū*, 235–249.

58. *Wŏnjong mullyu* 22, HPC 4:644c–645b.

59. Kalpa-ashes (*kŏphŭi*, Ch. *jiehui*) refers to one of the three kinds of destruction suffered at the end of a kalpa. At the time of the ruining of the kalpa (*hŭigŏp*, Ch. *huaijie*), seven suns appear in the heavens and burn the whole world to ashes up to the first dhyāna heaven. For a discussion of this idea, which is also called *kŏphwa*, *kŏbyo*, and *kŏpchinhwa*, see *Apidamo jushe lun* 12, T 1558, 29.63a.

60. *Wŏnjong mullyu* 22, HPC 4:645c–646a; quotation from 646a7–10.

61. *Wŏnjong mullyu* 22, HPC 4:646a–b.

62. *Wŏnjong mullyu* 22, HPC 4:646b–647b.

63. This is from a rubbing in the possession of Lee Ki-baik; see Kwak, *T'ongil Silla sidae ŭi chŏngch'i pyŏndong kwa Pulgyo*, 222–223.

64. Kwak, *T'ongil Silla sidae ŭi chŏngch'i pyŏndong kwa Pulgyo*, 225–231.

65. For instance, Wei Shou (506–572), in his famous "Monograph on Buddhism and Daoism" *(Shi Lao zhi)*, written about 551–554, places the Buddha's birth in 687 B.C.E. (Lu Zhuang Gong 7), records his nirvāṇa at age thirty (657 B.C.E.), and says he taught the Dharma for forty-nine years before entering *parinirvāṇa* (in ca. 608 B.C.E.). See *Wei shu* 114:3027. Buddhists involved in the official debates with Daoists in the early sixth century, countering the allegation that Laozi went to India where he became the Buddha, dated the birth of Śākyamuni to 1029 B.C.E. and his *parinirvāṇa* to 949 B.C.E., based on putative events in the annals of King Mu of Zhou. For a review of the various sources presenting this view see Whalen Lai, "Dating the *Hsiang-fa chüeh i ching*," 67–71. A similar opinion is propounded in an anecdote found in the hagiography of the Chinese monk Fashang (495–580), which reports that Fashang told an emissary from Koguryŏ that the Buddha was born in 1028 B.C.E. (Zhou Zhao Wang 24), left home at nineteen (1009 B.C.E.), and became enlightened at thirty (998 B.C.E.) and that word of his accomplishment reached China in 977 B.C.E. (Zhou Mu Wang 24). Fashang reports that the Buddha remained in the world for another forty-nine years (until 949 B.C.E.). However, he says that from the present time, the year 576 (Qi Wuping 7), it has been 1,465 years since his entering *parinirvāṇa*, which

would place that event in 889 B.C.E. See *Xu gaoseng zhuan* 8, T 2060, 50.485b. Fei Changfang (fl. 597), reports two separate dates: relying on Pāli materials, he places the *parinirvāṇa* in 485 B.C.E. (975 years back from Qi Yongming 7 [490 C.E.]); relying on Chinese materials, he suggests 687 B.C.E. (Zhou Zhuang Wang 10) as the year of the Buddha's birth. See *Lidai sanbao ji* 11, T 2034, 49.95b, 101b. Other Chinese Buddhist literature places the birth of the Buddha at the beginning of the classical Zhou kingdom, in 1132 B.C.E. See "Mingfo lun" in *Hongming ji* 2, T 2110, 52.9b–16a, and Whalen Lai, "The Three Jewels in China," 275. Other medieval Buddhist compositions appear to support this view by locating the Buddha's birth during the golden age of the early Zhou: "The Buddha was born at the beginning of the flourishing Zhou and Laozi was born at the end of the Ji (the family name of the Zhou rulers) season." See *Bian zheng lun* 6, T 2110, 52.528b15, and *Guang hongming ji* 13, T 2103, 52.179b15.

Korean Buddhist literary sources, as well, present a variety of different dates for the birth and death of the Buddha. At least two different dates are given for his birth: 1027 B.C.E. (see *Haedong kosŭng chŏn* 1, T 2065, 50:1015b; and *Chōsen jisatsu shiryō* 1:105; 2:274, 392) and 1024 B.C.E. (see *Chōsen kinseki sōran* 1:263). Four different dates are provided for his death: 960 B.C.E. (see *Chōsen kinseki sōran* 1:54), 950 B.C.E., 949 B.C.E. (see *Haedong kosung chon* 1, T 2065, 50:1015b; *Chōsen jisatsu shiryō* 1:263), and 941 B.C.E. See Fujita Ryōsaku, "Chōsen no nengō to kinen," 364–366. See also Peter Lee, *Lives*, 20–22.

66. Jan Nattier, *Once upon a Future Time*, 65–118.

67. See *Sinjŭng Tongguk yŏji sŭngnam* 44:30b5–31a2. In this story Pŏmil is referred to by his other name, P'umil.

68. For more on Kyŏrŏn see Kim Sang-hyun, "Samhwasa ch'ŏlbul kwa Hwaŏmŏp Kyŏrŏn taedaedŏk."

69. Kwak, *T'ongil Silla sidae ŭi chŏngch'i pyŏndong kwa Pulgyo*, 232–234.

70. *Huayan jing* 78–79, T 279, 10.434c–438a; see Cleary, *The Flower Ornament Scripture*, 1490–1498; for a similar discussion see Kwak, *T'ongil Silla sidae ŭi chŏngch'i pyŏndong kwa Pulgyo*, 236–238.

71. Kwak, *T'ongil Silla sidae ŭi chŏngch'i pyŏndong kwa Pulgyo*, 241–242.

72. The term "life-force of wisdom" (*hŭimyŏng*, Ch. *huiming*) is, in this case, an allusion to the Dharmakāya as in the following passages: "They will also lovingly see *rākṣasa*s and not injure the Dharmakāya, the life-force of wisdom" and "If you injure the life-force of wisdom you will lose the Dharmakāya"; see *Dafangguang huayan jing shu* 5, T 1735, 35.539b15–16; see also *Tiantai sijiao yi* 1, T 1931, 46.775c12.

73. The four graces (*saŭn*, Ch. *sien*) are the grace of parents, father, and mother; the grace of living beings; the grace of kings of countries; and the grace of the three jewels (*triratna*): the Buddha, the Dharma, and the Saṃgha. See *Dasheng bensheng xindi guan jing* 2, T 159, 3.297a–98b.

74. *Yujŏmsa ponmalsa chi* 326–330; see also Kwak, *T'ongil Silla sidae ŭi chŏngch'i pyŏndong kwa Pulgyo*, 242–244.

Chapter 5: The Hwaŏm Synthesis of Buddhist Cults

1. See, for instance, *Huayan jing* 1, T 278, 9.371a7–8; and 11, T 278, 9.471a11–13.

2. See Hibino Takeo and Ono Katsutoshi, *Godaisan*, 54–97; Kenneth Ch'en, *Buddhism in China*, 218, 276–277, 284; Raoul Birnbaum, "Thoughts on T'ang Buddhist Mountain Traditions and Their Context," 5–23, and "The Manifestation of a Monastery," 119–137; and Robert M. Gimello, "Chang Shang-ying on Wu-t'ai Shan," 89–149.

3. I am following Iryŏn's interlinear note that the King Chŏngsin of this account is actually a conflation of his posthumous reign name (viz. Sinmun) and his given name Ilcho. *Samguk yusa* 3, T 2039, 49.998c; SYKY 3:293–294.

4. Ri Sangho suggests that the Yusa River may be an allusion to the Yŏnghae area in North Kyŏngsang Province. See Ri Sangho, *Sinp'yŏn Samguk yusa*, 282n12. The other places—Changch'ŏn Grotto and Ulchin'guk—are found nowhere else in Buddhist hagiographical literature. Nevertheless, Ulchin-guk may refer to Ulchin district, which is on the east coast of Korea in present-day Kangwŏn Province and was part of Myŏngju during the Silla period. See *Samguk sagi* 35:341; *Sinjŭng Tongguk yŏji sŭngnam* 45:25a3–b4.

5. If this account is historically accurate, the version of the *Mahāpratisarā Dhāraṇī* that Poch'ŏn would have had access to would have been Ratnacinta's translation made at Tiangong Monastery in Chang'an in 693, viz. *Suiqiu jide dazizai tuoluoni shenzhou jing*, T 1154, 20.637b–644b. However, this particular dhāraṇī was also a spell sūtra retranslated by Amoghavajra during the mid-eighth century. *Pubian guangming qingjing zhizheng ruyi baoyinxin wuneng sheng damingwang suiqiu tuoluoni jing*, T 1153, 20.616a–637b.

6. What I have translated as "five virtuous monastic acolytes" is a paraphrastic translation of *pokchŏn o wŏn*, the *pokchŏn* part of which is literally "field of merit," a common term referring to both the Buddha and members of the monastic community. They are fields of merit because ordinary individuals acquire merit by making offerings to them. Here the term refers expressly to monks.

7. The text literally reads "eight roll golden sūtra" (*p'algwŏn kŭm-gyŏng*), which I have taken to be an abbreviation referring to the *Hebu jinguangming jing*, in eight rolls (T 664, vol. 16), translated by Baogui of the Sui in 597. Fei Changfang (fl. 595) also refers to a *Jinguang jing* in eight rolls; see *Lidai sanbao ji* 13, T 2034, 49.109c17. It would make sense for this sūtra to be read along with the *Renwang jing* since both texts were chanted in state-protection rituals. Here I differ from Murakami Yoshio who suggests, following earlier Japanese scholars, that it refers to the esoteric *Jinguangding jing;* see Mishina Shōei and Murakami Yoshio, *Sangoku iji kōshō* vol. 3/1:370.

8. Here I am in general agreement with Murakami Yoshio, who suggests that *Inwang panya* here is a reference to either the *Renwang bore boluomi jing* translated by Kumārajīva, ca. 402–409 (T 245, vol. 8), or the *Renwang huguo bore boluomiduo jing* by Amoghavajra, in 765 (T 246, vol. 8); see Mishina and Murakami, *Sangoku*

iji kōshō vol. 3/1:370. However, I am partial to the position that the writer is referring to the former one by Kumārajīva.

9. The four necessities *(sasa)* are food, clothing, lodging (bedding), and medicine.

10. *Samguk yusa* 3, T 2039, 49.998b–999c; SYKY 3:297–300; for an alternate translation of the record of religious observances on Mount Odae see Peter Lee, *Sourcebook*, 97–99.

11. In a broad sense, however, "coursing in a sūtra" (Kor. *chŏn'gyŏng*, Ch. *zhuanjing*) is merely one way of rendering the idea of sūtra recitation or sūtra chanting into Buddhist Chinese. Other compounds include "reading sūtras" *(dujing)*, "chanting sūtras" *(fengjing)*, "chanting and reciting [sūtras]" *(fengsong)*, "reciting sūtras" *(songjing)*, "looking at sūtras" *(kanjing)*, and "contemplating sūtras" *(nianjing)*. Many Buddhist scriptures speak of the merit generated from reciting or chanting a Mahāyāna sūtra, such as the famous passage in the chapter "Dhāraṇī" in the *Lotus Sūtra* in which the Buddha teaches that people who chant, recite, or copy that sūtra will earn immeasurable amounts of merit. See *Miaofa lianhua jing* 7, T 262, 9.58b10–12. Furthermore, in the *Larger Pure Land Sūtra* *(Sukhāvatīvyūhasūtra)* is a passage teaching that people will achieve the highest level of enlightenment if they accept this sūtra wholeheartedly in faith, chant this sūtra, and practice in accordance with its teachings. See *Wuliangshou jing* 2, T 360, 12.279a3–6.

12. See McBride, "Dhāraṇī and Spells," and, "Buddhist Cults in Silla Korea in Their Northeast Asian Context," 204–277.

13. *Samguk yusa* 3, T 2039, 49.999c–1000a; SYKY 3:300–302.

14. See Rhi, *Aux origines du "tch'an houei"*; Kyoto Tokuno, "Byways in Chinese Buddhism," 169, 247–256; see also Whalen Lai, "The Earliest Folk Buddhist Religion in China," 20.

15. For Zhiyi's repentance rituals see *Fangdeng sanmei xingfa* (The method of Vaipulya samādhi), T 1940, 46, 943c–944a. The spell procedures outlined in the foregoing text are based on the *Dafangdeng tuoluoni jing* (The great Vaipulya dhāraṇī) 4, T 1339, 21.656a–661a, a dhāraṇī sūtra translated by the śramaṇa Fazhong of the Northern Liang regime (ca. 402–413); for Shandao see *Guannian Amituofo xianghai sanmei gongde famen*, T 1959, 47.22b–30b, and Stevenson, "Pure Land Buddhist Worship and Meditation in China," 377–379; for Daoxuan see *Sifenlü shanfan buque xingshi chao* 2/4, T 1804, 40.96a16–104b27; *Sifenlü shanbu suiji jiemo* 2, T 1808, 40.506c1–508b29; for Daoshi see *Fayuan zhulin* 60, T 2122, 53.737c11–743c25 (for dhāraṇī used in repentance rituals); and 86, T 2122, 53.912b–921a (for "repentance practices," *chanhui*).

16. *Jizhujing lichanyi*, two rolls, T 1982, 47.456b–74c.

17. *Samguk yusa* 4, T 2039, 49.1006a; SYKY 4:352–353.

18. *Song gaoseng zhuan* 4, T 2061, 50.729a.

19. *Linjian lu* 1, X 148:295c.

20. *Samguk yusa* 4, T 2039, 49.1006a; SYKY 4:350–351.

21. *Song gaoseng zhuan* 4, T 2061, 50.729a3–c3; for a French translation of Ŭisang's biography see Herbert Durt, "La biographie du moine Coréen Ŭi-Sang d'après le Song kao seng tchouan," 411–422.
22. Han'guk Pulgyo Yŏn'guwŏn, *Pusŏksa*, 20–21, 84–94; Kamata Shigeo, *Shiragi Bukkyōshi josetsu*, 394.
23. *Huayan jing* 60, T 278, 9.786b11–12.
24. See, for instance, *Huayan jing* 4, T 278, 9.418b1, and 41, T 278, 9.759c18.
25. *Chōsen kinseki sōran* 1:271. The suggestion that the missing character should represent "buddhas and bodhisattvas" comes from Kim Pohyŏn, Pae Pyŏngsŏn, and Pak Tohwa, *Pusŏksa*, 44.
26. See Pulgyo Munhwa Yŏn'guwŏn, *Han'guk Chŏngt'o sasang yŏn'gu*, 453.
27. Great Compassion Spell (Ch. *dabei zhou*), in *Qianyan qianbi Guanshiyin pusa tuoluoni shenzhou jing* 1, T 1057, 20.84a–c, 90b–91a; *Qianshou qianyan Guanshiyin pusa guangda yuanman wuai dabeixin tuoluoni* 1, T 1060, 20.107b–c.
28. *Paekhwa toryang parwŏn mun*, HPC 2:9a.
29. *Qianshou qianyan Guanshiyin pusa guangda yuanman wuai dabeixin tuoluoni* 1, T 1060, 20.107a.
30. According to the *Foundation Record,* which claims that its information comes from the otherwise unknown *Basic Annals of Cock Grove [Silla] (Kyerim pon'gi),* Silla king Pŏphŭng began constructing the monastery, originally as a nunnery, in 528, merely one year after Ich'adon's martyrdom, on behalf of his mother and queen dowager Lady Yŏngje and his wife and queen Lady Kiyun. Since Lady Yŏngje's religious name (dharma name) was Pŏmnyu, the nunnery was called Hwaŏm Pulguk Nunnery or Hwaŏm Pŏmnyu Nunnery. See *Pulguksa kogŭm ch'anggi*, in *Pulguksa chi (oe)*, 43 (Liang Datong 2; Silla Pŏphŭng 27). Then, the text cites the likewise unknown *Lives of Monks from the Eastern Country (Tongguk sŭng chŏn),* which may be another name for the *Lives of Eminent Korean Monks (Haedong kosŭng chŏn),* and reports that King Chinhŭng's mother, Lady Chiso, apparently rebuilt the nunnery in 574 and that the king's wife became a nun whose religious name was Pŏbyun. In honor of a monk named Winant'a, who had arrived from the Chinese state of Jin, the king retiled the roof of Hŭngnyun Monastery; commissioned two Buddhist images, one of Vairocana and one of Amitābha; and enshrined these images at Pulguk Nunnery. See *Pulguksa kogŭm ch'anggi*, in *Pulguksa chi (oe)*, 44 (Chen Xiandi Dada 6; Silla Chinhŭng 36). Furthermore, referring to the lost but previously mentioned *Basic Biography of Marquis Ch'oe [Ch'iwŏn] (Ch'oe hu ponjŏn)* and the now lost *Record of Conduct of Master Wŏnhyo (Hyosa haengjang),* the lecture hall *(kangdang),* called the Hall of No Talking *(musŏlchŏn),* was constructed in 670 specifically for lectures on the *Avataṃsaka Sūtra;* later, P'yohun (fl. eighth century), one of Ŭisang's ten important disciples, was housed there by the Silla government. See *Pulguksa kogŭm ch'anggi*, in *Pulguksa chi (oe)*, 44 (Tang Gaozong Xianheng 1; Silla Munmu 10).
31. My skepticism regarding the validity of the early statements made in the *Foundation Record of Pulguk Monastery Old and New* runs contradictory to main-

stream Buddhist scholarship on Pulguk Monastery, which tends to follow the monastery record despite its claims that contradict other earlier textual evidence. Scholars do not support the *Foundation Record*'s claims with any evidence, but merely state that "if we follow what the records say . . ." See Han'guk Pulgyo Yŏn'guwŏn, *Pulguksa*, 15–19; see also Kim Sang-hyun, Kim Tonghyŏn, and Kwak Tongsŏk, *Pulguksa*, 15–24. These apologetic scholars clearly follow what was perhaps the original intent of the compiler of the *Foundation Record:* to provide Pulguk Monastery with a history that places its founding at the beginnings of Buddhist history in Silla, therefore providing the monastery with precedence over other extant monasteries that might have claim on royal endowments and funds for the construction and reconstruction of monastic buildings.

32. See Cho Aegi, "Shiragi ni okeru Miroku shinkō no kenkyū," 250–253.

33. *Samguk yusa* 5, T 2039, 49.1018a–b; SYKY 4:430–433.

34. Han'guk Pulgyo Yŏn'guwŏn, *Pulguksa*, 33.

35. *Samguk yusa* 5, T 2039, 49.1018b; SYKY 5:433.

36. *Miaofa lianhua jing* 4, T 262, 9.32b–34b.

37. *Huayan jing* 2–3, T 278, 9.405a–418a.

38. For this assertion, see www.bulguksa.or.kr/bulguksa/html_korea/208.htm.

39. *Wŏnjong mullyu* 22, HPC 4.647b14–c2.

40. *Koun chip* 3:30a–31a; *Pulguksa kogŭm ch'anggi*, in *Pulguksa chi (oe)*, 55–56; cf. *Pulguksa sajŏk*, in *Pulguksa chi (oe)*, 30–31.

41. See *Xinjiao zhengqie Song-ben Guangyun* 2:419a. It is also a mountain in Gansu province.

42. The traditional list of the eight groups of protector beings *(babu)* is heavenly dragons, yakṣas, asuras, garuḍas, kinnaras, mahoragas, humans, and nonhumans; see, for instance, *Miaofa lianhua jing* 1, T 262, 9.2b13–15; *Huayan jing* 27, T 278, 9.573c25–26.

43. *Da Tang xiyu ji* 8, T 2087, 51.918b; see also *Da Tang xiyu ji* 9, T 2087, 51.946c4–5. See also Wriggins, *Xuanzang*, 107–111, for a description of Mahābodhi Monastery.

44. Kang Woo-bang, "Sŏkkuram Pulgyo chogak ŭi tosangjŏk koch'al," 44; see also his "Sŏkkuram Pulgyo chogak ŭi tosang haesŏk," 60–64.

45. See Kang, "Sŏkkuram Pulgyo chogak ŭi tosang haesŏk," 64–72. See also *Fangguang da zhuangyan jing* 8–9, T 187, 3.584b–597a, specifically 586c, which lists the names of most of the figures surrounding the Buddha: the eight groups of gods, the four heavenly kings, Śakra, Brahmā, and so forth.

46. Kang, "Sŏkkuram Pulgyo chogak ŭi tosang haesŏk," 87–91. The conceptual and practical ideas of this "comprehensive Buddhism" are treated in Wŏnhyo's *Treatise on the Reconciliation of Disputes in Ten Approaches (Simmun hwajaeng non)*. For more on this see Oh Young Bong, *Wŏnhyo's Theory of Harmonization*, 194–204; and Yi Chongik, *Wŏnhyo ŭi kŭnbong sasang*.

47. For Hwang's views see Han'guk Pulgyo Yŏn'guwŏn, *Sŏkkuram*, 26, 38–41;

and Kim Lena, "Sŏkkuram pulsanggun ŭi myŏngch'ing kwa yangsik e kwanhayŏ," 6-7. For a more popular description of the grotto see Edward B. Adams, *Korea's Golden Age*, 114-133.

48. Ko Ikchin, *Han'guk kodae Pulgyo sasangsa*, 240-248.

49. James Huntley Grayson, "Religious Syncretism in the Shilla Period," 187-198.

50. Kang, "Sŏkkuram Pulgyo chogak ŭi tosang haesŏk," 66-70.

51. Lee Ki-baik, *Silla chŏngch'i sahoesa yŏn'gu*, 196-204; Hong Sunch'ang, "Shiragi no sansan gogaku to Shiragijin no sangaku sūhai ni tsuite," 247-264.

52. *Tang Taech'ŏnboksa kosaju pŏn'gyŏng taedŏk Pŏpchang hwasang chŏn* 1, T 2054, 50.285a29-b2; HPC 3.775c20-22.

53. *Samguk yusa* 4, T 2039, 49.1007a; SYKY 4:353.

54. Lee Ki-baik, *Silla chŏngch'i sahoesa yŏn'gu*, 210-214.

55. Kim Sang-hyun, "Silla chungdae chŏnje wanggwŏn kwa Hwaŏmjong," 85-89.

56. See Ch'oe Pyŏnghŏn, "Koryŏ sidae Hwaŏmhak ŭi pyŏnch'ŏn," 66; cited in Kim Sang-hyun, "Silla chungdae chŏnje wanggwŏn kwa Hwaŏmjong," 88n107.

57. Kim Sang-hyun, "Silla chungdae chŏnje wanggwŏn kwa Hwaŏmjong," 88.

58. Kim Sang-hyun, "Silla chungdae chŏnje wanggwŏn kwa Hwaŏmjong," 89.

59. Rhi Ki-yong lists ten objects depicting the buddhas of the four directions, including the famous Hermitage of the Seven Buddhas (Ch'ilburam) on Kyŏngju's Namsan; see Rhi, *Han'guk Pulgyo yŏn'gu*, 524-534.

60. *Huayan jing* 45, T 279, 10.241b23-26.

61. *Huayan jing tanxuan ji* 15, T 1733, 35.391a24-27; cf. *Huayan jing* 29, T 278, 9.590a13-16; see Rhi, *Han'guk Pulgyo yŏn'gu*, 518-521.

62. Sadāprarudita is the name of the famous bodhisattva who is featured most prominently as the hero of the *Perfection of Wisdom in Eight Thousand Lines*. His name is translated as "Ever Weeping" *(changti)* in Xuanzang's translation of the *Mahāprajñāpāramitā Sūtra*, *Da bore boluomiduo jing* 398-400, T 220, 6.1059a-1073b. For similarities between Sadāprarudita and Silla monks see McBride, "The Vision Quest Motif," 20-21, passim.

63. *Dafanggung fo huayan jing shu* 47, T 1735, 35.860a6-10 (a10-19 also contains relevant material); see also Rhi, *Han'guk Pulgyo yŏn'gu*, 521-522.

64. *Sinjŭng Tongguk yŏji sŭngnam* 47:12b4 (P'yohunsa).

65. *Huayan jing* 1, T 278, 9.395b-397b; *Huayan jing* 1, T 279, 10.2a-5a.

66. *Samguk yusa* 3, T 2039, 49.999c; SYKY 3:300; see also Kim Poksun, *Silla Hwaŏmjong yŏn'gu*, 115-121.

67. *Samguk yusa* 3, T 2039, 49.1001a-b; SYKY 3:309; "Mujangsa Amit'a yŏrae chosang sajŏk pi," in *Samguk Silla sidae Pulgyo kŭmsŏngmun kojŭng*, 120-125; *Chōsen kinseki sōran* 1:44-47; *Han'guk kŭmsŏk chŏnmun* 1:152-155.

68. *Pŏmŏsa sajŏk ki;* see also Kim Sang-hyun, *Silla Hwaŏm sasangsa yŏn'gu,* 140–141.

69. *Tongmunsŏn* 68:1b10–2a3; see also Kim Sang-hyun, *Silla Hwaŏm sasangsa yŏn'gu,* 141.

70. "Paeksŏngsansa chŏnt'ae Kilsangt'ap chung nappŏp ch'imgi," in *Samguk Silla sidae Pulgyo kŭmsŏngmun kojŭng,* 263.

71. Nam Tongsin, "Namal Yŏch'o Hwaŏm chongdan ŭi taeŭng kwa *(Hwaŏm) sinjung kyŏng* ŭi sŏngnip," 151–153.

72. Other historical records do not corroborate that Kyŏnhwŏn (fl. 892–936), king of Later Paekche, had a son with the name Wŏlgwang. Wŏlgwang is, in fact, more probably an allusion to the famous and formidable bodhisattva "Prince Moonlight" (Yueguang pusa), the hero of a series of apocryphal Buddhist sūtras that show a confluence of millennial Buddhist and millenarian Daoist ideas. See Zürcher, "Prince Moonlight." What is significant is that writers of the early Koryŏ period remembered the struggle for power among the later Three Kingdoms in such terms. See McBride, "Why did Kungye claim to be the Buddha Maitreya?"

73. *Chōsen jisatsu shiryō* 1:495–496; see also Kim Sang-hyun, *Silla Hwaŏm sasangsa yŏn'gu,* 142.

74. *Koryŏsa* 1:17b5–6. See also Han Kimun, *Koryŏ sawŏn ŭi kujo wa kinŭng,* 39, 47.

75. See *Kyunyŏ chŏn,* HPC 4:511a, 511c. See also Buzo and Prince, *Kyunyŏ-jŏn,* 24, 30.

Concluding Reflections

1. See, for instance, the discussions in James Ketelaar, *Of Heretics and Martyrs in Meiji Japan,* 177–207; and Abé, *The Weaving of Mantra,* 399–428.

2. See, for instance, Shim Jae-ryong, *Korean Buddhism,* 161–182; and Robert E. Buswell, Jr., "Imagining 'Korean Buddhism.'"

3. On the five schools see Kwŏn Sangno, "History of Korean Buddhism," 10; Richard A. Gard, "The Mādhyamika in Korea," 1173–1174n62; Lee Ki-baik, *A New History of Korea,* 81; Robert E. Buswell, Jr., *The Korean Approach to Zen,* 6–9; and Buswell, "Buddhism in Korea," 153–155. For Silla scholasticism see Kim Tonghwa, "Silla sidae ŭi Pulgyo sasang" (parts 1, 2, and 3); Cho Myŏnggi, "Silla Pulgyo ŭi kyohak"; and Ahn Kye-hyŏn, "Buddhism in the Unified Silla Period." This is not to say that scholars have not identified putative purveyors of the other intellectual traditions such as Sarvāstivādin Abhidharma, Chinese Madhyamaka (Samnon, Ch. Sanlun), Tattyasiddhi *(Chengshi lun).* Also added to this are the imagined tantric traditions, Myŏngnang's Divine Seal school (Sininjong) and Hyet'ong's (fl. 660–700) Dhāraṇī school (Ch'ongjijong) as well as a Pure Land school (Chŏngt'ojong). See Kim Tonghwa, "Silla sidae ŭi Pulgyo sasang (il)," 43–53; and Han Kidu, *Han'guk Pulgyo sasang,* 32–44. Also see the studies in Lewis R. Lancaster and C. S. Yu, *Introduction of Buddhism to Korea* and *Assimilation of Buddhism in Korea.*

4. For a treatment of the case against Chajang's being the founder of the Vinaya school see Kim Jongmyung, "Chajang (fl. 636–650) and 'Buddhism as National Protector' in Korea," 39–41; against Wŏnhyo as belonging to any school see McBride, "*Muryangsu-gyŏng chongyo* (Thematic Essentials of the *Larger Sukhāvatīvyūhasūtra*)."

5. *Samguk yusa* 3, T 2039, 49.988b–989a, 989b–c; SYKY 3:220–225, 232.

6. See, for instance, Buswell, *The Korean Approach to Zen*, 23–25; and Buswell, "Chinul's Systematization of Chinese Meditative Techniques in Korean Sŏn Buddhism," 210–213; see also Keel, *Chinul*, 27–31, passim.

7. Lee Ki-baik, *Silla sasangsa yŏn'gu*, 75–95; see also Lee, "Early Silla Buddhism and the Power of the Aristocracy," 161–185.

8. See, for instance, John B. Duncan, "The Formation of the Central Aristocracy in Early Koryŏ," 39–61; Duncan, *The Origins of the Chosŏn Dynasty;* and James B. Palais, "Confucianism and the Aristocratic/Bureaucratic Balance in Korea," 427–468.

Glossary of Sinitic Logographs

Abiji 阿非知
Ado 阿道
Aejang 哀莊
Amit'agul 阿彌陀窟
Amituo guyin shengwang tuoluoni jing 阿彌陀鼓音聲王陀羅尼經
An Lushan luan 安祿山亂
Ansang 安常
Anyangmun 安養門
Apidamo jushe lun 阿毘達磨俱舍論
Asuka 飛鳥
asurasin 阿修羅神
babu 八部
baguanzhai hui 八關齋會
Bailian she 白蓮社
Baiyi 白衣
bajiezhai 八戒齋
Baoyu jing 寶雨經
Bei Qi 北齊
Bei Song 北宋
Bei Wei 北魏
Bei Zhou 北周
bendi fen 本地分
benti 本體
Budai 布袋
Bukong juansuo Guanyin 不空羂索觀音
Bukong juansuo shenbian zhenyan jing 不空羂索神變眞言經
Bukong juansuo tuoluoni jing 不空羂索陀羅尼經

chabi 慈悲
chaegye ch'iril 齋戒七日
Chagung 紫宮
Chahamun 紫霞門
Chajang 慈藏
Chajang chŏn 慈藏傳
Cha jing 茶經
Chajiu lun 茶酒論
ch'alli chong 刹利種
Chan 禪
Changansa 長安寺
Changch'ŏn'gul 掌天窟
Changch'un 長春
Changgyŏngbong 長慶峯
Changnyŏngsan 長嶺山
changnyuk 丈六
Changnyukchŏn 丈六殿
changnyuk chonsang 丈六尊像
Chang Pogo 張保皐
Changsan 獐山
changsang 莊上
Changsusa 長壽寺
changti 常啼
Ch'angun 昶雲
Ch'angwŏn 昌原
Chassi 慈氏
ch'e 體
Chen 陳
Chengguan 澄觀
Chengshi lun 成實論
Cheng zhengjue pin 成正覺品

179

Chigwi 志鬼
Chihae 智海
chihye 智慧
Chiisan 智異山
Chijang 地藏
Ch'ilburam 七佛庵
Ch'ilpogyo 七寶橋
Chin Chinŭng 陳震應
Chindŏk 眞德
chin'gol 眞骨
Chinhŭng 眞興
Chinja 眞慈
Chinjang 眞藏
Chinji 眞智
Chinjŏng 眞定
Chinjugun 鎭州郡
Chinnaemal 眞乃末
Chinp'yo 眞表
Chinp'yŏng 眞平
chinsin 眞身
Chinul 知訥
Chinyŏwŏn 眞如院
Chirisan 智理山
Chirosan 地盧山
chisin 地神
Chiso 只召
Chit'ong 智通
Chitoumo 翅頭末
Ch'oe Ch'iwŏn 崔致遠
Ch'oe hu ponjŏn 崔候本傳
Ch'oe Sŭngno 崔承老
Ch'oe Ŭnham 崔殷諴
chokhaengsin 足行神
Ch'ok hyangbun yebul kyŏlsa mun 髑香墳禮佛結社文
Ch'ŏlbu 哲夫
Chŏlla namdo 全羅南道
Chŏlla pukto 全羅北道
Chŏmgae 漸開
Ch'ŏnbu Kwanŭm 千部觀音
chŏndang 前堂
chŏngbŏp 正法
Ch'ŏngdamsa 青潭寺

Ch'ŏngdogun 清道郡
Chŏnggang 定康
chŏnggŏ ch'ŏnjung 淨居天衆
Ch'ŏnggu saman 青丘沙門
Ch'ŏngha 清河
Chŏnghyŏn 定玄
Ch'ongjijong 總持宗
Ch'ŏngmuk 聽默
Chŏngsin 淨神
Ch'ŏngsongsan 青松山
chŏngsu 正受
Chŏngt'ojong 淨土宗
Ch'ŏngt'osa 淨土寺
ch'ŏn'gung 天宮
Ch'ŏngun'gyo 青雲橋
Ch'ŏn'gwansan ki 天冠山記
Ch'ŏngyangnu 青陽樓
chŏn'gyŏng 轉經
Ch'ŏn'gyŏngnim 天鏡林
chŏn Hwaŏm kyŏng 轉華嚴經
Ch'ŏnin 天因
Chŏnju 全州
Ch'ŏnsan 千山
ch'ŏnsa oktae 天賜玉帶
chŏnsu chu 千手呪
Ch'ŏnsu kyŏng 千手經
Ch'ŏrwŏn'gun 鐵圓郡
Chosin 調信
Chosŏn 朝鮮
Cho Sunsang 超巡相
Chowŏnjŏn 朝元殿
chuang 幢
chuanguoxi 傳國璽
chubangsin 主方神
Ch'udong 錐洞
Ch'udong ki 錐洞記
chugasin 主稼神
chugongsin 主空神
chuhaesin 主海神
chuhasin 主河神
chuhwasin 主火神
Chukchi 竹旨
Chukchiryŏng 竹旨嶺

Glossary of Sinitic Logographs

Chung'ak 中嶽
chungalch'an 重閼粲
Ch'ungch'ŏng pukto 忠清北道
chungdae 中代
Ch'ungdam 忠談
chunggo 中古
Chungsaengsa 眾生寺
chungsam chunggu 重三重九
chujisin 主地神
chujusin 主晝神
chup'ungsin 主風神
churimsin 主林神
chusansin 主山神
chusŏngsin 主城神
chususin 主水神
chuyaksin 主藥神
chuyasin 主夜神
cibei 慈悲
Cien 慈恩
Cishi 慈氏
Daban Niepan jing 大般涅槃經
dabei zhou 大悲呪
Dafangdeng tuoluoni jing 大方等陀羅尼經
Dafangguang fo huayan jing 大方廣佛華嚴經
Dafangguang fo huayan jing suishu yanyi chao 大方廣佛華嚴經隨疏演義鈔
Daikan Daiji 大官大寺
Daiwa sansan 大和三山
Dali 大曆
daochang 道場
Daochuo 道綽
Daode jing 道德經
Daolin 道林
daoren tong 道人統
Daoshi 道世
Daowu 道武
Daoxuan 道宣
daqian 大千
Dari rulai 大日如來
Da Tang xiyu ji 大唐西域記
datong 大統

Dayun jing 大雲經
Dazhong 大中
Dazu 大足
dengjue 等覺
dengzhengjue 等正覺
Dengzhou 登州
Dezong 德宗
Di lun 地論
Dizang 地藏
Dong Jin 東晉
Doushuaitian 兜率天
dujing 讀經
Dunhuang 敦煌
Dunhuang bianhua 敦煌變化
Dunhuang Pusa 敦煌菩薩
Duobao rulai 多寶如來
Dushun 杜順
duweina 都維那
Emeishan 峨嵋山
Fachang 法常
Faguo 法果
Fahua zhuanji 法華傳記
fajie 法界
fanben 梵本
fangbian 方便
Fangdeng sanmei xingfa 方等三昧行法
Fangguang bore jing 放光般若經
Fangguang da zhuangyan jing 方廣大莊嚴經
Fangshan 房山
Fanjingyuan 翻經院
Fanmayue 梵摩越
Fanwang jing 梵網經
fa puti xin 發菩提心
Faqi 法起
fashang 法尚
fashen 法身
Fashen 法深
fasheng 法生
Fashun 法順
Faxian 法顯
Faxiang 法相
Faxing 法興

fayong 法湧
Fayuan zhulin 法苑珠林
Fazang 法藏
Fazhong 法衆
fengjing 諷經
fengsong 諷誦
Fengxiansi 鳳先寺
Foshoujisi 佛授記寺
Fozu tongji 佛祖統紀
Fu Jian 符堅
Gaoseng Faxian zhuan 高僧法顯傳
Gaoseng zhuan 高僧傳
Gaowang Guanshiyin jing 高王觀世音經
gongyang Mile, fengxian Guanyin 供養彌勒, 奉獻觀音
Guan Mile pusa shangsheng Doushuaitian jing 觀彌勒菩薩上生兜率天經
Guan Mile shangsheng jing 觀彌勒上生經
Guannian Amituofo xianghai sanmei gongde famen 觀念阿彌陀佛相海三昧功德法門
Guanshiyin 觀世音
Guanshiyin jing 觀世音經
Guanshiyin pusa pumen pin 觀世音菩薩普門品
Guanshiyin yingyan ji 觀世音應驗記
Guan Wuliangshou jing 觀無量壽經
Guanyin 觀音
Guanzizai 觀自在
hadae 下代
Haedong 海東
Haedong Hwaŏm ch'ojo kisin wŏnmun 海東華嚴初祖忌晨願文
Haedong kosŭng chŏn 海東高僧傳
Haeinsa 海印寺
haein sammae 海印三昧
Haein sammae ron 海印三昧論
haesin 海神
Haewŏn 海圓
Hagasan 下柯山
hago 下古
Hagok-hyŏn 河曲縣

Hahŏe pyŏlsin kamyŏn 河回別神假面
Haitong 海通
haiyin sanmei 海印三昧
Han'giri 漢歧里
hangma ch'okchi in 降魔觸地印
Hangzhou 杭州
Hanju 漢州
hankashiyui-zō 半跏思惟象
hasin 河神
Hasŏbu 河西府
Hebei 河北
Heian 平安
hoehyang 廻向
hŏgong pŏpkye 虛空法界
hŏgongsin 虛空神
hoguk pulgyo 護國佛教
Hŏnan 憲安
Hŏn'gang 憲康
Hongjin 洪震
Hon'gu 混丘
Horim 虎林
Hossō 法相
Huayan jing 華嚴經
Huayan jing tanxuan ji 華嚴經潭玄記
huguo fojiao 護國佛教
Huguo pin 護國品
Huichang 會昌
hŭigŏp 懷劫
huiming 慧命
Hŭimyŏng 希明
Hŭirang 希朗
Huixiang 慧祥
Huiyun 慧雲
Hu Koguryŏ 後高句麗
Hŭngdŏk 興德
Hŭngnyunsa 興輪寺
hwabaek 花白
Hwagaesan 花開山
hwahyŏng 化形
Hwajangsa 華藏寺
Hwangboksa 皇福寺
Hwanghaedo 黃海道
Hwangnyongsa 皇龍寺/ 黃龍寺

Glossary of Sinitic Logographs

Hwangnyongsa kuch'ŭngt'ap ch'alchu pon'gi 皇龍寺九層塔刹柱本記
Hwanhŭi 歡喜
Hwaŏm 華嚴
Hwaŏm chongyo 華嚴宗要
Hwaŏm-gyŏng so 華嚴經疏
Hwaŏmhoe 華嚴會
Hwaŏm ibul myŏngho 華嚴二佛名號
Hwaŏm ilsŭng pŏpkye to 華嚴一乘法界圖
Hwaŏmjong 華嚴宗
Hwaŏmŏp Kyŏrŏn taet'ae[dŏk] 華嚴業決言大太[德]
Hwaŏm Pŏmnyusa 華嚴法流寺
Hwaŏm Pulguksa 華嚴佛國寺
Hwaŏmsa 華嚴寺 (monastery)
Hwaŏmsa 華嚴社 (shrine)
Hwaŏm sammae 華嚴三昧
Hwaŏm sinang 華嚴信仰
Hwaŏm sinjung yech'am 華嚴神衆禮懺
Hwaŏm toryang 華嚴道場
hwarakch'ŏnwang 化樂天王
hwarang 花郎
Hwasansa 華山寺
hwasin 火神
hyangch'al 鄕札
hyangga 鄕歌/ 響歌
hyangjŏn 鄕傳
hyangsa 香社
Hyegong 惠恭
Hyehun 惠訓
Hyehyŏnnyŏng 蟹縣嶺
Hyeryang 惠亮
Hyet'ong 惠通
Hyŏllye 穴禮
Hyomyŏng 孝明
Hyŏngnyŏn Chŏng 赫蓮挺
Hyŏnjun 賢俊/ 賢儁
hyŏnsin sŏngdo 現身成道
Hyosa haengjang 曉師行狀
Hyoso 孝昭
Ich'adon 異次頓
idu 吏讀

Ijae 異才
Ijŏng 理貞
Iksan 益山
Ilcho 日照
ilch'ŏnja 日天子
Illyŏm 一念
Ilsŭng pŏpkye-do wŏnt'ong ki 一乘法界圖圓通記
in'gi rusŏk 禋祈累夕
Injang 仁章
Inp'yŏng 仁平
Inwang toryang 仁王道場
Inyongsa 仁容寺
Iryŏn 一然
Jiaoran 皎然
Jiaqing 嘉慶
Jiazhou 嘉州
Jieshan 界山
jin 金
Jin 晉
Jinguang jing 金光經
Jingying Huiyuan 淨影慧遠
jinlun 金輪
Jinshizi zhang 金獅子章
Jitoumo 雞頭摩
jiuding 九鼎
Jiusheng Guanshiyin jing 救生觀世音經
Jiushi 久視
Jizhujing lichanyi 集諸經禮懺儀
Jōjitsu 成實
Kaenyŏnggun 開寧郡
Kaesŏng 開城
Kaet'aesa 開泰寺
Kaewŏn 愷元
Kaguyama 香久山
Kagwi 可歸
kaigen 開眼
Kaishu 楷書
Kaiyuan 開元
Kaiyuan shijiao lu 開元釋教錄
Kakhwangjŏn 覺皇展
Kakhyŏn 覺賢
Kaktŭk 覺得

Kalgyŏngsa 葛項寺
Kamsansa 甘山寺
Kamŭnsa 感恩寺
k'an/kan 間
kangdang 講堂
Kangju 康州
Kangssi 康氏
Kangwŏndo 江原道
kanjing 看經
karurawang 伽留羅王
Kayahyŏp 迦耶峽
Kayasan 加耶山/ 迦耶山
Kayasan Haeinsa kojŏk 伽倻山海印寺古蹟
Kegon 華嚴
Kegon engi emaki 華嚴緣起繪卷
Kibichi 吉備池
Kim Chisŏng 金志誠
Kim Ch'unch'u 金春秋
Kim Hŭn 金昕
Kim Inmun 金仁問
Kim Kungye 金弓裔
Kim Mullyang 金文亮
Kim Murim 金武林
Kim Pŏmmin 金法敏
Kim Pusik 金富軾
Kim Taemun 金大問
Kim Taesŏng 金大城
Kim Yang 金陽
Kim Yangdo 金良圖
Kim Yusin 金庾信
kinnarawang 緊那羅王
Kirinsan 麒麟山
Kiyun 己尹
Koguryŏ 高句麗
Koihyŏn 古伊峴
kojŏn 古傳
Koksan'gun 谷山郡
koksin 穀神
Kokubunji 国分寺
kolp'umje 骨品制
kŏndalp'awang 乾闥婆王
Kongju 公州

kongyang 供養
Kŏnwŏn 建元
kŏphŭi 劫灰
Koramsa 鵠嵒寺
Korhwa 骨火
Koryŏ 高麗
Kosu Namsan ŏm hwasang poŭn sahoe wŏnmun 故修南山儼社會願文
Koun chip 孤雲集
ku 九
kubanch'awang 鳩槃荼王
kuch'ŭng mokt'ap 九層木塔
Kudara Kannon 百濟觀音
Kudara Ōdera 百濟大寺
Kuiji 窺基
Kukhak 國學
Kukpan 國飯
kuksa 國師
Kuksa 國史
Kuksinsa 國神寺
kukt'ong 國統
kŭn'gu Mirŭk 勤求彌勒
kŭmdang 金堂
Kŭmgangnyŏng 金剛嶺
Kŭmgangsa 金剛社
Kŭmgang sammae-gyŏng non 金剛三昧經論
Kŭmgangsan 金剛山
kŭmgangsin 金剛神
kŭmgang yŏksa 金剛力士
Kŭmgyo 金橋
Kŭmjŏngsan 金井山
Kŭmnyun 金輪
Kŭmsansa 金山寺
kŭn 斤
Kŭngnakchŏn 極樂殿
kungno 國老
Kusha 俱舍
Kwalchiji 括地志
Kwangdŏk 廣德
kwanggwach'ŏn wang 廣果天王
kwangŭmch'ŏnwang 光音天王
Kwanseŭm 觀世音

Glossary of Sinitic Logographs 185

Kwanŭm 觀音
Kwanŭmjŏn 觀音殿
Kwanŭm toryang 觀音道場
kwasil ch'ŏnja 果實天子
Kwijŏngmun 歸正門
kwisinwang 鬼神王
kyedan 戒壇
Kyeduma 雞頭摩
Kyejoksan 雞足山
Kyeramsan 鷄藍山
Kyerim 鷄林
Kyerim chapchŏn 雞林雜傳
Kyerim pon'gi 雞林本記
Kyeryongsan 雞龍山
Kyeyulchong 戒律宗
Kyōkai 景戒
kyŏl 結
kyŏl wi Hwaŏmsa 結為華嚴社
Kyŏngdŏk 景德
Kyŏnghŭng 憬興
Kyŏngjo 慶祖
Kyŏngju 慶州
Kyŏnhwŏn 甄萱
Kyŏngmun 景文
Kyŏngsang pukto 慶尚北道
Kyŏngsun 敬順
kyŏngt'ap 敬塔
Kyŏrŏn 決言
Kyŏrŭng 決凝
Kyunyŏ 均如
Kyunyŏ chŏn 均如傳
Liang 梁
Liang lu 梁錄
lichan 禮懺
Lingfu 靈府
Lingjiu shan 靈鷲山
Lingyunsi 陵雲寺 / 凌雲寺
Liu-Song 劉宋
longhua 龍華
Longmenku 龍門窟
Lu Gao 陸杲
luohan 羅漢
Luoyang 洛陽

Luoyang qielan ji 洛陽伽藍記
Lushan Huiyuan 廬山慧遠
Lu Yu 陆羽
maaebul 磨崖佛
maengsun 孟旬
Mahajindan 摩訶震旦
mahoragawang 摩睺羅伽王
Majin 摩震
Majŏnggyesa 摩頂溪寺
malbŏp 末法
Malgal 靺鞨
Manwŏlsan 滿月山
Maranat'a 摩羅難陀
Maya puin 摩耶夫人
Miaofa lianhua jing 妙法蓮華經
miaojue 妙覺
miaojuezhe wushangdi 妙覺者無上地
Miaoshan 妙善
mijiao 密教 (esoteric teaching)
mijiao 秘教 (secret teaching)
Milbon 密本
milchang 密藏
Mile dachengfo jing 彌勒大成佛經
Mile dage 彌勒大閣
Mile xiasheng jing 彌勒下生經
Miminashi 耳梨
Mingtang 明堂
Minjangsa 敏藏寺
Mirisa 美理寺
Mirŭk 彌勒
Mirŭkchŏn 彌勒殿
Mirŭkkok 彌勒谷
Mirŭkpong 彌勒峰
Mirŭksa 彌勒寺
Mirŭk toryang 彌勒道場
Misi 彌尸
Misŭng 味勝
Misungsan 美崇山
Mit'a ch'ali 彌陀利
Mi'ta toryang 彌陀道場
Moaksan 母岳山
mofa 末法
Mohe 靺鞨

Mohezhendan 摩訶震旦
Monijŏm 牟尼岾
Moryangni 牟梁里
Mosan 母山
Mu 武
Muae 無碍
Muae ka 無碍歌
Mudŭnggok 無等谷
Mugŭk 無極
Mujangsa 鍪藏寺
Mujangsa Amit'a yŏrae chosang sajŏk pi 鍪藏寺阿彌陀如來造像事蹟碑
Mukhoja 墨胡子
munduru pimil chi pŏp 文豆婁秘密之法
Munjong 文宗
Munmu 文武
Muningnim 文仍林
Munsŏng 文聖
Munsu 文殊
Munsugapsa 文殊岬寺
muryang chŏnggŏch'ŏn 無量淨居天
Muryangsu 無量壽
Muryangsujŏn 無量壽殿
Musŏlchŏn 無說殿
Muyŏl 武烈
Muyŏm 無染
Myōe 明惠
Myŏnghyo 明曉
Myŏnghyo' 明皛
Myŏngju 溟州
Myŏngnang 明朗
Naemul 奈勿
Naeryŏk 奈歷
nahan 羅漢
Naksan 落山
Naksansa 洛山寺
Nalligun 捺己郡
Namhae 南海
Namhangsa 南巷寺
Namgan puin 南澗夫人
Namgansa 南澗寺
Namsan 南山
nangdo 郎徒
Nanghye 郎慧
Nangsan 狼山
Nanhai jigui neifa zhuan 南海寄歸內法傳
Nan Qi 南齊
Nansŭng 難勝
Nara 奈良
neidaochang 內道場
nianjing 念經
Nihon ryōiki 日本靈異記
Nizhiduo 昵枳多
Nohil Pudŭk 努肹夫得
Nosana 廬舍那
Nulchi 訥祇
Nŭngin 能仁
oak 五岳
obang sin 五方神
Obongsan 五峯山
Odaesan 五臺山
oesa 外寺
Ojin 悟眞
Ojisan 污知山
Okch'ŏnsa 玉泉寺
ŏmjang 嚴莊
Ongnyong chip 玉龍集
Orisan 鳧山
Oryesan 烏禮山
Osan 吳山
Paegun'gyo 白雲橋
Paegwŏlsan 白月山
Paekche 百濟
Paekchŏng 白淨
Paekhwa toryang parwŏn mun 白花道場法願文
paekkojwa kanghoe 百高座講會
Paekpan 伯飯
Paeksan 白山
Paeksŏngsan 百城山
Paeksŏngsansa chŏnt'ae Kilsangt'ap chung nappŏp ch'imgi 百城山寺前臺吉祥塔中納法琛記
Paektusan 白頭山
Paengnyŏnsa 白蓮社
Paengnyulsa 栢栗寺

Glossary of Sinitic Logographs 187

p'ajinch'an 波珍湌
Pak Yŏmch'ok 朴厭髑
p'al 八
p'albusin 八部神
Palchŏng 發正
P'algongsan 八公山
p'algwanhoe 八關會
p'algwŏn kŭm-gyŏng 八卷金經
pal pori sim 發菩提心
p'al pujŏngjae 八不淨財
p'al puljŏngmul 八不淨物
palsim tanwŏl 發心旦越
Paryŏnsu 鉢淵藪
pibŏp 秘法
pido 犀道
P'ijŏn 皮田
Piluzhena zhuangyan da louge 毘盧遮那莊嚴大樓閣
Pimara 毗摩羅
pin 品
pindao 貧道
Pirojana 毘盧遮那
Pirojŏn 毘盧殿
Pisŭlsan 毗瑟山
Poanhyŏn 保安縣
Pŏbyun 法雲
poch'ŏ 補處
Poch'ŏn 寶川
Poch'ŏnam 寶川庵
Podŏk 普德
Pogae 寶開
Pogan 福安
Pogwangsa 普光寺
pokchŏn o wŏn 福田五員
Pŏmil 梵日
Pŏmma 梵摩
Pŏmnyu 法流
Pŏmnyunsa 法輪社
Pŏmŏsa 梵魚寺
Pŏmŏsa sajŏk ki 梵魚寺事蹟記
Pŏmsu 梵修
ponch'e 本體
Pongdŏksa 奉德寺

Ponghwangsan 鳳凰山
Pongsŏng chi 鳳城誌
Ponjŏn 本傳
ponjon pul 本尊佛
Pŏp 法
Pŏpchusa 法主寺
Pŏphae 法海
Pŏphŭng 法興
Pŏpki 法起
Pŏpp'il 法弼
Pŏpsangjong 法相宗
Pŏpsŏngjong 法性宗
posal mahasal 菩薩摩訶薩
Poŭnhyŏn 報恩縣
Powŏnsa 普願寺
Pua 負兒山
Puak 父岳
Puan'gun 扶安郡
Pugak 北嶽
puik pangga chi sa 輔益邦家之事
Pulgong kyŏnsak Kwanŭm 不空羂索觀音
Pulguksa 佛國寺
Pulguksa kogŭm ch'anggi 佛國寺古今創記
Pulsan 佛山
Pulsaŭibang 不思議房
P'umil 品日
pun 分
P'ungak 楓岳
P'ungnosan 風盧山
p'ungnyu 風流
p'ungsin 風神
Punhwangsa 芬皇寺
Puryerang 夫禮郎
Pusan 浮山
Pusa yingluo benye jing 菩薩瓔珞本業經
Pusŏksa 浮石寺
Pusŏksa Wŏnyung kuksa pi 浮石寺圓融國師碑
Putuoshan 普陀山
Puyŏgun 扶餘郡
Puyunch'on 浮雲村

P'yohun 表訓
P'yohunsa 表訓寺
p'yŏnjŏngch'ŏnwang 遍淨天王
Pyŏnsan 邊山
Qianbu Guanyin 千部觀音
Qian Qin 前秦
Qianshou 千手
Qianshou jing 千手經
Qianshou qianyan Guanshiyin pusa
    guangda yuanman wuai dabeixin
    tuoluoni jing 千手千眼觀世音菩薩廣
    大圓滿無礙大悲心陀羅尼經
qianshou zhou 千手呪
Qianyan qianbi 千眼千臂
Qianyan qianbi Guanshiyin pusa
    tuoluoni shenzhou jing 千眼千臂觀
    世音菩薩陀羅尼神呪經
Qiefandamo 伽梵達磨
Qinghe Cui 清河崔
Qingliang 清涼
Qingliangshan 清涼山
Qixin lun 起信論
Renwang bore boluomi jing 仁王般若波
    羅密經
Ritsu 律
Ru fajie pin 入法界品
rulai zang 如來藏
ruyi baozhu 如意寶珠
sabangbul 四方佛
Sach'ŏnmi 沙川尾
sach'ŏnwang 四天王
Sach'ŏnwangsa 四天王寺
saenae norae 詞腦歌
Saichō 最澄
saji 寺志/ 寺誌
saju 寺主
saju p'alcha 四柱八字
Sakchu 朔州
sallyŏng 山靈
sambo 三寶
Samch'ŏn'gi 三川歧
Samgongsa 三公寺
Samguk sagi 三國史記

Samguk yusa 三國遺事
Samhwaryŏng 三花嶺
Samhwasa 三和寺
Sam Mirŭk kyŏng 三彌勒經
Samnon 三論
samsan 三山
samsipsamch'ŏnwang 三十三天王
sangbŏp 像法
sangdae 上代
sangdaedŭng 上大等
sanggo 上古
Sangju 尙州
sangmal 像末
Sangsa chŏn 相師傳
Sangwangsan 象王山
Sangwŏn 相源
Sang Yulsa 廂律師
Sanron 三論
Sap'o 絲浦
Saryangbu 沙梁部
Saryun 舍輪
sasa 四事
sasa muae 事事無礙
saŭn 四恩
Segyusa 世逵寺
Sehŏn kakkan 世獻角干
sengdu 僧都
Sengxiang 僧詳
sengzheng 僧正
sengzhu 僧主
Shancai 善財
Shandao 善導
Shandong 山東
Shang Tianzhusi 上天竺寺
Shanmiao 善妙
Shanxi 山西
Shengli 聖歷
Shengmeishan 省眉山
shengren 聖人
Shenseng zhuan 神僧傳
shenzhong 神眾
Shibishan 石壁山
Shi Daoan 釋道安

Glossary of Sinitic Logographs

shidi 十地
Shidi jing lun 十地經論
shi huixiang 十廻向
Shi huixiang pin 十廻向品
Shiji 史記
shijing 石經
Shingon 眞言
shishi wuai 事事無礙
shiwang 十王
shixin 十信
shixing 十行
Shiyimian 十一面
shizhu 十住
Shoulengyan jing 首楞嚴經
Shundao 順道
Shusheng Miaoyan 殊勝妙顏
si 寺
Sibilmyŏn Wŏnt'ong sang 十一面圓通象
Sichuan 四川
Sidumal 翅頭末
Sifenlü shan busui ji jiemo 四分律刪補隨機羯磨
Sifenlü shanfan buque xingshi chao 四分律刪繁補闕行事鈔
Sil 實
Silla 新羅
Silla Such'anggun hoguksŏng p'algak tŭngnu ki 新羅壽昌郡護國城八角燈樓記
Sillim 神琳
sillok 實綠
Sima Qian 司馬遷
Sima Tan 司馬談
simch'o 心礎
Simmun hwajaeng non 十門和諍論
simnyu sinjung yŏlmyŏng 卅類神衆列名
Simsang 審祥
Simwŏn chang 心源章
Sininjong 神印宗
sinjung 神衆
Sinjung'ak 神衆岳
Sinjung kyŏng 神衆經
sinjungsin 身衆神
Sinjungwŏn 神衆院
Sinmu 神武
Sinmun 神文
Sinmyo changgu tae tarani 神妙章句大陀羅尼
Sinsŏng'gul 神聖窟
Sinyurim 神遊林
siwang 十王
Sobaekhwa 小白華
Sobaeksan 小白山
Sŏch'ŏngjŏn 婿請田
Soga no Umako 蘇我馬子
Soji 炤智
Sŏkch'ong 釋聰
Sŏkkat'ap 釋迦塔
Sŏkkuram 石窟庵
Sŏkpulsa 石佛寺
Sŏk Saengŭi 釋生義
Sŏkssi 釋氏
Sŏn 禪
Sŏndŏk 善德
Song 宋
Songak 松嶽
Songdo 松都
Sŏngdŏk 聖德
Song gaoseng zhuan 宋高僧傳
sŏnggol 聖骨
songgyŏng 誦經
songjing 誦經
Songnisan 俗離山
Sŏngop'yŏng 省烏坪
Sŏng yusing-non hakki 成唯識論學記
Song Zixian 宋子賢
Sŏnjae 善財
Subŏm 修梵
Such'anggun 壽昌郡
Sugwangjŏn 壽光殿
Sui 隋
Suiqiu tuoluoni 随求陀羅尼
Sujŏngsa 水精社
Sulchong 述宗
Sundo 順道
Sŭnggŏ 乘炬

Sŭngjŏn 勝詮
Sŭngman 勝曼
sŭngnyŏ nangdo 僧侶郎徒
sŭngt'ong 僧統
Sunje 順濟
Sunŭng 順應
Susa 岫寺
susin 樹身
Susŏnggu 壽城區
Suwŏnsa 水源寺
Tabot'ap 多寶塔
T'aebaeksan 太白山
Taebi 大悲
taebi chu 大悲呪
taebŏmch'ŏnwang 大梵天王
T'aebong 泰封
t'aedae kakkan 太大角干
taedŏk 大德
taedoyuna 大都維那
Taegu 大邱
taegukt'ong 大國統
Tae Hwaŏmsa sajŏk 大華嚴寺史蹟
Tae Hwaŏm sujwa wŏnt'ong yangjung taesa Kyunyŏ chŏn pyŏngsŏ 大華嚴首座圓通兩重大師均如傳
Taehyŏn 大賢
T'aehyŏn 太賢
Taehyŏn *salch'an* 大玄薩喰
Taeil yŏrae 大日如來
taejajaech'ŏn wang 大自在天王
T'aejo 太祖
T'aejong Muyŏl 太宗武烈
Tae Kaya 大加耶
tae posal 大菩薩
taesŏsŏng 大書省
Taeungjŏn 大雄殿
Taewangam 大王岩
t'ahwajajaech'ŏnwang 他化自在天王
Taihe 太和
Taihechi 太和池
Taiyuan 太原
Talbulsŏng 達佛城
Taltal Pakpak 怛怛朴朴

tam'gye 談戒
Tammugal 曇無竭
Tane 曇噁
Tang 唐
Tang Taech'ŏnboksa kosaju pŏn'gyŏng taedŏk Pŏpchang hwasang chŏn 唐大薦福寺故寺主翻經大德法藏和尚傳
Tanŏmsa 曇嚴寺
Tanqian 曇遷
Tanwujie 曇無竭
Tao Qian 陶潛
Tao Yuanming 陶源明
Tendai 天台
Tianbao 天寶
Tiancheng 天成
Tiangongsi 天宮寺
Tianjian 天監
Tiantai 天台
Tiantai Zhiyi 天台智顗
tielun 鐵輪
Toch'o 道初
Tōdaiji 東大寺
T'ohamsan 吐含山
Tojŭng 道證
Tojungsa 道中寺
tokkyŏng 讀經
tong 統
Tongch'uksa 東竺寺
T'ongdosa 通道寺
Tongguk sŭng chŏn 東國僧傳
Tonghae 東海
Tonghaesi 東海市
tongi 東夷
tonglun 銅輪
Tŏngman 德曼
Tongnyun 銅輪
t'ong Pulgyo 通佛教
Top'iansa 到彼岸寺
Torich'ŏn 切利天
toryangsin 道場神
Tosolch'ŏn 兜率天
Tosolt'ach'ŏnwang 兜率天王

toyunanyang 都維那娘
Toyung 道融
tŭngji 等持
Tuoluoni zaji 陀羅尼雜集
Tut'asan 頭陀山
Ugokhyŏn 羽曲縣
Ŭich'ŏn 義天
Ŭijŏk 義寂
Ŭisang 義湘
Ulchin'guk 蔚珍國
Ulchinhyŏn 蔚珍縣
Ulsan 蔚山
Unebi 畝傍
Ungch'ŏn 熊川
Ungju 熊州
Ugŭmni 禺金里
Wando 莞島
wang 王
Wanghŭngsa 王興寺
Wang Kŏn 王建
wangnyŏk 王曆
wangsa 王師
wangsheng 往生
Wanli 萬曆
Weimojie jing 維摩詰經
Weishi 唯識
Wendi 文帝
Wenshu 文殊
Wihŭn 魏昕
Winant'a 韋難陀
Wŏlchang 月藏
wŏlch'ŏnja 月天子
Wŏlgwang 月光
Wŏlmyŏng 月明
wŏlsin ch'ŏnja 月身天子
Wŏlsŏng 月城
wŏn 員
Wŏnch'uk 圓測
Wŏn'gwang 圓光
Wŏnhyo 元曉
Wŏnjong mullyu 圓宗文類
Wŏnju 原州
Wŏnp'yo 元表

wŏnsil 圓室
Wŏnsŏng 元聖
Wŏnt'ongsa 圓通社
Wŏnyungjong 圓融宗
Wu 武
Wuliangshou jing 無量壽經
wuming 無明
Wutaishan 五臺山
wuyue 五嶽
Wuyue 吳越
Wu Zetian 武則天
xian 仙
xiangfa 像法
Xiangguosi 相國寺
Xiang Haiming 向海明
Xiangmo pin 降魔品
xianjiao 顯教
Xianqing 顯慶
Xianshou 賢首
Xiantong 咸通
xin 心
Xinxiu kefen luxue seng zhuan 信修科分六學僧傳
Xiufanma 修梵摩
Xuanzang 玄奘
Xuanzong 玄宗
Xu gaoseng zhuan 續高僧傳
yach'awang 夜茶王
yakch'osin 藥草神
Yaksajŏn 藥師殿
Yamach'ŏnwang 夜摩天王
Yangdi 陽帝
Yangju 良州
Yangwŏn 良圓
Yangyanggun 壤陽郡
Yanzi 崦嵫
ya yŏm Hwaŏm sinjung 夜念華嚴神衆
yech'am 禮懺
Yemaek 濊貊
yenyŏm Mit'a 禮念彌陀
Yijing 義淨
Yijing 易經
yinlun 銀輪

yishi 遺事
Yŏlbanjong 涅槃宗
yŏmbul sammae 念佛三昧
yŏm posal myŏng 念菩薩名
Yongbo 龍寶
Yŏngbyŏn 靈卞
Yŏngch'ŏn 永川
yongchu 湧出
yŏnggang ch'illyŏn se ch'a kap 永康七年歲次甲
Yonggung 龍宮
Yŏnghae 寧海
Yonghui 永徽
Yŏnghŭngsa 永興寺
yonghwa hyangdo 龍華香徒
Yonghwasan 龍華山
Yŏn'gi 緣起/ 煙氣
Yongjangsa 茸長寺
Yŏngje 迎帝
Yŏngju 榮州
Yŏngmyosa 靈妙寺/ 零妙寺
Yongningsi 永寧寺
yongsin 龍神
yongwang 龍王
Yŏnhwagyo 蓮花橋
yŏn kukt'o 緣國土
yŏnjwa-sŏk 宴坐石
Yŏnsan 連山
yŏnsŭng 緣僧
yŏrae chang 如來藏
yŏŭi poju 如意寶珠
Yuanhe 元和
Yuanxiang 圓香
Yueguang pusa 月光菩薩
Yueshang Zhuanlun Shengwang 月上轉輪聖王
Yuezhou 越州
Yuga 瑜伽
Yuga shidi lun 瑜伽師地論
yuktup'um 六頭品
Yumedono Kannon 夢殿觀音
Yumenguan 玉門關
Yungangku 雲岡窟
Yunhuasi 雲華寺
Yusagang 流沙江
Yu Tang Sillagukko yangjo kuksa kyoik tae Nanghye hwasang paegwŏl pogwang chi t'appimyŏng pyŏngsŏ 有唐新羅國故朝國師教諡大郎慧和尙白月葆光之塔碑銘幷序
Zanning 贊寧
Zhancha jing 占察經
Zhancha shane yebao jing 占察善惡業報經
Zhejiang 浙江
zhengfa 正法
Zhenguan 貞觀
zhenyan 眞言
Zhenyuan 貞元
Zhidan 枳怛
Zhidanna 枳怛那
Zhi Dun 支遁
zhihui 智慧
Zhi putichang pin 指菩提場品
Zhisheng 智昇
Zhitishan 支提山
Zhitong 智通
zhixin 至心
Zhiyan 智儼
Zhongnanshan 終南山
Zhou 周
zhouwen 呪文
Zhuangyanku 莊嚴窟
zhuanjing 轉經
zhuannian 專念
Zhu Qian 竺潛
Zongchimen 摠持門
Zongmi 宗密

Selected Bibliography

Classical and Canonical Sources

Amituo guyin shengwang tuoluoni jing 阿彌陀鼓音聲王陀羅尼經 (*Aparimitāyurjñānahṛdaya Dhāraṇī*). One roll. Translator unknown. Liang 梁 dynasty (502–557). T 370, 12.352b–353a.

Apidamo jushe lun 阿毘達磨俱舍論 (*Abhidharmakośabhāṣya*). 30 rolls. By Vasubandhu (Shiqin 世親, 400–480). Translated by Xuanzang 玄奘 (ca. 600–664). T 1558, 29.1a–159b.

Bore boluomiduo xin jing 般若波羅蜜多心經 (*Prajñāpāramitāhṛdaya Sūtra*, *Heart Sūtra*). One roll. Translated by Xuanzang 玄奘 (ca. 600–664) in 649. T 251, 8.848c.

Bukong juansuo shenbian zhenyan jing 不空羂索神變眞言經 (*Amoghapāśakalparāja*). 30 rolls. Translated by Bodhiruci (Putiliuzhi 菩提流志, d. 727) in 707. T 1092, 20.227a–398c.

Bukong juansuo tuoluoni jing 不空羂索陀羅尼經 (*Amoghapāśa Dhāraṇī*). One roll. Translated by Li Wuchan 李無諂 in 700. T 1096, 20.409b–421b.

Chōsen jisatsu shiryō 朝鮮寺刹史料 (Historical materials in Korean monasteries). Modern compilation edited by Chōsen Sōtokufu Naimubu Chihōkyoku 朝鮮總督府內務部地方局 (Japanese Colonial Administration of Korea, Internal Affairs Department, Provincial Bureau). 2 vols. Keijō (Seoul): Keijō Insatsujo 京城印刷所, 1911.

Chōsen kinseki sōran 朝鮮金石聰覽 (Comprehensive collection of Korean epigraphy). Modern compilation edited by Chōsen Sōtokufu 朝鮮聰督府 (Japanese Colonial Administration of Korea). 2 vols. Keijō (Seoul): Chōsen Sōtokufu, 1919.

Da bore boluomiduo jing 大般若波羅蜜多經 (*Mahāprajñāpāramitā Sūtra*). 600 rolls. Translated by Xuanzang 玄奘 (ca. 600–664) between 660 and 663. T 220, 5.1a–7.1110b.

Dafangdeng tuoluoni jing 大方等陀羅尼經 (*Pratyutpannabuddhasammukhāvasthitasamādhi Sūtra*). Four rolls. Translated by Fazhong 法衆 between 402 and 413. T 1339, 21.641a–661a.

Dafangguang huayan jing shu 大放光華嚴經疏 (Commentary on the Flower Garland

Sūtra). 60 rolls. By Chengguan 澄觀 (ca. 720/38–837/38) between 784 and 787. T 1735, 35.503a–963a.

Dafangdeng tuoluoni jing 大方等陀羅尼經 (The great Vaipulya dhāraṇī). Four rolls. Translated by Fazhong 法衆 between 402 and 413. T 1339, 21.641a–661a.

Da Tang xiyu ji 大唐西域記 (Record of a journey to the west during the mighty Tang). 12 rolls. By Xuanzang 玄奘 (ca. 600–664) and compiled by Bianji 辨機 in 646. T 2087, 51.867b–947c.

Dunhuang bianwen jiaozhu 敦煌變文校注 (Annotated collection of Dunhuang transformation tales). Modern compilation edited by Huang Wang 黃徃 and Zhang Yongquan 張涌泉. Beijing: Zhonghua shuju, 1997.

Fangdeng sanmei xingfa 方等三昧行法 (The method of Vaipulya samādhi). One roll. Explained by Zhiyi 智顗 (538–597) and recorded by Guanding 灌頂 (561–632). T 1940, 46, 943a–949a.

Fangguang da zhuangyan jing 方廣莊嚴經 *(Lalitavistara)*. 12 rolls. Translated by Dīvakara (Dipoheluo 地婆訶羅, Rizhao 日照, 613–687) between 683 and 685. T 187, 3.539a–617b.

Fayuan zhulin 法苑珠林 (A forest of pearls in the garden of the Dharma). 100 rolls. Compiled by Daoshi 道世 (ca. 596–683); completed in 668. T 2122, 53.269a–1030a.

Fozu tongji 佛祖統紀 (Chronicle of the Buddhas and patriarchs). 54 rolls. By Zhipan 志磐 (fl. 1258–1269). T 2035, 49.129b–475c.

Gaoseng Faxian zhuan 高僧法顯傳 (Life of the eminent monk Faxian). One roll. By Faxian 法顯 (d. after 423 C.E.) after 405. T 2085, 51.857a–866c.

Gaoseng zhuan 高僧傳 (Lives of eminent monks). 13 rolls. Compiled by Huijiao 慧皎 (497–554); completed ca. 519–554. T 2059, 50.322c–418a.

Guan Mile pusa shangsheng Doushuaitian jing 觀彌勒菩薩上生兜率天經 (Sūtra on the visualization of Maitreya's rebirth above in Tuṣita Heaven). One roll. Translated by Juqu Jingsheng 沮渠京聲 in 455. T 452, 14.418b–420c.

Guan Mile shangsheng Doushuaitian jing zan 觀彌勒上生兜率天經贊 (Commentary on the Sūtra on the Visualization of Maitreya's Rebirth above in Tuṣita Heaven). Two rolls. By Kuiji 窺基 (632–682). T 1772, 38.272b–299a.

Guannian Amituofo xianghai sanmei gongde famen 觀念阿彌陀佛相海三昧功德法門 (The meritorious Dharma approach of the samādhi involving visualization of the ocean-like marks of the Buddha Amitābha). One roll. Compiled by Shandao 善導 (613–681). T 1959, 47.22b–30b.

Guan Wuliangshou jing 觀無量壽經 (Book on the visualization of Amitāyus). One roll. T 365, 12.340b–346b.

Haedong kosŭng chŏn 海東高僧傳 (Lives of eminent Korean monks). Five rolls (two rolls extant). Compiled by Kakhun 覺訓 in 1215. T 2065, 50.1015a–1023c.

Haein sammae non 海印三昧經論 (Treatise on the ocean-seal samādhi). One roll. By Myŏnghyo 明皛 (Wŏnhyo?). X 103.299c–301b; HPC 2.397b–399b.

Han'guk kŭmsŏk chŏnmun 韓國金石全文 (Complete Korean epigraphy). Modern

Selected Bibliography

compilation edited by Hŏ Hŭngsik 許興植. 3 vols. Seoul: Asea Munhwasa, 1984.

Han'guk kŭmsŏk yumun 韓國金石遺文 (Addendum of Korean epigraphy). Modern compilation edited by Hwang Suyŏng 黃壽永. 5th ed. Seoul: Ilchisa, 1994.

Han'guk Pulgyo chŏnsŏ 韓國佛教全書 (Complete works of Korean Buddhism). 12 vols. Seoul: Tongguk Taehakkyo Ch'ulpansa, 1979[–2000].

Hebu jinguangming jing 合部金光明經 (*Suvarṇaprabhāsa*, Sūtra of golden light). Eight rolls. Translated by Baogui 寶貴 in 597 and combined with the earlier translation by Dharmakṣema (Tanwuchen 曇無讖, 385–433) completed between 414 and 421. T 664, 16.359b–402a.

Huayan jing 華嚴經 = *Dafangguang fo huayan jing* 大方廣佛華嚴經 (*Buddhāvataṃsaka Sūtra, Flower Garland Sūtra*). 60 rolls. Translated by Buddhabhadra (Juexian 覺賢, 359–429) between 418 and 422. T 278, 9.395a–788b.

Huayan jing 華嚴經 = *Dafangguang fo huayan jing* 大方廣佛華嚴經 (*Buddhāvataṃsaka Sūtra, Flower Garland Sūtra*). 80 rolls. Translated by Śikṣānanda (Shichanantuo 實叉難陀, 652–710) between 695 and 699. T 279, 10.1a–444c.

Huayan jing tanxuan ji 華嚴經探玄記 (Searching the mysteries of the Flower Garland Sūtra). 20 rolls. By Fazang 法藏 (643–712) between 687 and 695. T 1733, 35.107a–492c.

Hwaŏmgyŏng so 華嚴經疏 (Commentary on the Flower Garland Sūtra). Originally either ten or eight rolls; only preface and roll three extant. By Wŏnhyo 元曉 (617–686). T 2757, 85.234c–236a; HPC 1.495c–498b.

Hwaŏm ilsŭng pŏpkye to 華嚴一乘法界圖 (Seal-diagram symbolizing the reality of the world as the one vehicle of the *Flower Garland Scripture*). One roll. By Ŭisang 義湘 (625–702). T 1887, 45.711a–716a; X 103.294a–299b; HPC 2.1a–8c.

Ilsŭng pŏpkye to Wŏnt'ong ki 一乘法界圖圓通記 (Wŏnt'ong Kyunyŏ's commentary on the seal-diagram symbolizing the reality of the world as the one vehicle). Two rolls. By Kyunyŏ 均如 (923–973). HPC 4:1a–39a.

Jizhujing lichanyi 集諸經禮懺儀 (Rituals of worship and repentance collected from all the scriptures). Two rolls. Compiled by Zhisheng 智昇 (fl. 700–740). T 1982, 47.456b–74c.

Kaiyuan shijiao lu 開元釋教錄 (Record of Śākyamuni's teachings compiled during the Kaiyuan period). 20 rolls. By Zhisheng 智昇 (fl. 700–740) in 730. T 2154, 55.477a–723a.

Koryŏsa 高麗史 (History of Koryŏ). 137 vols. Compiled in 1451 by Chŏng Inji 鄭麟趾 (1396–1478) et al. Photolithic reprint in 3 vols. Seoul: Asea Munhwasa, 1972.

Koryŏ taejanggyŏng 高麗大藏經 (Korean Buddhist canon). Edited by Sugi 守其, 1236–1251. Photolithic reprint. Modern edition in 47 vols. Seoul: Tongguk University Press, 1976.

Kyunyŏ chŏn 均如傳 (The life of Kyunyŏ) = *Taehwaŏm sujwa Wŏnt'ong yangjung taesa Kyunyŏ chŏn* 大華嚴首座圓通兩重大師均如傳 (The life of the Kyunyŏ, the great

Hwaŏm master and head monk Wŏnt'ong). One roll. By Hyŏngnyŏn Chŏng 赫蓮挺 (fl. 1074–1105) in 1075. HPC 4:511a–517a.

Lidai sanbao ji 歷代三寶紀 (Record of the three treasures throughout successive generations). 15 rolls. By Fei Changfang 費長方 in 597. T 2034, 49.22c–127c.

Linjian lu 林間錄 (Anecdotes from the Groves of Chan). By Juefan Huihong 覺範慧洪 (1071–1128) in 1107. X 148.293a–324a.

Luoyang qielan ji 洛陽伽藍記 (Record of Buddhist monasteries in Luoyang). Five rolls. By Yang Xuanzhi 楊衒之 about 547. T 2092, 51.999a–1022b.

Miaofa lianhua jing 妙法蓮花經 (*Saddharmapuṇḍarīka Sūtra, Lotus Sūtra*). Seven rolls. Translated by Kumārajīva (Jiumoluoshi 鳩摩羅什, 343–413) in 406 or 405. T 262, 9.1a–62c.

Mile dachengfo jing 彌勒大成佛經 (Sūtra on Maitreya's great attainment of Buddhahood). One roll. Translated by Kumārajīva (Jiumoluoshi 鳩摩羅什, 343–413) in 402. T 456, 14.428b–434b.

Mile xiasheng jing 彌勒下生經 (Sūtra on Maitreya's rebirth below). One roll. Translated by Dharmarakṣa (Zhu Fahu 竺法護, ca. 265–313) in 303. T 453, 14.421a–423c.

Mile xiasheng chengfo jing 彌勒下生成佛經 (*Maitreyavyākaraṇa*, Sūtra on Maitreya's descent and attainment of Buddhahood). One roll. Translated by Kumārajīva (Jiumoluoshi 鳩摩羅什, 343–413) between 402 and 412. T 454, 14.423c–425c.

Nihon shoki 日本書記 (History of Japan). 30 rolls. Compiled by imperial command in 720. Edited by Sakamoto Tarō 坂本太郎 et al. Nihon Koten Bungaku Taikei 日本古典文学体系 (Japanese classical literature system) 67–68. Tokyo: Iwanami Shoten, 1966.

Paekhwa toryang parwŏn mun 白花道場發願文 (Vow made at the White Lotus enlightenment site). Fragments. By Ŭisang 義湘. HPC 2.9a–b.

Pŏmŏsa sajŏk ki 梵魚寺事蹟記 (Record of historical traces at Pŏmŏ monastery). In *Pŏmŏsa chi* 梵魚寺誌 (Records of Pŏmŏ monastery). Compiled by Han'gukhak Munhŏn Yŏn'guso 韓國學文獻研究所 (Research center for Korean studies materials). Seoul: Asea Munhwasa, 1989.

Pubian guangming qingjing zhizheng ruyi baoyinxin wuneng sheng damingwang suiqiu tuoluoni jing 普遍光明清淨熾盛如意寶印心無能勝大明王大隨求陀羅尼經 (*Mahāpratisarā Dhāraṇī*). Two rolls. Translated by Amoghavajra (Bukong 不空, 705–774). T 1153, 20.616a–637b.

Pulguksa chi (oe) 佛國寺誌（外） (Records of Pulguk Monastery and addendum). Seoul: Asea Munhwasa, 1983.

Pusa yingluo benye jing 菩薩瓔珞本業經 (Sūtra on the original acts that serve as a bodhisattva's adornments). Two rolls. Translated by Zhu Fonian 竺佛念 between 374 and 417. T 1485, 24.1010b–1023a.

Qianyan qianbi Guanshiyin pusa tuoluoni shenzhou jing 千眼千臂觀世音菩薩陀羅尼神呪經 (*Nīlakaṇṭha*). One roll. Translated by Zhitong 智通 between 627 and 649. T 1057, 20.83b–96b.

Selected Bibliography

Qianshou qianyan Guanshiyin pusa guangda yuanman wuai dabeixin tuoluoni jing 千手千眼觀世音菩薩廣大圓滿無礙大悲心陀羅尼經 (*Nīlakaṇṭha*). One roll. Translated by Bhagavaddharma (Qiefandamo 伽梵達磨) between 650 and 661. T 1060, 20.105c–111c.

Quan Tang shi 全唐詩 (Complete Tang poetry). Compiled by Peng Dingqiu 彭定求 (1645–1719) et al. in 1705. Modern edition in 25 vols. Beijing: Zhonghua shuju, 1960. Reprint, 1992.

Renwang bore boluomi jing 仁王般若波羅蜜經 (Perfection of wisdom sūtra for humane kings). Two rolls. Translated by Kumārajīva (Jiumoluoshi 鳩摩羅什, 343–413) between 402 and 409. T 245, 8.825a–834a.

Renwang bore boluomi jing 仁王般若波羅蜜經 (Perfection of wisdom sūtra for humane kings). Two rolls. Translated by Amoghavajra (Bukong 不空, 705–774) in 765. T 246, 8.834a–845a.

Sam Mirŭk-kyŏng so 三彌勒經疏 (Commentary on the three Maitreya scriptures). One roll. By Kyŏnghŭng 憬興. T 1774, 38.303a–327a; X 35.381a–406b; HPC 2.77b–114b.

Samguk sagi 三國史記 (History of the Three Kingdoms). 50 chapters. By Kim Pusik 金富軾 (1075–1151); completed between 1136 and 1145. Edited by Yi Pyŏngdo 李丙燾. Seoul: Ŭryu Munhwasa 乙酉文化社, 1977.

Samguk Silla sidae Pulgyo kŭmsŏngmun kojŭng 三國新羅時代佛教金石文考證 (Compilation of Buddhist epigraphy from the Three Kingdoms and Silla periods). Modern compilation edited by Kim Young-tai 金煐泰. Han'guk Pulgyo kŭmsŏngmun kojŭng 韓國佛教金石文考證 (Annotated compilations of Korean Buddhist epigraphy) 1. Seoul: Minjoksa, 1992.

Samguk yusa kyogam yŏn'gu 三國遺事校勘研究 (Critical edition of the *Samguk yusa*). Five chapters. Compiled initially by Iryŏn 一然 (1206–1289) and emended further by later editors. Modern critical edition edited by Ha Chŏngnyong 河廷龍 and Yi Kŭnjik 李根直. Seoul: Sinsŏwŏn, 1997.

Shenseng zhuan 神僧傳 (Biographies of divine monks). Nine rolls. Compiler unknown. T 2064, 50.948b–1015a.

Shoulengyan jing 首楞嚴經 = *Dafoding rulai miyin xiuzheng liaoyi zhu pusa wanxing shoulengyan jing* 大佛頂如來密因修證了義諸菩薩萬行首楞嚴經 (*Śūraṃgama Sūtra*). 10 rolls. Translation by Pāramiti (Banlamidi 般剌蜜帝) in 705. T 945, 19.105c–155b.

Sifenlü shanbu suiji jiemo 四分律刪補隨機羯磨 (Karmic practices added and removed according to spiritual capacity in the four-part vinaya). Three rolls. Compiled by Daoxuan 道宣 (596–667). T 1808, 40.492a–511b.

Sifenlü shanfan buque xingshi chao 四分律刪繁補闕行事鈔 (Comments on practices and services not included in the four-part vinaya). 12 rolls. Compiled by Daoxuan 道宣 (596–667). T 1804, 40.1a–156c.

Silla sui chŏn 新羅殊異傳 (Tales of the bizarre from Silla). Only reconstructed fragments are extant. Attributed to Pak Illyang 朴寅亮 (d. 1096). In *Wang och'ŏn ch'ukkuk chŏn (wae)* 往五天竺國傳（外）(Diary of a journey to the five regions of India and other works), translated by Yi Sŏkcho 李錫造, 111–174. Ŭryu mungŏ 乙酉文庫 (Ŭryu pocket edition) 46. Seoul: Ŭryu Munhwasa, 1970.

Sinjŭng Tongguk yŏji sŭngnam 新增東國輿地勝覽 (Augmented survey of Korean geography). 55 vols. Originally *Tongguk yŏji sŭngnam* 新增東國輿地勝覽 (Survey of Korean geography). 50 vols. Compiled by No Sasin 盧思慎 (1427–1498) et al. between 1445 and 1481. Revised by Kim Chongjik 金宗直 et al. in 1530–1531. Photolithic reprint. Seoul: Tongguk Munhwasa, 1957.

Song gaoseng zhuan 宋高僧傳 (Lives of eminent monks compiled during the Song). 30 rolls. Compiled by Zanning 贊寧 (919–1001); completed in 988. T 2061.50.709a–900a.

Sŏng yusing-non hakki 成唯識論學記 (Study notes to the treatise on the completion of consciousness-only). Six rolls. T'aehyŏn 太賢 (fl. 742–765). X 80.1a–100b; HPC 3:483b–690c.

Suiqiu jide dazizai tuoluoni shenzhou jing 隨求即得大自在陀羅尼神呪經 *(Mahāpratisarā Dhāraṇī)*. One roll. Translated by Baosiwei 寶思惟 (Manicintana?, d. 721) in 693. T 1154, 20.637b–644b.

Taedong unbu kunok 大東韻府群玉 (Korean rhyming dictionary). 20 vols. Compiled by Kwŏn Munhae 權文海 (1534–1591); published by Kwŏn Chillak 權進洛 in 1798. Seoul: Asea Munhwasa, 1976.

Taishō shinshū dai zōkyō 大正新修大藏經 (Taishō edition of the Buddhist canon). Edited by Takakasu Junjirō 高楠順次郎 et al. 100 vols. Tokyo: Taishō Issaikyō Kankōkai, 1924–1932[–1935].

Tang Taech'ŏnboksa kosaju pŏn'gyŏng Taedŏk Pŏpchang hwasang chŏn 唐大薦福寺故寺主翻經大德法藏和尚傳 (Life of the *upadhyāya* Fazang, *bhadanta* of the Sūtra Translation Bureau and late overseer of Dajianfu monastery of the Tang). One roll. By Ch'oe Ch'iwŏn 崔致遠 (857–d. after 908). T 2054, 50.280a–289c; HPC 3:769c–777c.

Tiantai sijiao yi 天台四教儀 (An outline of the fourfold teachings of Tiantai). One roll. By Ch'egwan 諦觀 (d. 970). T 1931, 46.774a–780c.

Tongguk t'onggam 東國通鑑 (Comprehensive mirror of the Eastern Country [Korea]). 57 vols. Compiled by Sŏ Kŏjŏng 徐居正 (1420–1488) et al. between 1458 and 1484. 3 vols. Seoul: Chosŏn Kwangmunhoe, 1911.

Tongmunsŏn 東文選 (Anthology of Korean literature). 130 vols. Compiled by Sŏ Kŏjŏng 徐居正 (1420–1488) et al.; first edition published in 1478; second edition (*Sok Tongmunsŏn* 續東文選 [Continued anthology of Korean literature], an extra 3 vols.) published in 1517; third edition (*Sinch'an Tongmunsŏn* 新撰東文選 [New selections for the anthology of Korean literature], an extra 35 vols.) published in 1713. *Yŏngin p'yojŏm Tongmunsŏn* 影印標點東文選 (Photolithic reprint of the anthology of Korean literature), 4 vols. Seoul: Minjok Munhwa Ch'ujinhoe, 1999. Photolithic reprint in 5 vols. Tokyo: Tōyō Bunko Kenkyūso, 1970. Reprint, Seoul: Hyŏpsŏng Munhwasa, 1985.

Tuoluoni zaji 陀羅尼雜集 (Dhāraṇī miscellany). 10 rolls. Translator unknown. T 1336, 21.580c–637c.

Wei shu 魏書 (History of the Wei). 114 rolls. Compiled by Wei Shou 魏收 (506–572) between 551 and 554. 8 vols. Beijing: Zhonghua shuju, 1974.

Wŏnjong mullyu 圓宗文類 (Literature of the perfect [Hwaŏm] tradition). Originally 23 rolls; roll 14 and roll 22 extant. Compiled by Ŭich'ŏn 義天 (1055–1101). HPC 4:644c–645b.

Wuliangshou jing 無量壽經 (*Sukhāvatīvyūha Sūtra, Larger Pure Land Sūtra*). Two rolls. Translated by Saṅghavarman (Kang Sengkai 康僧鎧, d. 280) in 262. T 360, 12.265c–279a.

Xinjiao zhengqie Song-ben Guangyun 新校正切宋本廣韻 (Newly revised Song-dynasty edition of the *Expanded Rhyming Dictionary*). Five rolls. By Chen Pengnian 陳彭年 (961–1017). Modern edition revised by Lin Yin 林尹. Taipei: Liming wenhua shiye gongsi yinxing, 1987.

Xinxiu kefen luxue seng zhuan 信修科分六學僧傳 (Newly edited and compiled biographies of monks of the six learnings). 30 rolls. By Tane 曇噩 (1285–1373). X 133.210a–490c.

Xu gaoseng zhuan 續高僧傳 (Further lives of eminent monks [compiled during the Tang]). 30 rolls. Compiled by Daoxuan 道宣 (596–667); completed in 649. T 2060, 50.425a–707a.

Xuzangjing 續藏經 (Hong Kong reprint of *The Kyoto Supplement to the Canon* [*Dai Nihon zokuzōkyō* 大日本續藏經]). 150 vols. Hong Kong: Hong Kong Buddhist Association, 1967.

Yuga shidi lun 瑜伽十地論 (*Yogācārabhūmi*, Treatise on the stages of the Yogācāra). 100 rolls. Attributed to Maitreya (Mile 彌勒), translated by Xuanzang 玄奘 (ca. 600–664) between 646 and 648. T 1579, 30.279a–882a.

Yujŏmsa ponmalsa chi 楡岾寺本末寺誌 (Records of the main and branch monasteries associated with Yujŏm Monastery). Compiled and edited by Kim T'anwŏl 金坦月 in 1942. Reprint, Seoul: Asea Munhwasa, 1977.

Zizhi tongjian 資治通鑑 (Comprehensive mirror for aid in government). 294 chapters. By Sima Guang 司馬光 (1019–1086). 20 vols. Beijing: Zhonghua shuju, 1995.

Secondary Sources

Abé Ryūichi. *The Weaving of Mantra: Kūkai and the Construction of Esoteric Buddhist Discourse*. New York: Columbia University Press, 1999.

Adams, Edward B. *Korea's Golden Age: Cultural Spirit of Silla in Kyongju*. Seoul: International Publishing House, 1991.

Ahn Kye-hyŏn (An Kyehyŏn) 安啟賢. "Buddhism in the Unified Silla Period." In *Assimilation of Buddhism in Korea: Religious Maturity and Innovation in the Silla Dynasty*, edited by Lewis R. Lancaster and C. S. Yu, 1–45. Berkeley, Calif.: Asian Humanities Press, 1991.

———. "Koguryŏ Pulgyo ŭi chŏn'gae" 高句麗佛敎의 展開 (The development of Koguryŏ Buddhism). *Han'guk sasang* 韓國思想 7 (1964): 65–76.

———. "P'algwanhoe ko" 八關會考 (Study of the Assembly of the Eight Prohibitions). *Tongguk sahak* 東國史學 4 (1956): 31–54.

———. "A Short History of Ancient Korean Buddhism." In *Introduction of Buddhism to Korea: New Cultural Patterns*, edited by Lewis R. Lancaster and C. S. Yu, 1–27. Berkeley, Calif.: Asian Humanities Press, 1989.

———. *Silla chŏngt'o sasangsa yŏn'gu* 新羅淨土思想史研究 (Research on the history of Pure Land thought in Silla). Seoul: Asea Munhwasa, 1976. Reprint, Seoul: Hyŏnmunsa, 1987.

Aston, William G., trans. *Nihongi: Chronicles of Japan from the Earliest Times to A.D. 697*. 2 vols. Reprint, Rutland, Vt., and Tokyo: Charles E. Tuttle, 1972.

Bell, Catherine. *Ritual Theory, Ritual Practice*. New York: Oxford University Press, 1992.

Benn, James A. "Temperance Tracts and Teetotalers under the T'ang." M.A. thesis, University of London, School of Oriental and African Studies, 1994.

Best, Jonathan. "Buddhism in Paekche: A Cultural Approach to Early Korean History and Sculpture." Ph.D. diss., Harvard University, 1976.

———. "Early Korean Buddhist Bronzes and Sui Regional Substyles: A Contextual Study of Stylistic Influence in the Early Seventh Century." In *Sambul Kim Wŏllyong kyosu chŏngnyŏn t'oeim kinyŏm nonch'ong II* 三佛金元龍教授停年退任記論念叢 II (Festschrift commemorating the retirement of Sambul Prof. Kim Wŏllyong, vol. 2), compiled by Sambul Kim Wŏllyong Kyosu Chŏngnyŏn T'oeim Kinyŏm Nonch'ong Kanhaeng Wiwŏnhoe 三佛金元龍教授停年退任記念論叢 (Committee for the publication of the festschrift commemorating the retirement of Sambul Prof. Kim Wŏllyong), 476–512. Seoul: Ilchisa, 1987.

———. "Early Korea's Role in the Stylistic Formulation of the Yumedono Kannon, a Major Monument of Seventh-Century Japanese Buddhist Sculpture." *Korea Journal* 30, no. 10 (October 1990): 13–26.

———. "Imagery, Iconography and Belief in Early Korean Buddhism." *Korean Culture* 13, no. 3 (Fall 1992): 23–33.

———. "Tales of Three Paekche Monks Who Traveled Afar in Search of the Law." *Harvard Journal of Asiatic Studies* 51, no. 1 (1991): 139–197.

Birnbaum, Raoul. "Thoughts on T'ang Buddhist Mountain Traditions and Their Context." *T'ang Studies* 2 (1984): 5–23.

———. "The Manifestation of a Monastery: Shen-ying's Experiences on Mount Wu-t'ai in T'ang Context." *Journal of the American Oriental Society* 106, no. 1 (1986): 119–137.

Brock, Karen. "Tales of Gishō and Gangyō: Editor, Artist, and Audience in Japanese Picture Scrolls." Ph.D. diss., Princeton University, 1984.

Brown, Peter. *The Cult of the Saints: Its Rise and Function in Latin Christianity*. Chicago: University of Chicago Press, 1981.

Buswell, Jr., Robert E. "Buddhism in Korea." In *Buddhism and Asian History*, edited by Joseph M. Kitakawa and Mark D. Cummings, 151–158. New York: Macmillan, 1987.

———. "Chinul's Systematization of Chinese Meditative Techniques in Korean Sŏn Buddhism." In *Traditions of Meditation in Chinese Buddhism,* edited by Peter N. Gregory, 199–242. Studies in East Asian Buddhism, no. 4. Honolulu: University of Hawai'i Press, 1986.

———. "The Chronology of Wŏnhyo's Life and Works: Some Preliminary Considerations." In *Wŏnhyo yŏn'gu nonch'ong: kŭ ch'ŏrak kwa in'gan ŭi modŭn kŏt* 元曉研究論叢: 그哲學과 人間의 모든 것 (Compendium of studies on Wŏnhyo: Aspects of his philosophy and humanism), edited by Kuksa Ch'ongirwŏn Chosa Yŏn'gusil 國史統一調查研究室, 931–964. Seoul: Kuksa Ch'ongirwŏn Chosa Yŏn'gusil, 1987.

———. *The Formation of Ch'an Ideology in China and Korea: The Vajrasamādhi-Sūtra, a Buddhist Apocryphon.* Princeton: Princeton University Press, 1989.

———. "Hagiographies of the Korean Monk Wŏnhyo." In *Buddhism and Practice,* edited by Donald S. Lopez, Jr., 553–562. Princeton Readings in Religions. Princeton: Princeton University Press, 1995.

———. "Imagining 'Korean Buddhism.'" In *Nationalism and the Construction of Korean Identity,* edited by Hyung Il Pai and Timothy R. Tangherlini, 73–107. Korea Research Monograph 26. Berkeley, Calif.: Institute of East Asian Studies, University of California, 1998.

———. *The Korean Approach to Zen: The Collected Works of Chinul.* Honolulu: University of Hawai'i Press, 1983.

———. *The Zen Monastic Experience: Buddhist Practice in Contemporary Korea.* Princeton: Princeton University Press, 1992. Reprint, 1994.

Buzo, Adrian, and Tony Prince, trans. *Kyunyŏ-jŏn: The Life, Times and Songs of a Tenth Century Korean Monk.* University of Sydney East Asian Series 6. Canberra: Wild Peony, 1993.

Ch'ae Inhwan 蔡印幻. *Shiragi Bukkyō kairitsu shisō kenkyū* 新羅佛教戒律思想研究 (Studies on Buddhist precepts in Silla Buddhism). Tokyo: Kokusho Kankōkai, 1975.

Chen Jinhua. *Monks and Monarchs, Kinship and Kingship: Tanqian in Sui Buddhism and Politics.* Kyoto: Italian School of East Asian Studies, 2002.

———. "More Than a Philosopher: Fazang (643–712) as a Politician and a Miracle Worker." *History of Religions* 42, no. 4 (May 2003): 320–358.

———. "The Tang Buddhist Palace Chapels." *Journal of Chinese Religions* 32 (2004): 101–173.

Ch'en, Kenneth. *Buddhism in China: A Historical Survey.* Princeton: Princeton University Press, 1964.

Chen Yuzhen 陳昱珍. "Daoshi yu *Fayuan zhulin*" 道世與法苑珠林 (Daoshi and the *Fayuan zhulin*). *Zhonghua foxue xuebao* 中華佛學學報 5 (July 1992): 233–261.

Cho Aegi 趙愛姬. "Shiragi ni okeru Miroku shinkō no kenkyū" 新羅における弥勒信仰の研究 (Research on the cult of Maitreya in Silla). In *Shiragi Bukkyō kenkyū* 新羅佛教研究 (Research on Silla Buddhism), edited by Kim Chigyŏn 金知見 and Ch'ae Inhwan 蔡印幻, 236–281. Tokyo: Sankibō Busshorin, 1973.

Cho Insŏng 趙仁成. "Kungye ŭi seryŏk hyŏngsŏng kwa Mirŭk sinyang" 弓裔의 세력 형성과 彌勒信仰 (The formation of Kungye's power and the Maitreya cult). *Han'guk saron* 韓國史論 36 (2002): 23–52.

Cho Myŏnggi 趙明基. "Silla Pulgyo ŭi kyohak" 新羅佛敎의 敎學 (Scholasticism in Silla Buddhism). In *Han'guk Pulgyo sasangsa: Sungsan Pak Kilchin paksa hwagap kinyŏm* 韓國佛敎思想史: 崇山朴吉眞華甲記念 (History of Korean Buddhist thought: In commemoration of the 60th birthday of Sungsan Dr. Pak Kilchin), 149–175. Iri (Chŏlla pukto): Wŏn Pulgyo sasang yŏn'guwŏn, Wŏn'gwang Taehakkyo, 1975.

Cho Oh-kon. *Traditional Korean Theatre*. Berkeley, Calif.: Asian Humanities Press, 1988.

Ch'oe Pyŏnghŏn 崔柄憲. "Koryŏ sidae Hwaŏmhak ŭi pyŏnch'ŏn" 高麗時代華嚴學의 變遷 (The transformation of Hwaŏm learning in the Koryŏ period). *Han'guksa yŏn'gu* 韓國史研究 30 (1980): 61–76.

Ch'oe Wŏnsik 崔源植. "Silla hadae ŭi Haeinsa wa Hwaŏmjong" 新羅下代의 海印寺와 華嚴宗 (Haein Monastery and the Hwaŏm school during the late Silla period). *Han'guksa yŏn'gu* 韓國史研究 49 (1985): 1–27.

Ch'oe Yŏngsŏng 崔英成, trans. *Yŏkchu Ch'oe Ch'iwŏn chŏnjip* 譯註崔致遠全集 (Translated and annotated collected works of Ch'oe Ch'iwŏn). 2 vols. Seoul: Asea Munhwasa, 1998–1999.

Chŏng Pyŏngjo 鄭柄朝. "Silla sidae Chijang sinhaeng ŭi yŏn'gu" 新羅時代地藏信行의 研究 (Study of Kṣitigarbha cultic practices in the Silla period). *Pulgyo hakpo* 佛敎學報 19 (1982): 327–344.

Chou Yi-liang. "Tantrism in China." *Harvard Journal of Asiatic Studies* 8 (1945): 241–332.

Cleary, Thomas, trans. *The Flower Ornament Scripture: A Translation of* The Avataṃsaka Sutra. Boston: Shambhala, 1993.

de Visser, Marimus Willem. *Ancient Buddhism in Japan: Sūtras and Ceremonies in Use in the Seventh and Eight Centuries A.D. and Their History in Later Times*. 2 vols. Leiden: E. J. Brill, 1935.

Deuchler, Martina. *The Confucian Transformation of Korea: A Study of Society and Ideology*. Harvard-Yenching Monograph Series 36. Cambridge: Council on East Asian Studies, Harvard University, 1992.

Duncan, John B. "The Formation of the Central Aristocracy in Early Koryŏ." *Korean Studies* 12 (1988): 39–61.

———. *The Origins of the Chosŏn Dynasty*. Seattle: University of Washington Press, 2000.

Durt, Herbert. "La biographie du moine Coréen Ŭi-Sang d'après le Song kao seng tchouan." In *Kim Chaewŏn paksa hoegap kinyŏm nonch'ong* 金載元博士回甲紀念論叢 (Essays presented in commemoration of Dr. Kim Chaewŏn's 60th birthday), edited by Yŏdang Kim Chaewŏn Paksa Hoegap Kinyŏm Sach'ong Wiwŏnhoe 藜堂金載元博士回甲紀念事業委員會 (Committee for the commemoration of the 60th birthday of Yŏdang Kim Chaewŏn), 411–422. Seoul: Tong Wiwŏnhoe, 1969.

Edkins, Joseph. *Chinese Buddhism: A Volume of Sketches, Historical, Descriptive, and Critical.* 2nd ed. London: Kegan Paul, Trench, Trübner, 1893. Reprint, New York: Paragon Book Reprint, 1968.

Emmerick, R. E., trans. *The Sūtra of Golden Light; Being a Translation of the Suvarṇabhāsottamasūtra.* London: Luzac, 1970.

Forte, Antonino. "Un gioiello della rete di Indra. La lettera che dalla Cina Fazang inviò a Ŭisang in Corea." In *Tang China and Beyond: Studies on East Asia from the Seventh Century to the Tenth Century*, edited by Antonino Forte, 35–93. Kyoto: Instituto Italiano di Cultura Scuola di Studi sull'Asia Orientale, 1988.

———. *A Jewel of Indra's Net: The Letter of Fazang in China to Ŭisang in Korea.* ISEAS Occasional Papers Series 8. Kyoto: Italian School of East Asian Studies, 2000.

———. *Political Propaganda and Ideology in China at the End of the Seventh Century.* Naples: Instituto Universitario Orientale Seminario di Studi Asiatci, 1976.

Fujita Ryōsaku 藤田亮策. "Chōsen no nengō to kinen" 朝鮮の年号と記念 (Korean reign dates and commemorations). *Tōyō gakuhō* 東洋学報 41 (1958): 335–373.

Gard, Richard A. "The Mādhyamika in Korea." In *Paek Sŏnguk paksa songsu kinyŏm Pulgyohak nonmunjip* 白性郁博士頌壽記念佛教學論文集 (Festschrift in commemoration of the long life of Dr. Paek Sŏnguk), edited by Paek Sŏnguk Paksa Songsu Kinyŏm Saŏp Wiwonhoe 白性郁博士頌壽記念事業委員會 (Committee for the Commemoration of the Long Life of Dr. Paek Sŏnguk), 1155–1174. Seoul: Tongguk Taehakkyo, 1959.

Gimello, Robert M. "Chang Shang-ying on Wu-t'ai Shan." In *Pilgrims and Sacred Sites in China*, edited by Susan Naquin and Chün-fang Yü, 89–149. Berkeley, Los Angeles, and London: University of California Press, 1992.

———. "Chih-yen (智儼, 602–668) and the Foundations of Hua-yen (華嚴) Buddhism." Ph.D. diss., Columbia University, 1976.

Grayson, James Huntley. "Religious Syncretism in the Shilla Period: The Relationship between Esoteric Buddhism and Korean Primeval Religion." *Asian Folklore Studies* 53, no. 2 (1984): 187–198.

Gregory, Peter N. *Tsung-mi and the Sinification of Buddhism.* Princeton: Princeton University Press, 1991.

Guisso, R. W. L. *Wu Tse-t'ien and the Politics of Legitimation in T'ang China.* Bellingham: Western Washington University, 1978.

Ha Tae-Hung and Grafton K. Mintz, trans. *Samguk Yusa: Legends and History of the Three Kingdoms of Ancient Korea.* Seoul: Yonsei University Press, 1972.

Han Chongman 韓鍾萬. "Koun ŭi Pulgyogwan" 孤雲의佛教觀 (Koun's views on Buddhism). In *Koun Ch'oe Ch'iwŏn* 孤雲崔致遠, edited by Kim Injong 金仁宗 et al., 87–120. Seoul: Minŭmsa, 1989.

Han Kidu 韓基斗. *Han'guk Pulgyo sasang* 韓國佛教思想 (Korean Buddhist thought).

Iri (Chŏlla pukto): Wŏn Pulgyo sasang yŏn'guwŏn, Wŏn'gwang Taehakkyo, 1973.
Han Kimun 韓基汶. *Koryŏ sawŏn ŭi kujo wa kinŭng* 高麗寺院의 構造와 機能 (The structure and function of Korean monasteries). Seoul: Minjoksa, 1998.
Han'guk Pulgyo Yŏn'guwŏn 韓國佛教研究院, ed. *Hwaŏmsa* 華嚴寺 (Hwaŏm Monastery). Han'guk ŭi sach'al 韓國의사刹 8. Seoul: Ichisa, 1976.
———. *Kŭmsansa* 金山寺 (Kŭmsan Monastery). Han'guk ŭi sach'al 韓國의 寺刹 韓國의 寺刹 韓國의 寺刹 11. Seoul: Ilchisa, 1977.
———. *Naksansa* 洛山寺 (Naksan Monastery). Han'guk ŭi sach'al 韓國의 寺刹 韓國의 寺刹 韓國의 寺刹 14. Seoul: Ilchisa, 1978.
———. *Pŏpchusa* 法主寺 (Pŏpchu Monastery). Han'guk ŭi sach'al 韓國의 寺刹 韓國의 寺刹 韓國의 寺刹 5. Seoul: Ilchisa, 1975.
———. *Pulguksa* 佛國寺 (Pulguk Monastery). Han'guk ŭi sach'al 韓國의 寺刹 韓國의 寺刹 韓國의 寺刹 1. Seoul: Ilchisa, 1974.
———. *Pusŏksa* 浮石寺 (Pusŏk Monastery). Han'guk ŭi sach'al 韓國의 寺刹 韓國의 寺刹 韓國의 寺刹 9. Seoul: Ilchisa, 1976.
———. *Silla ŭi p'esa I* 新羅廢寺 I (Monastery ruins of Silla 1). Han'guk ŭi sach'al 韓國의 寺刹 韓國의 寺刹 韓國의 寺刹 3. Seoul: Ilchisa, 1974.
———. *Silla ŭi p'esa II* 新羅廢寺 II (Monastery ruins of Silla 2). Han'guk ŭi sach'al 韓國의 寺刹 韓國의 寺刹 韓國의 寺刹 12. Seoul: Ilchisa, 1977.
———. *Sŏkkuram* 石窟庵 (The stone Buddhist grotto Sŏkkuram). Han'guk ŭi sach'al 韓國의 寺刹 韓國의 寺刹 韓國의 寺刹 2. Seoul: Ilchisa, 1974.
———. *T'ongdosa* 通道寺 (T'ongdo Monastery). Han'guk ŭi sach'al 韓國의 寺刹 韓國의 寺刹 韓國의 寺刹 4. Seoul: Ilchisa, 1974.
Hayami Tasuku 速水侑, ed. *Kannon shinkō* 觀音信仰 (The Avalokiteśvara cult). Minshū shūkyōshi sōsho 民衆宗教史叢書 7. Tokyo: Yuzankaku Shuppan, 1982.
———. *Miroku shinkō: mo hitotsu no jōdo shinkō* 弥勒信仰: もう一つの浄土信仰 (The Maitreya cult: One more Pure Land cult). Tokyo: Hyoronsha, 1971.
———. "Narachō no Kannon shinkō ni tsuite" 奈良朝の観音信仰について (On the Avalokiteśvara cult in the Nara period). In *Kannon shinkō* 觀音信仰 (The Avalokiteśvara cult), edited by Hayami Tasuku. Minshū shūkyōshi sōsho 民衆宗教史叢書 7. Tokyo: Yuzankaku Shuppan, 1982.
Hibino Takeo 日比野丈夫 and Ono Katsutoshi 小野勝年. *Godaisan* 五台山 (Mount Wutai). Tōyō Bunko 593. Tokyo: Heibonsha, 1995.
Hŏ Hŭngsik 許興植. *Koryŏ Pulgyosa yŏn'gu* 高麗佛教史研究. Seoul: Ilchogak, 1986.
Hong Sunch'ang 洪淳昶. "Shiragi no sansan gogaku to Shiragijin no sangaku sūhai ni tsuite" 新羅の三山五岳と新羅人の山岳崇拝について (On the three mountains and five peaks of Silla and mountain worship by the people of Silla). In *Mikami Tsugio hakushi kiju kinen ronbunshū* 三上次男博士喜寿記念論文集 (Festschrift in commemoration of the 77th birthday of Dr. Mikami Tsugio), edited by Mikami Tsugio Hakushi Kiju Kinen Ronbunshū Iinkai 三上次男博士喜寿記念論文集委員会, 1: 247–264. Tokyo: Heibonsha, 1985.
Hong Yunsik 洪潤植. "Silla sidae Hwaŏm sinang ŭi sŏngkyŏk kwa kŭ yŏnghyang"

新羅時代 華嚴信仰의 性格과 그 影響 (The characteristics and influence of the Hwaŏm cult in the Silla period). *Silla munhwa* 新羅文化 6 (1989): 109–129.

Howard, Angela. "Tang and Song Images of Guanyin from Sichuan." *Orientations* 21, no. 1 (1990): 49–57.

Hucker, Charles O. *A Dictionary of Official Titles in Imperial China.* Stanford: Stanford University Press, 1985.

Hurvitz, Leon, trans. *Scripture of the Lotus Blossom of the Fine Dharma.* Translated from the Chinese of Kumārajīva. New York: Columbia University Press, 1976.

Hwang Suyŏng 黄壽永 et al., comps. *Han'guk pulsang sambaeksŏn* 韓國佛像三百選 (Selection of 300 Korean Buddhist images). Seoul: Han'guk Chŏngsin Munhwa Yŏn'guwŏn, 1982.

———. "Silla Kyŏngdŏk wangdae ŭi paekchi hŭksŏ Hwaŏm kyŏng" 新羅 景德王代의 白紙黑書 華嚴經 (The *Avataṃsaka Sūtra* in black ink on white paper from the reign of King Kyŏngdŏk of Silla). *Yŏksa hakpo* 歷史學報 83 (September 1979): 121–126.

Inagaki Hisao. *The Three Pure Land Sutras.* Berkeley, Calif.: Numata Center for Buddhist Translation and Research, 1995.

Inoue Hideo. "The Reception of Buddhism in Korea and Its Impact on Indigenous Culture." In *Introduction of Buddhism to Korea: New Cultural Patterns,* edited by Lewis R. Lancaster and C. S. Yu, 29–78. Berkeley, Calif.: Asian Humanities Press, 1989.

Jackson, Roger. "Terms of Sanskrit and Pali Origin Acceptable as English Words." *Journal of the International Association of Asian Studies* 5 (1982): 141–142.

Jamieson, John Charles. "The *Samguk Sagi* and the Unification Wars." Ph.D. diss., University of California, Berkeley, 1969.

Kamata Shigeo 鎌田茂雄. *Chūgoku Kegon shisōshi no kenkyū* 中國華嚴思想史の研究 (Research on the intellectual history of Chinese Huayan). Tokyo: Tokyō Daigaku Tōyō Bunka Kenkyūjo, 1965.

———. *Kegon no shisō* 華厳の思想 (Huayan thought). Tokyo: Kōdansha, 1983.

———. *Shiragi Bukkyōshi josetsu* 新羅仏教序說 (An introduction to Silla Buddhism). Tokyo: Daizō Shuppan, 1988.

Kamstra, Jacques H. *Encounter or Syncretism: The Initial Growth of Japanese Buddhism.* Leiden: E. J. Brill, 1967.

Kanaoka Shōkō 金岡照光. "Donkō bunken yori mitaru Miroku shinkō no ichishokumen" 敦煌文獻より見たる彌勒信仰の一側面 (A survey of the Maitreya cult as seen in Dunhuang materials). *Tōhō shūkyō* 東方宗教 53 (May 1979): 22–48.

Kang Woo-bang (Kang Ubang) 姜友邦. "Sŏkkuram Pulgyo chogak ŭi tosang haesŏk" 石窟庵佛教彫의圖像解釋 (Iconology of the Buddhist images at Sŏkkuram). *Misul charyo* 美術資料 57 (June 1996): 43–94.

———. "Sŏkkuram Pulgyo chogak ŭi tosangjŏk koch'al" 石窟庵 佛教彫의 圖像的考察 (An iconographical analysis of the Buddhist images at Sŏkkuram). *Misul charyo* 美術資料 56 (December 1995): 1–48.

Kasahara Kazuo 笠原一男, ed. *Nihon shūkyōshi* 日本宗教史 (History of Japanese religions). 2 vols. Seikai shūkyōshi 世界宗教史 11–12. Tokyo: Yamakawa Shuppansha, 1977.

Keel, Hee-Sung. *Chinul: The Founder of the Korean Sŏn Tradition*. Berkeley Buddhist Studies Series, no. 6. Berkeley, Calif.: Center for South and Southeast Asian Studies and Seoul: Po Chin Chai, Ltd., 1984.

Kegasawa Yasunori 氣賀沢保規. "Zuimatsu Mirokukyō no ran o meguru ichikōsatsu" 隋末弥勒教の乱をめぐる一考察 (A study of the rebellions caused by Maitreya teachings at the end of the Sui). *Bukkyō shigaku kenkyū* 仏教史學研究 23, no. 1 (1981): 15–32.

Ketelaar, James Edward. *Of Heretics and Martyrs in Meiji Japan: Buddhism and Its Persecution*. Princeton: Princeton University Press, 1990.

Kim Ch'ŏlchun 金哲埈. "Silla sangdae sahoe ŭi Dual Organization (sang)" 新羅上代社會의 Dual Organization (上) (The dual organization of the ancient society of Silla 1). *Yŏksa hakpo* 歷史學報 1 [1, no. 1] (July 1952): 15–47.

―――. "Silla sangdae sahoe ŭi Dual Organization (ha)" 新羅 上代社會의 Dual Organization (下) (The dual organization of the ancient society of Silla 2). *Yŏksa hakpo* 歷史學報 2 [1, no. 2] (October 1952): 85–113.

Kim Jongmyung. "Buddhist Rituals in Medieval Korea (918–1392)." Ph.D. diss., University of California, Los Angeles, 1994.

―――. "Chajang (fl. 636–650) and 'Buddhism as National Protector' in Korea: A Reconsideration." In *Religions of Traditional Korea*, edited by Henrik H. Sørensen, 23–55. Copenhagen: Seminar for Buddhist Studies, University of Copenhagen, 1995.

Kim Lena (Kim Rina) 金理那. "Sŏkkuram pulsanggun ŭi myŏngch'ing kwa yangsik e kwanhayŏ" 石窟庵佛像群의 名稱과 樣式에 관하여 (On the names and styles of the Buddhist images of Sŏkkuram). *Chŏngsin munhwa yŏn'gu* 精神文化研究 15, no. 3 (1992): 3–32.

Kim Pohyŏn 김보현, Pae Pyŏngsŏn 배병선, and Pak Tohwa 박도화. *Pusŏksa*. Seoul: Taewŏnsa, 1995.

Kim Poksun 金福順. *Silla Hwaŏmjong yŏn'gu* 新羅華嚴宗研究 (Research on the Hwaŏm school in Silla). Seoul: Minjoksa, 1990.

Kim Samyong 金三龍. *Han'guk Mirŭk sinang ŭi yŏn'gu* 韓國彌勒信仰의研究 (Research on the Maitreya cult in Korea). Seoul: Tonghwa Ch'ulpan Kongsa, 1983.

Kim Sanggi 金庠基. "Hwarang kwa Mirŭk sinang e taehayŏ" 花郎과 彌勒信仰에 對하여 (On the *hwarang* and the Maitreya cult). In *Yi Hongjik paksa hwagap kinyŏm Han'guk sahak nonch'ong* 李弘植博士花甲紀念韓國史學論叢 (Festschrift on Korean history in commemoration of the 60th birthday of Dr. Yi Hongjik), compiled by Yi Hongjik Paksa Hoegap Kinyŏm Munjip Kanhaeng Wiwŏnhoe 李弘植博士甲回紀念文集干行委員會 (Committee for the publication of the festschrift in commemoration of the sixtieth birthday of Dr. Yi Hongjik), 3–12. Seoul: Sin'gu Munhwasa, 1969.

Kim Sang-hyun (Kim Sanghyŏn) 金相鉉. "Silla chungdae chŏnje wanggwŏn kwa Hwaŏmjong" 新羅 中代專制王權과 華嚴宗 (Autocratic royal power and the Hwaŏm school in the mid-Silla period). *Tongbang hakchi* 東方學志 44 (1984): 59–91.

———. "Silla Hwaŏm haksŭng ŭi kyebo wa kŭ hwaltong" 新羅 華嚴 學僧의 系譜와 그 活動 (The lineage and activities of the scholastic Hwaŏm monks of Silla). *Silla munhwa* 新羅文化 新羅文化 1 (1984): 43–86.

———. *Silla Hwaŏm sasangsa yŏn'gu* 新羅華嚴思想史研究 (Research on the history of Hwaŏm thought in Korea). Seoul: Minjoksa, 1991.

———. *Silla ŭi sasang kwa munhwa* 신라의 사상과 문화 (Silla thought and culture). Seoul: Ilchisa, 1999.

———. "T'ongil Silla sidae ŭi Hwaŏm sinang" 統一新羅時代의 華嚴信仰 (The Hwaŏm cult in the Unified Silla period). *Silla munhwa* 新羅文化 新羅文化 2 (1985): 65–88.

Kim Sang-hyun, Kim Tonghyŏn, and Kwak Tongsŏk. *Pulguksa*. Seoul: Taewŏnsa, 1992.

Kim Sayŏp 金思燁, trans. and annot. *Sankoku shiki: kan'yaku* 三国史記: 完訳 (History of the Three Kingdoms: A complete translation). Tokyo: Akashi Shoten, 1997.

Kim Tonghwa 金東華. "Silla sidae ŭi Pulgyo sasang (il)" 新羅時代의 佛教思想 (一) (Buddhist thought in the Silla period, part 1). *Asesa yŏn'gu* 亞世亞研究 5, no. 2 (December 1962): 1–62.

———. "Silla sidae ŭi Pulgyo sasang (i)" 新羅時代의 佛教思想 (二) (Buddhist thought in the Silla period, part 2). *Asesa yŏn'gu* 亞世亞研究 亞世亞研究 6, no. 1 (May 1963): 367–421.

———. "Silla sidae ŭi Pulgyo sasang (sam)" 新羅時代의 佛教思想 (三) (Buddhist thought in the Silla period, part 3). *Asesa yŏn'gu* 亞世亞研究 亞世亞研究 6, no. 2 (December 1963): 127–168.

Kim Tujin 金杜珍. *Kyunyŏ Hwaŏm sasang yŏn'gu: Sŏngsang yunghoe sasang* 均如華嚴思想研究: 性相融會 思想 (Research on Kyunyŏ's Hwaŏm thought: The interfusion of nature and characteristics thought). Seoul: Ilchogak, 1983.

———. *Silla Hwaŏmsasangsa yŏn'gu* 신라화엄사상사연구 (Research on the history of Hwaŏm thought in Silla). Seoul: Seoul Taehakkyo Ch'ulp'anbu, 2002.

Kim Young-tai (Kim Yŏngt'ae) 金煐泰. "Chŏmch'al pŏphoe wa Chinp'yo ŭi kyobŏp sasang" 占察法會와 眞表의 教法思想 (Divination dharma assemblies and Chinp'yo's thought on teaching the dharma). In *Han'guk Pulgyo sasangsa: Sungsan Pak Kilchin paksa hwagap kinyŏm* 韓國佛教思想史: 崇山朴吉眞華甲記念 (History of Korean Buddhist thought: In commemoration of the 60th birthday of Sungsan Dr. Pak Kilchin), 383–405. Iri (Chŏlla pukto): Wŏn Pulgyo sasang yŏn'guwŏn, Wŏn'gwang Taehakkyo, 1975.

———. "Mirŭk sŏnhwa ko" 彌勒仙花考 (Study of the transcendent flower of Maitreya). *Pulgyo hakpo* 佛教學報 佛教學報 3, no. 4 (1966): 135–149.

———. "Silla chŏmch'al pŏphoe wa Chinp'yo ŭi kyobŏp yŏn'gu" 新羅占察法會와 眞表의教法研究 (A study of Buddhist fortune-telling assemblies and the missionary work of Chinp'yo). *Pulgyo hakpo* 佛教學報 佛教學報 9 (1972): 99–136.

———. "Silla Paegwŏl-san isŏng sŏrhwa ŭi yŏn'gu" 新羅白月山二聖說話의研究 (Study on the narrative on the two sages of Mount Paegwŏl in Silla). In *Hyŏsong Cho Myŏnggi paksa hwagap kinyŏm Pulgyo sahak nonch'ong* 曉城趙明基博師華甲紀念 佛教史學論叢 (Festschrift in Buddhist historical studies in commemoration of Dr. Cho Myŏnggi's sixtieth birthday), compiled by Hyŏsong Cho Myŏnggi Paksa Hwagap Kinyŏm Pulgyo Sahak Nonch'ong Kanhaeng Wiwŏnhoe 曉城趙明基博師華甲紀念佛教史學論叢刊行委員會 (Committee for the publication of the festschrift on Buddhist history commemorating the 60th birthday of Hyŏsong Cho Myŏnggi), 33–65. Seoul: Tongguk Taehakkyo Ch'ulpanbu, 1965.

———. "Sŭngnyŏ Nangdo ko: Hwarang-do wa Pulgyo wa ŭi kwan'gye ilgoch'al" 僧侶郎徒考: 花郎道와의 佛教關係一考察 (Study of the monk Nangdo: Treatment of the relationship between the way of the *hwarang* and Buddhism). *Pulgyo hakpo* 佛教學報 佛教學報 7 (1970): 255–274.

Kimura Toshihiko 木村俊彦 and Takenaka Chitai 竹中智泰. *Zen no darani* 禅宗の陀羅尼 (Dhāraṇī of the Zen school). Osaka: Daitō Shuppansha, 1998.

Ko Ikchin 高翊晉. *Han'guk kodae Pulgyo sasangsa* 韓國古代佛教思想史 (Intellectual history of ancient Korean Buddhism). Seoul: Tongguk Taehakkyo Ch'ulp'anbu, 1989.

Kobayashi Taichirō 小林太市郎. "Tōdai no Daihi Kannon" 唐代の大悲観音 (The Avalokiteśvara of Great Compassion in the Tang period). In *Kannon shinkō* 觀音信仰, edited by Hayami Tasuku 速水侑, 43–68. Tokyo: Yuzankaku Shuppan, 1982.

Kodama Daien. "Serindia and Paekche Culture." In *Introduction of Buddhism to Korea: New Cultural Patterns,* edited by Lewis R. Lancaster and C. S. Yu, 109–142. Berkeley, Calif.: Asian Humanities Press, 1989.

Komatsu Shigemi 小松茂美, comp. *Kegonshū soshi eden (Kegon engi)* 華嚴宗祖師絵伝 (華嚴緣起) (Scroll paintings of the patriarchs of the Huayan school [origins of Huayan]). Tokyo: Chūō Kōronsha, 1990.

Kwak Sŭnghun 郭丞勳. *T'ongil Silla sidae ŭi chŏngch'i pyŏndong kwa Pulgyo* 統一新羅時代의 政治變動과 佛教 (Buddhism and the transformation of government in the Unified Silla period). Seoul: Kukhak Charyowŏn, 2002.

Kwŏn Sangno. "History of Korean Buddhism." *Korea Journal* 4, no. 5 (May 1964): 8–14.

Lai, Whalen. "The *Chan-ch'a ching*: Religion and Magic in Medieval China." In *Chinese Buddhist Apocrypha,* edited by Robert E. Buswell, Jr., 175–206. Honolulu: University of Hawai'i Press, 1990.

———. "Dating the *Hsiang-fa chüeh i ching.*" *Annual Memoirs of the Otani University Shin Buddhist Comprehensive Research Institute* 4 (1986): 61–91.

———. "The Earliest Folk Buddhist Religion in China: *T'i-wei Po-li Ching* and Its Historical Significance." In *Buddhist and Taoist Practice in Medieval Chinese So-*

ciety: Buddhist and Taoist Studies II, edited by David W. Chappell, 11–35. Honolulu: University of Hawai'i Press, 1987.

———. "The Three Jewels in China." In *Buddhist Spirituality I: Indian, Southeast Asian, Tibetan, Early Chinese,* edited by Takeuchi Yoshinori, 275–342. New York: Crossroad, 1997.

Lancaster, Lewis R. "Maitreya in Korea." In *Maitreya, the Future Buddha,* edited by Alan Sponberg and Helen Hardacre, 135–153. Cambridge: Cambridge University Press, 1988.

———. "The Rock Cut Canon in China: Findings at Fang-shan." In *Buddhist Heritage: Papers delivered at the SOAS in November 1985,* edited by Tadeusz Skorupski, 143–156. Tring: Institute of Buddhist Studies, 1989.

Lancaster, Lewis R., and C. S. [Chai-shin] Yu, eds. *Assimilation of Buddhism in Korea: Religious Maturity and Innovation in the Silla Dynasty.* Berkeley, Calif.: Asian Humanities Press, 1991.

———. *Introduction of Buddhism to Korea: New Cultural Patterns.* Berkeley, Calif.: Asian Humanities Press, 1989.

———, comp., with Sung-Bae Park. *The Korean Buddhist Canon: A Descriptive Catalogue.* Berkeley, Los Angeles, and London: University of California Press, 1979.

Ledderose, Lothar. "Ein Programm für den Weltuntergang: Die steinerne Bibliothek eines Klosters bei Peking." *Heidelberger Jahrbücher* 36 (1992): 15–33.

Lee Jong-Wook (Yi Chonguk) 李鍾旭. *Silla kolp'umje yŏn'gu* 新羅骨品制研究 (Research on the bone-rank system of Silla). Seoul: Ilchogak, 1999.

Lee Ki-baik (Yi Kibaek) 李基白. "Early Silla Buddhism and the Power of the Aristocracy." In *Introduction of Buddhism to Korea: New Cultural Patterns,* edited by Lewis R. Lancaster and C. S. Yu, 161–185. Berkeley, Calif.: Asian Humanities Press, 1989.

———. *A New History of Korea.* Translated by Edward W. Wagner. Cambridge, Mass.: Harvard University Press, 1984.

———. *Silla chŏngch'i sahoesa yŏn'gu* 新羅政治社會史研究 (Studies in the sociopolitical history of Silla). Seoul: Ilchisa, 1974. Reprint, 1984.

———. "Silla Kyŏngdŏk wangdae Hwaŏm kyŏng sagyŏng kwanyŏja e taehan koch'al" 新羅 景德王代 華嚴經 寫經 關與者에 대한 考察 (A study on the people associated with the illustrated edition of the *Avataṃsaka Sūtra* from the period of King Kyŏngdŏk of Silla). *Yŏksa hakpo* 歷史學報 83 (September 1979): 126–139.

———. *Silla sasangsa yŏn'gu* 新羅思想史研究 (Studies in the intellectual history of Silla). Seoul: Ilchogak, 1986.

Lee Kidong (Yi Kidong) 李基東. "Hwarangsang ŭi pyŏnch'ŏn e kwanhan kaksŏ" 花郎像의 變遷에 관한 覺書 (A note on the transformation of the image of the *hwarang*). *Silla munhwa* 新羅文化 新羅文化 5 (1989): 103–119.

———. *Silla kolp'umje sahoe wa hwarangdo* 新羅骨品制社會와 花郎道 (The bone-rank society and the *hwarang*). Seoul: Ilchogak, 1984.

———. "Silla sahoe wa hwarangdo" 新羅社會와 花郞徒 (Silla society and the *hwarang* order). *Silla munhwa* 新羅文化 新羅文化 1 (1984): 27–41.
Lee, Peter H., trans. *Lives of Eminent Korean Monks: The* Haedong Kosŭng Chŏn. Cambridge, Mass.: Harvard University Press, 1969.
———, ed. *Sourcebook of Korean Civilization*. Volume I: *From Early Times to the Sixteenth Century*. New York: Columbia University Press, 1993.
———. *Studies in the Saenaenorae: Old Korean Poetry*. Rome: Istituto Italiano per Il medio ed Estremo Oriente, 1959.
Lee Yu-Min. "Ketumati Maitreya and Tuṣita Maitreya in Early China." Pt. 1: *National Palace Museum Bulletin* 19, no. 4 (September/October 1984): 1–11; pt. 2: *National Palace Musem Bulletin* 19, no. 5 (November/December 1984): 1–11.
Legge, James, trans. *A Record of Buddhistic Kingdoms*. Oxford: Clarendon Press, 1886. Reprint, New York: Dover, 1965.
Lew, Walter Kyu-sung. "Against Counting Up the Verses: An Analysis and Translation of the *Haein sammae-ron*, a Silla Treatise on the Ocean Seal Samádhi." M.A. thesis, University of California, Los Angeles, 1992.
Link, Arthur E. "Biography of Shih Tao-an." *T'oung Pao* 46, no. 1–2 (1958): 1–48.
Luk, Charles (Lu K'wan Yü), trans. *The Śūraṅgama Sūtra*. New York: Altai Press, 1966.
Makita Tairyō 牧田諦亮. *Rikuchō koitsu Kanzeon ōikenki no kenkyū* 六朝古 觀世音應驗 記の研究 (Research on the *Guanshiyin yingyan ji*, a lost book from the Six Dynasties period). Kyoto: Heirakuji Shoten, 1970.
——— and Suwa Gijun 諏訪義純, ed. *Tō kosōden sakuin* 唐高僧傳索引 (Index to the Tang and Song *Lives of Eminent Monks*). Kyoto: Heirakuji Shoten, 1973–1975.
Matsunaga, Daigan and Alicia. *Foundation of Japanese Buddhism*. 2 vols. Los Angeles and Tokyo: Buddhist Books International, 1974–1976.
McBride, II, Richard D. "Buddhist Cults in Silla Korea in their Northeast Asian Context." Ph.D. diss., University of California, Los Angeles, 2001.
———. "Dhāraṇī and Spells in Medieval Sinitic Buddhism." *Journal of the International Association of Buddhist Studies* 28, no. 1 (2005): 85–114.
———. "Hidden Agendas in the Life Writings of Kim Yusin." *Acta Koreana* 1 (August 1998): 101–142.
———. The *Hwarang segi* Manuscripts: An In-Progress Colonial Period Fiction." *Korea Journal* 45, no. 3 (Autumn 2005): 230–260.
———. "Is the *Samguk yusa* reliable? Case Studies on Chinese and Korean Sources." *Journal of Korean Studies* 11, no. 1 (Fall 2006): 163–189.
———. "Is there really 'esoteric' Buddhism?" *Journal of the International Association of Buddhist Studies* 27, no. 2 (2004): 323–350.
———. "A Koreanist's Musings on the Chinese *Yishi* Genre." *Sungkyun Journal of East Asian Studies* 6, no. 1 (April 2006): 31–59.
———. "*Muryangsu-gyŏng chongyo* (Thematic Essentials of the *Larger Sukhāva-*

tīvyūhasūtra): Annotated Translation and Introduction." In *Arouse Your Mind and Practice: Wŏnhyo's Pure Land, Ritual, and Didactic Texts. The Collected Works of Wŏnhyo*, vol. 3, edited by Robert E. Buswell, Jr. Honolulu: University of Hawai'i Press, forthcoming, 2008.

———. "The Vision-Quest Motif in Narrative Literature on the Buddhist Traditions of Silla." *Korean Studies* 27 (2003): 16–47.

———. "What is the Ancient Korean Religion?" *Acta Koreana* 9, no. 2 (July 2006): 30.

———. "Why did Kungye claim to be the Buddha Maitreya? The Maitreya Cult and Royal Power in the Silla-Koryŏ Transition." *Journal of Inner and East Asian Studies* 2, no. 1 (2004): 35–62.

Mishina Shōei 三品彰英. *Shiragi karō no kenkyū* 新羅花郎の研究. Tokyo, 1943. Reprinted in Mishina Shōei Ronbunshū 6. Tokyo: Heibonsha, 1974.

——— and Murakami Yoshio 村上四男. *Sangoku iji kōshō* 三国遺事考証 (Textual research on the *Samguk yusa*). 3 books in 5 vols. (book 3 in 3 parts). Tokyo: Hanawa Shobō, 1975–1995.

Mochizuki Shinkō 望月信亨. *Bukkyō kyōten seiritsu shiron* 佛教經典成立史論 (Exposition on the compilation of the Buddhist canon). Kyoto: Hōzōkan, 1946.

Mun Myŏngdae 文明大. "Silla Hwaŏm kyŏng sagyŏng kwa kŭ pyŏnsangdo ŭi yŏn'gu" 新羅華嚴經寫經과 그 變相圖의 研究 (Research on the Silla-period illustrated edition of the *Avataṃsaka Sūtra* and its illustrations). *Han'guk hakpo* 韓國學報 14 (1979): 27–64.

Nakai Shinkō 中井真孝. "Shiragi ni okeru Bukkyō tōsei kikan ni tsuite" 新羅における仏教統制機関について (On the organs for controlling Buddhism in Silla). *Chōsen gakuhō* 朝鮮学報 59 (1971): 1–21.

Nakamura Hajime 中村元, Kasahara Kazuo 笠原一男, and Kanaoke Shuyu 金岡秀友, eds. *Ajia Bukkyōshi Nihon hen I: Asuka-Nara Bukkyō, kukka to Bukkyō* アジア仏教史日本編 I 飛鳥奈良仏教―国家と仏教 (The history of Asian Buddhism, Japanese Buddhism 1: Asuka-Nara Buddhism, the state and Buddhism). Tokyo: Kōsei Shuppansha, 1972.

Nakamura Kyoto Motomuchi, trans. and ed. *Miraculous Stories from the Japanese Buddhist Tradition: The Nihon ryōiki of the Monk Kyōkai*. Cambridge, Mass.: Harvard University Press, 1973. Reprint, Surry, England: Curzon, 1997.

Nam Tongsin 南東信. "Namal Yŏch'o Hwaŏm chongdan ŭi taeŭng kwa *(Hwaŏm) Sinjung kyŏng* ŭi sŏngnip" 羅末麗初 華嚴宗團의 대응과 (華嚴)神衆經의 성립 (The establishment of the *[Hwaŏm] Sinjung kyŏng* and the response of the Hwaŏm school in late Silla and early Koryŏ). *Oedae sahak* 外大史學 5 (1993): 143–174.

Nattier, Jan. "The Meanings of the Maitreya Myth: A Typological Analysis." In *Maitreya, the Future Buddha*, edited by Alan Sponberg and Helen Hardacre, 23–47. Cambridge: Cambridge University Press, 1988.

———. *Once Upon a Future Time: Studies in a Buddhist Prophecy of Decline*. Berkeley, Calif.: Asian Humanities Press, 1991.

Oh Young Bong. *Wŏnhyo's Theory of Harmonization (Wŏnhyo ŭi hwajaengsasang yŏn'gu)*. Seoul: Korea Research Foundation, 1989.
Orzech, Charles D. *Politics and Transcendent Wisdom*. University Park: Pennsylvania State University Press, 1998.
Palais, James B. "Confucianism and the Aristocratic/Bureaucratic Balance in Korea." *Harvard Journal of Asiatic Studies* 44, no. 2 (December 1984): 427–468.
Pankaj, Narendra M (Pankaj N. Mohan). "The Life and Times of the Silla King Chinhung." *Korean Culture* 17, no. 1 (Spring 1996): 12–23.
Park Youngbok. "The Monastery Hwangnyongsa and Buddhism of the Early Silla Period." Translated by Karen Hwang and Rick McBride. In *Transmitting the Forms of Divinity: Early Buddhist Art from Korea and Japan*, edited by Washizuka Hiromitsu, Park Youngbok, and Kang Woo-bang, 140–153. New York: Japan Society, 2003.
Pulgyo Munhwa Yŏn'guwŏn 佛教文化研究院 (Buddhist Culture Research Center), ed. *Han'guk Chŏngt'o sasang yŏn'gu* 韓國淨土思想研究 (Research on Korean Pure Land thought). Seoul: Tongguk Taehakkyo Ch'ulpanbu, 1985.
Reis-Habito, Maria. "The Great Compassion Dhāraṇī." In *The Esoteric Buddhist Tradition: Selected Papers from the 1989 SBS Conference*, edited by Henrik H. Sørensen, 31–49. SBS Monographs 2. Copenhagen and Aarhus: Seminar for Buddhist Studies, 1994.
Rhi Ki-yong (Yi Kiyŏng) 李箕永. *Aux Origines du "tch'an houei": Aspects Bouddhiqques de la pratique pénitentielle*. Seoul: The Korean Institute for Buddhist Studies, 1982.
———. "Brief Remarks on the Buddha-land Ideology in Silla during the Seventh and Eighth Centuries." Translated by Antonino Forte. In *Tang China and Beyond: Studies on East Asia from the Seventh to the Tenth Century*, edited by Antonino Forte, 163–179. Kyoto: Istituto Italiano di Cultura Scuola di Studi sull'Asia Orientale, 1988.
———. *Han'guk Pulgyo yŏn'gu* 韓國佛教研究 (Research on Korean Buddhism). Seoul: Han'guk Pulgyo Yŏn'guwŏn, 1982.
———. "Sangjingjŏk p'yohyŏn ŭl t'onghaesŏ pon 7–8 segi Silla mit Ilbon ŭi Pulgukto sasang" 象徵的 表現을 통해서 본 7-8 세기 新羅 및 日本의 佛國土 思想 (The Buddha-land ideology of Silla and Japan in the seventh and eighth centuries as seen through symbolic representations). *Chonggyosa yŏn'gu* 宗教史研究 2 (1971). Reprinted in *Han'guk Pulgyo yŏn'gu* 韓國佛教研究, 507–534. Seoul: Han'guk Pulgyo Yŏn'guwŏn, 1982.
———. "Shōchōteki hyōgen o tōshite mitaru shichi hasseki Shiragi oyobi Nihon no Bukkokuto shisō" 象徴的表現を通して見たる七八世代新羅及び日本の仏国土思想 (The Buddha-land ideology of Silla and Japan in the seventh and eighth centuries as seen through symbolic representations). In *Shiragi to Asuka-Hakuhō no Bukkyō bunka* 新羅と飛鳥白鳳の仏教文化, edited by Tamura Enchō

田村圓澄 and Hong Sunch'ang 洪淳昶, 1–44. Tokyo: Yoshikawa Kōbunkan, 1975

Ri Sangho, trans. *Sinp'yŏn Samguk yusa* 新編三國遺事 (Revised translation of *Memorabilia of the Three Kingdoms*). Pyongyang: Kwahagwŏn Ch'ulp'ansa, 1960. Reprint, Seoul: Sinsŏwŏn, 1994.

Rutt, Richard. "The Flower Boys of Silla *(Hwarang):* Notes on the Sources." *Transactions of the Royal Asiatic Society, Korea* 38 (1961): 1–66.

Schopen, Gregory. *Bones, Stones, and Buddhist Monks: Collected Papers on the Archeology, Epigraphy, and Texts of Monastic Buddhism in India.* Honolulu: University of Hawai'i Press, 1997.

———. *Buddhist Monks and Business Matters: Still More Papers on Monastic Buddhism in India.* Honolulu: University of Hawai'i Press, 2004.

Sen, Tansen. *Buddhism, Diplomacy, and Trade: The Realignment of Sino-Indian Relations, 600–1400.* Honolulu: University of Hawai'i Press, 2003.

Sharf, Robert H. *Coming to Terms with Chinese Buddhism: A Reading of the Treasure Store Treatise.* Kuroda Institute Studies in East Asian Buddhism 14. Honolulu: University of Hawai'i Press, 2002.

Shim Jae-ryong. *Korean Buddhism: Tradition and Transformation.* Seoul: Jimoondang, 1999.

Sin Chongwŏn 辛鐘遠. *Silla ch'ogi Pulgyosa yŏn'gu* 新羅初期佛教史研究 (Research on the early Buddhist history of Silla). Seoul: Minjoksa, 1992.

Sørensen, Henrik H. "On the Sinin and Ch'ongji Schools and the Nature of Esoteric Buddhist Practice under the Koryŏ." *International Journal of Buddhist Thought and Culture* 5 (February 2005) 49–84.

———. "Problems with using the *Samguk yusa* as a source for the history of Korean Buddhism." *Cahiers d'Études Coréennes* 7 (2000): 271–288.

Stein, Rolf A. "Avalokiteśvara/Kouan-yin: un exemple de transformation d'un dieu en deesse." *Cahiers d'Extreme-Asie* 2 (1986): 17–80.

Stevenson, Daniel B. "Pure Land Buddhist Worship and Meditation in China." In *Buddhism and Practice,* edited by Donald S. Lopez, Jr., 359–379. Princeton Readings in Religions. Princeton: Princeton University Press, 1995.

Strickmann, Michel. *Chinese Magical Medicine.* Stanford: Stanford University Press, 2002.

———. "The *Consecration Sūtra:* A Buddhist Book of Spells." In *Chinese Buddhist Apocrypha,* edited by Robert E. Buswell, Jr., 75–118. Honolulu: University of Hawai'i Press, 1990.

———. "India in the Chinese Looking-Glass." In *The Silk Route and the Diamond Path: Esoteric Buddhist Art on the Trans-Himalayan Trade Routes,* edited by D. Klimberg-Salter, 52–63. Los Angeles: UCLA Art Council, 1982.

———. *Mantras et Mandarins: le bouddhisme tantrique en Chine.* Paris: Éditions Gallimard, 1996.

Sueki Fumihiko 末木文美士. *Nihon Bukkyōshi shisōshi toshite no apurōchi* 日本仏教史：

思想史としてのアプローチ (Japanese Buddhist history: An intellectual history approach). Tokyo: Shinchōsha, 1992.

Suh Yoon-kil (Sŏ Yun'gil) 徐閨吉. "Silla Mit'a sasang" 新羅彌陀思想 (Pure Land thought of Silla). In *Han'guk Pulgyo sasangsa: Sungsan Pak Kilchin paksa hwagap kinŏm* (History of Korean Buddhist thought: In commemoration of the 60th birthday of Sungsan Dr. Pak Kilchin), 287–304. Iri (Chŏlla pukto): Wŏn Pulgyo sasang yŏn'guwŏn, 1975.

Takakusu Junjirō. *The Amitāyur-dhyāna-sūtra: The Sūtra on the Meditation of Amitāyus.* In *Sacred Books of the East* 49, pt. 2, edited by F. Max Müller, 169–199. Oxford: Clarendon Press, 1894. Reprinted in *Buddhist Mahāyāna Texts,* pt. 2, edited by E. B. Cowell, 169–199. New York: Dover, 1969.

Tamura Enchō 田村圓澄. *Bukkyō denrai to kodai Nihon* 仏教伝来と古代日本 (The transmission of Buddhism and ancient Japan). Tokyo: Kodansha, 1986.

———. *Kodai Chosen Bukkyō to Nihon Bukkyō* 古代朝鮮仏教と日本仏教 (Ancient Korean Buddhism and Japanese Buddhism). Tokyo: Yoshikawa Kobunkan, 1980.

———. "Kodai Chōsen no Miroku shinkō" 古代朝鮮の弥勒信仰 (Maitreya cult in ancient Korea). *Chōsen gakuhō* 朝鮮學報 102 (1982): 1–28.

Tanabe, Jr., George J. *Myōe the Dreamkeeper: Fantasy and Knowledge in Early Kamakura Buddhism.* Harvard East Asian Monographs 136. Cambridge, Mass.: Harvard University Press, 1992.

———, and Willa Jane Tanabe. *The Lotus Sutra in Japanese Culture.* Honolulu: University of Hawai'i Press, 1989.

Teiser, Stephen F. *The Ghost Festival in Medieval China.* Princeton: Princeton University Press, 1988.

———. "T'ang Buddhist Encyclopedias: An Introduction to *Fa-yŭan chu-lin* and *Chu-ching yao-chi.*" *T'ang Studies* 3 (1985): 109–128.

Tsukamoto Zenryū 塚本善隆. *A History of Early Chinese Buddhism.* Translated by Leon Hurvitz. 2 vols. Tokyo, New York, and San Francisco: Kodansha, 1985.

———. *Shina Bukkyōshi kenkyū: Hokugi hen* 支那佛教史研究：北魏篇 (Studies in Chinese Buddhist history: Northern Wei). Tokyo: Kōbundō, 1942.

———. "The Śramaṇa Superintendent T'an-yao and His Time." Translated by Galen E. Sargent. *Monumenta Serica* 16 (1957): 363–396.

von Glahn, Richard. *The Sinister Way: The Divine and the Demonic in Chinese Religious Culture.* Berkeley and Los Angeles: University of California Press, 2004.

Waley, Arthur. *The Real Tripitaka: And Other Pieces.* London: George Allen and Unwin, 1952.

Ware, James R. "Wei Shou on Buddhism." *T'oung Pao* 通報 30 (1933): 100–181.

Weinstein, Stanley. *Buddhism under the T'ang.* London: Cambridge University Press, 1987.

Wriggins, Sally Hovey. *Xuanzang: A Buddhist Pilgrim on the Silk Road.* Boulder, Colo.: Westview Press, 1996.

Xue Zhongsan 薛仲三. *Liangqiannian Zhong-Xi li duizhao biao* 兩千年中西曆對照表

(A Sino-Western calendar for two thousand years). Revised edition. Beijing: Shangwu yinshuguan chuban, 1957. Reprint, Taipei: Xuehai chubanshe, 1993.

Yang Chŏngsŏk 梁正錫. *Hwangnyongsa ŭi choyŏng kwa wanggwŏn* 黃龍寺의 造營과 王權 (The construction of Hwangnyongsa and royal authority). Seoul: Sŏgyŏng Munhwasa, 2004.

———. "Silla Hwangnyongsa, Puk Wi Yŏngnyŏngsa kurigo Ilbon Taegwan Taesasa: 5–7 segi Tongasia tusŏngje wa kwallyŏn hayŏ" 新羅 黃龍寺・北魏 永寧寺 그리고 日本 大官大寺: 5–7 세기 동아시아 都城制와 관련하여 (Silla's Hwangnyongsa, the Northern Wei's Yongningsi, and Japan's Kudara Ōdera: On the management of capitals in East Asia from the fifth–seventh centuries). *Han'guksa hakpo* 韓國史學報 9 (September 2000): 9–56.

Yao Chang-shou (Yang Zhangshou) 姚長壽. "Bōzan sekikyō ni okeru Kegon tenseki ni tsuite" 房山石經における華嚴典籍について (On the Huayan literature in the Fangshan lithic canon). In *Chūgoku Bukkyō sekikyō no kenkyū* 中國佛教石経の研究 (Research on Chinese Buddhist lithic canons), edited by Kegasawa Yasunori 気賀澤保規, 411–437. Kyoto: Kyōdo Daigaku Gakujutsu Shuppansha, 1996.

Yi Chŏng 李政, ed. *Han'guk Pulgyo sach'al sajŏn* 韓國佛教寺刹事典 (Dictionary of Korean Buddhist monasteries). Seoul: Pulgyo Sidaesa, 1996.

Yi Chongik 李鍾益. *Wŏnhyo ŭi kŭnbon sasang: Sinmun hwajaeng non yŏn'gu* 元曉의 根本思想: 十門和諍論研究 (Wŏnhyo's fundamental ideology: Research on the *Treatise on the Reconciliation of Disputes in Ten Approaches*). Seoul: Tongbang Sasang Yŏn'guwŏn, 1977.

Yi Haenggu 李杏九. "Kankoku Bukkyō ni okeru Kegon shinkō no tenkai: Kegon hōe o chūshin toshite" 韓国仏教における華厳信仰の展開―華厳法会の中心として (The development of the Hwaŏm cult in Korean Buddhism: Focusing on the Hwaŏm dharma assembly). *Chōsen gakuhō* 朝鮮學報 114 (January 1985): 77–119.

Yi Hongjik 李弘植. "Silla sŭnggwanje wa Pulgyo chŏngch'aek ŭi chemunje" 新羅僧官制佛教政策諸問題 (Issues associated with the system of monastic regulation in Silla and government policies toward Buddhism). In *Paek Sŏnguk paksa songsu kinyŏm Pulgyohak nonmunjip* 白性郁博士頌壽記念佛教學論文集 (Festschrift on Buddhist studies commemorating the long life of Prof. Paek Sŏnguk), edited by Paek Sŏnguk Paksa Songsu Kinyŏm Saŏp Wiwŏnhoe 白性郁博士頌壽記念事業委員會, 661–679. Seoul: Tongguk Taehakkyo, 1959.

Yi Kŏmguk 李劍國 and Ch'oe Hwan 崔桓, comp., ed., trans., and annot. *Silla sui chŏn chipkyo wa yŏkchu* 新羅殊異傳 輯校와 譯註 (Translated and annotated critical edition of *Tales of the Bizarre from Silla*). Kyŏngsansi: Yŏngnam Taehakkyo Ch'ulp'anbu, 1998.

Yi Pyŏngdo 李丙燾, trans. *Kugyŏk Samguk sagi* 國譯三國史記 (Official Korean translation of the *History of the Three Kingdoms*). Seoul: Ŭryu Munhwasa, 1977.

Yi Yŏngja 李永子. "Namal Hu Samguk Mirŭk sinang ŭi sŏngkyŏk" 羅末後三國

彌勒信仰의 性格 (The character of the Maitreya cult in late Silla and the Later Three Kingdoms period). In *Han'guk Miruk sasang yŏn'gu* 韓國彌勒思想研究 (Research on Korean conceptions of Maitreya), edited by Pulgyo Munhwa Yŏn'guwŏn 佛教文化研究院 (Buddhist Culture Research Center), 101–143. Seoul: Tongguk Taehakkyo Ch'ulp'anbu, 1987.

Yü Chün-fang. "Guanyin: The Chinese Transformation of Avalokiteshvara." In *Latter Days of the Law: Images of Chinese Buddhism, 850–1850,* edited by Marsha Weidner, 151–181. Honolulu: Spencer Museum of Art, University of Kansas in association with University of Hawai'i Press, 1994.

———. *Kuan-yin: The Chinese Transformation of Avalokiteśvara.* New York: Columbia University Press, 2001.

———. "P'u-t'o Shan: Pilgrimage and the Creation of the Chinese Potalaka." In *Pilgrimages and Sacred Sites in China,* edited by Susan Naquin and Chünfang Yü, 190–245. Berkeley and Los Angeles: University of California Press, 1992.

Yun Changsŏp 尹張燮. *Han'guk kŏnch'uksa* 韓國建築史 (History of Korean architecture). Seoul: Tongmyŏngsa, 1973.

Zimmer, Heinrich Robert. *Myths and Symbols in Indian Art and Civilization.* Edited by Joseph Campbell. Princeton: Princeton University Press, 1946.

Zürcher, Erik. *The Buddhist Conquest of China: The Spread and Adoption of Buddhism in Medieval China.* 2nd ed. 2 vols. Leiden: E. J. Brill, 1972.

———. "Buddhist Influence on Early Taoism: A Survey of Scriptural Evidence." *T'oung Pao* 通報 通報 96, no. 1–3 (1980): 84–147.

———. "Prince Moonlight: Messianism and Eschatology in Early Medieval Chinese Buddhism." *T'oung Pao* 通報 通報 98, no. 1–3 (1982): 1–71.

Index

Abiji, 29
Acala, 113
Ado, 14–15, 22–23
Aejang, K., 94, 97, 131, 136
Amitābha, 55, 124; and
  Avalokiteśvara cult, 62–64, 66,
  68–69, 70; cult of, 5, 10, 35, 36,
  83, 103, 141–144; images of, 124,
  135; and Maitreya cult, 43–47,
  55; and Mount Odae, 110, 115,
  116; Pulguksa and, 122–124; Sŏk-
  kuram image as, 126–128; and
  Ŭisang and, 92, 100, 118–120
Amitāyus, 36, 111, 113, 118. *See also*
  Amitābha
Amoghapāśa. *See under* Avalokiteśvara
An Lushan rebellion, 53, 89
Ansang, 75
Aśoka, K., 18, 25–26
Assembly of the Eight Prohibitions.
  See under Dharma Assemblies
Asuka, 29, 155n46
Asuka and Nara periods (Japan),
  33, 65
asura, 126, 147, 149
August Dragon Monastery. *See*
  Hwangnyong Monastery
Avalokiteśvara, 62–85; Amoghapāśa,
  76–77, 164n49; eleven-headed
  (Ekadaśamukha), 11, 63, 78,
  84–85, 128; thousand-armed
  (Sahasrabhuja), 11, 63, 71,
76, 85, 113, 161n6; thousand-
  armed and thousand-eyed, 11,
  63, 67–68, 80–81; white-robed
  (Pāṇḍaravāsinī), 11, 63, 73–74
Avataṃsaka Sūtra, viii, 11–12; coursing
  in, 112, 115, 172n11; Diamond
  Mountains and, 132–133; and
  Divine Assembly cult, 133–138,
  140–141, 144, 147–151; in healing
  ritual, 78; *Lotus Sūtra* and, 64–65,
  72; Maitreya and all buddhas
  preach, 106, 108–110; Mount
  Odae and, 112–115; Pulguksa and,
  122–123, 125–126, 131; Sŏkkuram
  and, 128; Wang Kŏn and, 60

baguanzhai hui. *See* Dharma Assemblies, Feast of Eight Prohibitions
baguanzhi. *See* Dharma Assemblies,
  Feast of Eight Prohibitions
Bailian she, 103
Baiyi Guanyin. *See* Avalokiteśvara,
  white-robed
bajiezhai, 27–28. *See also* Assembly of
  the Eight Prohibitions
Baoyu jing, 59
Best, Jonathan, 65
Bhaiṣajyaguru, Hall of, 80
bodhi tree: of Maitreya, 21, 37, 41; of
  Śākyamuni, 69
bodhicitta, arousal of, 89, 91, 105–106,
  117, 141

bodhimaṇḍa. *See* enlightenment site
Bodhisattva Dharma Arouser. *See*
 Bodhisattva Dharmodgata
Bodhisattva Dharmodgata, 132–133
bodhisattvas, eight great, 111, 113
bodhisattva: path, viii, 46–47, 86, 89,
 108, 141, 166n8; precepts, 53, 112
Bohai. *See* Parhae
bone-rank system, 20, 30, 75
Brown, Peter, 2, 142
Budai, 56
Buddha Maitreya. *See* Maitreya
Buddha, the, 4, 17–18, 89; dates
 of in China, 169n65; image in
 Sŏkkuram, 126–128; preaches
 in Lotus Storehouse Realm, 86,
 106; preaches on Vulture Peak,
 124, 126. *See also* Śākyamuni
buddhahood, 19, 34, 45–46, 50, 79,
 91, 97, 102, 106, 107, 112, 118
buddhakṣetra. *See* Buddha-land
Buddha-land: Hwaŏm inspired, 116,
 133; Silla as, 22–27, 32, 57, 141;
 Sukhāvatī and Tuṣita as, 35. *See
 also* propaganda, Buddha-land
buddha-nature, 45–46, 88, 141
Buddhaśarīra. *See* relics
Buddhāvataṃsaka Sūtra. *See*
 Avataṃsaka Sūtra
Buddhist Overseer, xii, 5, 26, 31,
 136–137, 154n29
Buddhist studies, vii, 139–140
Buddhist symbols and symbolism, 3,
 10, 14, 20, 32, 86, 105; Maitreya,
 21, 59–60; political legitimation
 by, 2, 7, 9, 14, 16–19, 32, 143. *See
 also* Hwaŏm, symbolism
Bukong juansuo tuoluoni jing, 77

cakravartin, 13–14, 17–21, 71
Central Peak, 41–42
Cha jing, 51
Chajang, 7, 29, 31, 43; and
 Avataṃsaka Sūtra, 88, 93; birth
 of, 67–68; and Chinese culture,
 162n24; and Mount Wutai, 1, 19,
 26, 110, 114; and Vinaya school,
 139, 140, 177n4
Chajiu lun, 52
Chang Pogo, 136
Changch'un, 79–80
Changnyŏng, Mount, 111
Chassi. *See* Maitreya
Chen (dynasty), 18
Chigwi, 54
Chijang. *See* Kṣitigarbha
Chindŏk, Q., 19
chin'gol, 19–21; and Avalokiteśvara
 cult, 62, 67, 70, 74, 75, 77; and
 Maitreya cult, 39, 40, 41, 43, 46;
 and Silla society, 31, 100, 131
Chinhŭng, K., 17–18, 23–27, 31, 40
Chinja, 21, 38–39, 42, 43
Chinjang, 99
Chinji, K., 17–18, 38
Chinjŏng, 99
Chinese Northern dynasties, vii, xii,
 10, 14; church and state relations
 in, 19, 27; invest Silla kings, 18;
 Maitreya cult in, 31–32, 33–36,
 43; Mount Wutai cult in, 110,
 142. *See also* Northern Qi; Northern Wei; Northern Zhou
Chinese Southern dynasties, vii, 16,
 18, 63, 64, 115. *See also* Liang;
 Southern Qi
Chinp'yo, 47, 50, 55, 115, 140
Chinp'yŏng, K., 13, 17, 19, 37
Chinul, 140
Chinyŏ Cloister, 111–113
Chiri, Mount, 97, 98, 129
Chiro, Mount. *See* P'ungno, Mount
Chit'ong, 93, 99
Ch'oe Ch'iwŏn, 8, 11; Haeinsa and,
 136; and Hwaŏm communities,
 100–103; Hwaŏm monasteries
 and, 129–131; lost books by, 120;
 Maitreya cult and, 56–57; and
 Pulguksa, 124–125; and Qinghe
 Cui clan, 101, 169n54
Ch'oe Sŭngno, 84
Ch'oe Ŭnham, 84

Ch'ŏlbu, 17
Chŏlla Province: North, 37, 50, 129; South, 97, 136
Ch'ŏn, Mount, 38
Ch'ŏnbu Kwanŭm. *See* Avalokiteśvara, thousand-armed and thousand-eyed
Chŏnggang, K., 98, 103
Chŏnghyŏn, 101
Ch'ŏngsong, Mount, 22
Ch'ŏnin, 135–136
ch'ŏnsu chu. See Great Compassion Spell
Ch'ŏnsu kyŏng. See Nīlakaṇṭha
Chōsen kinseki sōran, 98
Chosin, 82–83
Chosŏn period, 38, 72, 98, 143
Ch'udong ki, 93, 99
Chukchi, 21, 40
Chukchi Pass, 40
Chung'ak, 41–42
chungalch'an, 57
Ch'ungdam, 50–52, 55
Chungsaeng Monastery, 84
cintāmaṇi, 65
Cishi, 52. *See also* Maitreya
Convocation for the Recitation of the *Sūtra for Humane Kings*. *See under* Dharma Assemblies

Da Tang xiyu ji, 126
dabei zhou. See Great Compassion Spell
Dalai Lama, 62
dānapati, 105–106, 124
Daoan, 34–35, 64
daochang. See enlightenment site
Daochuo, 119
Daode jing, 46–47
Daoshi, 7, 115
Daoxuan, 7, 67, 115
Daśabhūmika, 87, 89
Dayun jing, 58, 59, 89
Dengzhou, 117
devotional practices, Buddhist: circumambulation, 53, 100, 112, 141, 142; commissioning copies of sūtras, 78, 99, 108; commissioning images, 10, 34, 36, 38, 42–43, 46–47, 50, 52, 56, 63, 67–69, 108, 154n45, 173n30; commissioning monasteries, 25, 46, 83, 93, 109, 115–116, 127, 142; making offerings, 5, 10–11, 36, 42, 44, 50–53, 55, 64, 78, 111–112, 121, 149; merit-making practices, 6, 142; recollection, 45, 63, 70, 119–120, 148, 150; spell-chanting, 10, 54, 63, 70–72, 85, 112, 117, 119, 141–142; sūtra-chanting, 5, 43, 172n11; vocal recitation (chanting) of name, 5, 45, 53, 55, 63, 76, 142
Dezong, E., 90
dhāraṇī, viii, xii, 5, 10; and Avalokiteśvara cult, 63, 71–73, 76–78, 81, 85; *Mahāpratisāra*, 112, 115, 171n5; and Maitreya cult, 42, 54; in repentance rituals, 172n15; in Ŭisang seal-diagram, 91
Dharma, the three ages of: Final, 102–103, 105, 108; Semblance, 103, 105, 107, 108; True, 105
Dharma Assemblies: Assembly of the Eight Prohibitions, 18, 21, 27–29; Convocation for the Recitation of the *Sūtra for Humane Kings*, 27–28, 156n63; eye-opening ceremony, 90; Feast of the Eight Prohibitions, 71; Flower Garland Convocation, 93, 95, 102, 114–115; Hwaŏm inspired, 96, 141
Dharmadhātu, 72, 91–92, 106, 107, 118, 148
Dharmakāya, 72, 92, 105, 107, 108, 170n72
Diamond Ridge, 75
Diamond Sūtra, 81, 113
divination practices, 47–49
Divine Assembly, cult of, 12, 60, 109, 114, 133–137, 141, 144, 147–150

Dizang. *See* Kṣitigarbha
dragon(s): in Divine Assembly, 147, 150, 174n42; of East Sea, 73; in eight groups of gods, 126; and Hwangnyongsa, 18, 23, 29; King Munmu becomes, 30, 127; Shanmiao becomes, 117
Dragon Flower Aspirants, 21, 41
Dragon Palace, 23–25, 101
dreams, 1, 2; of Avalokiteśvara, 82–84; of buried images, 42; at conception/birth, 21, 67, 121; of Maitreya, 38–40, 57–58; religious, 44–45, 127, 154n45, 165n66
Dunhuang, 35, 52, 87, 110, 125
Dunhuang bianhua, 52

East Sea. *See* Tonghae
Eastern Barbarians, 19
eight groups of gods, 126, 174n42
Ekadaśamukha. *See under* Avalokiteśvara
Emei, Mount, 133
enlightenment site, 69; Avalokiteśvara in China, 64–65; Avalokiteśvara in Silla, 78; deities practice at, 147, 149; Hwaŏm and Maitreya, 60; for Humane Kings, 28; White Lotus, 70, 119
epigraphy, viii, xii, 7, 8, 98
esoteric Buddhism, 63, 128, 141
esoteric teaching, 77, 86
exegesis, Buddhist, vii, xii, 7, 88, 93, 94
exorcism, 43, 164n56

fa puti xin. See bodhicitta
Fachang, 93
Fahua zhuanji, 64
Fangguang da zhuangyuan jing. See Lalitavistara
Fanmayue, 44
Fanwang jing, 53
Faqi. *See* Bodhisattva Dharmodgata
Faxian, 64

Fayuan zhulin, 7
Fazang, 88–91, 101–102, 117, 129, 131–132
Fazheng, 64
Feast of the Eight Prohibitions. *See under* Dharma Assemblies
five directions, 110; spirits of, 30
five marchmounts. *See under* mountains
five sacred mountains. *See under* mountains
Flower Garland Sūtra. See Avataṃsaka Sūtra
Foundation Record of Pulguk Monastery Past and Present. See Pulguksa kogŭm ch'anggi
four directions, buddhas of, 132
four heavenly kings, 28, 30, 126
Fu Jian, 4, 16, 34
Further Lives of Eminent Monks. See Xu gaoseng zhuan

Gaṇḍavyūha Sūtra, 106
Gaowang Guanshiyin jing, 63
gāthā(s), 1, 93, 102
Gimello, Robert, 88
gods, of Silla, 15, 23, 27, 109, 133, 138
Great Cloud Sūtra. See Dayun jing
Great Compassion Spell, 11, 70–72, 81, 85, 119–120, 142, 163n36
Guan Mile shangsheng jing, 20
Guan Wuliangshou jing, 63–64, 124
Guanshiyin. *See* Avalokiteśvara
Guanshiyin jing, 63, 65, 137
Guanshiyin pusa pumen pin, 63–64
Guanshiyin yingyan ji, 64
Guanyin. *See* Avalokiteśvara

Haedong Hwaŏm ch'ojo kisin wŏnmun, 102
Haein Monastery: and Ch'oe Ch'iwŏn, 101–102; and Divine Assembly cult, 133, 136, 137; founding of, 97; and Hwaŏm monasteries, 129
Haewŏn, 122
hagiography, vii–viii, 7, 81

Hagok District, 25
haiyin sanmei, 97
head-rank six, 20, 21, 47, 48, 50, 54, 57
Heart Sūtra, 74, 81
Hemp-bag Bonze. *See* Budai
Hīnayāna, 77, 118
holy-bone elites, 19–20, 39, 43
Hŏnan, K., 59
Hŏn'gang, K., 103
Hon'gu, 8
Horim, Duke, 67
Huayan doctrine, 88–90, 91–93, 141; fifty-two stages, 88, 166n8; interconnection, 89, 91, 116; interpenetration, 88, 97, 109, 141
Huayan jing. See *Avataṃsaka Sūtra*
Huayan jing tanxuan ji, 132
Huguo pin, 28
Hŭimyŏng, 80
Hŭirang, 136–137
Huiyun, 52
Humane Kings' Enlightenment Site, 28
Hŭngdŏk, K., 135
Hŭngnyun Monastery, 17–18, 22–23, 38–39, 43
Hwang Suyŏng, 98, 127
Hwangnyong Monastery, 13, 18–19, 22–26, 141; lectures on *Avataṃsaka* at, 95–97; nine-story pagoda, 13, 25, 29, 30; state protection ritual at, 28–30
Hwanhŭi, 26
Hwaŏm: cosmology, 22, 26, 100, 114, 116, 123–125, 132, 141; and mountain monasteries, 128–130, 141–142; and Pulguksa, 118, 120, 122, 124, 125; symbolism, 60, 90, 97, 103, 108, 109–110, 123, 141; tradition, 1–2, 60–61, 70, 87–88, 92, 93–108, 109, 114
Hwaŏm chongyo, 95
Hwaŏm cult, 114; of Divine Assembly, 12, 133–138; Mount Odae, 110, 116, 132, 133, 135, 140
Hwaŏm ilsŭng pŏpkye to, 91

Hwaŏm Monastery, 97–98, 129–130
Hwaŏm-gyŏng so, 94, 117
Hwaŏm/Huayan school, 87, 90
hwarang, 10, 14, 18, 20–21; and Maitreya cult, 21, 32, 38–41, 43, 56–57; and native songs, 50, 54–55; and wandering in mountains, 74–75, 114
hyangch'al, 54
hyangga, 50–51, 54–55, 80–81
Hyegong, K., 96, 131
Hyehyŏn Ridge, 82–83
Hyeryang, 27
Hyet'ong, 32, 176n3
Hyŏngnyŏn Chŏng, 101, 137, 169n54
Hyŏnjun, 101, 103
Hyoso, K., 75, 110

icchantika, 88
Ich'adon. *See* Pak Yŏmch'ok
iconography, 53, 76, 85, 127–128
idu, 54
images and icons, 2, 11, 25, 32, 34, 78; in pensive pose, 34, 36, 42
inscriptions: on images, 11, 36, 46–47, 103–108; on stele, 8, 22–23, 48, 50, 54, 56, 94–95, 118, 135
Iryŏn, 8, 14, 22–26, 29, 37, 67, 72, 122, 129, 135. See also *Samguk yusa*

Jambudvīpa, 25, 59
Japan, 2, 4, 5, 11, 29; and Avalokiteśvara cult, 65, 76; colonial period, 98, 127; and Eastern Buddhism, 139–140; and esoteric Buddhism, 77; and Hwaŏm/Kegon, 90–91; and Maitreya cult, 33, 36, 37; mountain worship in, 155n46; rulers of, 4; Sea of, 30, 125; and state protection ritual, 96
Jinguang jing, 53, 96, 113, 115
Jingying Huiyuan, 93
Jinshizi zhang, 88

Kaenyŏng Commandery, 95
Kaewŏn, 46

Kagwi, 95
Kaiyuan shijiao lu, 77
Kalgyŏng Monastery, 95
Kamsan Monastery, 46
Kamŭn Monastery, 28, 30, 96
Kang Woo-bang, 126–127
Kāśyapa, 22, 23, 24, 26, 57, 141
Kaya, 16, 18, 21
Kaya, Mount, 97, 129, 131, 137
Kaya Ravine, 129
Kegon engi emaki, 91
Kibi Pond, 29
Kim Chisŏng, 46–47
Kim Ch'unch'u, viii, 28, 31, 41, 68, 92, 97, 131
Kim Hŭn, 82, 165n65
Kim Injang, 46
Kim Inmun, 68–70, 74, 76, 158n32
Kim Kungye, 59–60, 105
Kim Mullyang, 121
Kim Murim, 67–68, 83
Kim Pusik, 7
Kim Sang-hyun, 8, 92, 130
Kim Taesŏng, 78, 120–122, 125
Kim Yangdo, 43
Kim Yusin, 21, 41, 74
King Gao's Sūtra of Avalokiteśvara. See *Gaowang Guanshiyin jing*
Koguryŏ (dynasty), 3–4; and adoption of Buddhism, 14, 15, 16; Later, 59; Maitreya cult in, 36–37; Parhae succession of, 114; state-protection Buddhism and, 19, 27
Koryŏ (dynasty), 8; Avalokiteśvara cult in, 73, 84; Buddhist court ritual in, 28; Divine Assembly cult in, 136, 137; Haeinsa in, 97; *hwarang* disappear in, 21; Maitreya cult in, 38, 58–60; Pulguksa in, 118
Koryŏsa, 137
Koun chip, 124
kṣatriya caste, 19
Kṣitigarbha, 47–49, 111, 113, 116
Kudara Kannon, 65
Kudara Ōdera, 29

Kukhak, 21
kuksŏn, 39, 74
Kungye. *See* Kim Kungye
Kŭmgang, Mount: in Kangwŏn, 50, 132–133; in Kyŏngju, 21–22
Kŭmgang sammae-gyŏng non, 94
Kŭmsan Monastery, 48, 50
Kwalchiji, 129
Kwanseŭm. *See* Avalokiteśvara
Kwanŭm. *See* Avalokiteśvara
Kwijŏng Gate, 50
Kyejoksan, 57
Kyerim, 57
Kyŏngdŏk, K., 46, 50, 54, 95–98, 99
Kyŏnghŭng, 5–6, 31–32, 78
Kyŏngju, 15, 17, 22, 42, 43, 46, 53, 67, 80, 127, 129
Kyŏngmun, K., 59
Kyŏngsun, K., 98
Kyŏnhwŏn, 59–60, 84, 99
Kyŏrŏng, 118
Kyunyŏ chŏn, 101, 137

Lalitavistara, 126–127
Lantern Festival, 28
Later Paekche, 59, 84, 99
Later Three Kingdoms, 33
laypeople, Buddhist, vii, 1–2, 5, 142–143; and Avalokiteśvara cult, 66–67; in China, 110, 117; and eight prohibitions, 27; and Great Compassion Spell, 120; and Hwaŏm communities, 93, 102, 105, 108; and Maitreya cult, 34, 35, 40, 57–58
Lee Ki-baik, 21, 91, 92
Liang (dynasty), 14, 16, 18, 28, 64,
Liang lu, 73–74
lithic canon, 99, 166n18, 168n47
Lives of Eminent Monks Compiled in the Song. See Song gaoseng zhuan
Longmen caves, 35, 36, 89, 110, 125
Lotus Storehouse World System, 86, 107, 124–126
Lotus Sūtra: and Avalokiteśvara cult, 69, 75–76, 80, 82, 85; and

Index 223

Avataṃsaka, 63–64, 67, 122–124, 126, 128, 137; and Mount Odae, 113
Luoyang, 29, 52, 70
Lushan Huiyuan, 64, 103

maaebul, 56
Mahācīnasthāna, 59
Mahamegha Sūtra. See Dayun jing
Mahāpratisarā Dhāraṇī, 112, 171n5
Mahāyāna, vii, 3, 7, 62, 70, 76, 77, 79, 103, 106, 107–108, 117, 138; sūtra literature, 19, 27, 47, 86
Maitreya: appearance in Avataṃsaka Sūtra, 103–106; as bodhisattva, 33–61; Empress Wu claims to be, 52, 58, 59; as future Buddha, 5, 19, 20, 27, 33, 34, 37, 41, 56, 58, 60, 106; incarnations of (Misi, Budai), 21, 27, 39, 41, 56; symbolism of, 59
masks, 78, 94, 164n56
Miaoshan myth, 85
Majin, 59
Malgal, the, 29, 40, 41, 114
maṇḍala, 128
Mañjuśrī, 1, 19, 26, 72, 90, 106, 110–116, 135
mantra, 3, 78
Maranant'a, 15
mārga, 89. See also bodhisattva path
Mathurā, 64
Maya puin, 19
Medicine Buddha. See Bhaiṣajyaguru
meditation (samādhi), 5, 6, 7, 34; Avataṃsaka, 134, 137; Kāśapa in, 57; ocean-seal, 97; recollecting the Buddha, 148
Memorabilia of the Three Kingdoms. See Samguk yusa
merit, transference of, 76
merit-making practices. See devotional practices
messianism, 21, 58–61
Mile dage, 53
Mile xiasheng jing, 20
Mingtang, 13

Mirŭk. See Maitreya
Mirŭkchŏn, 50
Mirŭkkok, 42–43
Mirŭkpong, 50
Misŭng, 44
Misŭng, Mount, 137
Moak, Mount, 50
Mohe, the. See Malgal, the
monastic precepts, 27, 74
monastic records, 8, 98, 127, 137
Moon City. See Wŏlsŏng
Moryang Village, 121–122
mountains: five marchmounts in China, 129; five sacred, 12, 41–42, 128–133; three sacred mountains in Silla, 22, 129, 154n45, 155n46
mountain god(s), 39, 42, 149
mountain spirit, 42
Mu, K., 37
Muae ka, 94
mudrā, māratarjanabhūmisparśa, 126, 128
Mugŭk, 8
Mukhoja, 14–15
munduru pimil chi pŏp, 30
Munjong K., 118
Munmu, K., 23, 30, 31, 43, 68, 98, 116, 117, 127
Munsŏng, K., 82
Muryangsujŏn, 118
Muyŏl, K. See Kim Ch'unch'u
Muyŏm, 56
Myŏnghyo, 77
Myŏngnang, 30, 67, 176n3

Naemul, K., 96
nāgapuṣpa, 21, 37, 41
Nalli Commandery, 82
Namgan, Lady, 67
Namhae, 25
Namhang Nunnery, 78
Namsan, Mount, 22, 42, 50, 51, 53, 134fig3
Nang, Mount, 84, 155n46
Nansŭng, 41–42
Nīlakaṇṭha, 70, 72, 119

nirvāṇa, 6, 57, 77, 88, 105, 118, 169n65
Nirvāṇa Sūtra, 92, 113, 116, 140
Nohil Puduk, 44–46, 79
North Kyŏngsang Province, 22, 42, 116
Northern Qi (dynasty), 18, 31, 35, 168n47
Northern Song (dynasty), 117
Northern Wei (dynasty): Buddhism and state in, 10, 18–19, 27, 29, 154n29; ecclesiastical positions in, 31; enlightenment site in, 69; Maitreya cult in, 35–36, 58, 64
Northern Zhou (dynasty), 78
Nulchi, K., 14
Nŭngin, 99, 133

Obong, Mount, 72
ocean-seal samādhi, 97
Odae, Mount, 12, 71, 102, 110–116, 132, 133, 135, 140–141
Oji, Mount, 22
Ojin, 99
One Vehicle, 91, 118, 119
Ōno Genmyō, 127

Paekche (dynasty), 4; adoption of Buddhism in, 15–16; Avalokiteśvara cult in, 64–66, 84, 86, 99; Hwangnyongsa and, 29–30; Later, 59, 60, 84, 137; Maitreya cult in, 33, 36–39, 41, 43, 47
Paengnyul Monastery, 75
pagoda(s). *See* stūpa(s)
Pak Yŏmch'ok. *See* Ich'adon
pal pori-sim. See *bodhicitta*
p'albusin. *See* eight groups of gods
Palchŏng, 64–65
P'algong, Mount, 41, 129, 158n29
p'algwanhoe. See Dharma Assemblies, Assembly of the Eight Prohibitions
pāramitā, 79, 147
Parhae, 114, 144

pariṇāmanā. See merit, transference of
Pāṇḍaravāsinī. *See under* Avalokiteśvara
Paryŏn Monastery, 48, 50
P'ijŏn, 22
pilgrimage, 42, 50, 54, 72, 73, 74
Poch'ŏn, 110–115, 118
Poch'ŏn Hermitage, 111, 113
Podŏk, 139–140
poetry, 8, 73, 122
Pogae, 79–80
Pŏmil, 74, 105, 170n67
Pŏmŏ Monastery, 129, 135
Pongdŏk Monastery, 28
Pongsŏng chi, 98
Pŏp, K., 37
Pŏphŭng, K., 15–17, 23, 39, 153n11, 173n30
popular Buddhism, 6, 7, 143
poṣadha, 27
Potalaka, Mount, 72, 123, 141
Poŭn District, 50
Prākṛit, 54
Prince Moonlight, 59, 176n72
propaganda, Buddha-land, 9, 11, 14, 22, 27, 54, 116, 128, 141
Pulguk Monastery, 120–128; *Avataṃsaka Sūtra* preached at, 95, 100; and five sacred mountains, 130–131
Pulguksa kogŭm ch'anggi, 120–121, 173n30
P'ungno, Mount, 111
p'ungnyu, 20
Punhwang Monastery, 23, 80, 93, 94
Pure Land Sūtra, 63, 64; Larger, 124
purification practices, 41, 73–74
Purple Palace. *See* Chagung
Puryerang, 74–76, 80
Pusŏk Monastery, 99, 109, 116–120, 129, 130
Putuo, Mount, 72
P'yohun, 99, 122, 133, 173n30

qianshou zhou. See Great Compassion Spell

Index 225

Qianyan qianbi Guanshiyin pusa tuoluoni shenzhou jing. See *Nīlakaṇṭha*
Qingliang, Master, 90
Qingliang, Mount, 1, 110. *See also* Wutai, Mount

Ratnamegha Sūtra, 59
relics, 1, 2, 18, 71, 136, 144
religious services. *See* Dharma Assemblies
Renwang bore boluomi jing, 28
repentance rituals, 2, 10, 47–48, 71, 115–116, 140, 141, 172n15
Rhi Ki-yong, 132
ritual, 3, 6; Buddhist, 3, 5, 7; and Divine Assembly cult, 133, 135; enlightenment site, 69; Great Compassion Spell, 71; Hwaŏm, 96, 102–103, 112–116, 120; *hwarang* and, 41; incense, 14; state sponsored, 21, 27–28, 30, 54; tantric ritual unnecessary, 141; texts, 76. *See also* dhāraṇī; divination; purification practices; repentance rituals
Room of Inconceivable Meaning, 50
rosary beads, 55, 73
royal authority, 13–14, 17, 35, 43, 58, 89
royal preceptor, 51
Ru fajue pin, 72, 106
ruyi baozhu, 65

Sach'ŏnwang Monastery, 23, 28, 30
sacred space, transformation of, 22–23, 57, 128–133, 137–138. *See also* mountains, five sacred; mountains, three sacred in Silla
saenae norae. See *hyangga*
Saengŭi, 42, 50
Sahasrubhuja. *See under* Avalokiteśvara
Saichō, 90
Sakchu, 40, 129
Śākyamuni, 17–19; *Avataṃsaka* and, 86; enlightenment site, 69; images of, 25–26; and Kāśapa, 57; and Mount Odae cult, 111, 113; Sŏkkuram image as, 126–128; stūpa at Pulguksa, 123; traditional views of dates of, 105, 169n65
Sam Mirŭk kyŏng, 5–6
saṃgha chief, 31
saṃgha overseer, 31, 136–137
saṃgha rectifier, 31
saṃghārāma, 22, 24, 118
Samgong Monastery, 105
Samguk sagi, 7
Samguk yusa, 7, 8, 79
Samhwa Ridge, 42, 50, 51, 53, 105
sangdaedŭng, 13, 17, 36, 121, 131
Sangsa chŏn, 101
Sangwŏn, 99
Sap'o, 25
Saryun, 18, 153n20
schools of Buddhism, vii; in academic discourse, vii–viii; in China, 90, 139–140; in Japan, 90–91, 140; in Korea, 9, 53, 87, 139–140, 176n3
Schopen, Gregory, viii, 2, 6, 7, 83, 144
seal-diagram, 91, 166nn18–19
Segyu Monastery, 82
Sengxiang, 64
sexigesimal calendar, 51
shamanism, 43, 128
Shancai. *See* Sudhana
Shandao, 50, 115, 119
Shanmiao, 117
Shengmai, Mount, 52
Shenseng zhuan, 48
Shi Daoan. *See* Daoan
Shinjō. *See* Simsang
Shiyimian. *See* Avalokiteśvara, eleven-headed
Shundao, 4, 15
Shusheng Miaoyan, 44
Siddhārtha, 18, 36. *See also* Śākyamuni
Śikṣānanda, 88
Silk Road, 52, 125
Silla-Tang alliance, 16, 31, 41, 43, 68; relations, 68–69

Simmun hwajaeng non, 95
Simsang, 90–91
Simwŏn chang, 95
sinjung. See Divine Assembly
Sinjung kyŏng, 137
Sinmu, K., 136
Sinmun, K., 30, 31, 43, 78, 110–111
Sinyu Forrest, 23, 30
Sobaek, Mount, 93, 116
Sobaekhwa, 72
Soga no Umako, 36
Soji, K., 14
Sŏkkuram Grotto, 78, 85, 95, 120–122, 125–128
Sŏkpul Monastery. *See* Sŏkkuram Grotto
Sŏn (Chan/Zen), 9, 100, 105, 107, 140, 144
Sŏndŏk, Q., 19, 23, 26, 29, 42, 54, 67, 80
Song gaoseng zhuan, 47–48, 92, 94, 116
Sŏng yusing-non hakki, 53
Song Zixian, 58
Sŏngdŏk, K., 28, 44, 111, 115
Songni, Mount, 50
Sŏngo Plains, 111
Southern Monastery of White Moon Mountain, 46
Southern Qi (dynasty), 31, 64
spells, viii, 2, 5, 7, 10, 62, 72–73, 76, 81. *See also* dhāraṇī
Śrīmālā, 19
state elder, 5, 31, 78,
state preceptor, 31, 32, 118
state-protection Buddhism, 10–11, 14, 27–32, 96, 109, 115, 133, 135, 171n7
Strickmann, Michel, 2, 3
stūpa(s), xii; Great Compassion Spell and, 71; Haeinsa, 136; Hwangboksa, 100; Hwangnyongsa nine-story, 29–30; Maitreya enters, 55; Pulguksa, 122–123; Punhwangsa, 80; worship of, 5–6
Sudhana, 72, 106, 136
Sui (dynasty), 35; Buddhist developments in, 87, 93, 110, 115; iconic influences of, 65; Emperor Yang of, 69; Maitreya cult in, 58
Sukhāvatī, 5, 35, 46, 55, 69–70, 72, 120, 123–125, 172n11; as Amitābha's *kṣetra,* 55
Sukhāvatīvyūha Sūtra, Larger. *See Pure Land Sūtra,* Larger
Sulchong, Lord, 40, 42
Sundo. *See* Shundao
Sŭngjŏn, 88, 95
sŭngnyo nangdo, 20. *See also hwarang*
sŭngt'ong. See saṃgha overseer
Sunje, 50
Sunŭng, 97
Śūraṃgama Sūtra, 63
Survarṇaprabhāsa Sūtra, 53, 96, 113, 115
Suwŏn Monastery, 38
symbolic resources, 13, 15, 16, 19, 20, 21, 143
symbolism, 7, 9, 14, 17–20, 32, 59–60, 86
syncretism, 90, 116, 119–120

Tabot'ap, 123
Tae Hwaŏmsa sajŏk, 98
T'aebaek, Mount, 116, 129
taebi chu. See Great Compassion Spell
T'aebong, 59
taegukt'ong, 31
T'aehyŏn, 53, 74, 96
T'aejo, K., 137
T'aejong Muyŏl, K. *See* Kim Ch'unch'u
Taewangam, 30, 127
Taihe, Lake, 29, 56
Talbul Fortress, 57
Taltal Pakpak, 44, 79
Tang (dynasty), 4; Avalokiteśvara cult in, 70, 74; Buddhist caves in, 35; Chajang in, 1, 29–31; Huayan in, 87–90, 100; Maitreya cult in, 52, 58, 59; Mount Wutai cult in, 110; Silla relations with, 68–69; Ŭisang in, 116, 117

Tang-Silla alliance. *See* Silla-Tang alliance
Tanqian, 93
tantric Buddhism, 63–64, 73, 77, 87, 123, 126, 128, 141
tea, offerings of, 10, 11, 42, 44, 50–52, 55, 111–112
thaumaturgy, viii, 6, 13, 15, 32, 37, 43, 51, 54, 58, 89, 91, 96, 125
Three Kingdoms, Korean, vii, xi, 20, 37, 66, 140; Later, 33
three mountains. *See* mountains, three sacred mountains of Silla
three treasures of Silla, 13
Tiantai Zhiyi, 115, 172n15
Tōdaiji, 90–91
T'oham, Mount, 95, 120–122, 125, 127–129
Tojŭng, 53
Tojung Monastery, 42
Tomb-Rock of the Great King. *See* Taewangam
t'ong Pulgyo, 127
Tongch'uk Monastery, 25–26
T'ongdo Monastery, 31
Tonghae, 30, 73, 96, 125
Top'ian Monastery, 103–105
toryang. See enlightenment site
Toyung, 99
true-bone status. See *chin'gol*
Tsukamoto Zenryū, 35
tuoluoni. See dhāraṇī
Tuoluoni zaji, 73
Tuṣita Heaven, 5–6, 20; and Hwaŏm beliefs, 102–103, 142, 148, 150; and Maitreya cult, 33–36, 41, 46, 52, 55
Tut'a, Mount, 105

Ŭich'ŏn, 95, 101, 124–125
Ŭijŏk, 99
Ŭisang, 7; and his disciples, 95, 99–101, 129–131, 133; and Divine Assembly cult, 135; and Great Compassion Spell, 70–74; and Hwaŏm tradition, 85, 87, 88, 91–93, 102–103, 108, 109, 114–116; and Pusŏksa, 116–121, 123; and schools of Korean Buddhism, 140–142
Ungch'ŏn, 31, 38

Vairocana, 11, 88–90, 141; and Divine Assembly cult, 136, 147, 149; inscriptions on images, 103–108; Mount Odae cult of, 111–114; and Pulguksa, 122–124, 173n30; Sŏkkuram image as, 126, 128
visions, 10, 38, 50, 57–58
visualization. *See also* meditation practices, samādhi
vow-text, 70–71, 101–103, 119–120

Wang Kŏn, 59–60, 137
Wanghŭng Monastery, 37
Weimojie jing, 52
Wen, Sui Emperor, 87
White Tārā, 73
Wŏlchang, 44
Wŏlgwang, 137. *See also* Prince Moonlight
Wŏlmyŏng, 54–55
Wŏlsŏng, 22, 24
Wŏnch'ŭk, 53
Wŏn'gwang, 28, 43
Wŏnhyo, 7; and Avalokiteśvara cult, 73–74; and Hwaŏm Buddhism, 93–95; and Punhwangsa, 80; and schools of Buddhism, vii–viii, 139–140; and Ŭisang, 91, 116–117
Wŏnjong mullyu, 101, 124
Wŏnsŏng, K., 96
Wu, Liang Emperor, 22
Wu, Empress, 52, 58, 59, 69; patronizes Huayan Buddhism, 88–89
Wuliangshou jing. See Pure Land Sūtra, Larger
Wutai, Mount, 1, 12, 19, 26, 50, 53, 110, 114, 133, 141

Xiang Haiming, 58
Xiangguo Monastery, 52

Xianshou, Master. *See* Fazang
Xinxiu kefen luxue seng zhuan, 48
Xu gaoseng zhuan, 7, 67, 68
Xuanzang, 7, 53, 74, 76, 88, 116, 126
Xuanzong, Emperor, 52

Yangwŏn, 99
Yemaek, 29
Yijing (Tang monk), 88, 159n50
Yijing, 49
Yoga monks, 30
Yogācāra school, 7, 53, 87, 105, 122, 140
Yonggung, 23–25, 101
Yonghwa, Mount, 37
yonghwa hyangdo, 21, 41
Yŏn'gi, 97

Yongjang Monastery, 53
Yŏngmyo Monastery, 23, 39
Yongning Monastery, 29
Yuanxiang, 29
yuktup'um. See head-rank six
Yumedono Kannon, 65
Yun'gang caves, 110, 125
Yunhua Monastery, 88

Zhancha jing/Zhancha shane yebao jing, 49, 113
zhenyan, 77–78. *See also* dhāraṇī
Zhisheng, 116
Zhiyan, 87–88, 91, 93, 101–102, 117–118, 166n18
Zhongnan, Mount, 29, 101, 133
Zongmi, 90

About the Author

RICHARD D. MCBRIDE, II, earned his doctorate in East Asian Languages and Cultures at the University of California, Los Angeles, in 2001. He has published studies on medieval Sinitic Buddhism, ancient Korean religion, the *Samguk yusa,* and the *Hwarang segi* manuscripts. He is also a member of the International Association for Wŏnhyo Studies. He is currently doing a Fulbright research grant in Korean history at Dongguk University in Seoul, Korea.

Production Notes for McBride / *Domesticating the Dharma*

Jacket design by Santos Barbasa Jr.

Text design by Paul Herr with text in New Baskerville and display in Clearface

Text composition by Tseng Information Systems, Inc.

Printing and binding by The Maple-Vail Book Manufacturing Group

Printed on 55 lb. Glatfelter Offset B18, 360 ppi